DEPARTMENT OF THE NAVY
Headquarters United States Marine Corps
Washington, DC 20380-1775

17 February 2005

CHANGE 1 to MCWP 3-13

1. Marine Corps Warfighting Publication (MCWP) 3-13, *Employment of Amphibious Assault Vehicles*, should be changed as follows:

   a. On page 1-7 of Chapter 1, in "Assault Amphibian Section," delete sentences two and three and replace with, "The Rifle Platoon Commander exercises maneuver control of his platoon through the AAV Section Leader. While mounted or dismounted, the Rifle Platoon Commander coordinates AAV direct fires through the AAV Section Leader."

   b. On page 2-2 of Chapter 2, in "Assault Amphibian Platoon," paragraph 2, delete sentences three, four and five and replace with, "The Rifle Company Commander exercises maneuver control of his company through the AA Platoon Commander. While mounted or dismounted, the Rifle Company Commander coordinates AAV direct fires through the AAV Platoon Commander."

   c. On page 3-7 of Chapter 3, in "Planning," delete sentence three, which currently reads, "During this period, the AA unit leader maintains TACON over the unit."

   d. On page 3-17 of Chapter 3, in "The Assault," delete the first sentence, which currently reads, "AA unit leaders, in conjunction with the designated PCO, maintain TACON of AAVs and embarked troops during waterborne movement."

2. Reviewed and approved this date.

BY DIRECTION OF THE COMMANDANT OF THE MARINE CORPS

J. N. MATTIS
Lieutenant General, U.S. Marine Corps
Commanding General
Marine Corps Combat Development Command

PCN: 143 000103 01

DEPARTMENT OF THE NAVY
Headquarters United States Marine Corps
Washington, D.C. 20380-1775

10 September 2003

FOREWORD

Marine Corps Warfighting Publication (MCWP) 3-13, *Employment of Amphibious Assault Vehicles*, provides the doctrinal basis for the use of amphibious assault vehicles (AAVs) in support of Marine air-ground task force (MAGTF) operations. This publication addresses the mechanized capability of the assault amphibian unit, section, and platoon in support of MAGTF missions. These missions include seizure and defense of naval and air bases, conduct of land operations essential to naval operations, and sustained operations ashore that support joint or combined force land operations.

The target audience for MCWP 3-13 is officers and staff noncommissioned officers serving as members of MAGTF staffs and assault amphibian battalions. The publication provides information for consideration in the planning and employment of AAVs in combat operations and military operations other than war.

Reviewed and approved this date.

BY DIRECTION OF THE COMMANDANT OF THE MARINE CORPS

EDWARD HANLON, JR.
Lieutenant General, U.S. Marine Corps
Commanding General
Marine Corps Combat Development Command

Publication Control Number: 143 000103 00

TABLE OF CONTENTS

Chapter 1. Fundamentals

AAV Capabilities 1-1
   Armor Protection. 1-1
   Land Operation 1-1
   Water Operation 1-1
Types of AAVs 1-2
   AAVP7A1 and AAV7A1 Reliability, Availability, and
      Maintainability/Rebuild to Standard 1-2
   AAVC7A1. 1-3
   AAVR7A1. 1-3
Organization 1-4
   Assault Amphibian Battalion 1-4
   Assault Amphibian Battalion, Headquarters and Service Company. . . 1-4
   Assault Amphibian Company 1-6
   Assault Amphibian Platoon. 1-7
   Assault Amphibian Section. 1-7
   Assault Amphibian Crew 1-7

Chapter 2. Operational Principles

Command Relationships 2-1
   Operational Control. 2-1
   Administrative Control 2-1
   Assault Amphibian Battalion 2-1
   Assault Amphibian Company 2-2
   Assault Amphibian Platoon. 2-2
   Assault Amphibian Section. 2-2
Task Organization 2-2
   Fundamentals 2-3
   Cross Attachment 2-3
   Combat Support. 2-4
   AAV Allocations. 2-6
Movement 2-7
   Control. 2-7
   Considerations. 2-7

Chapter 3. Amphibious Operations

Types of Operations.   3-1
    Assault   3-1
    Raid   3-1
    Demonstration   3-2
    Withdrawal.   3-2
    Military Operations Other Than War.   3-2
Intelligence Requirements   3-2
    Hydrography   3-2
    Enemy Defenses.   3-6
    Sources of Hydrographic Information   3-7
Planning   3-7
    Assault Amphibian Unit Special Staff Officer   3-7
    Organization for Amphibious Assaults   3-8
    Landing Plan   3-10
    Preparation of Landing Documents   3-10
    Organization of the Amphibious Objective Area   3-10
    Launch Planning   3-12
    AAV Maximum Ship-to-Shore Swim Distance.   3-12
Embarkation.   3-12
    Amphibious Shipping Characteristics   3-12
    Embarkation Planning   3-12
    Embarkation of AAVs   3-13
    Securing AAVs   3-15
Rehearsal and Movement.   3-15
    Planning Considerations   3-16
    Types   3-16
    Preoperational Briefing and Security.   3-17
    Unit Preparation   3-17
The Assault   3-17
    Command and Control.   3-17
    Fundamentals of the Assault   3-19
    Infantry Concept Determination   3-19
    Debarkation Procedures.   3-20
    Grid Reference System   3-22
    Quiet Landing Procedures   3-22
    Position Location Reporting System   3-22
    Global Positioning System.   3-23
    Formations   3-23
    Rate of Advance.   3-23
    Screening   3-25
    Actions on the Beach   3-25
Shore-to-Objective Maneuver   3-25
    Planning   3-25
    Execution   3-25
    Operations in Navigable Waters   3-25

Night and Low Visibility Operations 3-26
    Preparation 3-26
    Night Launches. 3-26
    Formations and Speed 3-26
    Beach Markings 3-27

Chapter 4. Offensive Operations

Section I. Forms of Offensive Maneuver

Frontal Attack. 4-1
Flanking Attack 4-1
Envelopment. 4-1
Turning Movement. 4-2
Penetration 4-2
Infiltration. 4-2

Section II. Types of Operations

Movement to Contact 4-2
    Security Elements. 4-2
    Main Body 4-3
    Actions on Contact in Meeting Engagement 4-3
    Actions on Contact in a Bypass 4-3
Attack 4-3
    Deliberate Attack 4-3
    Hasty Attack. 4-10
    Reconnaissance in Force 4-10
    Feint 4-10
    Demonstration 4-11
    Raid. 4-11
    Spoiling Attack. 4-11
    Counterattack 4-11
Exploitation 4-11
    Characteristics 4-11
    Planning 4-11
Pursuit. 4-11

Section III. Mechanized Operations

Mutual Support. 4-12
Employment Methods. 4-12
    Tanks and Mechanized Infantry Attack Together 4-13
    Tanks and AAVs Support by Fire Only 4-13
    Multiaxis Attack. 4-14
Mechanized Movement 4-14

Maneuver Considerations 4-15
    Tanks Lead 4-15
    Infantry Mounted 4-15
    Infantry Dismounted 4-15
Dismount Points 4-16
    Short of the Objective 4-16
    On the Objective 4-16
    After Passing Through the Objective 4-17
Base of Fire and Maneuver 4-17
    Elements 4-17
    Attacks 4-17
Assault 4-18
    Mounted 4-18
    Dismounted 4-18
Consolidation and Reorganization 4-19

Section IV. Role of the Reserve

Section V. Conduct of Passage of Lines

Planning 4-20
Unit Responsibilities 4-20
Command and Control 4-20
Rearward Passage of Lines 4-20

Chapter 5. Defensive Operations

Defense Fundamentals 5-1
    Maneuver 5-1
    Preparation 5-1
    Concentration of Combat Power 5-1
    Flexibility 5-1
    Offensive Actions 5-1
    Use of Terrain 5-1
    Security 5-2
    Mutual Support 5-2
    Defense in Depth 5-2
    Fire Support and Obstacle Plans 5-2
Defensive Position Variations 5-2
    Reverse-Slope Defense 5-2
    Perimeter Defense 5-2
Organization of the Battlespace 5-2

Organization of the Force. 5-2
    Security Forces. 5-3
    Main Battle Forces 5-3
    Rear Area Forces 5-3
Types of Missions. 5-3
    Security. 5-3
    Defend in Sector 5-3
    Defend a Battle Position. 5-3
    Defend a Strong Point. 5-4
    Reserve 5-5
    Counterattacks 5-6
Planning 5-6
    Intelligence 5-6
    Maneuver 5-7
    Fires 5-7
    Direct fire 5-7
    Positioning 5-7
    Methods of Engagement. 5-8
    Fire Control. 5-8
    Preparations for the Defense. 5-10
    Engineering. 5-11
    Logistics 5-12
    Command and Control 5-12
Types of Defense 5-12
    Mobile and Position Defense 5-12
    Deployment Methods in Position Defense 5-12

Chapter 6. Logistics Operations

Logistic Trains 6-1
    Types of Trains. 6-1
    Command and Control 6-2
    Battalion Support Area. 6-3
    Replenishment Methods 6-3
    Recovery and Repair 6-5
AA Battalion Organic Logistic Support 6-6
    Supply. 6-6
    Maintenance 6-7
    Transportation. 6-7
    Engineering. 6-8
    Health Services. 6-8
    Services. 6-8
Logistic Support Requirements 6-8
    Supply. 6-8
    Maintenance 6-9
    Transportation. 6-9

AAV-Unique Planning Considerations. 6-10
  Refueling. 6-10
  Preventive Maintenance 6-10
  Environmental Effects. 6-10

Chapter 7. Special Operations

Marine Expeditionary Unit Operations. 7-1
  Organization 7-1
  Training. 7-1
  Missions 7-1
Nuclear, Biological, and Chemical Defense Operations. 7-2
  Organization 7-2
  Nuclear, Biological, and Chemical Environmental Effects 7-3
  Nuclear Defense 7-3
  Chemical/Biological Defense 7-4
  Decontamination Procedures 7-4
Road March Operations 7-9
Military Operations Other Than War 7-9
  Types. 7-10
  Employment Advantages 7-10
  Employment Disadvantages 7-10
Breaching Operations 7-10
  MK-154 Linear Mine Clearing System 7-11
  Organization of Mobility, Countermobility Assets. 7-12
  Mobility, Countermobility Precepts 7-13
  Preparations for Amphibious Operations 7-13

Chapter 8. AAV Gunnery and Fire Control

Weapons System Employment 8-1
  Fire Control Responsibilities 8-1
  Classes of Fire. 8-2
  Weapons Effectiveness 8-2
  Water Gunnery 8-4
  Range Determination Methods 8-4
  Principles of Fire Distribution. 8-5
  Fire Control Techniques 8-6
  Range Cards 8-7
  Fire Commands. 8-9
  Infantry Calls for Fire 8-10
  Antiaircraft Gunnery. 8-10

Smoke Generation 8-10
    Engine Generating System 8-10
    M-257 Smoke Grenade Launcher. 8-11

Chapter 9. Operations in Special Terrain

Jungle Operations 9-1
    Intelligence 9-1
    Combat Service Support 9-1
    Tactical Planning 9-2
    Fire Support 9-2
    Engineer 9-2
    Communications. 9-2
Riverine Operations 9-3
    Environment 9-3
    Concept of Operations 9-6
    Missions 9-7
    Command Relationships. 9-7
    Organization Fundamentals 9-8
    Plan of Attack. 9-8
    Control Measures 9-8
    Movement Techniques 9-9
    Tactics. 9-9
    Combat Service Support Employment 9-9
River Crossing Operations 9-11
    Planning Factors 9-12
    Types of Crossings 9-14
Urbanized Terrain Operations 9-16
    Types of Urbanized Terrain 9-16
    Hub Phenomenon 9-17
    Offense 9-17
    Defense. 9-17
Desert Operations 9-18
    Maintenance Considerations. 9-18
    Tactical Considerations 9-19
Mountain and Cold Weather Operations 9-19
    Mobility 9-19
    Logistic Considerations 9-21
    Vehicular Considerations 9-21
    Tactical Employment Considerations. 9-22
    Individual Equipment Considerations 9-23

Chapter 10. Communications

Forms of Communications 10-1
   Visual Signals 10-1
   Radio 10-1
   Wire 10-2
   Messenger 10-2
AAV Assets 10-2
   AAVP7A1 10-2
   AAVC7A1 10-3

Chapter 11. Safety Guidelines

General Safety 11-1
   Responsibilities 11-1
   Vehicle Employment 11-1
   Preventive Maintenance 11-2
   Operational Briefs 11-2
   Passenger Orientation 11-2
Waterborne Safety 11-2
   Required Equipment 11-2
   Operational Requirements 11-3
   Rescue Teams 11-4
   Safety Criteria 11-4
   Water Operating Speeds and Distances 11-4
   Emergency Signals 11-4
   Embarked Troops 11-4
Land Safety 11-4
   Crew Composition 11-5
   Operating Speeds 11-5
   Operating Distances 11-5
   Road Crossings 11-5
   Operational Environments 11-5
Other Safety Considerations 11-6
   Weather 11-6
   Nuclear, Biological, and Chemical Operations 11-6
   Medical Evacuation 11-6
   Lasers 11-6
   Up-Gunned Weapon Station 11-6
   Linear Mine Clearing 11-7
   Onboard Vehicle Fires 11-7

Appendices

A. AAVP7A1 Data. A-1
B. AAVP7A1 (RAM/RS) Data B-1
C. AAVC7A1 Data. C-1
D. AAVR7A1 Data. D-1
E. Rescue Procedures for Disabled AAVs E-1
F. Landing Documents F-1
G. Grid Reference System G-1
H. Amphibious Ship AAV Capacities H-1
I. Embarkation and Debarkation Procedures I-1
J. Standard Flags, Lights, and Markers Used to Control AAVs. J-1
K. Hand and Arm Signals for Control of AAVs K-1
L. Sample Time Schedule for Ship-to-Shore Movement of AAVs L-1
M. Amphibious Ship Launch Tracks M-1
N. Glossary. N-1
O. References and Related Publications. O-1

Tables

2-1. AAV Allocation 2-6

3-1. Sea State Conditions 3-3
3-2. Safe Breaker Heights and Breaker Periods 3-4
3-3. Notional Boat Team for an AAVP7A1 3-9
3-4. AAV Launch Intervals 3-21
3-5. RPM/Speed Conversions. 3-25

7-1. M/CM Organization 7-12

8-1. MK-19 Time of Flight Table. 8-3
8-2. Grenades for the AAV M-257 Grenade Launcher 8-11

9-1 Freshwater Ice Crossing. 9-21

Figures

1-1. H&S Company 1-5
1-2. AA Company. 1-6

2-1. Tank-Heavy Force. 2-4
2-2. Mech-Heavy Force 2-4

3-1. Amphibious Operations Area 3-11
3-2. Tactical Launch Diagram 3-14
3-3. Single Grip 3-15
3-4. Double Grip. 3-16
3-5. AAV Formations. 3-24

Figures (Continued)

5-1. Defense-in-Sector Plan 5-4

6-1. Service Station Method 6-4
6-2. Tailgate Issue Method 6-5

7-1. M11 DAP. 7-5
7-2. M13 DAP. 7-5
7-3. M17 LDS 7-6
7-4. M100 SDS 7-7
7-5. Thorough Decontamination Site 7-9
7-6. MK-154 LMC 7-11

8-1. Range Card Example 8-8

9-1. AAVs Moving on Opposite Shorelines 9-10

10-1. AAVC7A1 Layout 10-3

CHAPTER 1. FUNDAMENTALS

The amphibious assault vehicle (AAV) is employed to conduct mechanized (mech) operations and related combat support in subsequent operations ashore. A fully-tracked amphibian, the AAV is used by the assault amphibian (AA) battalion to accomplish its mission to land the surface assault elements of the landing force (LF) and their equipment in a single lift from assault shipping during amphibious operations to inland objectives. The AA battalion and subordinate units perform the following tasks:

- Transport assault elements, selected equipment, and supplies ashore in mech ship-to-shore movement, and other combat support operations.
- Participate in the planning, coordination, and execution of mech, linkup, riverine, landing, and other operations as directed.
- Use organic weapon systems to provide fire support during amphibious operations.
- Provide support by clearing lanes through minefields and other obstacles during amphibious operations and subsequent operations ashore.
- Execute the missions associated with AAV special mission kits.

AAV Capabilities

Understanding the capabilities and limitations of the AAV are important to maximizing its operational utility on the battlefield. An amphibious armored personnel carrier (APC), the AAV is capable of open ocean operation from offshore shipping through rough seas and plunging surf; and without modification, it is capable of traversing beaches, crossing rough terrain, and performing high speed operations on improved roads. AAVs provide the ground combat element (GCE) with armor protection as well as land and water operation capabilities.

Armor Protection

The AAV provides armor-protected mobility to the embarked infantry who will dismount to carry the fight to the enemy, while the AAV crew fights from overwatch. The hull of the AAV is constructed from welded plates of ballistic aluminum and will provide a high degree of protection against small arms fire, up to .30 caliber at 300 meters and 105-millimeter high explosive (HE) (variable time) fragmentation at 15 meters.

Land Operation

The AAV is capable of worldwide operation in nearly any terrain. Possessing a ground pressure of roughly 9.1 pounds per square inch, the AAV is capable of operating in soft soil that is inaccessible to the M1A1 tank or light armored vehicle-25 (LAV-25). The AAV has a 300-mile operating range at a cruising speed of 25 miles per hour on a flat, hard surface road with a maximum land speed of 45 miles per hour. The vehicle can operate on forward slopes of 60 percent and side slopes of 40 percent. It can cross an 8-foot trench and a 3-foot vertical obstacle.

Water Operation

The AAV is the most seaworthy personnel landing craft in military service. It is capable of operating in calm to moderate seas. Depending on the cargo load, the AAV can negotiate up to 10-feet plunging surf and can self-right from a 180-degree roll. Powered by two 21-inch water-jets, the AAV has a maximum water speed of 8.2 miles per hour and is capable of a waterborne range in excess of 45 miles in calm seas. Although relatively slow in the water, the vehicle is capable of safe, long distance water marches that are limited only by extremely rough seas and associated effects of motion sickness on embarked personnel.

=== CAUTION ===

The AAV was not designed as an infantry fighting vehicle (IFV) and should not be employed as such. It lacks the armor protection, stabilized weapons station, low silhouette, and means for the infantry to fight from the vehicle without exposing themselves to direct fire.

Types of AAVs

Three AAV7A1 family variants provide personnel transport, command, and recovery functions.

AAVP7A1 and AAV7A1 Reliability, Availability, and Maintainability/Rebuild to Standard

The AAVP7A1 and the AAV7A1 reliability, availability, and maintainability/rebuild to standard (RAM/RS) are designed to provide combat support and armor-protected mobility for a reinforced rifle squad and associated combat equipment for operation on land or sea. Although the vehicles are principally personnel carriers, they may be employed to transport cargo in support of combat service support (CSS) operations. Appendices A and B provide additional data and specifications.

Load Capabilities

The maximum troop load (TL) for both vehicles consists of 3 crewmen and 21 combat-loaded infantrymen. The maximum cargo payload for the AAVP7A1 is 10,000 pounds and the AAV RAM/RS is 8,000 pounds. Typical cargo loads include—

- 17, 55-gallon drums.
- 400 cases of meals, ready to eat.
- 138 cases of .50-caliber machine gun ammunition.
- 2, 500-gallon fuel bladders.

Special Mission Kits

Five special mission kits add to the capabilities of the vehicle.

Enhanced Appliqué Armor Kit. The enhanced appliqué armor kit (EAAK) consists of a series of bolt-on armor panels that provide additional armor protection to the vehicle. With the EAAK mounted, the vehicle receives a substantial increase in ballistic protection. The EAAK adds 4,400 pounds to the vehicle. The EAAK also mounts to the AAVC7A1 but not the AAVR7A1. The following EAAK data applies:

- No penetration for 7.62-millimeter and smaller weapons at muzzle velocity.
- 95 percent probability of no penetration for 12.7-millimeter armor piercing at muzzle velocity.
- 95 percent probability of no penetration for 14.5 millimeters at 300 meters.
- 99 percent probability of no penetration for 155-millimeter HE at 50 feet.
- Substantially decreases the effectiveness of shape charge weapons by reducing the fragmentation debris cone from 110 degrees to 35 degrees.

Litter Kit. The litter kit provides space for up to six litters and is installed by the vehicle crew when the vehicle is to be used by medical support personnel as a mobile aid station and/or medical evacuation vehicle. For use only with the AAVP7A1 and AAV RAM/RS, the litter kit is installed using straps and is secured to existing hull brackets and deck plate slots.

MK-154 Linear Mine Clearing Kit. The MK-154 linear mine clearing (LMC) kit is a three-shot system designed for use in breaching operations. The kit functions as a rocket launcher, and an initial ammunition issue and subsequent reload is required to permit the kit to operate. Each of the three rockets, when launched, pulls a series of tubing from the cargo/personnel area of the AAVP7A1 and AAV RAM/RS; each series of tubing contains 1,750 pounds of C-4 explosive.

Upon detonation, the system is capable of opening a 100-meter long, 16-meter wide lane, at 95-percent proof, through the minefield.

Winterization Kit. The winterization kit helps the vehicle operate in temperatures to -45 degrees Fahrenheit. The kit consists of an engine coolant heater, winterization personnel heater, and battery box heat exchanger.

Visor Kit. Used when the AAV is operated under extreme cold weather conditions, the visor kit protects the driver from the elements and provides a greater field of vision. The kit consists of a visor, windshield wiper and motor, defroster hose, and attaching hardware. The visor kit may be installed on the driver's hatch opening of AAV7A1 and AAV RAM/RS variants.

Communications

The AAVP7A1 and AAV RAM/RS are equipped with single-channel ground and airborne radio systems (SINCGARSs) for use by the crew and embarked infantry commander. A vehicle intercommunications system provides the capability for the crew and infantry commander to pass information while the vehicle is in operation.

Firepower

AAVP7A1 and AAV RAM/RS vehicles are equipped with the up-gunned weapons station (UGWS) that mounts an M2, .50-caliber, heavy-barreled (HB) machine gun and an MK-19, 40-millimeter grenade launcher. The UGWS provides an effective mix of firepower for offensive and defensive requirements.

AAVC7A1

As the command and control (C2) variant of the AAV7A1 family, the AAVC7A1 is employed by the supported unit at the battalion and regimental headquarters level as a mobile command echelon/fire support coordination center (FSCC). The AAVC7A1 is not configured for the Advanced Field Artillery Tactical Data System.

Communications

The AAVC7A1 is equipped with six very high frequency (VHF), one ultrahigh frequency (UHF), and one high frequency (HF) radio transmitters and receivers to allow secure communications with subordinate, adjacent, and higher units, as well as with supporting arms and logistic agencies. It includes workstations for up to five staff officers and five radio operators. The AAVC7A1 intercommunications assets provide the embarked commander and staff with the capability to communicate with each other while stationary or moving and to remotely operate radio assets from staff positions within the vehicle. Appendix C provides additional AAVC7A1 technical data and specifications.

Firepower

While the AAVC7A1 is not an offensive weapons system, it is equipped with the current 7.62-millimeter machine gun for self-defense.

AAVR7A1

The AAVR7A1 is the maintenance and recovery variant of the AAV7A1 family. It is organic to the AA company and battalion as well as the maintenance battalion of the force service support group (FSSG). The AAVR7A1 supports vehicle recovery and maintenance in the field through third echelon.

Capabilities

The principal equipment of the AAVR7A1 includes a hydraulic, telescoping, boom crane with a 6,000-pound capacity, 30,000-pound capacity recovery winch, as well as cutting, welding, and other portable maintenance equipment. Appendix D provides additional technical data and specifications.

Firepower

Although the AAVR7A1 is not an offensive weapons system, it is equipped with the current 7.62-millimeter machine gun for self-defense.

Organization

AA units are organized and equipped to land the surface assault elements of the LF and their equipment in a single lift from assault shipping during amphibious operations to inland objectives and to conduct mech operations and related combat support in subsequent operations ashore. In addition, AA units can conduct shore-to-shore assault operations, riverine operations, sea control operations in littoral areas, and other missions in support of Marine air-ground task force (MAGTF) operations. AA units may be tasked-organized as a maneuver element for riverine operations and operations in littoral areas for the conduct of rear area security. These varied missions reflect the flexibility and operational utility of the AAV on the modern battlefield.

Assault Amphibian Battalion

The AA battalion is assigned to a Marine division. The battalion and/or its subordinate units are attached to or placed in support of a GCE commander to provide ship-to-shore lift of the surface assault elements of the LF. Once ashore, the battalion provides tactical mobility and communications to the supported force. The AA battalion augments the AA company's organic logistic capability by providing personnel, medical, resupply, and overflow second and third echelon maintenance. Although primarily employed to mechanize the surface assault elements of a regimental landing team (RLT), AA battalion elements may be employed in a CSS role forward of the forward edge of the battle area (FEBA) or in the beach support area. The AA battalion has the command, staff, and resources necessary to plan and execute mech operations as a maneuver control headquarters when augmented with combat, combat support forces, and FSCC representatives (i.e., air officer, naval guns liaison officer, 81-millimeter mortar forward observers [FOs], and artillery FO).

The I Marine Expeditionary Force (MEF) and II MEF each have a full AA battalion. The III MEF possesses one AA company that is part of the unit deployment program. This program is sourced from I MEF. Marine Corps Forces Reserve has one AA battalion (minus) consisting of two line companies and one headquarters and service (H&S) company.

Assault Amphibian Battalion, Headquarters and Service Company

The H&S company, AA battalion, provides the AA battalion commander the means to effect C2 of the battalion. Through its subordinate platoons and sections, the H&S company provides maintenance, communications, administrative, medical, supply, and other service support functions to the AA battalion. See figure 1-1.

Headquarters Platoon

The headquarters platoon includes the medical, chaplain, and headquarters sections as well as the company staff.

Medical Section. The medical section includes medical personnel organic to the battalion. In addition to their medical qualifications, these personnel are familiar with the capabilities and limitations of the AAV. Section personnel provide advice on the employment of AAVs as mobile aid stations and casualty evacuation vehicles and operate the vehicles in support of such missions.

Chaplain Section. The chaplain section is responsible for the spiritual welfare of the battalion.

Headquarters Section. The headquarters section contains those assets associated with the AA battalion staff functions, e.g., manpower staff officer (S-1)/communications and information systems officer (S-6).

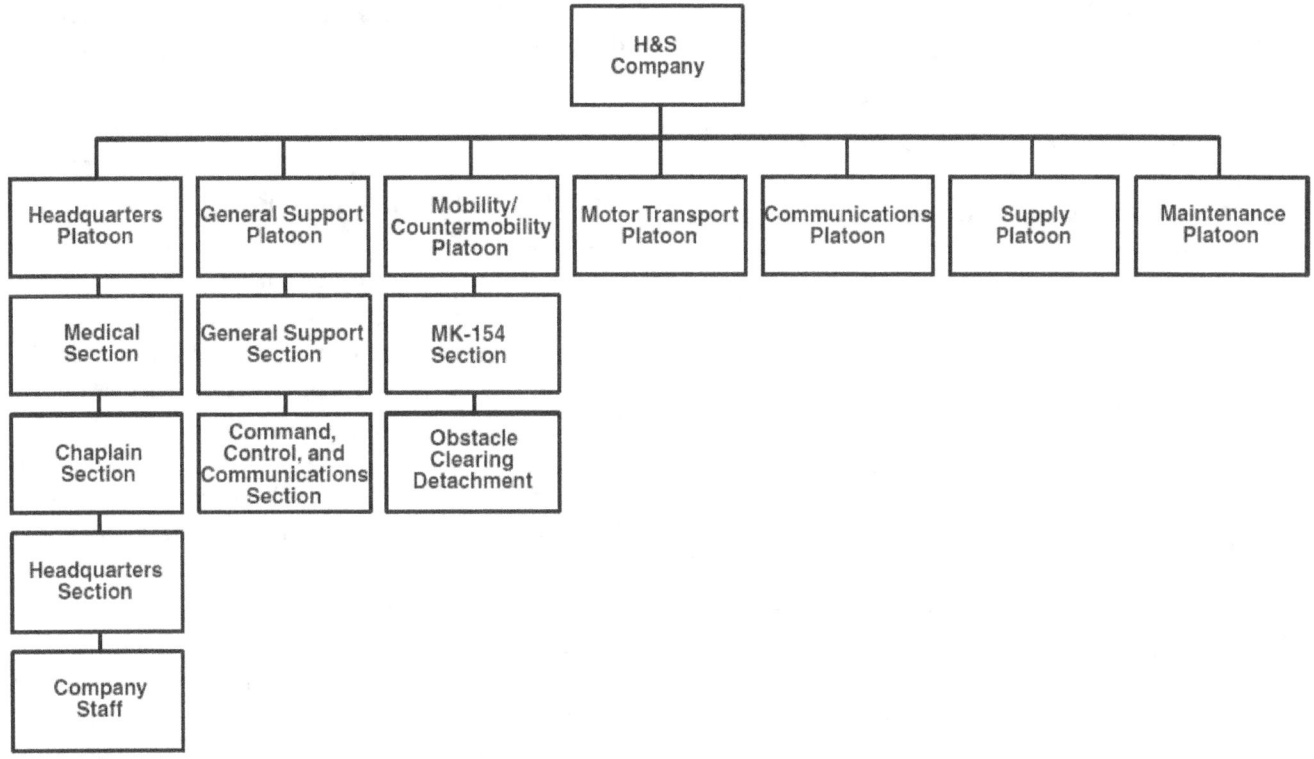

Figure 1-1. H&S Company.

Company Staff. In addition to exercising command over H&S company, the company staff conducts functions associated with supporting and coordinating personnel, logistics, and training requirements for personnel attached to the H&S company. The company staff also exercise command functions over the general support (GS) platoon and mobility, countermobility (M/CM) platoon when it is located at the battalion level.

General Support Platoon

This unit is composed of a GS section and a command, control, and communications section.

General Support Section. Composed of nine AAVP7A1s organized into three sections of three vehicles, the GS section provides support to the battalion logistic trains.

Command, Control, and Communications Section. Composed of six AAVC7A1 communication vehicles and three AAVP7A1 chase vehicles,

the command, control, and communications section supports the C2 requirements of the AA battalion and supported GCE maneuver units.

Mobility/Countermobility Platoon

The M/CM platoon is composed of 24 AAVP7A1s with 12 MK-154 LMC kits that are divided between the MK-154 section and the obstacle clearing detachment. The mission of the M/CM platoon is to land combat engineer elements from ship-to-shore or from shore-to-shore to support the breaching of beachhead defenses and provide M/CM support to subsequent operations ashore.

Motor Transport Platoon

The motor transport platoon is responsible for the operation and maintenance of wheeled vehicles in the battalion except those assigned to the AA companies.

Communications Platoon

The communications platoon installs, operates, and maintains the communication system for the battalion headquarters. The platoon is responsible for repairs through second echelon to communications equipment organic to the battalion headquarters. In addition, the platoon supports the company communications sections as required.

Supply Platoon

The supply platoon is organized to provide supply support for organic battalion units.

Maintenance Platoon

The maintenance platoon is responsible for third echelon maintenance of tracked vehicles in the battalion. The maintenance platoon operates and maintains the battalion's two AAVR7A1s.

Assault Amphibian Company

The AA company consists of three line platoons, a headquarters platoon, and a maintenance platoon. See figure 1-2. Each of the line platoons has 12 AAVP7A1s. The headquarters platoon provides the company administrative and logistic support. The headquarters platoon includes the headquarters section, command tractor section that provides AAVC7A1 assets to the supported unit headquarters, and GS section that provides tactical mobility and logistic train assets to the AA company. The maintenance platoon provides the AA company maintenance capability through second echelon. The maintenance platoon includes the AAV maintenance section, communications section, and the retriever section that maintain the company's AAVR7A1. The AA company may be reinforced with M/CM assets from the AA battalion.

The AA company is usually employed to lift the assault elements of a reinforced infantry battalion. Whether attached or in direct support (DS)/GS, the AA company commander functions as a special staff officer in AAV employment. Infantry and AAVs are task-organized to create a single tactical combat unit. The AA company commander and subordinate commanders work in harmony with their supported unit counterparts to achieve unity of command and effort according to the supported infantry commander's concept of operation. One or two of the AA company's AAVC7A1s along with chase AAVP7A1s are employed by the infantry headquarters to support command echelon operations. The AA company's limited CSS capabilities, augmented by

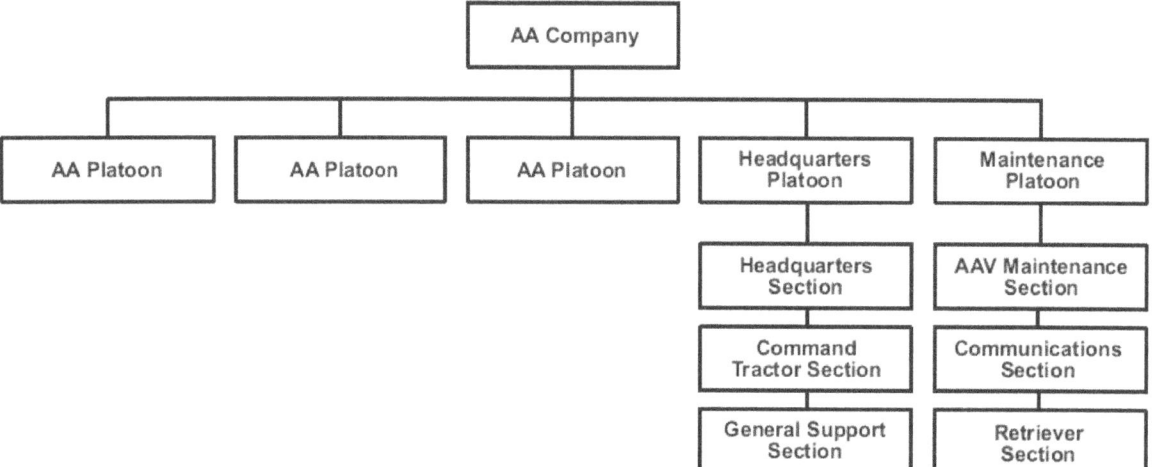

Figure 1-2. AA Company.

AA battalion resources, provide essential administrative and logistic support.

Assault Amphibian Platoon

Organized into four sections of three AAVP7A1s, the AA platoon normally conducts operations attached to or in DS/GS of the infantry company. The AA platoon commander directs the employment of the AA platoon according to the supported unit commander's concept of operations. The AA platoon employs AAVs to—

- Achieve mech mobility.
- Negotiate obstacles.
- Support the commander's plan of fires.
- Enhance the commander's communications capability.

As a general employment guideline, AAVs exploit cover and concealment provided by terrain to reduce the risk of antiarmor attack. To increase the security of the AAVs, particularly in limited visibility terrain, the vehicle should operate with cargo hatches in the open-and-locked position to enable the embarked infantry to provide added observation and fire protection.

Assault Amphibian Section

Organized with four AAVP7A1 vehicles, the AA section provides combat support to the infantry rifle platoon. The AA section leader exercises tactical control (TACON) of AAVs under the command of the AA platoon commander. The section leader is responsible for the section's fire control and responds to calls for fire from the supported infantry commander. An AA section may be used for transporting units (e.g., 81-millimeter mortar platoon, engineer platoon).

Assault Amphibian Crew

The three members of the AA crew and vehicle primarily support a reinforced infantry squad. The AA crewmen operate their vehicle under the direction of the AA section leader.

Senior Crewman (Vehicle Commander or Crew Chief)

Responsible for the employment of the AAV, the senior member commands the AAV from the UGWS and employs the weapon systems.

=== **CAUTION** ===
Only qualified and licensed crewmen with a military occupational specialty (MOS) 1833 are allowed to operate the UGWS.

Second Senior Crewman

As the vehicle driver, the second senior crewman operates the vehicle at the direction of the senior crewman and in accordance with factors such as the terrain, tactical situation, standing operating procedures (SOPs), and immediate action drills.

Third Crewman

The third crewman is positioned in the vehicle to support the mission. When required, the third crewman—

- Serves as the assistant gunner.
- Supplies ammunition to the vehicle commander.
- Maintains good order and discipline in the troop compartment.
- Warns of violations to the integrity of the watertight hull.
- Assists in embarking and debarking of the infantry.

CHAPTER 2. OPERATIONAL PRINCIPLES

Command relationships in amphibious operations should help cooperative planning between the supported infantry commander and the AAV commander/special staff officer to accomplish the specified mission. The supported infantry commander and the AAV commander/special staff officer must develop and train to the SOPs inherent to mech operations. The AAV commander/special staff officer must be involved with planning phases involving waterborne and ground movement to ensure the proper employment of the AAV unit. Once the commander's intent is established, the AAV commander/special staff officer will provide valuable guidance on the maneuver/employment of the AAV unit based on the capabilities and limitations of the AAV unit in relation to the weather, enemy, and terrain. During operations, AAVs can support in DS or GS.

DS is a mission requiring a force to support another specific force and authorizing it to answer directly to the supported force's request for assistance. The supported infantry unit maintains operational control (OPCON). DS is the dominant command relationship for AAV units in support of infantry units.

GS is support given to the supported force as a whole, not to a particular subdivision of that force. When in GS, the AAV unit maintains OPCON over its own unit and responds to support requests equally. GS is typically in large-scale amphibious operations that require AAVs to conduct multiple lifts.

Command Relationships

To maximize the capabilities of the AAV unit, the supported infantry commander should integrate the AAV unit and establish cohesive working command relationships. Keeping the lines of communications open will help C2 and foster the one-team, one-fight ethos. The command relationship options available to the supported unit commander include OPCON and administrative control (ADCON). In some situations, the supported infantry unit is responsible for logistical support for the attached AAV unit. Normally, an infantry company is not equipped to logistically support an AAV platoon. Hence, AAV units are seldom attached to units below the infantry battalion level. In most cases, an AAV platoon is attached to a battalion landing team (BLT) and is in DS of one of the infantry companies (mech infantry company).

Operational Control

The supported unit operationally controls the AAV unit. OPCON does not include authoritative direction for logistics or matters of administration, discipline, internal organization or unit training.

Administrative Control

The supported unit administratively controls the AAV unit.

Assault Amphibian Battalion

A separate battalion organic to the Marine division, the AA battalion possesses the assets to mechanize one infantry regiment or parts of multiple regiments. The AA battalion commander serves as a special staff officer to the commanding general of the Marine division and directs the maintenance and logistic efforts of the battalion to support operations and on-order missions. The AA battalion has the ability to function as a maneuver element headquarters when provided augmentation from higher headquarters for FSCC positions (i.e., air officer, naval gunfire [NGF] liaison officer, FOs, and fire support coordinator [FSC]).

Assault Amphibian Company

When the AA company is attached to another organization or given a support mission, the AA company commander works directly for the commanding officer of the supported unit and becomes a special staff officer to the supported infantry commander. When the company is 80 percent task-organized with the infantry, the AA company commander will directly command the remaining 20 percent of the company's assets. The commander's primary duties include simultaneously directing the maintenance and logistics support organic to the AA company and advising the supported commander on the employment of AAVs.

Assault Amphibian Platoon

When the AA platoon is attached to another organization or given a support mission, the AA platoon commander works directly for the supported company commander. In mech operations, the supported commander is normally the infantry, tank company or battalion commander. Based on mission, enemy, terrain and weather, troops and support available—time available (METT-T), the supported commander may be from another combat support unit or CSS service unit (e.g., AA platoon participating in foreign humanitarian assistance [FHA]/disaster relief operations).

The supported commander is collocated with the AA platoon commander in the command vehicle for ease of C2. Normally, the AA platoon commander occupies the AAV turret, while the supported commander is positioned in the hatch of the troop commander (TC). As the senior AA officer assigned to a battalion, the platoon commander serves as a special staff officer to the battalion commander and advises the supported commander on the tactical employment of AAVs. The AA platoon commander directs the platoon's

movement according to the supported commander's intent. During movements, the AA platoon commander maintains the TACON of the AA platoon and the individual employment of AAVs.

Assault Amphibian Section

The AA section leader is responsible to the AA platoon commander for the maintenance and readiness of the platoon's AAVs. The section leader occupies the AAV turret with the supported infantry platoon commander occupying the TC's hatch. In addition to duties similar to that of the AA platoon commander, the section leader serves as a focal point for rapid dissemination of the AA unit SOP to infantry platoon commanders and helps the infantry and AAV crews form into a cohesive team. The section leader is also the focal point for employing the AA section's weapons systems.

Task Organization

The Marine Corps is one of the few armed forces in the world that conducts mech operations with temporarily formed units of light infantry and armor/antiarmor units. These well-trained, general-purpose infantry units are capable of executing air assault, mech or other ground combat operations. The predominant method of employing AA units is through task organization, by which an AA unit possessing the required quantity and mix of assets is attached to the battalion and in DS/GS of the supported unit.

In mech operations, the AA unit provides the infantry commander with a ready pool of expertise and experience to assist in the accomplishment of the assigned mission. The established AA tactical organization, the AA unit leaders' experience and familiarity with the unit's strengths and weaknesses, and the established SOP provide the infantry commander with the tactical and logistical requirements for movement of embarked infantry.

To maximize the capabilities of the AAV and its crew, the supported unit should quickly integrate the AA unit, establish close working relationships at peer levels, and keep communications open between the supported unit and the supporting unit. The level of success or failure that the mech force will achieve is greatly dependent on the team concept, level of cooperation, and mutual trust.

Fundamentals

The process of task organization distributes available units to a supported headquarters by establishing various command and support relationships. A mechanized task force (MTF) is created by task-organizing mech infantry and/or tanks under the command of a single battalion or regimental commander. Air, artillery, light armored reconnaissance (LAR), motor transport, and other combat support and CSS units support the MTF. The following fundamentals apply to task organization:

- Flexibility—Task organization is based on the current situation but must also be prepared to meet new requirements due to rapidly changing events. The task-organized elements of a unit should have a similar degree of mobility.
- Unity of command—Mech forces normally operate at distances and a tempo that preclude centralized control of supporting units by the parent headquarters. To ensure positive control and unity of effort, supporting units should be attached to the base maneuver units. The commander must have the means and authority to control the employment of the combined arms force. Command and support relationships must provide the commander maximum flexibility to accomplish the assigned mission. To develop familiarity, teamwork, and trust within subordinate units, the commander should avoid making frequent changes to the task organization and strive to establish standing relationships among units.
- Self-sufficiency—Because subordinate units are highly mobile and may operate at considerable distance from one another, the higher commander should also assign sufficient combat support and CSS to accomplish the mission.
- Tactical integrity—To facilitate and simplify C2, the commander should maintain the tactical integrity of units when task-organizing. Maintaining tactical integrity of combat support units is secondary to the tactical integrity of combat units.

Cross Attachment

Task-organizing a force for a specific mission on a temporary basis creates cross attachment. For example, a tank battalion detaches a tank company that is subsequently attached to an infantry battalion mechanized in AAVs. The infantry battalion mechanized in AAVs detaches a company to the tank battalion to create two battalion task forces with complementary capabilities. Cross-attached units are described by their mix of tank and mech infantry.

Tank Heavy

A tank-heavy force has more subordinate tank units than infantry units. See figure 2-1 on page 2-4. The headquarters of a tank-heavy task force is usually that of a tank battalion. Tank-heavy forces are preferred when—

- Shock action and firepower are desired.
- Terrain is open with few obstacles.
- Enemy antitank (AT) fire is easily suppressed.

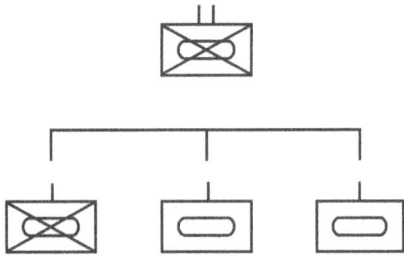

Figure 2-1. Tank-Heavy Force.

Mech Heavy

A mech-heavy force, also known as infantry-heavy force, has more subordinate infantry units mounted in tracked vehicles [AAVs] than subordinate tank units. See figure 2-2. The headquarters of a mech-heavy task force is usually that of an infantry battalion or regiment. Mech-heavy forces are employed—

● In the conduct of security operations suitable for LAR or mech infantry.
● When specific terrain must be seized and held.
● In built-up areas or other restrictive terrain.
● When visibility is limited.
● Against strong points.
● When heavy AT fires or obstacles are expected.

Balanced

A balanced force has an equal number of subordinate tank and mech infantry units. The headquarters of a balanced task force can be either that of a tank battalion or infantry battalion/regiment. A balanced task force enhances tank and infantry capabilities while retaining similar mobility.

Company-Size Maneuver

A company-size maneuver element is a team organized by cross attachment of one or more tank platoons and/or mounted or dismounted infantry platoons. An infantry or tank battalion commander receiving tank or mech infantry companies based on METT-T may tailor those units by cross-attaching tank platoons and mech infantry companies to form company teams. The company is the smallest element of a mech force task-organized with combined arms. A company-sized mech unit typically consists of a tank or infantry headquarters; a combination of several tank, infantry, and/or LAR platoons; and an attached AA unit supporting the infantry. Other supporting units, such as combat engineers, may also be attached. The following are types of mech company teams:

● Tank-heavy teams.
● Mech-heavy teams.
● Balanced teams.
● Mech-pure companies.
● Tank-pure companies.

Combat Support

In carrying out their mission of supporting the infantry, AA units typically receive combat support from various units. These combat support units may be attached, GS/DS or organic to the supported unit. Support will come from the GCE and other elements of the MAGTF, including the aviation combat element. The types of combat support provided will depend on METT-T.

Antiarmor

Antiarmor support is provided by tube-launched, optically-tracked, wire-command link guided missile (TOW) sections and Javelin sections of the antiarmor platoon located in the infantry battalion weapons company. The tank battalion maintains an AT platoon equipped with TOWs

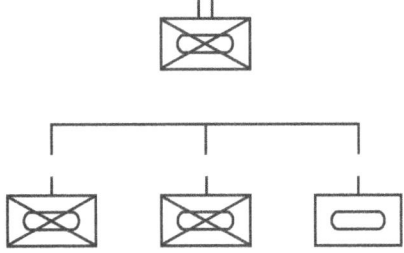

Figure 2-2. Mech-Heavy Force.

mounted on a high mobility multipurpose wheeled vehicle (HMMWV).

TOW. The TOW is used to engage enemy armor at ranges up to 3,750 meters and assigned missions to overwatch lead units or to cover flanks. HMMWV-mounted TOWs do not possess the same cross-country mobility as the AAV, tank or LAV. Because TOWs are vulnerable to suppressive fires, firing positions must be camouflaged to take advantage of the TOW's long firing range and to conceal the vulnerable TOW shooter.

Javelin. The Javelin is the replacement for the Dragon antitank guided munition (ATGM). It is a top-attack or direct-fire mode, man-portable, AT missile. The Javelin's lock-on-before-launch, fire-and-forget capability increases the probability of a hit because the gunner is not exposed to enemy suppressive fires while tracking the missile to its target. The Javelin's maximum effective range of 2,000-plus meters is beyond the maximum effective range of current threat tank and combat vehicle coaxial machine guns. The AAV provides the embarked infantry carrying these systems with mobility and limited armored protection.

81-Millimeter Mortar

The 81-millimeter mortar of the weapons company of the infantry battalion provides an ability to deliver immediate suppressive fires or target marking. Mortar squads may depend upon AAVs for transport during mech operations. Because of their limited range, mortar squads are usually placed well forward in the vehicle formation. If the entire mortar platoon is assigned, the two sections will bound to alternating firing positions to keep the lead elements of the force within their firing fan. If only one section is available, it will normally establish a firing position when required. This allows the fires of the section to be massed.

Heavy Machine Guns

The infantry battalion weapons company's MK-19, 40-millimeter grenade launcher and M2,

.50-caliber machine gun are normally employed in security missions and can provide direct fire support to dismounted infantry. When mounted on transport vehicles, the M2 and MK-19 can be used in the conduct of route reconnaissance. AAVs can also provide direct fire support with the M2 and MK-19 machine guns in the vehicles' UGWS.

Artillery

Artillery is the primary supporting arm for land operations. It provides most of the suppressive fire that allows assaulting elements to maneuver. A variety of projectiles (e.g., HE, smoke, illumination, chemical, dual purpose improved conventional munitions [DPICM], laser-guided munitions [Copperhead]) are available. The DPICM and Copperhead rounds have an antiarmor capability. FO teams from supporting artillery batteries originate calls for fire. In the absence of FO teams, AAV crews can call for and adjust artillery fires. Because towed artillery cannot displace as rapidly as the mech force, artillery must echelon firing units forward to provide continuous coverage for an advancing mech force. The artillery FO supporting the mech force should maintain close coordination to determine the exact status of artillery support. If mech units advance while their supporting artillery is displacing, early coordination with other supporting arms can potentially prevent gaps in fire support coverage.

Naval Gun Fire

Although the MAGTF does not have an organic NGF capability in most amphibious operations, Navy ships will provide NGF support to the forces ashore. AAVs may have their own NGF liaison officer attached that will coordinate NGF for the AAV unit or supported commander during amphibious operations or during subsequent operations that are conducted near the coastline.

Reconnaissance

GCE units provide reconnaissance support. Reconnaissance teams using organic assets are inserted by air or mech patrols of tanks and

AAVs/LAVs. Patrols will normally patrol forward and to the flanks not to exceed the supporting arms umbrella provided by the MAGTF.

Combat Engineers

Engineers conduct minefield breaching/emplacement and obstacle clearing/installation. To support the task force, engineers should be provided AAVs for transportation to have the same mobility as the maneuver elements. Combat engineers should be well forward in the mech force if choke points, obstacles, and minefields are expected.

To rapidly breach minefields and obstacles, engineers use the MK-154, LMC kit, that is organic to the H&S company, AA battalion. The MK-154 can be mounted on any AAVP7A1. The kit is composed of three rocket-propelled line charges containing 1,750 pounds of C-4 plastic explosive that is stored in the AAVP7A1 troop compartment. The MK-154 can clear a lane 100 meters by 16 meters. When attached to the mech force, the chase vehicles assigned to the MK-154 provide added mobility to breaching teams and combat engineers.

Antiair

Air defense for the mech force is a multilayered system. It includes long-range attack aircraft that strike enemy airfields and conduct combat air patrols to intercept enemy aircraft and the low altitude air defense (LAAD) battalion. LAAD teams using the Stinger surface-to-air missile are positioned around the force with overlapping sectors of fire to provide defense against enemy aircraft. Although the LAAD teams have their own transport, they may be carried in AAVs to increase their mobility to that of the mech force.

Air

Close air support (CAS) is provided to the mech force by both fixed- and rotary-wing aircraft. Rotary-wing aircraft allows overwatch of the MAGTF during mech operations and enhance situational awareness of the battlefield.

AAV Allocations

Each AA battalion has at least four letter companies and an H&S company. Each letter company is equipped with 43 AAVP7A1s, 2 AAVC7A1s, and 1 AAVR7A1. The AAVs used to support the GCE come from the three line platoons of each letter company. Each line platoon is equipped with 12 AAVP7A1s.

Approximately 42 AAVs are required to mechanize a reinforced infantry battalion; however, the AA company possesses only 36 AAVP7A1s dedicated for support. Table 2-1 shows the typical numbers of AAVs required to mechanize elements of the GCE.

Table 2-1. AAV Allocation.

Unit	Number Required
Three infantry companies (rein)	36 AAVP7A1s
81-millimeter mortar platoon	8 AAVP7A1s
Engineers	3 AAVP7A1s
Battalion aid station (BAS)	3 AAVP7A1s
Command	2 AAVP7A1s 2 AAVC7A1s

The AA company has 36 AAVP7A1s in 3 line platoons available for assignment to GCE units. Based on the mission and other transportation assets assigned, the GCE commander can assign four additional AAVP7A1s to the GS section of the AA company headquarters platoon. Normally, these vehicles provide support in towing disabled AAVs to the maintenance collection point for repair, support the company logistic train, and provide local security to the AA company headquarters.

The AA platoon is the basic building block for task organization. Generally, no more than 18 Marines should be assigned to any one vehicle since more than this number requires precise staging and seating arrangements that can degrade the ability of embarked personnel to respond to tactical situations. No more than 21 Marines should be contemplated for ship-to-shore movement. The established method of task organization is one AA section for each rifle platoon and one AA section for support missions. These support missions include the command AAV used by the infantry company commander and the AA platoon commander, logistic AAV, 60-millimeter mortar section, and engineer vehicle to provide mobility for any other assets attached to the company by higher headquarters.

Movement

Self-deploying AAVs allow the MAGTF to maneuver forces from ship to shore and inland in a seamless transition. The AAV provides the principal means of armored-protected land and water mobility for supported units.

Control

The AA unit movement is controlled through centralized and decentralized techniques.

Centralized

The centralized control technique enables the supported commander to control the movement of the mech force through verbal orders to the AA unit leader. This technique maximizes the experience and skill of the AA unit to facilitate the movement of the force. In addition, the centralized control technique may be employed for the conduct of tactical road marches or movement to contact when the unit is traveling together. Centralized control allows the supported commander to—

● Coordinate fire support.
● Plan.
● Issue orders to assigned unit leaders.
● Conduct liaison with other units on the march while retaining centralized control of the embarked force.

Decentralized Control

The decentralized control technique passes control of the movement of AA sections to subordinate leaders of the embarked force. For example, the infantry platoon commander would exercise the control of movement through the supporting AA section leader. The AA section leader receives direction from the infantry platoon leader and controls the movement of the AAVs in the section accordingly. This technique may be used in the following situations:

● Upon initiation of contact.
● In the approach to the point of debarkation.
● When the mech infantry platoons are operating away from the main body.

Considerations

Dispersion, speed, possible immediate actions, and the commander's location to effectively control the unit should be considered when maneuvering forces. During movement, the commander should—

● Use terrain to mask movement/noise and to avoid exposure to the enemy.
● Use supporting arms to suppress enemy antiarmor fires.
● Move quickly out of the impact area when encountering enemy indirect fire.
● Change the AAV's primary position after engaging the enemy.

Dispersion

The factors of METT-T greatly influence dispersion and mobility. For example, when operating in a traveling/column manner, a battalion-sized MTF can occupy over 17 kilometers from front to rear. Such an MTF cannot generate significant combat power quickly. If the point elements halt and engage the enemy, it could take 30 minutes for the remainder of the column to close the formation and join the fight. Commanders must minimize the effects of this dispersion of combat power. Having units maneuver on broader fronts when the terrain permits can reduce the effects of improper dispersion.

Speed

Mech columns routinely travel at speeds averaging 20 miles per hour. A meeting engagement of two opposing mech forces can occur at 40 miles per hour, and a single column can move quickly into the opposing force's antiarmor kill zone without notice. Speed has the following advantages:

● Permits the rapid massing of combat power from across a broad expanse of terrain at the decisive point in the battle.

● Supports the rapid exploitation of openings in the enemy's front, permitting the armor-protected movement of infantry into the enemy's rear.

● Permits the commander to maneuver forces swiftly and place them on crucial sections of the battlefield, thereby forcing the opposing commander to surrender the initiative.

Immediate Actions

The individual training of AAV crews and infantry will carry the first critical moments of the mech battle, while the mech force continues to maneuver by either advancing or seeking cover and concealment from enemy fire. Immediate action drills of fundamental responses to enemy actions must be wargamed and rehearsed to the point where they can be confidently carried out instantly. In mech operations, the commander's decisionmaking often is limited to a matter of seconds, and actions are executed by the forces in less time than it takes the commander to assess the situation and decide on a specific action.

Commander's Location

Normally positioned as far forward in the formation as feasible under the tactical situation, the MTF commander should position the command vehicle immediately behind the forward screening section of AAVs, tanks or LAVs. From an overwatch position, the commander will be able to employ supporting arms and direct additional mech forces forward to the developing tactical situation.

CHAPTER 3. AMPHIBIOUS OPERATIONS

During World War II, the amphibious and mech characteristics of the amphibious tractor made it the backbone of the Marine Corps' amphibious assault capability. The landing vehicle, tracked, was originally designed to operate primarily in the water and in a logistical role, but its demonstrated utility and versatility quickly led to improvements that largely reversed its initial concept of employment. Continuous upgrades enhanced its inherent ability to transition from an armored landing craft to an APC. Vast improvements were made to the vehicle's mobility and firepower ashore. These combined changes produced the highly capable AAV that is a critical part of the Marine Corps' amphibious doctrine.

Joint Publication (JP) 3-02, *Joint Doctrine for Amphibious Operations,* defines an amphibious operation as a military operation launched from the sea by an amphibious force, embarked in ships or craft with the primary purpose of introducing a landing force ashore to accomplish the assigned mission. Amphibious operations include assaults, withdrawals, demonstrations, raids, and other operations in a permissive, uncertain or hostile environment.

The AAV7A1's demonstrated ability to negotiate various surf conditions and obstacles while simultaneously withstanding small arms fire makes it uniquely suited to conducting the initial portion of any amphibious operation. These characteristics allow the Marine Corps the flexibility to exploit gaps in the enemy's coastal defenses and/or mass substantial combat power at a decisive place to create such gaps.

Once the enemy's defenses have been penetrated, the mech and highly mobile nature of the AAV enable the embarked assault forces to rapidly deploy to their inland objective. This dual nature of the AAV helps to generate an overwhelming operational tempo thus maintaining the overall momentum of the assault.

Types of Operations

There are five principal types of amphibious operations—the assault, raid, demonstration, withdrawal, and other operations. Various capabilities and functions of AAVs provide support for these amphibious operations.

Assault

The amphibious assault is the most important type of amphibious operation. It involves establishing a force on a hostile or potentially hostile shore for the immediate execution of inland maneuver. The unique combination of armor and amphibious capabilities of the AAV make it the mainstay of surface assault forces conducting amphibious assaults.

Raid

An amphibious raid is a landing from the sea involving swift incursion into hostile territory for a specified purpose that is followed by a planned withdrawal. Raids are conducted to—

- Inflict loss or damage.
- Secure information.
- Create a diversion.
- Capture or evacuate individuals and/or material.

Raid forces consist of individuals or unit(s) with the capabilities or skills required to accomplish the mission. Raid forces should be as small as possible to maximize stealth and speed and to achieve the desired effect. AAVs should be used when the mission requirements dictate the need for armor, firepower, and mobility. AAVs also have the ability to extract the raid force back to sea without the assistance of additional landing craft.

Demonstration

The amphibious demonstration is conducted to deceive the enemy by a show of force with the expectation of deluding the enemy into a course of action unfavorable to him. The effectiveness of a demonstration increases in direct proportion to the degree of realism involved in its execution. The AAVs' imposing presence enhanced through the utilization of their smoke generation system and noise signature makes AAVs a convincing show of force. The amphibious and mech nature of the AAV pressures the enemy to divert forces to deal with the threat, thus achieving the desired effect.

Withdrawal

The amphibious withdrawal involves the evacuation of land forces by sea in naval ships or craft from a hostile shore. Amphibious withdrawals may be conducted to extract a force under pressure, to assist in the repositioning of forces elsewhere in theater, to reconstitute forces afloat or to establish a reserve after introduction of follow-on forces. The armored and amphibious nature of AAVs makes them particularly well suited for withdrawing forces from hostile shores. Their self-sufficient amphibious capability enables them to act as a covering force for other assets withdrawing aboard landing crafts air cushion (LCACs), landing crafts, utility (LCUs) or landing craft, mechanized (LCMs).

Military Operations Other Than War

Amphibious operations in support of MOOTW may involve elements of both combat and noncombat operations. Some of these operations may parallel other types of amphibious operations (e.g., a noncombatant evacuation operation [NEO] may closely parallel an amphibious raid) and may

require minor adjustments to planning. Other MOOTW (e.g., FHA) may require considerable flexibility on the part of the planners. MOOTW are normally more sensitive to political considerations due to the overriding goal to prevent, preempt or limit potential hostilities. In addition to flexibility of platform, amphibious and mech capabilities, and force protecting armor, AAVs have a substantial cargo capacity to assist in conducting varied operations ranging from NEOs to relief operations.

Intelligence Requirements

The impact of environmental conditions and enemy defenses must be considered when AAVs are employed, because AAVs are typically the first assault wave in amphibious operations. Intelligence information on hydrography and enemy defenses will be required to effectively employ AAVs to negotiate the seaward approaches and to move from the surf zone to inland objectives.

Hydrography

Hydrography, the description and study of bodies of water and their touching land areas, is used to interpret sea, surf, and beach conditions on AAV employment. Many complex factors influence these conditions and have varying effects upon AAV operations. The success or failure of an amphibious landing using AAVs largely depends on the completeness and accuracy of intelligence data and upon the AAV unit leader's interpretation of that data. Although sea, surf, and beach characteristics contribute to the following AAV casualties, appendix E provides AAV recovery criteria:

- Swamping, flipping or capsizing by breakers when approaching the shore.
- Sinking due to structural damage sustained from impacting reefs or other natural obstructions.
- Broaching on a sandbar, obstacles or the beach.

Sea States

AAVs have a demonstrated ability to easily negotiate sea states 1 through 3 (see table 3-1), but will experience difficulty maintaining speed and maneuverability in sea state 4. AAVs can survive operations in sea state 5, but at reduced effectiveness. Troops should not be embarked aboard AAVs in sea state 5 conditions, and it is not advisable to conduct operations in sea state 5 or greater.

Sea Waves

Caused by high winds in storm areas, sea waves are usually steep, have a short period, and often crest and break in deep water. They are commonly referred to as white caps or combers if very large. Combers affect the speed and maneuverability of the AAV. In addition, the driver's visibility will be reduced because of the spray encountered. Operations in sea states 3 to 5 should be conducted with the driver's hatch closed to enable the driver to maintain speed. In these conditions, the vehicle commander, magnetic heading device or precision lightweight glo-

bal positioning system (GPS) receiver system (PLGRS) may be used to assist the driver in maintaining course. High seas must be anticipated in the navigation plan, landing formation, and landing schedule.

Swell

A swell is characterized by its lack of steepness and longer, rolling period. Depending on their size and orientation to the AAV, swells can impede the vehicle's speed and maneuverability. Swell conditions must be anticipated in the navigation plan, landing formation, and landing schedule. Heavy swells (sea state 5 or greater) may also make debarkation from naval shipping more difficult or dangerous. Swells more commonly affect embarked personnel by causing motion or seasickness and fatigue. Long waterborne movements (greater than 15,000 yards) in large swells (sea state 4 or greater) should be avoided as they reduce the combat effectiveness of embarked assault forces. Swells have the greatest effect upon AAVs once they reach the shore and form breakers.

Table 3-1. Sea State Conditions.

Sea State	Conditions
1	Wind speeds between 5 to 9 miles per hour (5 to 8 knots). Wave heights considered small wavelets between 0.5 and 1 feet (0.6093 to 0.304 meters. Small wavelets with glassy-appearing crests and no breaking.
2	Wind speeds between 10 to 11 miles per hours (9 to 10 knots). Wave heights considered large wavelets, between 1.5 and 2 feet (0.456 to 0.609 meters). Large wavelets, crests begin to break and whitecaps are scattered.
3	Wind speeds between 16 to 17 miles per hour (14 to 15 knots). Wave heights considered small, between 3.5 and 4 feet (1.06 to 1.21 meters). Small waves becoming longer and whitecaps are numerous.
4	Wind speeds between 19 to24 miles per hour (17 to 21 knots). Wave heights considered moderate, between 4 and 7.5 feet (1.24-2.5 meters). Moderate waves forming numerous white caps and some spray.
5	Wind speeds between 24 to 28 miles per hour (21 to 25 knots). Wave heights considered large, between 8 and 12 feet (2.43 to 3.65 meters). Large waves form and whitecaps are common, along with more spray.

Tides

The stage of tide affects the width of the beach and surf zone; therefore, in amphibious operations using AAVs, the high and low tides and the tide range must be known. Tides affect the type of surf, depth of water over sandbars and reefs, and the effectiveness of underwater obstacles. For example, high tides will enable AAVs to more easily overcome sandbars, reefs, and obstacles but may tend to increase the percentage of plunging breakers by shortening the surf zone. Low tides may have the direct opposite effect by increasing spilling breakers. Extreme highs and lows, which may remain unchanged over the course of several days, can occur and severely affect operations.

Surf

Various factors can greatly affect amphibious operations using AAVs in the surf zone. The minimum information on the surf conditions needed to safely conduct AAV operations should include the following:

- Significant breaker height.
- Maximum breaker height.
- Breaker period or interval in seconds.
- Breaker types (i.e., spilling, plunging or surging).
- Breaker angle.
- Littoral or long shore current in knots.
- Width of the surf zone.
- Number of breaker lines.

Before AAV operations, a surf observation report (SUROB) must be conducted. For large-scale operations, the SUROB should be conducted hourly for 4 hours before H-hour.

Surf Zone

The most dangerous portion of an amphibious landing is negotiating the surf zone. The energy of the wave is released at this point and most landing craft casualties occur at this time. Conditions in the surf zone are the combined result of the following factors:

- Breaker type.
- Maximum breaker height.

- Breaker period or interval.
- Vehicle load.

Table 3-2 illustrates the handling capabilities and safety criteria of the AAV under various conditions. This table represents the maximum safe breaker heights and breaker periods allowed for each type of AAV load. Exceeding these conditions is unsafe for AAV operations.

The load criteria is based on three internal cargo weights that act as a type of ballast for the AAV: combat load (CL) 10,000 pounds; TL 5,600 pounds; and combat equipped (CE), which is an empty vehicle. The vehicle can handle shorter intervals between breakers or right itself as the cargo or ballast increases. The listed breaker period should be read as the minimum interval in seconds.

Narrow surf zones can hinder AAV operations if the surf is high (4 to 6 feet) and moving in excess

Table 3-2. Safe Breaker Heights and Breaker Periods.

Type of AAV Load	Maximum Breaker Height (feet)	Breaker Period (seconds)
100 Percent Plunging Breakers		
CL	6 10*	9 9*
TL	6 10*	9 9*
CE	6 8*	13 13*
50 Percent Plunging/50 Percent Spilling Breakers		
CL	6	8
TL	6	8
CE	6	10
100 Percent Spilling Breakers		
CL	6	5
TL	6	5
CE	6	7
* Used when planning combat operations.		

of 8.5 knots. These combined conditions can cause the vehicle to contact the bottom quickly and sometimes violently, become swamped, and flip over.

Reefs, Sandbars, and Other Natural Obstructions

A distinct advantage AAVs have over conventional landing craft is their tracked suspension. This alone enables them to negotiate reefs, sandbars, and other natural obstructions that may impede boats. The surf beat, vertical climb, and breakers must be considered before AAVs are navigated through those obstructions. Information needed for AAV operations over reefs or bars should include the following:

- Nature or type of the obstruction.
- Distance offshore or location of the obstruction.
- Slope (seaward).
- Depth of water at various tidal stages or height of obstruction above water.
- Gaps or passages in the sandbar, reef or obstruction.
- Breaker height.

Surf Beat. Surf beat is the distinct rise and fall of the mean water level within the surf zone. Surf beat can be of significance to AAVs approaching submerged obstacles such as sandbars or reefs. Normally, surf beat is equal to 10 percent of the breaker height. This quick raising and dropping of almost a foot at times can throw an AAV against a reef hard enough to severely damage the suspension, because reefs can be composed of coral or rock. The damaging effects of surf beat upon a vehicle can be overcome if the tide provides sufficient water depth over the obstacle or if the composition of the sandbar or reef is soft material.

Vertical Climb. On land, AAVs can climb a 3-foot wall, but in water, the vertical distance is much less. The depth of the water over a steep gradient obstruction (e.g., reef, sea wall) should be at least 3 feet to allow the tracks to be able to engage and climb it. This is not a concern where the gradient is less steep (e.g., sandbars), since

the tracks will eventually contact the bottom and gain traction to transverse the obstacle. Because reefs are irregular and often contain many pockets or holes, care should be taken to avoid getting an AAV stuck in one without sufficient water depth to climb out.

Breakers. Despite the AAV's ability to climb sandbars and reefs, additional care should be taken whenever approaching these obstacles as swells may break violently upon them. Wherever bars or reefs are present, the wave crest will peak as the waves roll over them. The water depth over the sandbar or reef and the wave height determine whether or not breaking takes place on or near the obstruction. Generally, if the depth is less than one and a half times the breaker height, waves will break upon the sandbar or reef. For example, a 6-foot swell will break upon a sandbar or reef unless the water depth over that obstruction is a least 9 feet.

Currents

In conducting amphibious landings, planners are most often concerned with the effects of long shore or littoral current, but offshore seasonal currents can have a greater effect on AAVs. In conducting AAV operations, the speeds of long shore (littoral) and offshore currents should be collected and considered.

Offshore Currents. Tidal and nontidal offshore currents are found outside the surf zone. Currents in excess of 3 knots will adversely affect an AAV's navigation and speed.

Long Shore/Littoral Currents. Littoral currents are set up within the surf zone by the breaking waves. They flow parallel to the shoreline inside the breaker line. They increase with larger breaker angles, beach gradients, and breaker heights. Larger intervals between breakers tend to slow the velocity of littoral currents. These currents present little problem for AAVs since the vehicles have usually gained positive traction before reaching the point where they occur. These currents can cause conventional landing craft to broach along the shoreline. At this point, AAVs are out of the surf zone and past the high watermark.

Gradient

Gradient tends to have little effect upon AAV operations unless it is nearly vertical. Depth of the surf zone, number of breakers present, and type of breaker that will be encountered are gradient characteristics that may affect AAV operations. Steep gradients of more than 1:15 (7 percent) tend to produce a very high percentage of plunging breakers. Steep beaches normally have short surf zones with one line of breakers present. Moderate gradients of between 1:15 (7 percent) and 1:30 (3 percent) tend to produce spilling breakers, but often create a mixed percentage of both plunging and spilling breakers. Moderate gradients produce bars and extend the surf zone creating two to four lines of breakers. Mild gradients of greater than 1:30 (3 percent) tend to produce a very high percentage of spilling breakers. They also produce several bars that greatly extend the surf zone and lines of breakers.

Beach Composition

The beach may be composed of silt, mud, sand, gravel, boulders, rock, coral or any combination of these. The nature and composition of the beach foreshore, backshore, and hinterland may affect the trafficability for AAVs.

Foreshore. Coarser materials (i.e., gravel, rocks or cobblestones) from the surf zone to the high watermark provide poor traction for AAVs beginning to ground themselves and moving out of the water. Since AAVs are not fully grounded at the foreshore, they tend to slip on these coarse materials. The heavier the AAV and the steeper the gradient, the less traction an AAV will get. The most critical area of trafficability on the beach is the foreshore due to the increased gradient and looseness of the material. As the gradient increases to its peak, AAVs will tend to become stuck or mired in the loose bottom material.

Backshore. The composition of the backshore is usually soft, loose, and dry. Normally, the backshore does not present a problem to trafficability since it generally has a mild gradient, but AAVs may lose traction if the gradient is steeper.

Hinterland. The hinterland is the area just past the backshore behind the first line of permanent vegetation. AAVs may encounter trafficability problems in the hinterland if confronted with dunes or cliffs. If these obstacles are too steep, the AAV may advance only to the backshore.

Beach Exits

Avenues off the beach or beach exits allow AAVs to quickly move inland. Natural or man-made obstacles may channel or prevent AAVs from exiting the beach to move inland. The AAV can climb a 3-foot wall and cover an 8-foot span, but any obstacle greater than this must be breached or avoided.

Enemy Defenses

Amphibious operations will normally avoid concentrated enemy defenses or surfaces. The LF will require the armored, amphibious capabilities of the AAV. Enemy defenses against AAV landings can vary from AT mines and tetrahedrons to entrenched infantry with ATGM or a combination thereof. Operational considerations for using AAVs are the enemy situation and obstacles.

Enemy Situation

Enemy situation intelligence required when planning AAV landings includes—

- Tank and IFV threat.
- ATGM threat.
- Heavy machine gun (above 12.5 millimeters) threat.

- Hardened positions (e.g., bunkers, trenches).
- Enemy capability to observe beach-landing sites.
- Location of enemy mobile reserves.
- High-speed avenues of approach and lines of communications (LOC).

Obstacles

Manmade obstacles can range from AT and personnel mines to steel tetrahedrons and rock-filled cribs. Beach obstacles are typically laid out in belts from the low tide line to the high watermark and beyond. Overcoming these obstacles requires a high water depth, but even at high tide, vehicle casualties are likely to occur. Surface or submerged obstructions must be cleared before landing operations commence. If only narrow passages or lanes are cleared, AAVs commonly will use the column formation to safely traverse the cleared channels.

Sources of Hydrographic Information

The following resources should be used when planning for an operation involving AAVs:

- Confirmatory beach reports.
- SUROB.
- Mapping, charting, and geodesy materials (e.g., National Imagery and Mapping Agency maps, charts).
- Tourist guides and maps.
- Aerial observation and photos.
- Multispectral imagery.

Planning

See JP 3-02.1, *Joint Doctrine for Landing Force Operations,* for definition of amphibious force (AF), amphibious task force (ATF), and landing force (LF).

Although assigned as a component of the GCE, the AA unit is under the OPCON of commander, amphibious task force (CATF) or supported unit commander for the conduct of the operation. During this period, the AA unit leader maintains TACON over the unit. The AA unit leader is responsible to the CATF or supported unit commander for landing the embarked infantry on the correct beach at the proper time. See JP 3-02.1, for additional information on command relationships.

Assault Amphibian Unit Special Staff Officer

During planning for amphibious operations, the AA unit leader is a special staff officer to the GCE commander under the staff cognizance of the operations officer. As special staff officer to the GCE commander, the AA unit leader deals with matters pertaining to employment of the supported unit's AAVs in the conduct of amphibious operations and the subsequent operations ashore. The AA unit leader's responsibilities are varied but must include providing estimates of supportability to the ATF.

Coordination with CATF and CLF

Although a subordinate element of the GCE, the AA unit leader is responsible to CATF or the supported unit commander for the unit's safe operation of the ship-to-shore movement as well as waterborne operations conducted in the amphibious objective area (AOA). The AA unit leader must conduct the necessary coordination with the naval personnel responsible for planning and executing the operation. The AA unit leader will ensure adequate safety measures have been planned for launch, recovery, and coordination of emergency procedures. The coordination must be conducted with the concurrence of the GCE commander and commander, landing force (CLF), and it should support the GCE's scheme of maneuver. To ensure that the tenets of parallel and concurrent planning are occurring, the AA unit leader should always participate in the planning of the amphibious operation to provide appropriate recommendations and expertise regarding safe AA operation. The AA unit leader should be collocated with the supported commander during planning and in communication during the conduct phase of the operation.

Estimates of Supportability

Planning continues with receipt of the order alerting AF elements of upcoming operations. The AA unit leader is responsible for providing appropriate recommendations regarding the tactical employment, operational safety, and logistical support requirements of the unit. The estimates of supportability should be provided for each course of action considered by the GCE commander for the ship-to-shore operation and subsequent operations ashore. The AA unit leader must support operational planning and execution to ensure the safe accomplishment of the mission and should make recommendations regarding the following aspects of the operation:

- Overall mission and task organization for AAVs.
- Assignment to various classes of shipping.
- Request for essential elements of information from Navy component intelligence staff officer (N-2)/intelligence staff officer (S-2).
- Estimates of supportability for proposed GCE courses of action.
- Interactions with the Navy component operations staff officer (N-3)/operations staff officer (S-3) for scheme of maneuver for ship-to-shore movement.
- Development of the landing plan.
- Tactics/techniques of amphibious assault using AAVs.
- Waterborne assault breaching of obstacles and minefields.
- Night operations/landings.
- Rehearsals and associated prelanding/operation training.
- Logistical requirements.

- Communications considerations.
- Safety.
- Subsequent operations/tactics ashore.

Organization for Amphibious Assaults

An amphibious operation is inherently among the most complex operation to plan, involving air, naval, and land units. To facilitate planning for movement and landing, troops and equipment must be organized into various categories, serials, and boat teams.

Landing Categories

Personnel, equipment, and supplies are further subdivided into one of five categories based upon their importance to the operation and the times they will be needed.

Scheduled Waves. Scheduled waves are units that have a predetermined time and place of landing. They consist of AA units, landing craft or helicopters that carry the MAGTF assault troops and their initial combat supplies. AA units are generally employed as scheduled waves. After the waterborne waves have crossed the line of departure (LD), the landing of scheduled waves proceeds without change, except in an emergency. Scheduled waves land according to the assault schedule. AAVs and their embarked LFs are typically landed in scheduled waves because their time and place of landing are predetermined.

On-Call Waves. Units that may be required ashore soon, but with allowed discretion as to time and place of landing based on the assigned mission, are designated as on-call waves. On-call waves may contain infantry reserves, antimechanized units or combat support units. These waves are requested by serial number and are usually held in readiness for immediate landing. On-call waves are listed in the assault schedule, following the scheduled waves.

Nonscheduled Units. Nonscheduled units are generally held aboard ship in readiness to land. These units are usually comprised of troops and equipment not required ashore during the initial offloading. An example of a nonscheduled unit is a free boat. A free boat could be an AAV and/or landing craft designated to carry commanders, command/control groups or other LF personnel ashore. AAVs are not normally employed in the landing of nonscheduled units.

Prepositioned Emergency Supplies. Prepositioned emergency supplies are designated by the CLF to meet expected critical needs for CSS replenishment early in the ship-to-shore movement. These serialized supplies, available for immediate delivery ashore, are organized into floating dumps and prestaged, helicopter-lifted supplies. AAVs and/or other landing craft may be preloaded with critical combat supplies (e.g., ammunition, water, fuel) and positioned near the LD as floating dumps. AAVs are not normally employed as floating dumps.

Remaining Landing Force Supplies. This category consists of replenishment supplies and equipment not included in a unit commander's prescribed loads or floating dumps. This category is largely placed ashore during the general unloading period but can be selectively dispatched to replenish floating dumps or dumps ashore.

Serials

To provide a convenient means to identify elements of the LF, each grouping is given a serial number. A serial number is assigned to each unit, part of a unit, or grouping (including its equipment and initial combat supplies) embarked aboard one ship to be landed as a unit at the same time at one landing beach. Serial numbers are primarily reference numbers assigned by the CLF that act as a code to identify and control the unit or grouping for brevity in communications. An example of a serial might be an infantry company embarked aboard AAVs from the same ship that will land at the same beach at the same time.

Boat Teams

Serials are further broken down into boat teams. These are tactical divisions of the LF elements within that serial. Normally serials are assigned to landing craft or groups of landing craft. Boat teams are the tactical units or teams that are assigned to a particular landing craft; therefore, serials can have several boat teams or just one, depending on the number or capacity of the landing craft.

The serial designator of a boat team is a number followed by a dash and another number (e.g., 1-1, 1-2, 1-3). The first digit indicates the wave number and the second indicates the position in the wave. The AAV's position number indicates the vehicle farthest to the left facing the beach or the first craft in a column.

The notional tactical organization in table 3-3 largely composed of 1st Squad, is labeled Boat Team 1-1, thus being the left most vehicle of the first wave. Boat teams are made up of boat spaces that are variables, which account for the space and weight factor of personnel/equipment being assigned to a landing craft or amphibious vehicle. These spaces are based on the requirements of individual equipment (240 pounds occupying 13.5 cubic feet of space).

Table 3-3. Notional Boat Team for an AAVP7A1.

Boat Team	Personnel and Equipment	Boat Spaces
1-1	1st Squad, 1st Platoon, Company B	11
	Corpsman	1
	1st Machine Gun Team, Machine Gun Squad, Weapons Platoon, Company B	3
	81-millimeter FO Team	2
	Radio Operator	1
	Total	18

Landing Plan

The landing plan reflects the operational conduct of the amphibious operation and focuses on the establishment of the LF ashore. It is the product of extensive planning and coordination between the CATF and CLF and supports the maneuver of the GCE ashore. The AA unit commander will actively participate in the formulation and execution of the landing plan. The GCE scheme of maneuver ashore will be of primary concern in the development of the landing plan. The scheme of maneuver should be well understood by the AA unit Marines to facilitate planning and coordination of the ship-to-shore movement and subsequent operations ashore. Other factors are the CL of the infantry being supported, their assigned objectives, and the commander's intent.

Preparation of Landing Documents

The landing documents, completed by the LF in connection with waterborne movements from ship to shore, are of vital concern to participating AA units. These documents assign AA units to elements of the LF, prescribe loads, stipulate landing formations, and provide for AAV employment subsequent to the landing. See appendix F for landing documents of specific interest to AA units.

Organization of the Amphibious Objective Area

The AOA is organized into operating areas to meet tactical requirements and to facilitate control of the ship-to-shore movement. See figure 3-1. AA unit leaders must understand the TACON and administrative significance of these areas.

Line of Departure

The LD is a designated line offshore, parallel to the beach that represents the seaward extent of the boat lane. It is a coordinating line from which successive assault waves are dispatched for their final movement ashore. Topographic, oceanographic,

and tactical considerations determine the location of the LD. A separate LD may be provided for AAVs to reduce waterborne transit times.

Boat Lane

Boat lanes extend seaward from the landing beaches to the LD. The width of the landing beach determines the width of the boat lane. The typical length is from 2,000 to 2,700 yards. The width is usually 500 yards. See the grid reference system in appendix G. The flanks of the boat lane may be marked at the LD by a control ship, marker boats or buoys. The Navy is responsible for clearing mines or obstructions in the boat lane. AAV movement from the AAV launch area to the beach is controlled by the primary control ship (PCS) or secondary control ship (SCS) when designated.

Inner Transport Area

The inner transport area is an area located as close to the landing beach as depth of water, navigational hazards, boat traffic, and enemy action will permit assault shipping to move to expedite unloading.

AAV Launch Area

AAV launch areas are usually located as close to the seaward side of the LD as possible (within 1,500 yards). Amphibious ships carrying AAVs will conduct either static or underway launch of AAVs in this area. Upon entering the water, the AAVs will be directed to the LD or to an assigned maneuvering area to await dispatch to the LD. AA unit leaders should coordinate their launch to minimize loitering in the AAV launch area.

Control Ship Stations

Control ship stations are assigned to control ships for guiding and controlling the ship-to-shore movement. These stations are generally assigned as underway sectors to avoid shore-based threats. If the enemy situation permits, these stations may be located on either flank of the LD. During landing under quiet landing procedures (QLPs), AA unit

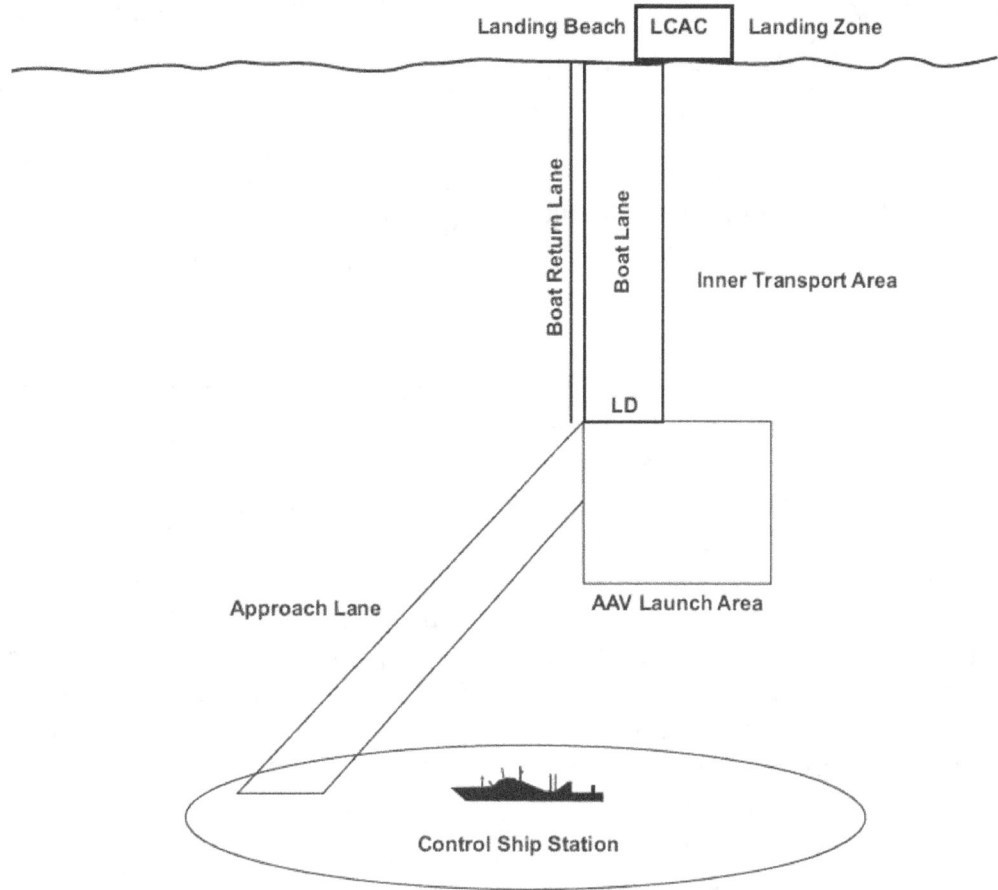

Figure 3-1. Amphibious Operations Area.

leaders receive visual control signals from control ship stations for the ship-to-shore movement.

Approach Lane

An approach lane is an extension of the boat lane from the LD toward the inner transport area. It indicates the route AAVs use to approach the LD and boat lane from the transport area. Generally, this lane is used when AAVs must launch further than 1,500 yards from the LD. The typical length is from 2,000 to 10,000 yards depending upon the deep-water hydrography.

Boat Return Lane

A boat return lane is designated to the left or right of the boat lane to facilitate the return of landing

craft or disabled AAVs seaward without interfering with the landing. AA units returning to their ships following a turn-away landing also use the boat return lane.

Landing Beach

The landing beach is the area assigned for the landing of troops and equipment by AAVs and landing craft. Beaches are colored and numbered to facilitate the identification and control of the force beachhead. Colored beaches are generally allotted for the landing of elements of one unit or a regimental-sized unit, with numbered beaches supporting the landing of battalion-sized units within the regimental (colored) beach. A landing beach is generally 500 to 1,000 meters in width.

Air Cushion Landing Zones

Air cushion landing zones (LZs) are the designated landing areas for LCAC. These areas are usually separate from beaches used by AAVs or conventional landing craft. AA units should avoid air cushion LZs to preclude possible mishaps or interference with LCAC operations.

Launch Planning

Launch planning is essential to the effective support of the established landing plan. It provides for the underway or static launch of AAVs from amphibious ships, the formation of waves, and the linkup with designated safety boats. This process can become more complex if the AAVs comprising the assault waves come from two or more ships. The AAV launch must be planned to facilitate the expeditious formation of waves to execute the landing plan. The AA unit leader must coordinate the proposed launch and ship-to-shore movement with the cognizant Navy ship-to-shore officer, ship operations officer, boat officers, and ship's first lieutenant. Considerations for coordination include—

- Ship's AAV launch/recovery safety criteria.
- Ship's ship-to-shore timeline.
- Serial number.
- Unit.
- Relation of the AAV launch area with respect to LD.
- Speed of ship (if launched underway).
- Well-deck lighting (if night launched).
- Staging of AAVs for launch.
- Communications and signals.
- Launch interval between vehicles.
- Location and dispositions of other amphibious ships in the AAV launch area, transport area, LD or boat lane.
- Location of safety boats.
- Coordination of safety procedures for AAV emergencies.

AAV Maximum Ship-to-Shore Swim Distance

The maximum range for an AAV in the water is 7 hours under normal operating conditions. The distance from amphibious ships that the AAV can launch is normally determined by the AAV commander, supported unit commander, and the ship's captain using METT-T with consideration for troop and crew fatigue.

Embarkation

AAVs are normally embarked and transported to the AOA on amphibious ships designed for AA operations. AAVS can be embarked on the following ship types: landing ship dock (LSD); landing ship, tank (LST); landing platform dock (LPD); landing helicopter dock (LHD); and general purpose amphibious assault ship (LHA). Employment of these ships to transport AAVs allow—

- Rapid embarkation/debarkation of AAVs.
- Ease of maintenance/preparation of vehicles for assault.
- High speed underway launch of AAVs on or near the LD.

Amphibious Shipping Characteristics

Amphibious ships have varying characteristics that affect their AAV transport capacity. Each ship has a published ship's loading characteristics pamphlet that details the AAV capacity and other limitations for the ship. Appendix H provides the estimated AAV capacities for the listed class and variant of ship for planning purposes only. Close liaison with the designated embarkation officer and ship's first lieutenant will provide the actual AAV spaces available for embarkation.

Embarkation Planning

Representatives of AA units must attend planning or presail conferences to advise supported unit commanders and naval representatives on shipping requirements and recommended methods of embarking and employing their units. Resulting plans appear as tables showing the types and number of AAVs to be carried by transport group or task force ships. Plans for the embarkation of AAVs are completed before the arrival of assault shipping. Embarkation planning considerations for AA units include—

- Embarkation of vehicles and crews.
- Coordination of plans for underway launch with respect to embarkation.
- Embarkation of command, maintenance, and communication personnel; equipment; and wheeled vehicles to support AAV operations.
- Loading of supplies; petroleum, oils, and lubricants (POL); repair parts or equipment to support embarked vehicles.
- Staffing and equipping ships designated as AAV repair ships.
- Preloading supported unit's equipment and cargo as required.

Embarkation of AAVs

AAVs can move on dry land without entering the water (dry loaded) pier side or at anchorage under the supervision of the embarkation officer or ship's first lieutenant; however, AAVs normally enter the water and transit out to the ship (wet loaded) offshore. In doing so, AAVs are normally grouped on the beach according to the ship on which they will embark. Upon notification that the ship is ready for embarkation, the AAVs proceed to the ship for loading. AA unit leaders must ensure the AAVs are embarked in the proper launching sequence for landing (e.g., first vehicle on, last vehicle off).

Launch Procedures

AAVs only enter the water after an SUROB has been sent to the controlling ship; the prewater operational checks have been performed; the passengers have been briefed, instructed, and

embarked; the manifest list has been submitted; and permission has been received to launch. A designated unit leader will control the launch of AAVs into the water. Before launching, the unit leader ensures that each crew chief inspects the AAV, conducts a prewater check, and completes a passenger manifest list. When satisfied that the AAVs are ready for waterborne operations, the unit leader launches the AAV by visual signal or radio. Launch interval will depend on conditions within the surf zone.

Tactical (Combat) Launch

The tactical (combat) launch is normally used when withdrawing from a hostile or potentially hostile beach or during training operations simulating such conditions. Under combat conditions, units typically form a defensive perimeter position before splashing back to amphibious shipping. Forming a defensive perimeter position can be done at the beach or at a secure site (e.g., assembly area located further inland). AAVs should enter the water soon after the prewater operations checklists have been completed. A prewater operations check ensures the watertight integrity of the vehicle and overall safety of the operation. Typically the defensive perimeter is used with infantry deployed slightly forward of the AAVs to provide local security. See figure 3-2 on page 3-14.

Forming a defensive perimeter position will spread the AA unit over several hundred meters and will rely heavily on the individual crew chiefs and section leaders for control and safety. Once personnel are in place, the AA unit leader will establish communications with the ship, designate personnel to conduct the surf report, and ensure that prewater operation checks are being conducted. The AA unit leader will coordinate the following information with the ship:

- Launch time. (When will the ship be ready?)
- Launch location. (Where is the unit located?)
- Surf report.
- Use of safety or guide boats.
- Recovery procedures for disabled vehicles.

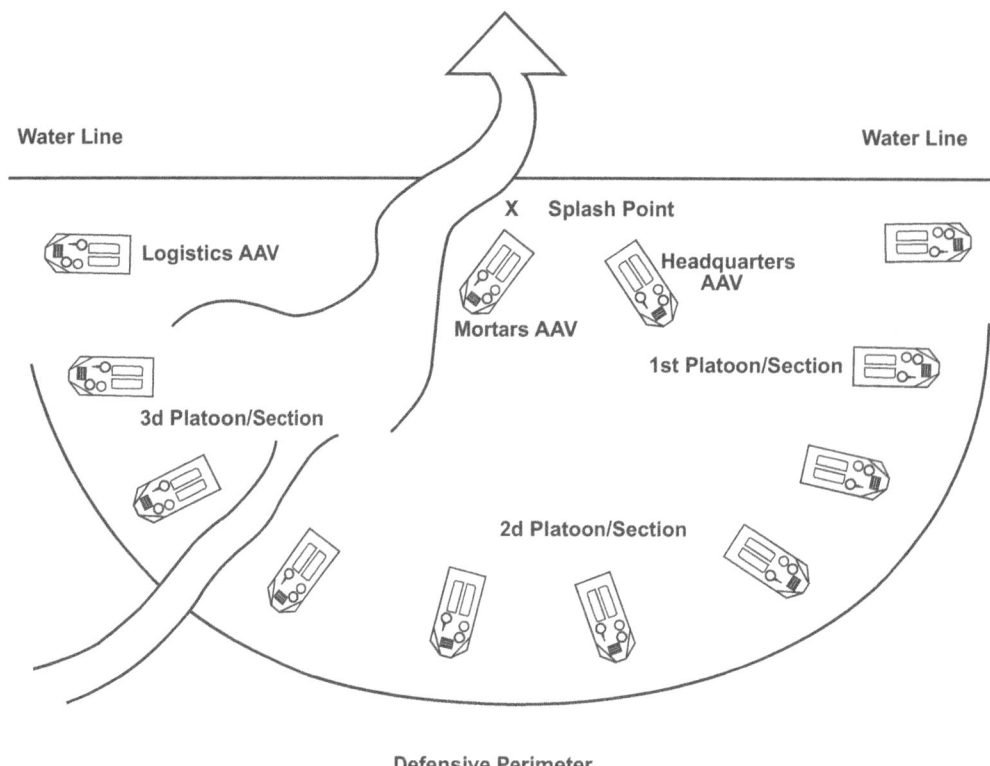

Figure 3-2. Tactical Launch Diagram.

Crew chiefs will complete the prewater operation checks, using a standard prelaunch checklist from the unit SOP and turn them over to each section leader or platoon commander. Passenger manifests, completed previously, should only require updating. Manifests will be turned over to the section leader or platoon sergeant. Once the AAVs are ready to launch, the crew chief will notify the section leader. When the AA unit leader orders the AAVs to launch, each section leader will move individual AAVs to the launch point. The launch point is a predetermined location on the beach from which vehicles will enter the surf. The AA unit leader's vehicle, chemical lights or a green range flag usually mark this point. For increased safety, a launch team, a group of three Marines organized to conduct standardized water safety checks to ensure watertight integrity and proper mechanical operation, may be collocated at the launch point to quickly

check each vehicle before it enters the water. Once waterborne, the individual sections transit to the ship and begin to embark. After all sections are waterborne, the AA unit leader's vehicle launches and transits to the ship. The platoon sergeant's vehicle is typically the first to board the ship. Once aboard, the platoon sergeant should further coordinate on-load and/or special recovery procedures if needed.

Nontactical (Administrative) Launch

Nontactical launches are used during basic training operations involving inexperienced crews and when other safety conditions dictate (e.g., limited visibility, high surf). This method involves lining the vehicles up either side by side or in a column on the beach and launching from that central point. The procedures are largely the same as for a tactical launch, except for the close proximity of vehicles and the use of launch teams.

The launch team will dispatch each vehicle, using either radio or hand and arm signal, in designated order once it determines the vehicle is ready to launch. This technique should only be used for training operations to establish basic safety procedures in preparation for the more advanced tactical launch. The open, linear formation makes it susceptible to attack from the ground and air and, therefore, unsuitable for combat conditions.

Ship Class

Wet well ships, such as LPDs, LSDs, LHDs, and LHAs, provide the easiest platforms for conducting embarkation and debarkation. AAVs will work mostly with LSDs and LPDs, but on occasion, will embark aboard LHDs and LHAs. LSTs provide the most challenge to embarkation because they are not wet well ships. Although the AAV has little difficulty in embarking LSTs, the narrow dimensions of the stern gate opening and the steepness of the ramp require greater driver skill than with other ships. For information concerning embarkation procedures aboard each class, see appendix I.

Securing AAVs

Aboard ship, AAV crews secure vehicles using gripping gear (furnished by the ship). Four clevises (1 1/8-inch screw-pin anchor shackles) will be provided by the AAV unit and attached to each towing eye to receive lashing cable eyes. AAVs are normally secured by four 70,000-pound, test-lashing assemblies. See figure 3-3.

Additional lashing may be required when the vehicles will be remaining aboard for long durations or when rough seas are expected. In this case, two lashing assemblies will be used on each towing eye for a total of eight. See figure 3-4 on page 3-16. Lashing assemblies will never be attached to or wrapped around the track, sprockets or idler assemblies of the AAVs. Rubber track pads eliminate metal-on-metal contact, and, in most circumstances, additional dunnage is not required. The commanding officer of the ship is ultimately responsible for ensuring that AAVs are properly secured and is the final authority on the procedures to be followed. The AA unit leader should ensure that daily checks of grips are conducted.

Rehearsal and Movement

A rehearsal is that phase of an amphibious operation in which one or more exercises are conducted by the AF, or elements thereof, under conditions simulating those of the anticipated amphibious operation. It is executed according to a plan that parallels the plan for the specific operation, and rehearsal participants should include

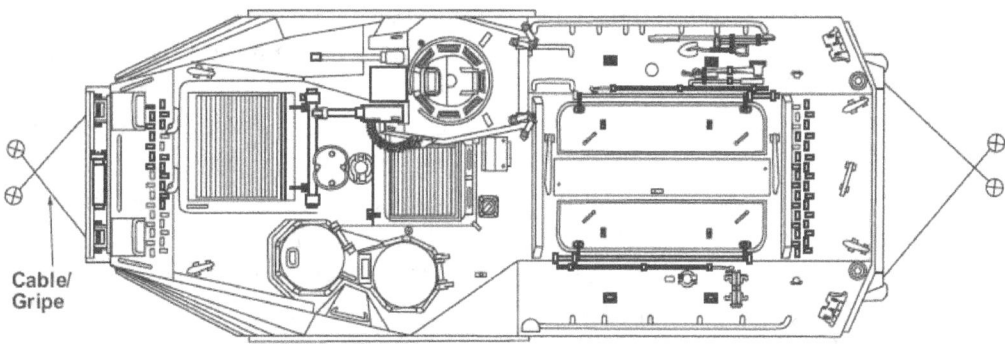

Cable/
Gripe

Figure 3-3. Single Grip.

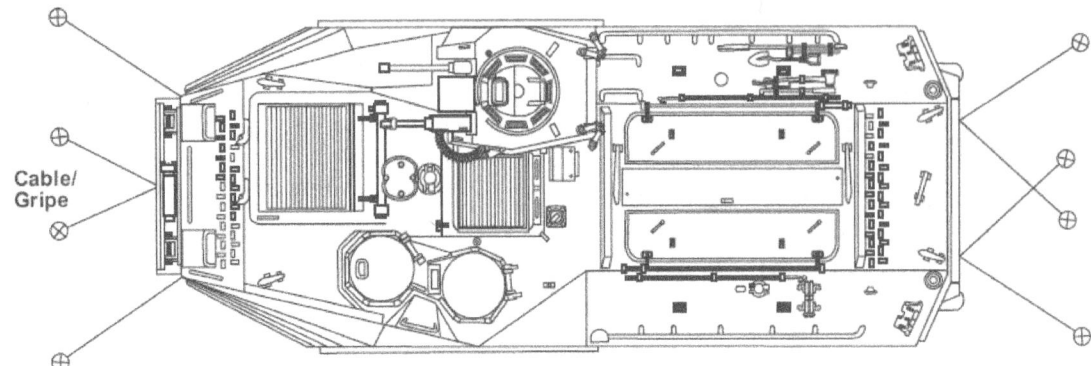

Cable/
Gripe

Figure 3-4. Double Grip.

units that are to take part in the operation. Rehearsals are used to test—

- Plan and procedures.
- Timing of detailed operations such as debarkation schedules.
- Combat readiness of vehicles and crews.
- Communications.

Planning Considerations

The AA unit leader may be called on to assist the CATF and CLF in the planning of rehearsals. Leaders planning rehearsals should consider the number, nature, and scope of rehearsals as well as the date, time, and location for each. AAV-specific considerations include—

- Delays involved in embarking and refueling AAVs aboard ship.
- Necessary repair or replacement of AAVs damaged during rehearsals.
- Additional requirements for fuel, repair parts, and other related supplies.

The AA unit leader must participate in AF debriefs to evaluate the exercise and correct mistakes from the AA perspective. Each rehearsal should also be critiqued within the AA unit.

Types

Given the complexity of the mission assigned, level of unit training, time available, and operational security considerations, every attempt should be made to conduct staff rehearsals, rehearsals without infantry, and rehearsals with infantry before the assault landing.

Staff Rehearsals

Staff rehearsals are conducted by staffs participating in the operation and take the form of war games or tactical exercises without troops. These rehearsals are conducted before integrated rehearsals and should include the use of AAVC7A1s, if available, and fire support teams.

Rehearsals Without Infantry

A rehearsal without infantry is an integrated rehearsal conducted by the AA unit. It generally involves a turn-away before the beach. Focusing on AAV and naval personnel, rehearsals without infantry are conducted to perfect the C2 of the ship-to-shore movement. Timing of the ship-to-shore movement is the most critical aspect to evaluate and is vital to the successful coordination of NGF and air support. The AA unit leader should adjust time and distance-to-shore factors with the

PCS as required. Most primary control officers (PCOs) plan on an average speed of 5 knots or less for timing AAV movement in the boat lane. This speed should be adjusted to allow for wind, currents, and sea conditions in the AOA and to maximize the AAV water speed.

Rehearsals With Infantry

The rehearsal with infantry is a final integrated rehearsal conducted, as nearly as possible, in accordance with the planned assault. The rehearsal should include extensive troop participation to include actions on objectives. Each rehearsal should be followed by a critique. Ships will conduct periodic embarkation drills, where the infantry are called away to the tank or well deck to practice embarking on their assigned AAV. During the rehearsal, crew chiefs will guide their assigned infantry squad in the proper loading of the AAV and will review waterborne safety and evacuation procedures. Embarking infantry leaders will allow them to practice with the communication equipment, view the boat lane, and identify targets inland.

Preoperational Briefing and Security

Before rehearsals, and again before the operation, preoperational briefings should be conducted to the lowest level. In addition to the regular operational briefs, AA unit personnel will receive special briefs concerning beach hydrography, weather, and the amphibious control measures.

Unit Preparation

During movement to the AOA, a maximum effort is made to prepare men and machines for combat considering both AA and supported unit SOPs. AA unit leaders should allow time for the following activities:

● Vehicle and equipment inspections.
● Preoperational checks and services.
● Communication checks.
● Weapon checks and test firing.
● Training for naval, infantry, and AAV personnel as required.

The Assault

AA unit leaders, in conjunction with the designated PCO, maintain TACON of AAVs and embarked troops during waterborne movement. The CATF accomplishes the movement of the LF to the beach through the AA unit and naval elements of the ATF. Landing ships and craft, helicopters, and AAVs may be employed in this mission. The waterborne formations of AAVs in the assault are similar to those of infantry formations. AAVs' low silhouette and armored hull make them very survivable against direct and indirect fire weapons if detected in the assault.

Command and Control

The waterborne portion of an amphibious assault is a highly controlled effort involving precise navigation, timing, and coordination by elements of the AF. The AA unit leader must understand the responsibilities and missions of the elements of the ATF.

Naval Control Group

The naval control group (NCG) consists of the personnel, ships, boats, and landing craft that are designated to plan and control the waterborne ship-to-shore movement. The AA unit leader, as the wave guide officer (WGO), is part of the NCG. The organization of the control group is based on the arrangement and number of landing beaches. Normally, the NCG includes a central control officer (CCO), a PCS and officer, SCS and officer, boat control team, boat group commander (BGC), WGO, and safety boats.

Central Control Officer. Designated by the CATF to plan and conduct the waterborne ship-to-shore movement, the CCO is responsible for organizing the control group to support the AF landing plan. The CCO directs the movement of scheduled waves to the beach and maintains close contact with the tactical-logistical group.

Primary Control Ship and Officer. A PCO and PCS are designated for each colored beach and transport organization landing an RLT or BLT. Their mission is to control the movement of AAVs, landing craft, and landing ships to and from the beach. When assault forces are to be landed over widely separated beaches, additional PCOs may be required for each beach. The PCO's responsibilities include—

● Directing scheduled waves over their assigned beach at a specified time.
● Designating the communications method to be used between boats, AAVs, and PCS.
● Maintaining current location and status of ships within the PCO's control area and of assigned boats, including safety and salvage boats.
● Monitoring surf conditions and long and short term weather reports, and making recommendations to CATF to terminate boating when surf or weather conditions dictate.
● Maintaining the status of debarkation/embarkation using the landing plan.
● Effecting liaison with the LF tactical logistics radio net for serial offload.
● Arranging for the refueling of boats and the feeding and rest of boat crews.

Secondary Control Ship and Officer. Secondary control officers and SCSs may be stationed on the LD to assist the PCOs and ships. They are usually stationed so that they mark the flank of the boat lane at the LD.

Boat Control Team. The boat control team plots, tracks, and controls the movements of scheduled waves from the PCS combat information center (CIC). The team is composed of the following:

● Supervisor.
● Wave controller.
● Grid plotter.
● Radio net operators (Alpha and Bravo).
● Radar operator.
● Visual bearing takers.
● Signalman for visual communications.

The boat control team uses the signals in appendices J and K, and the grid reference system in appendix G for wave control. See Marine Corps Warfighting Publication (MCWP) 3-31.5/Naval Warfare Publication (NWP) 3-02.1, *Ship-to-Shore Movement*, for additional signals information.

Boat Group Commander. The CATF employs boat groups to control AAVs and landing craft in scheduled waves for each numbered beach. Each boat group will have a BGC, and assistant BGC if required, to help guide the movement of the group to or from the beach. During the waterborne movement, boat groups are organized into waves that are groups of AAVs or landing craft, which are scheduled to land simultaneously. The BGC is a Navy officer. The BGC and assistant BGC are embarked aboard small naval craft that may be tasked to act as safety boats in the event of emergencies.

Wave Guide Officer. A WGO or wave commander will be assigned to each AAV wave. The senior AAV officer, staff noncommissioned officer or noncommissioned officer (NCO) in each wave is designated the WGO. The WGO leads the wave to the LD and assumes a position in the wave to best control movement. Responsibilities of the WGO include—

● Forming the AAVs into the proper organization for landing.
● Reporting to the PCS, giving any details concerning the wave readiness.
● Ensuring that the wave is maintaining proper position and interval in the boat lane.
● Controlling fires of AAVs during the ship-to-shore phase.
● Retracting AAVs from the beach.

Safety Boats. Safety boats may be employed to render assistance and pick up personnel from disabled or sinking AAVs. Safety boats are normally naval craft from the launching ship, but if not available, an empty AAV in each wave should be designated to act as a safety boat.

Communications

Communications for the ship-to-shore movement may be by radio, light and flag signals or hand and arm signals.

Radio. Radio will be the primary means of communication between the PCS and the wave and between units/vehicles within the wave. AA and naval units will use the following nets during the ship-to-shore movement:

- The boat B net is used by the WGO after the launch of AAVs to report to the PCS and to receive instructions for vectoring to the LD. The boat B net is used to control surface craft seaward of the LD.
- The boat A net is used by the wave commander after crossing the LD or on order from the PCS to report to the PCS for directions, vectors, and time hacks.
- The AAV safety net is established to coordinate the rescue of disabled or sinking AAVs. AAVs, safety boats, and the PCS should guard this frequency.
- The AAV command net is used by the AA unit for the C2 of the waves and for fire control in the assault. It is guarded by AAVs in the unit and is assigned as their tactical net.

Light and Flag Signals. Light and flag signals from the PCS are the secondary means used to control respective waves during QLPs. It is helpful for wave commanders or platoon communicator to have an understanding of semaphore or Morse code. See appendix J for illustrations of standard flags, lights, and markers used to control AAVs.

Hand and Arm Signals. Communications within the wave of AAVs may rely on hand and arm signals as a secondary means of control. AAV personnel must be familiar with the standard hand and arm signals used. See appendix K for illustrations of hand and arm signals used in AAV operations.

Fundamentals of the Assault

The AA unit focuses primarily on the seizure of LF and ATF objectives. The CLF's concept of operation determines the nature of the assault. The factors of METT-T will determine whether the amphibious operation will be conducted from near shore or from over the horizon (OTH). Space and logistic considerations are other factors of the operation that must be considered. The near shore assault is conducted from approximately 4,000 to 15,000 meters off the target landing beaches. Although the near-shore assault allows for the launch of AAVs outside of the range of direct fire AT weapons as well as allowing a short transit time in the ship-to-shore movement, it requires the amphibious ships to operate within the range of enemy artillery and antiship weapons (e.g., missiles, mines). The OTH assault provides for the launching of AAVs and landing craft outside of the range of enemy indirect fire weapons and short-range antiship missiles.

Infantry Concept Determination

If not previously involved in the operation development at the Marine expeditionary unit (MEU), RLT or BLT, the AA unit leader should find out the infantry's plans for reaching shore. The AA unit leader will need the following minimum information for planning the ship-to-shore movement:

- Infantry load plans.
- General infantry scheme of maneuver once ashore.
- Infantry communications plan.

Debarkation from Ship

The following procedures are a general outline for conducting debarkation from amphibious shipping. For detailed debarkation procedures, see appendix I. The NCG establishes the time for AAV launching and provides for the calculated launch time, formation of the waves, ship-to-shore transit, and landing in accordance with the assault schedule. Each ship publishes a ship-to-shore timeline that details the exact times each event will occur. See appendix L for a sample timeline. Normally, AAV crews board their vehicles at least 1 hour before the scheduled launch time to conduct the required prewater operations checks and needed repairs.

The officer in charge or petty officer in charge (POIC) of the well/tank deck orders the start and warmup of vehicles. The embarked TC ensures Marines are embarked according to the landing craft and amphibious vehicle assignment table and serial assignment table. AAV crew chiefs supervise the embarkation of their assigned passengers. A written manifest for each AAV must be prepared, life jackets must be issued and put on, and appropriate safety briefs must be given to the embarked troops. Before launching AAVs, designated naval personnel guide or stage each vehicle into their launch positions. AAV crewmen close the rear personnel and cargo hatches and plenums before staging. Hatches may be opened only in an extreme emergency. The topside driver, TC, and vehicle commander's hatches are closed no later than 2 minutes before launch. Naval personnel in the launch control station supervise and conduct the launching of AAVs. Light and flag signals are used to launch AAVs.

Underway Launch. The underway launch of AAVs combines the elements of speed and surprise. See appendix M for underway launch illustrations. This technique should be used whenever minimum exposure time is desired for the protection of the ATF. The underway launch does not require the congestion of ships anchored about the LD. As an example, two LSDs carrying 48 troop-laden AAVs can make a high speed (21.5 knots), angled approach to an LD that is 2,000 yards from a target beach. The AAVs can be launched in two columns at 5-second intervals, and in 2 minutes, 48 vehicles will be waterborne.

Within 11 minutes, 864 combat-equipped Marines will be ashore, and the delivery ships will be quickly approaching the horizon.

Static Launch. The near-static or at-anchor launch of AAVs may be required by the hydrographic, size or depth limitations of the AAV launch area. The static launch will require a greater launch interval between vehicles. AAVs should enter the water at a speed sufficient to clear the end of the stern gate without striking towing pintles.

(AAVs can be embarked for transit aboard LCACs and LCUs to close the distance for OTH movements. They can be launched from these craft, but special coordination is required and rehearsals are vital.)

Movement to the Line of Departure

After AAVs have entered the water in column, each wave commander will report to the PCO/PCS on boat B and commence the assault. Each wave, in turn, will form on line and maneuver across the LD by executing a flanking movement. During daylight landings, the PCS will hoist a numeral-one flag at half-mast 5 minutes before the first wave is to cross the LD. Wave one will then move to a position just seaward of the LD. Two minutes before crossing, the flag is hoisted to the top and when the flag drops, wave one crosses the LD. For succeeding waves, only the 2 minute warning and execute signals will be given, using the numerical flag corresponding to the wave being dispatched.

Debarkation Procedures

To debark AAVs from static or underway amphibious shipping, the AA unit leader will conduct close, small-unit liaison with the respective ship's personnel. Issuing the warning order and coordinating intelligence and launch information are vital to the success of the operation.

Issue the Warning Order

Upon being alerted that a launch may occur, the AA unit leader should issue a warning order to personnel. This will allow them to begin the following preparations for the actual launch:

- Draw personal weapons from ship's armory.
- Boresight/check crew-served weapons.
- Draw and stow ammunition aboard vehicles.
- Conduct preoperational checks and troubleshoot vehicles.
- Conduct communications checks.
- Ungrip vehicles and stow grips.

Coordinate Intelligence and Launch Information

The intelligence and launch information must be determined before launch.

Hydrographic/Surf Conditions. Intelligence requirements should be checked and updated before launch. At a minimum, a current SUROB must be analyzed to determine if it is or will be safe to launch AAVs.

Center Beach Location. Coordination as to the exact location of center beach should be conducted before launch. The AA unit leader should ensure that the Navy's plot for center beach is consistent with the LF's concept of operations ashore.

Boat Lane Length/Width. Boat lanes are normally between 2,000 and 2,700 yards long and 500 yards wide. The AA unit leader should check assigned boat lanes for accuracy.

Launch Track. If an underway launch is planned, the ship's approach to the launch site or launch track should be checked. The approach that the ship takes will greatly affect the launch and landing of AAVs. The underway launch tracks that the Navy employs are covered in appendix M.

Launch Speed and Interval. The speed of the ship will affect the interval between AAVs in time and distance. The interval is a function of ship speed at launch, width of the area AAVs are to be launched, and the number of AAVs to be launched.

The minimum safe interval between vehicles is 5 seconds. Intervals of at least 15 seconds are needed at speeds less than 10 knots to provide for a safe distance of 50 meters between vehicles in the water after launch. Launch control must ensure that each vehicle clears the ship's wake before another AAV is launched. AAVs may be launched singularly by amphibious ships and in two columns from LPDs, LSDs, LHAs, and LHDs. Table 3-4 can be used to adjust the spacing between vehicles in the water.

Table 3-4. AAV Launch Intervals.

Speed of Ship (knots)	50-Meter Interval (seconds)	60-Meter Interval (seconds)	70-Meter Interval (seconds)
0	12	14	16
2	11.2	13.1	15
4	10.2	12.2	14
6	9.5	11.3	13
8	8.9	10.5	12.2
10	7.5	9.5	11
12	6.3	8.7	10.1
14	5.5	7.5	8.8
16	5	6.7	7.8
18	5	6	7
20	5	5.3	6.2

Launch Criteria. The Navy will normally ensure proper safety criteria for launching AAVs are followed. Various types of ships have different criteria. See appendix I. The AA unit should know the correct safety procedures for the following criteria.

● Stern gate position.
● Vent fans status.
● Ship's ballast position.
● Water depth at the sill.
● Maximum ship speed.
● Turntable position (LSTs only).
● Stern anchor position (LSTs only).

Squat Draft. The Navy will be concerned with the effect the ocean's bottom has on the ship as it travels at high speeds. The launch track should avoid large variations in water depth, especially at depths less then 100 feet. Transiting from deep water to relatively shallow areas causes the ship to squat. The resulting increase in depth of water over the sill or in the well is undesirable and extremely dangerous, causing AAVs to lose steering control during launches, collide with the bulkheads, and get caught in the ship's wake. In some cases, this squat draft effect may increase the draft as much as 8.5 feet deeper than the preselected ballast draft. To reduce this effect, either a reduction in speed is required or the preselected draft must be reduced to allow for squat. The AA unit leader should be aware that significant squat draft will occur in depths less than 60 feet and higher speeds will increase the effect.

Approach Lane Length. CATF/CLF staff will determine approach lane length with METT-T and vehicle capabilities input from subordinate unit leaders, including AA leaders. The total approach lane and boat lane distance should not exceed the range of AAV unless underway fueling is planned.

Enemy Situation. Intelligence requirements for the enemy situation should be checked and updated before launch.

Grid Reference System

AA units use the grid reference system to control AAV waves moving across the LD and down the boat lane until the waves land on their assigned beach. A standard voice procedure is used to reduce voice transmission to a minimum, while transmitting accurate positions to the waves. See Appendix G.

Quiet Landing Procedures

QLPs allow the LFs to reduce or cease radio transmission during a landing. These procedures are used to counter enemy attempts to disrupt the ship-to-shore movement through beaconing, intrusion, jamming, and interference. Grid position messages will be passed from the PCS to the various scheduled waves using flashing lights, flag hoist or semaphore. Only corrections to the wave's position in the boat lane will be passed. QLPs are rarely used because AA units must conduct extensive training, and each wave must have some personnel who can read Morse code and/or semaphore to successfully conduct QLPs. See NWP 3-02.1 for additional information.

Position Location Reporting System

The position location reporting system (PLRS) is a UHF radio system. It can provide for precise AAV waterborne navigation, as well as PCS control in the ship-to-shore movement. The PCS must be equipped with a PLRS master station and each wave commander must have a PLRS basic user unit to conduct the operation. The boat lane and its approaches can be established as way points on the master station. Each wave commander's basic user unit would receive boat lane guidance from the PCS master station. Additional tactical information can be transmitted via PLRS, and the PCO can modify timing or boat lane data by changing the way points via the PCS master station.

Global Positioning System

If PLRS is not available, the NCG may allow the use of a GPS device for the precise guidance of AAVs during the ship-to-shore movement. The WGOs would enter their assigned way points (from the projected boat lane) into their GPS units or PLGRS. Once launched, GPS would provide the wave commander with constant position and guidance updates. Using the magnetic heading device, the WGO can vector the wave and provide speed information to correct timing. While GPS does not provide the PCO with the capability to control or monitor each wave's progress as they move down the boat lane, GPS does provide a more accurate navigational aid than the traditional employment of radar guidance. GPS with advisory control from PCS is the primary method for controlling waves to the beach.

Formations

The WGO's senior AAV leader in each wave will establish the formation, vehicle interval, speed, and direction of movement within the boat lane. The on-line, column, wedge, and echelon formations may be employed in conducting landings. See figure 3-5 on page 3-24.

On-Line

On-line formations are typically used to assault defended beaches. In this formation, vehicles approach the beach abreast of each other and parallel to the shoreline. This formation is used when—

- Landing on defended beaches.
- Rapid buildup of combat power ashore is desired.
- Firepower to the front is needed.
- Tactical integrity of units must be maintained.

Disadvantages of using on-line formations are—

- Difficult to control over long distances, at night or during periods of limited visibility.
- Vulnerable to fire from the flanks.
- Requires large frontages.

Column

Column formations are commonly used on beaches that are undefended or during movement through breached lanes. Advantages of column formations are—

- Increased firepower to the flanks.
- Ease of control over long distances, at night or during periods of limited visibility.
- Adapted to narrow beaches or lanes.

Disadvantages of column formations are—

- Firepower to the front is very limited.
- Requires extended amounts of time and space in the boat lane.
- Slow buildup of combat power ashore.

Wedge

The wedge, like the column, provides good security and firepower to the flanks and front. This formation does not provide the most rapid buildup of combat power ashore, and it takes up more room in the boat lane.

Echelon (Left/Right)

Echelon left or right can be used to protect an exposed flank. This formation is difficult to control and not often used over long distances or in poor visibility.

Rate of Advance

Speed afloat will depend on the wave's scheduled progress down the boat lane and should average slightly over 5 knots. Each driver within the wave can set uniform engine revolutions per minute (RPM) to establish and maintain the desired speed. The initial speed or RPM should be set before launch. Upon reaching a point 1,000 yards from the beach, the wave commander orders battle speed. At this point, AAVs close hatches and advance to maximum speed. Normally, the formation breaks at battle speed, as some vehicles are faster than others. Once inside small arms range, speed is more important. Table 3-5 on page 3-25 lists calm water speed for each designated engine RPM.

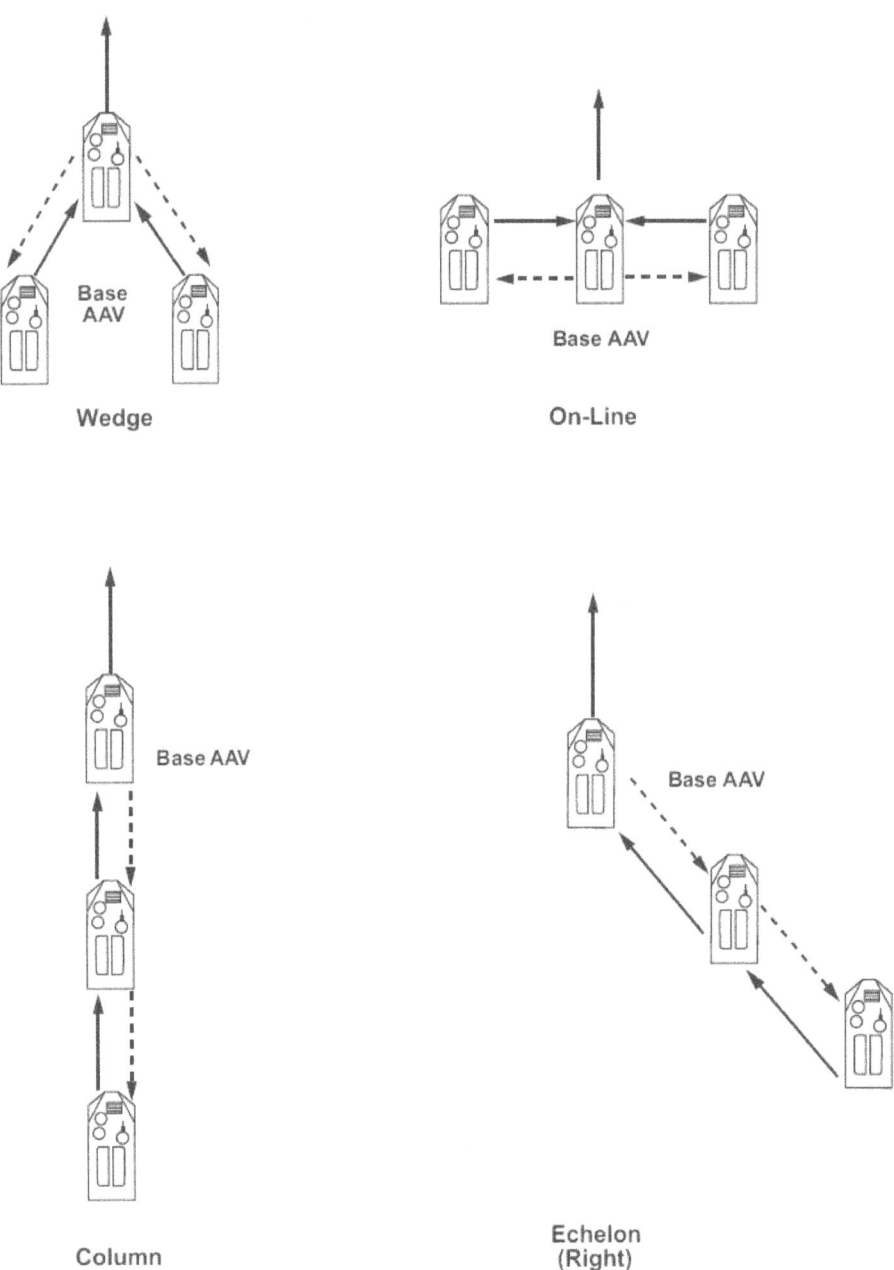

Note: Interval for all formations is adjusted off the base vehicle.

———————————▶ Close up distance

- - - - - - ▶ Extend or open up

Figure 3-5. AAV Formations.

Table 3-5. RPM/Speed Conversions.

RPM	Miles Per Hour	Knots
1,500	5.7	5
1,700	6.4	5.6
1,900	7.3	6.4
2,000	7.6	6.7
2,300	7.7	6.8
2,500	8.1	7.2
2,800	8.2	7.2

Screening

AAVs are equipped with a smoke generation system. The effective use of this system can afford the assaulting force a means of screening its advance and that of follow-on waves. The system is very effective with an onshore wind. The employment of the AAV smoke generators is normally ordered at the same time as battle speed. Drivers should use magnetic compasses when moving through the smoke screen to maintain proper direction. The vehicle's smoke grenade launchers should be saved for the obscuration of a specific threat once ashore.

Actions on the Beach

Once a wave lands, the wave commander will report touchdown to the boat control group over the boat A net. If the enemy situation permits, the AAVs should continue through the beach inland to make room for subsequent landing craft and to avoid providing a lucrative target for enemy artillery. When AAVs are required to dismount infantry, they should avoid stopping in the open. Upon the infantry's debarkation, AA units will continue to provide fire support as required. Once ashore, the AA unit reestablishes its command relationship with the supported infantry commander.

Shore-to-Objective Maneuver

Shore-to-objective assault operations can be executed from different locations along the coastline, from the mainland to nearby islands, from island to island or anywhere AAVs are employed from land to land.

Planning

The AAV's maximum range in the water, condition of crew and passengers, as well as METT-T are planning considerations for shore-to-objective maneuvers. LCACs can be used to ferry AAVs in shore-to-shore operations. A primary concern of waterborne maneuvers is security, because the force is vulnerable in the water.

Execution

Execution will be similar to a ship-to-shore amphibious assault. The same safety considerations apply as for any waterborne movement.

Operations in Navigable Waters

Because an AAV is considered a ship or boat when afloat, AA unit leaders are expected to follow the international rule of the road when the AAV is waterborne in coastal waters, rivers, and bays. For further information concerning riverine operations, see chapter 9.

Waterway Rules

AAVs involved in waterborne operations in navigable waters are subject to the same international rules of the road as powerboats. However, during combat assaults, crafts in the boat lane are to be avoided if possible, but the execution of the mission takes precedence. The following international rules of the road regulations are applicable:

- When an AAV and a sailboat are approaching in such a direction as to involve risk of collision, the AAV shall avoid the sailboat.

- When AAVs or powered boats are approaching bow to bow, each shall pass on the port side of the other by steering to the starboard.
- When two AAVs or powered boats are on crossing courses that involve risk of collision, the AAV or boat that has the other on starboard shall give way to avoid the other.
- When safe and practical, AAVs in narrow channels shall keep to the right of the channel.
- During night operations, AAVs shall clearly exhibit a searchlight in time to prevent collisions.

Navigational Aids

Various channel markers can be found along local waterways. The local rules of the road and regulations should be clarified before launching and conducting operations. The red-right-returning rule applies in most parts of the world. However, in some parts of the world these rules are reversed. Under the red-right-returning rule, vessels moving up river will keep red channel markers on the right and green markers on the left. When going out to sea, vessels keep red markers on the left and green markers on the right.

Night and Low Visibility Operations

The concept of night and low visibility operations must be simple and provide for the seizure of easily recognizable objectives. A desire to minimize AF vulnerabilities to threat weapons systems, to attain secrecy in landing raid or reconnaissance units, and to achieve tactical surprise are the principal factors motivating the conduct of night and low visibility ship-to-objective operations. Planning for a night or low visibility landing is similar to that for other amphibious operations. However, plans must provide the greatest possible detail on the landing beaches, seaward approaches, terrain, enemy situation, and obstacles to movement. Planners should consider the preparation, night launches, formations and speed, as well as beach markings.

Preparation

AA units should be trained in night operations before the conduct of an operation with embarked troops. Personnel must be thoroughly briefed on the operation to include emergency procedures. Communications and signals for the AAV launch and ship-to-shore movement must be coordinated with the PCO and ship's launch control. If safety boats are used to mark the boat lane, they should stay clear of the landing AAV waves.

Each vehicle should be equipped with night vision equipment. Based on METT-T, vehicle lights or chemical lights may be used to mark each vehicle in the unit. After preoperational checks are made and approximately 30 minutes prior to launch, the lighting in the well deck should be changed to red to enable AAV crews to adjust to the dark. Lights in the well deck should be switched off when the stern gate is lowered to minimize the ship's visual signature during the launch of AAVs.

Night Launches

Appendix J contains the light signals to be employed for the staging of vehicles and subsequent night launch. To avoid a possible collision in the darkness, the launch control officer must ensure that each waterborne AAV clears the ship's wake before launching the next AAV. The last vehicle to enter the water should provide a predetermined signal to the wave commander. Appendix I contains detailed information concerning the launch procedures for each class of ship. These procedures remain largely unchanged for night operations.

Formations and Speed

Depending on the degree of visibility, on-line or wedge formations may be used during a night operation, but the close column is the preferred formation for ease of control at night. The wave can form a close wedge formation before landing. The vehicle interval should be between 30 to 50 meters, depending on the limit of visibility.

Before launch, the WGO should establish the engine RPM setting for the ship-to-shore movement to maintain an established speed and minimize the accordion effect within the column.

Beach Markings

The ATF commander, in coordination with the LF commander, plans the necessary approach and retirement lanes, checkpoints, rendezvous points, and aids to navigation to help control and coordinate ship-to-shore movement. In addition, the ATF commander and staff should consider METT-T when planning for the center and flank markings of the landing beach. Appendix J contains standard light symbols used to indicate various parts of the beach. Infrared (IR) strobe lights or chemical light used to mark the beach will assist the wave in reaching center beach during periods of reduced visibility.

CHAPTER 4. OFFENSIVE OPERATIONS

Offense is the decisive form of war. Success in battle is achieved by offensive action. Even though defensive operations are often necessary, a commander must take every opportunity to seize the initiative by offensive action. The purpose of offensive operations is the destruction of the enemy and his will to fight. The attacker has the initiative and can concentrate enough combat power at a decisive place to overcome the defender.

A mech force is primarily offensive in nature; only in the offense can the commander fully exploit the mobility, firepower, and shock action of mech forces.

The AA unit provides an important component of the requisite armor-protected mobility and firepower to enable the MAGTF commander to conduct offensive mech operations.

AA sections and platoons participate in the offense as part of a team or task force that will be conducting movement to contact, attack, exploitation or pursuit, which are types of offensive operations.

SECTION I. FORMS OF OFFENSIVE MANEUVER

To best accomplish the offensive mission, the AA unit will decide which form of offensive maneuver to use. The decision is based on the mission and METT-T. Frontal attack, flanking attack, envelopment, turning movement, penetration, and infiltration are the forms of offensive maneuver used to accomplish an offensive mission.

Frontal Attack

For explanation of frontal attack, see MCDP 1-0, Chapter 7. The speed and armor protection of combat vehicles may reduce the mech force's exposure to enemy fire. Tank-heavy forces may be able to force a rupture in an enemy's hasty defense, while mech-heavy forces will be required against a deliberate defense. After a rupture is created, mech-heavy forces are best used to hold and widen the gap, while the tank-heavy forces exploit quickly by attacking suitable objectives in the depth of the enemy position.

Flanking Attack

For explanation of flanking attack, see MCDP 1-0, Chapter 7. To exploit advantages of speed and cross-terrain mobility, the majority of a mech force will normally be put in the main effort while less mobile forces are in a supporting role.

Envelopment

For explanation of envelopment, see MCDP 1-0, Chapter 7. The most mobile forces are typically distributed in the main effort, and those forces with less mobility are in the supporting effort. The majority of combat power, usually including most

4-2 ──────────────────── MCWP 3-13

of the tanks, will be placed in the main effort. Deep envelopments may require the displacement of artillery to provide continuous support.

Turning Movement

For explanation of turning movement, see MCDP 1-0, Chapter 7. Normally, a turning movement is executed by a division-sized force and would involve large mechanized units attacking to deep objectives.

Penetration

For explanation of penetration, see MCDP 1-0, Chapter 7. The shock action and mobility of a mech force, in conjunction with aviation forces,

are useful in rupturing the enemy's position and exploiting the rupture. Tank-heavy forces may be able to force the rupture in an enemy's hasty defense, while mech-heavy forces will normally be required against a deliberate defense. After a rupture is created, mech-heavy forces are most suitable to attack.

Infiltration

For explanation of infiltration, see MCDP 1-0, Chapter 7. Mech forces are ideally employed to conduct infiltrations when the enemy is arrayed in defensive positions scattered across a wide frontage. AAVs provide a unique capability to infiltrate by taking advantage of marshlands and bodies of water.

SECTION II. TYPES OF OPERATIONS

Movement to contact, attack, exploitation, and pursuit are the four types of offensive operations. At the small unit level, particularly at the individual AAV level, the crew actions are essentially the same for these operations. The movement techniques and forms of maneuver distinguish crew actions. The AA unit must be trained and organized to pass immediately from one type of operation to another. In a successful battle, the four types of offensive operations should be conducted in sequence.

Movement to Contact

A force conducting a movement to contact is organized in an approach march formation with advance, flank, and rear security elements protecting the main body. The main body contains the bulk of the force's combat power. The advance force, flank, and rear security formations may consist of aviation or ground combat units (one or

both as individual elements or as a task-organized combined arms team) and appropriate CSS organizations based on METT-T. For a detailed explanation of movement to contact, see MCDP 1-0, Chapter 7.

Security Elements

The security element protects the unit from surprise by observing and reporting enemy activity. The security force—

- Reports enemy contact to the unit commander.
- Collects and reports information about the enemy.
- Selects tentative fighting positions for oncoming units.
- Attempts to penetrate enemy security elements to reach and identify the enemy main force.
- Performs chemical and engineer reconnaissance.
- Bypasses or breaches (in stride) obstacles.

Main Body

In relatively open terrain, a tank-heavy team augmented by combat engineers permits the greatest amount of flexibility. This force has enough combat power to develop the situation after contact with the enemy. In addition, the team can breach minor obstacles, secure terrain, and clear small villages and wooded areas. Even if the situation is developed properly during a movement to contact, the commander may be faced with a meeting engagement.

Actions on Contact in Meeting Engagement

A combat action that occurs when a moving force, incompletely deployed for combat, engages the enemy at an unexpected time and place. The basic principle of a meeting engagement is seizing or retaining the initiative. To increase the odds of adhering to this principle, the commander utilizes the immediate action or battle drills. The infantry unit commander controls unit movement through the AA unit leader.

Successes in most meeting engagements are determined in the opening moments and depend on the ability of the commander to quickly use available combat power. Reacting immediately, the element first making contact engages the enemy by fire, deploys, reports, and develops the situation. The side that brings effective fire to bear on the enemy first has a significant advantage. Overwatch elements and supporting arms suppress the enemy. When possible, the leading elements fight to eliminate the enemy and continue the advance. When faced with a meeting engagement, the commander may—

- Continue to develop the situation.
- Conduct an ambush.
- Order the lead element to fix the enemy in place and bypass with the rest of the force.
- Conduct a hasty attack.
- Adopt a hasty defense or delay while the next higher commander reacts to the situation.
- Disengage.

Actions on Contact in a Bypass

One of the options available to a commander when contact is made with the enemy is to bypass. This would typically be appropriate if the enemy does not present a meaningful threat and bypass routes are available. Stopping to engage the enemy could result in premature employment of the main body. This can cause the force to slow down the tempo of operations and may cause the loss of initiative. Light enemy resistance should not be allowed to slow momentum. The commander's guidance will normally specify if light enemy resistance may be bypassed. The mech forces with fires may still engage bypassed forces.

For example, if tanks were part of the mech force they would suppress while on the move. The AAVs would likely be directed to suppress also. The infantry normally remain mounted and the mech force commander would call for indirect fire and smoke to screen the unit's movement past the enemy position. Whenever enemy is bypassed, the commander informs higher headquarters so following forces are not surprised.

Attack

For explanation of attack, see MCDP 1-0, Chapter 7.

Deliberate Attack

For explanation of deliberate attack, see MCDP 1-0, Chapter 7.

AA sections and platoons will generally be part of a larger mech force when a deliberate attack is ordered. A deliberate attack is required to destroy or penetrate a well-prepared enemy defense. The longer preparation time allows for more detailed fire planning, including scheduled fires, and more specialized task organization. The purpose of a deliberate attack is to break through the enemy's main defensive zone into his rear area to destroy artillery positions, command posts (CPs), logistics support areas, air defense artillery positions, and LOC.

When preparing for a deliberate attack, the mech company commander and AA platoon commander must first reconnoiter the area as much as time permits. They try to locate obstacles between the LD and objective area, covered routes into or around enemy positions, and positions from which direct fire weapons can support an assault. The unit commander then develops a scheme of maneuver and a fire support plan based on METT-T in the operations area.

Scheme of Maneuver

The unit commander's scheme of maneuver must—

- Allow rapid closing with the enemy, using terrain to avoid enemy fire.
- Use terrain features and other measures to keep control of maneuver and fires.
- Keep infantry mounted as long as possible to use the mobility and protection of the AAV.
- Strike the enemy flank, rear, or other known weak points.

Fire Support Plan

To achieve the effects of combined arms, the scheme of maneuver and fire support plan are developed concurrently and take advantage of available direct, indirect, and aviation-delivered fires. The unit commander's fire support plan should—

- Designate planned, on-call targets for immediate suppression and for shifting during movement.
- Use priority targets that can be activated/deactivated on order or by event.
- Plan for use of smoke to obscure dismount points (DPs) and/or assault positions.
- Consider the use of series targets for movement/attack.
- Use fires to place the enemy in a dilemma.

Engagement Priorities

The commander of the mech force provides guidance in the form of engagement priorities based on METT-T. Different weapon systems within the mech force have different priorities of engagement based on lethality of the respective weapon system and the scheme of maneuver. Engagement priorities are especially useful in fire control where there are overlapping sectors of fire or when communication is lost. The following are examples of engagement priorities:

- Tanks fire at enemy tanks, AT/crew-served weapon systems, and infantry.
- AAVs fire at AT weapons, crew-served weapons positions, and enemy soldiers.
- Individual small arms and crew-served weapons fire at unarmored AT weapons and exposed enemy soldiers.
- AT weapons fire at tanks, AT, and fortified positions from concealed overwatch positions.
- Artillery and mortars fire to suppress enemy fires, kill enemy AT crews and other exposed soldiers, and conceal friendly movement with smoke.
- Air defense weapons fire at enemy aircraft.

Control Measures

The control measures that apply to a specific AA unit will depend on the scheme of maneuver and fire support plan. See Marine Corps Reference Publication (MCRP) 5-12A, *Operational Terms and Graphics*, for additional information. Normally, control measures include—

- Time of departure from the assembly area.
- Route of advance.
- Location of DP.
- Location of checkpoints and phase lines if applicable.
- Sector of fire for supporting the attack and specific instructions for shifting fires during the assault.
- Consolidation and reorganization instructions.

Preparations

Available time should be used for preparing the AAVs and crews for the attack. Combat trains should be available for logistic needs (e.g., fuel, ammunition). Operational condition of systems should be checked during the time available. After everyone, down to the last AAV crew, has been briefed, the unit leaders must ensure that everyone understands his/her role. The optimum preparatory measure would be to conduct a rehearsal if the time available and tactical situation permits.

AAV Employment Considerations

Employment considerations are METT-T dependent. Detailed knowledge of the terrain and the enemy will aid in determining how to best employ the AAVs when departing the assembly area. Key decisions involve—

- Formations.
- Movement techniques.
- Terrain driving.
- Method of attack.
- Mounted or dismounted considerations.

Actions in the Attack Position

The purpose of an attack position (AP) is to have a covered and concealed location short of the LD where last minute instructions are issued and final coordination is made. Normally, an AP is planned but may be bypassed if the attacking unit is engaged with the enemy earlier than anticipated, or if no final coordination is required before crossing the LD, which is the area where the infantry normally dismounts when conducting attacks on foot.

Crossing the Line of Departure

An LD is designated to coordinate the departure of attack elements. It is one of the standard control measures used in a deliberate attack. A time is normally attached to the LD that specifies when it is to be crossed. This makes coordination easier with adjacent and supporting units.

Supporting the Attack

AAVs can support the attack through a variety of methods. An example of the standard support role is using AAVs to deceive the enemy. After dismounting the rifle sections, the AAVs should maneuver away from the main point of the attack to make the enemy think that the attack is coming from another direction.

Attacks During Limited Visibility

Limited visibility includes smoke, haze, snow, rain, fog, and darkness. The mech force commander must be prepared to take advantage of limited visibility to continue functions of combat. Not only do attacks during limited visibility require more detailed preparation than attacks during good visibility, objectives are normally smaller and distances to them shorter. Plans must be simple, complete, and understood. If time and the enemy situation permit, leaders should reconnoiter routes and observe the objective area during good visibility. Night attacks, the most common type of limited visibility operation, are conducted to—

- Achieve surprise.
- Avoid heavy losses.
- Exploit success and maintain momentum.
- Keep the pressure on the enemy.
- Exploit the advantage of night vision devices.

The physical and psychological effects of limited visibility reduce individual effectiveness and increase the difficulty in performing most tasks. The mech unit commander must anticipate control, movement, and navigational problems, and must plan additional time to accomplish the mission. Success in night operations depends principally on leadership, training, planning, and surprise.

Leadership. Due to the negative psychological effects and inherent difficulty in control, navigation, and coordination of fires during darkness, leadership is the most important element in success or failure of night operations. Strong leadership will help compensate for the natural sense of isolation felt during darkness and will contribute to the confidence and esprit that will create a psychological advantage over the enemy.

Training. Training is the tool that leaders must use to develop individual and unit confidence in operating at night. In addition, training will help the individual Marine overcome natural apprehension and stress common during night operations. Individual training standards, training and readiness manuals, and Marine Corps Combat Readiness Evaluation System are the basis for individual and unit training.

Planning. Planning must compensate for the increased difficulty in control and coordination characteristics of night operations. Indirect fire should be planned for suppression and for illumination during darkness. Whether the attack is mounted or dismounted, every Marine should participate in a rehearsal of the plan. For night operations, planners should—

● Detail intelligence.
● Detail control measures.
● Plan target reference points (TRPs) along the route of attack.
● Enforce noise and light discipline.
● Use short count to start AAVs.
● Use GPS.

Surprise. Surprise multiplies combat power far beyond the weapon systems at hand. Darkness and limited visibility provide the concealment that will assist in creating surprise.

Special Equipment Requirements. The nature of night movement will be greatly affected by the amount and types of night vision equipment available to the mech force. Currently, tanks, LAVs, and AAVs are equipped with thermal night vision devices for drivers. Vehicle commanders and personnel assigned to vehicles that

are not equipped with organic night viewing devices should be issued night vision goggles. Tanks and LAV gunner stations have a thermal imaging capability that can greatly assist in maneuver and enemy targeting at night. While night vision devices greatly enhance the ability to move at night, they do not eliminate the need for control techniques.

Mounted Formation. The column and wedge formations are the easiest to control. The line formation is the most difficult to control because of the limited flank vision of the driver when using a night vision device. Therefore, the line formation should be limited to moving short distances, as when rapidly crossing a danger area or assaulting a position. The AAV leader should be in a position to best support the mech infantry commander and C2 the unit.

Dismounted Formation. In dismounted formations, infantry units should move closer together for better control. Marines should be close enough to see each other. Leaders should place themselves near the front of the formation for movement control.

Movement Techniques. When visibility is limited by darkness only, the mech unit should be able to use any movement technique. When smoke, fog or falling snow limits visibility, the unit's ability to provide overwatch may be reduced. In limited visibility, the loss of security to the flanks and rear is a major consideration in movement planning.

When using bounding overwatch, the platoon should consider bounding a section instead of one vehicle to increase the security of the bounding element. This would allow one vehicle to observe to the left front and another to the right front, making up for the driver's limited field of view. An AAV platoon or section moving by traveling overwatch keys its movement on the lead AAV. The distance between the lead AAV and the platoon or section is based on the ability of the driver and vehicle commander of the overwatch vehicles to keep the lead vehicle in sight. When the traveling technique is used, the lack of flank security becomes an even more important consideration. Because a unit traveling in a staggered column is vulnerable, this technique would be used only when the chance of enemy contact is slight and speed of movement is necessary.

Illuminated Attack

Illumination during a night attack makes control easier and allows rapid movement. It also improves the enemy's ability to detect advancing units. Illumination fires are planned and called as needed, normally for the final assault. Smoke can cut down the effectiveness of enemy battlefield illumination and some of his night vision devices. Indirect HE fire may be used to hide the sound of the AAVs as well as to suppress enemy gunners.

If attacking during darkness, the commander may illuminate the battlefield using indirect fire. To take advantage of limited visibility conditions or when illumination is not possible, the commander may order a mounted attack and dismount short of the objective. The commander may also decide to attack dismounted and use stealth to gain surprise.

The commander may decide to attack mounted to maintain momentum against an enemy occupying hastily prepared positions. This allows the infantry to close rapidly on the objective, and to conserve strength. The mech unit moves mounted to the last covered and concealed position short of the objective. Infantry units may then dismount and assault the objective while the AAVs provide covering fire.

During the assault, the AA leader must closely control the direct and indirect fires to avoid endangering the dismounted Marines. A signal, such as a pyrotechnic device, should be prearranged to designate when the AAVs should lift or shift fires from the objective. As soon as the objective is seized, the AAVs should quickly move to the objective area. The infantry should

have a prearranged coded signal such as a blinking, filtered flashlight to help AAVs locate and join with the dismounted troops. The rifle unit leader should select positions on the objective for the AAVs and require each rifle squad to provide a ground guide to simplify the AAVs' movement into positions.

Nonilluminated Attack

Even though a nonilluminated attack is planned, the mech unit leader should plan illumination from the LD to the objective so it is available if needed. The mech unit leader also should plan for the use of smoke during the attack. If the enemy fires illumination, the mech unit leader can call for indirect fire smoke or use smoke grenades to screen movement. Smoke also will reduce the effectiveness of some of the enemy's night vision devices.

The main advantage gained by attacking without illumination is surprise. Nonilluminated attacks can be conducted during any condition of reduced visibility. The concept of a dismounted attack without using illumination is to get as close as possible to the enemy's position without a fight, then, before he can react, surprise and overwhelm him. The objective will be relatively close to the LD, usually within range of supporting fires from the AAVs.

AAVs in Limited Visibility Attacks

The mission of the AAVs during limited visibility is usually to support the rifle units by fire or by fire and movement. In the mech unit's operation order (OPORD), the AAVs, tanks, and TOWs are normally assigned firing positions, sectors of fire, and routes to the objective. The firing position may be along the LD or to the rear of the LD.

The OPORD should specify how the AA unit leader plans to control the AAV fire, the route that the dismounted infantry will move, and the portions of the objective to be occupied by the direct fire units (e.g., AAVs, tanks, TOWs). If the noise of the vehicles will alert the enemy, vehicles move as close as they can to the overwatch position and halt until ordered to occupy overwatch position. From that position, a dismounted observer can be sent forward to observe the sector of fire and assist the direct fire units when they move into the position. The AAVs can then support the dismounted infantry by fire, or by fire and movement, as directed by the mech unit commander. Once the objective is seized, the direct fire units should move as quickly as possible to the objective with dismounted infantry providing guides and occupy hull-down positions. When planning a nonilluminated attack by stealth, the mech force commander normally uses the following control measures:

- The AP should be short of the LD, provide cover and concealment, and permit easy entry and exit. The AP may be occupied only long enough for the unit to receive final instructions and ensure coordination. Normally, the infantry dismounts in this area before the conduct of the attack.
- An LD is designated to coordinate the commitment of attacking units or scouting elements at a specified time of attack.
- Point of departure is assigned to rifle sections for crossing over the LD, because it is critical that movements be closely coordinated.
- Probable line of deployment (PLD) is planned by the company commander before moving forward. If the attack is not discovered at the PLD, the unit advances quietly until discovered or ordered to assault. The PLD is generally along an easily identifiable terrain feature perpendicular to the direction of attack.
- Release points (RPs) are designated points for releasing control. Each company commander releases control of platoons to the platoon commanders at the platoon RP. RPs are far enough back to let units deploy before they reach the squad RPs and the PLD. Platoon/squad RPs are used during dismounted attacks.

- Route is selected by the company commander, who normally picks the route from the company RP to the platoon RP. Platoon leaders pick routes from the platoon RP to the squad RP.
- Objectives are assigned by the company commander to each platoon. The objectives should be easily identifiable terrain features.
- Limit of advance (LOA) is designated by the company commander to keep friendly supporting fires from falling on friendly dismounted troops. The LOA should be a terrain feature that is easy to recognize even during limited visibility. The assaulting elements must not advance beyond this feature. This LOA allows use of supporting fires beyond the objective without endangering friendly troops.
- DP should be a planned point that is either outside the range of effective enemy AT weapons or within range but covered to allow for safe dismount of the infantry.
- Support by fire position (SFP) must be located within the maximum effective range of the UGWS.

When planning a nonilluminated attack by stealth, the mech force commander normally uses the following techniques:

- The speed of march should be maintained at approximately 15 miles per hour, since greater speeds normally result in broken intervals between vehicles.
- Map distances should be converted to tenths of miles and the odometer used to determine distances.
- Units should make extensive use of GPS.
- When possible, routes should be marked with luminous devices or chemical lights.
- Check points located on terrain that are identifiable at night should be used as control measures.
- Guides should be provided along the route to assist the moving force.

● The driver of a vehicle that becomes disabled should immediately notify the vehicle to the rear, allowing it to bypass and continue movement. The driver must then assist with traffic control, directing other following vehicles to bypass the disabled vehicle. The driver awaits the recovery vehicle.

Attacking a Strong Point

A strong point is a key point in a defensive position; a strong point is usually fortified and heavily armed with at least automatic weapons, around which other positions are grouped for its protection. A strong point defense is a defensive system that contains numerous strong points disposed in depth and width in such a manner as to be mutually supporting. The following are principles of attacking a strong point:

● Suppress enemy observation points and frontline units.
● Obscure the enemy with smoke concentration.
● Secure breach point and initial positions.
● Reduce frontline positions, roll flanks, and rear areas.
● Never attack a strong point defense with infantry-mounted armored vehicles.

Once a reconnaissance has provided the commander with sufficient detail of the enemy position, the commander will eventually arrive at a general concept of operations and task-organize the force. The commander's planning sequence is task-organize, isolate, breach, and exploit.

Task-Organize. The task organization for an attack of a strongpoint defense is not just the temporary grouping of forces to accomplish a mission. Companies and platoons are normally assigned the role of breach force, support force, or assault force. Each role implies certain tasks, techniques, and procedures that must be developed and rehearsed regardless of the specific objectives tasked by the completed OPORD. The task organization is done as soon as possible, usually before the completion of the OPORD. This allows units the time to rehearse those general techniques and procedures implied by the following role assignments:

● Breach Force—Normally the main effort, the breach force makes the initial breach and the assault force passes through. The battalion task force normally assigns a mech company as the breach force; the company assigns a mech infantry platoon. Engineers are normally assigned to the battalion breach force, and if available, to the company breach force.
● Support Force—The support force provides supporting fires to the breach force initially, and then to the assault force. The support force usually consists of tank companies or tank-heavy company teams and TOW assets. At the company level, the support force consists of tanks and AAVs providing a base of fire for the maneuver elements.
● Assault Force—The assault force attacks through the breach and destroys the enemy position. The assault force is usually a mech-infantry company. The assault force may be required to breach enemy close-in obstacles and should include infantry and engineers. At the company level, the assault force is one or more mech-infantry platoons. The assault force may provide security for the breaching force. After the obstacle is breached, the assault force moves through the breach and assaults the enemy position. Each squad may be given an objective to assault.

Isolate. The site of penetration is the point of the initial breach of the enemy position. It should be the weakest point. This location is isolated by intense direct and indirect fires, CAS, and smoke to destroy enemy positions and to prevent lateral movement to reinforce the position. Indirect fires and smoke are planned to ensure continuous fires isolate the enemy.

Breach. The main effort is directed toward the breach or penetration of the strong point. Objectives are assigned in the area of the point of penetration forward of the enemy's platoon and company defensive positions. Normally, the infantry and engineers dismount beyond the range of enemy direct fire weapons and move by cover and concealment. The penetration is made on a narrow front. The breach force penetrates the enemy's protective obstacles, gains a foothold in the trench line, and creates a gap in the strong point large enough to pass through the assault force. The gap is then widened and deepened to allow for exploitation.

The tanks and AAVs support by fire during the initial breach. If sufficient obstacle lanes have been cleared, tanks follow and support the dismounted infantry by fire. Tanks move quickly to exploit the initial breach. AAVs should be brought forward only when the antiarmor defenses are destroyed. The AAVs then assist in holding the shoulders of the penetration. Mutual support between attacking elements is maintained so that they are not isolated and defeated. The attacking elements will be subject to counterattacks that attempt to cut off the penetration.

Exploit. The main effort is shifted from the breach force to the assault force following a successful breach. The assault force passes rapidly through the breach, supported by the fires of the support force and the breach force. The task force objective is normally an isolated platoon position. At every level, the envelopment is the preferred form of maneuver. If the task force assault force can get to the rear of the strong point, the remainder of the task force can neutralize the remaining platoon strong points by attacking from positions on the flank or rear.

As subsequent platoon positions are encountered, the task force assault force (company team) may repeat the breaching process. As in the initial breach, AAVs support by fire while the tanks and dismounted infantry complete the reduction of the strong point and associated trench lines. The task force commander may commit the reserve to complete the destruction of the strong point and prepare for a counterattack or continue to attack.

Hasty Attack

For explanation of hasty attack, see MCDP 1-0, Chapter 7. By necessity, hasty attacks do not employ complicated schemes of maneuver and require a minimum of coordination. Habitual support relationships, SOPs, and battle drills contribute to increased tempo and the likelihood of success of the hasty attack.

Actions on Contact

The specific actions in a hasty attack will depend on the enemy's response to the contact. In a hasty attack, there will be little time for preparations. On receipt of an order to attack, actions could include delivering suppressive fires and maneuvering to cover and concealment.

Conduct of the Attack

The attack may be conducted mounted or dismounted. Once the attack has begun and the tactical situation changes, it may be necessary to alter the plan. The commander must place himself in the most advantageous position from which he can C2 the unit. He must go wherever he feels his presence is most needed. The commander should attempt to make maximum use of fire support assets available to support the movement.

Reconnaissance in Force

See MCDP 1-0, Chapter 7 for explanation.

Feint

See MCDP 1-0, Chapter 7 for explanation.

Demonstration

See MCDP 1-0, Chapter 7 for explanation.

Raid

See MCDP 1-0, Chapter 7 for explanation.

Spoiling Attack

See MCDP 1-0, Chapter 7 for explanation.

Counterattack

See MCDP 1-0, Chapter 7 for explanation.

Exploitation

For explanation of exploitation, see MCDP 1-0, Chapter 7.

A mech force is ideally suited for exploitation operations because of its inherent speed, mobility, and shock action. Mech forces may be held in reserve, when working with non-mech forces, and committed to an exploitation operation after a deliberate attack. The purpose of the exploitation is to take advantage of the enemy's loss of a defensive position by continuing the attack, increasing the tempo of operations, restricting his time to react, and destroying his cohesion. An exploitation operation ends when—

● The enemy loses his ability and will to fight and a pursuit operation is initiated.
● Enemy resistance increases requiring a deliberate attack.
● The force conducting the exploitation can no longer be supported or sustained.

Characteristics

The operation is conducted similar to a movement to contact with numerous hasty attacks. The exploitation is normally assigned to no less than a battalion-size unit. Direction is provided by a fragmentary order that emphasizes decentralized execution of orders. Deep objectives are selected. Company-size mech units normally attack on a narrow front with task forces and regiments employing multiple axes. Enemy resistance of insufficient strength to jeopardize the mission is normally suppressed, bypassed, and cleared by follow-on units. The operation is fast paced, continues day and night, and creates extended supply lines. High consumption rates of class III and V are normal.

Planning

Initial planning begins before the deliberate attack and anticipates a successful attack. Planning develops a reconnaissance plan, analyzes terrain suitable for mech operations beyond the objective, and identifies potential deep objectives. Fire support and CSS planning must also be conducted before the deliberate attack. The final plan is completed when the deliberate attack is successfully completed. The planning must be accomplished rapidly to reduce enemy reaction time. METT-T analysis confirms the locations of units, identifies enemy location and intentions, and confirms anticipated objectives and axes of advance.

Pursuit

For explanation of pursuit, see MCDP 1-0, Chapter 7. AAVs as part of a mech force help provide the force with the ability to move rapidly to encircle enemy forces attempting to flee or strike the enemy in his flanks.

SECTION III. MECHANIZED OPERATIONS

Within the Marine Corps, mech forces are task-organized within the structure of the MAGTF. The mech and tank company team is a common ground maneuver element that normally attacks as part of a larger mech force such as a battalion- or regimental-sized task force. The company team can be used to support by fire the movement of another unit, serve as a maneuver element or operate in reserve. To achieve the effects of combined arms, mech forces supporting arms, organic fires, and maneuver must be combined to ensure that any action the enemy takes to avoid one threat makes him more vulnerable to another. While the strengths of the various arms complement and reinforce each other, the weaknesses and vulnerabilities of each arm are protected or offset by the capabilities of the other.

Mutual Support

To best exploit the mech force's offensive capabilities, infantry, tanks, and AAVs must work together in pursuit of a common goal. Each element of the mech force provides a degree of mutual support to the other element.

AA units and tank units support the infantry by—

- Providing mobile protected firepower.
- Neutralizing or destroying hostile weapons by fire and movement.
- Clearing paths for dismounted infantry through wire.
- Neutralizing fortified positions with direct fire.
- Supporting dismounted infantry by direct fire.
- Providing protection against long-range, anti-armor fires.
- Leading the attack whenever possible.
- Assisting in the consolidation of the objective.

Infantry assists AA and tank units by—

- Breaching or removing antiarmor obstacles.

- Assisting in the neutralization or destruction of enemy antiarmor weapons.
- Designating targets for tanks and AAVs.
- Protecting tanks and AAVs from enemy infantry and antiarmor weapons.
- Leading the attack, dismounted when necessary.
- Clearing bridges and fording areas.
- Clearing restrictive terrain such as urban, swamp, or woodland areas.
- Conducting dismounted security patrols.

Based on METT-T, the mech force's combination of tanks, AAVs, and infantry provides the commander with the options of—

- Mounted maneuver with tanks.
- Mounted maneuver with AAVs.
- Mounted maneuver with tanks and AAVs.
- Dismounted maneuver alone.
- Dismounted maneuver combined with mounted maneuver options.

Employment Methods

Tank and mech infantry (mounted or dismounted in AAVs) attack together or support by fire. Based on METT-T, a combination of the two methods may be employed in a multiaxis attack.

Prior planning ensures communication can be maintained between the base of fire element(s) and dismounted infantry during the attack. Prepositioned retransmission sites and preplanned radio relay procedures are examples of techniques that can overcome a potential loss of communications during the attack.

The scheme of maneuver and fire support plan (direct fire, indirect fire, and aviation-delivered fires) must be developed concurrently and understood by elements of the mech force. Primarily used to engage targets on the objective, fires are also planned to isolate the objective by engaging targets on adjacent positions or likely enemy avenues of approach and to provide illumination and obscuration.

Tanks and Mechanized Infantry Attack Together

This method allows tanks and mech infantry to advance together within mutually supporting distances of each other. Normally, tanks lead the formation, while the infantry remains mounted in AAVs until the forward defensive positions of the enemy have been breached. However, the infantry should only remain mounted in AAVs when enemy resistance is weak or his defensive positions are overextended. Employing tanks and mech infantry to attack together—

● Exploits the mobility, speed, armor-protected firepower, and shock action of the mech force.

● Reduces enemy reaction time.

● Disorganizes the enemy's defense (his positions have normally been breached before the infantry dismounts).

● Conserves the energy of the mech infantry (they are carried by AAVs to DPs short of, on or behind the objective).

● Reduces the amount of time that the infantry is exposed to enemy fires.

When employing tanks and mech infantry to attack together there is a greater potential for casualties among elements of the mech force if enemy antiarmor fires cannot be bypassed or effectively reduced by suppressive fires. AAVs are vulnerable to antiarmor weapons and may be destroyed if employed as a tank. AAV armor can provide protection against hand grenades, shell fragments, and some small arms fire. However, even when EAAK is installed, the AAV can be vulnerable to the fires of tank and AT guns, ATGMs, and rockets.

Tanks and AAVs Support by Fire Only

During planning, the commander of the mech force may decide to attack using the tanks-and-AAVs-support-by-fire-only method. During a mounted assault, if surprise antiarmor fire is received that available fire support resources cannot suppress and if continuing the assault would result in unacceptable casualties, the infantry is dismounted in defilade locations. Tanks and AAVs then adopt the tanks-and-AAVs-support-by-fire-only method. Commanders should devise a plan of action that incorporates the tanks-and-infantry-attack-together method and has the flexibility to incorporate the tanks-and-AAVs-support-by-fire-only method if the situation changes unexpectedly.

The tanks-and-AAVs-support-by-fire-only method should be used when—

● Obstacles prevent mounted movement and cannot be quickly breached or bypassed.

● Enemy antiarmor capability poses significant threat to both tanks and AAVs.

● Terrain canalizes mounted movement into likely enemy ambush sites and minefields.

● Visibility is limited.

The base of fire element can deliver the following types of direct fires to support the dismounted infantry:

● Point fire is directed against a specific identified target (e.g., machine gun position, ATGM position).

● Area fire is distributed over an area when enemy positions are more numerous and less obvious. Fire is distributed in width and depth to keep parts of the target under fire.

Positive control of supporting fires between the dismounted infantry and base of fire element(s) must be maintained throughout the attack. The infantry uses radio communication, prearranged visual signals (e.g., pyrotechnic), and/or messengers to designate targets and coordinate supporting fires. AAVs, tanks, and other available direct fire support assets normally displace forward to new SFPs as they become available.

Momentum of the dismounted infantry attack is achieved by a sustained, accurate, and heavy volume of fires. Suppressive fire helps compensate for the infantry's lack of armor protection and decreased mobility. Long-range precision fires (e.g., TOWs) are employed against enemy vehicles, protected AT guns and ATGMs, and other priority hard targets.

The base of fire element ideally supports from concealed positions, (hull down, turret defilade). To avoid presenting the enemy with easily acquired stationary targets, units comprising the base of fire element should constantly reposition themselves to different support-by-fire positions.

Dismounted infantry should advance on a route that provides cover and concealment and prevents or minimizes masking of the base of fire element's fires. If available, engineers should accompany the dismounted infantry to breach obstacles and destroy fortified positions.

A disadvantage of the tanks-and-AAVs-support-by-fire only method is that the infantry loses the mobility, shock action, and close support of the tanks and AAVs. The infantry is also unsupported on the objective itself when the tanks and AAVs shift or cease fires. In addition, tanks and AAVs are not initially available on the objective to cover the consolidation.

Multiaxis Attack

A multiaxis attack is a combination of the two general methods of employment based on METT-T. A primary consideration is the availability of suitable avenues of approach for the tanks, AAVs, and the infantry. The multiaxis attack is often used to exploit the amphibious capability of the AAV in crossing streams, rivers, lakes, and marshes. In addition, multiaxis attack may be used when a single avenue of approach is too narrow to accommodate the entire mech force.

Normally, the tanks follow the more open terrain, while the infantry advance follows an axis offering cover and concealment. Tanks initially support the infantry advance by fire and join the infantry as soon as practicable. Movement of the tanks is normally timed so that the tanks assault the objective slightly in advance of the infantry to take maximum advantage of their shock effect. The greatest challenge to employing this method is achieving proper timing among the various elements and coordination of fires during the attack.

Mechanized Movement

Tanks normally lead the mech formation because they have better armor protection and main gun firepower than AAVs. When the situation permits, AAVs can support the mech force by following the tanks close enough to fire around the tanks and deliver suppressive fire against enemy infantry and antiarmor weapons encountered on exposed flanks.

Order of movement is generally based on the following criteria:

- Tanks lead in open areas or when faced with a significant armor threat.
- Mech infantry leads mounted only if mech infantry is pure with no other antiarmor reinforcements or capabilities.

The desired distance between tanks and AAVs should be determined before starting the attack based on the following METT-T situations:

- Mission—If the mission requires rapid, closely controlled movement and closely coordinated dismounted infantry action, the AAVs may closely follow the tanks.

- Enemy—The capabilities of the enemy force influence the location of the tanks and AAVs in the assault. If the enemy force possesses a substantial antiarmor capability, both the tanks and AAVs may be better employed in providing direct fire support to dismounted infantry.
- Terrain and weather—When visibility is poor and/or terrain provides numerous defilade positions and short fields of fire, AAVs may closely follow tanks. However, there are situations where mech infantry mounted in AAVs may lead tanks. For example, mech infantry mounted AAVs may lead while crossing an unfordable body of water or a marshy area that tanks cannot ford to seize an objective from a more favorable direction (e.g. bridge, other key terrain). In addition, when the mech force is confronted with close terrain (e.g., woodland, urban areas), dismounted infantry should clear this terrain before AAVs and tanks move through it. This clearing facilitates frequent and rapid dismounting and protects the AAVs and tanks from enemy infantry and antiarmor fires.
- Troops and support available—Task organization will also influence the formations and relative positions of the AAVs. Few or no tanks, other available direct fire weapons, and supporting arms may require that AAVs lead the assault.
- Time available—The less time there is, the closer the AAVs normally are to the tanks. This cuts down reaction time and response time but may permit faster reorganization.

Maneuver Considerations

In mech attacks, speed is essential and maintained to the greatest degree possible. The critical decision of whether the infantry attacks mounted or dismounted is based on METT-T.

Tanks Lead

When tanks lead, they and mech infantry maneuver together, supported by the base of fire element and available supporting arms. The AAV-mounted or dismounted infantry normally follows tanks. Normally, tanks lead and infantry stays mounted when—

- Enemy antiarmor fires can be effectively bypassed or suppressed by fire.
- Terrain is relatively open or manmade and natural obstacles can be easily overcome.
- Terrain and weather affords good trafficability and visibility.

Infantry Mounted

The mobility and limited armor protection of AAVs help the infantry cross the battlefield quickly. Normally, the mech infantry remains mounted when—

- Enemy resistance is extremely light.
- Enemy is in hasty positions.
- Suppressive fires have reduced enemy antiarmor fires.
- Terrain near the objective allows rapid movement onto and across the objective.

Infantry Dismounted

Dismounted infantry may designate targets for the overwatching AAVs and tanks. Dismounted infantry cover the flanks and rear of the mech force by employing organic fires, directing fires from the base of fire element, and providing supporting arms against enemy positions. Infantry normally moves far enough behind tanks to avoid being hit by enemy fire directed at the tanks. This technique permits close coordination and maximum mutual support but sacrifices the speed and mobility of the AAVs and tanks. Infantry leads dismounted when—

- Terrain and vegetation are restrictive. For example, when terrain and vegetation canalize movement into likely enemy ambush sites and minefield (e.g. urban areas, woodland terrain).
- Visibility is limited.

- Antiarmor fire can't be bypassed or suppressed by fire.
- Significant obstacles or fortified positions are encountered that may prevent mounted movement and cannot be bypassed.

Dismount Points

The mech force commander must decide to dismount the infantry before being committed to the final assault. After the decision is made, the mech force commander chooses when and where the infantry dismounts. Commanders normally stay well forward to judge the situation and make an appropriate decision of whether or not to change the DP. Timing is critical; dismounting too early will slow down the force's momentum and unnecessarily expose the infantry to hostile fire. Speed can provide for the security of a mech force already committed to the final assault.

Ideally, the infantry is dismounted after forward defensive positions have been breached. The DP should provide good cover and concealment, yet be as near the objective as possible. AA unit leaders must ensure that their vehicles do not halt in the open and are properly dispersed. This reduces the amount of time that the dismounted infantry is exposed to fires while closing with the enemy.

Rapid dismount and good vehicle dispersion reduces the mech force's vulnerability to enemy fires. Well-understood SOPs and well-rehearsed battle drills provide a foundation for rapid dismount and good vehicle dispersion. DPs may be short of the objective, on the objective, or after passing through the objective.

Short of the Objective

Tactical conditions may require seeking a DP short of the objective that is usually not within range of small arms and handheld antiarmor weapons. Ideally, the DP should be located on easily recognizable terrain that provides cover from enemy direct fires.

Advantages

- Dismounted infantry are protected from small arms and observed indirect fires while dismounting.
- Infantry can be oriented as they approach the objective.
- Control can be established in the DP.
- Organic and supporting fires can suppress the enemy while the infantry is dismounting.

Disadvantages

- Dismounted infantry are exposed longer to enemy small arms and indirect fire as they move forward in the assault.
- Suitable DPs forward of enemy positions may be targeted by enemy direct and indirect fires.

On the Objective

This DP is used when the mech force has achieved surprise or the enemy antiarmor defense is weak.

Advantages

- Greater speed and shock effect are achieved.
- Mech infantry remains protected longer by AAV light armor from the fires of enemy small arms.
- Supporting fires can continue while the mech force approaches its objective since mounted infantry have greater protection against shell fragments and other small projectiles.

Disadvantages

- Mech infantry is difficult to orient to specific objectives.
- Control is difficult to establish at the DP due to potentially close enemy fires.

- Supporting fires are difficult to direct against enemy positions in close proximity to friendly dismounted infantry.
- AAVs are vulnerable to short-range antiarmor weapons.
- High volume of suppressive fire is required to support dismounted infantry.

After Passing Through the Objective

Dismount after passing through the objective is employed when a mounted attack is more effective. The capabilities of the enemy antiarmor defense will dictate whether this is feasible.

Advantages

- Dismounted infantry fights from an area and direction unexpected by the enemy.
- Control is usually more easily established when not on the objective.
- Shock effect on the enemy caused by a mech force moving through its position is likely to be considerable.

Disadvantages

- This method may conflict with enemy positions in depth.
- Enemy indirect and direct fires may target suitable DPs.
- Turning AAVs around in close proximity to enemy fires can make the AAVs more vulnerable to flank shots and may reverse the relative positions of the tanks, AAVs, and infantry.

Base of Fire and Maneuver

Fires are primarily employed to suppress, neutralize, destroy, and demoralize enemy forces. As movement supported by fire, maneuver brings firepower into positions from which it extends and completes the destruction. To facilitate fire and maneuver attacks, mech forces normally organize into base of fire element(s) and maneuver element(s).

Elements

The composition of base of fire and maneuver elements is determined by the commander's task organization of the mech force.

Base of Fire

The base of fire element covers the maneuver element's advance toward the enemy position by engaging known or suspected targets. Upon opening fire, the base of fire element seeks to gain fire superiority over the enemy. Fire superiority is gained by subjecting the enemy to fire of such accuracy and volume that the enemy fire ceases or becomes ineffective.

Maneuver

The mission of the maneuver element is to close with and destroy or capture the enemy. The maneuver element advances and assaults under maximum concealment and covering fire of the base of fire element. Fire superiority is maintained throughout the attack to ensure the success of any maneuver.

Attacks

When maneuvering to close range of the enemy is not required, attack by fire is employed to destroy the enemy from a distance. This task is usually given to the supporting element during the offensive and as a counterattack option for the reserve during defensive operations. An attack by fire is not done in conjunction with a maneuvering force. When assigning this task, the commander of the mech force specifies the intent of fires, to destroy, fix or suppress. Attacks consist of fire and maneuver and fire and movement.

Fire and Maneuver

Fire and maneuver is the process of one or more elements establishing a base of fire to engage the enemy, while the other element(s) maneuver to an advantageous position from which to close with and destroy or capture the enemy. Supporting fires from weapons not organic to the maneuver unit may be provided. Supporting fires may consist of direct, indirect, and aviation-delivered fires, which are integrated to achieve the effects of combined arms. Supporting fires should be followed closely by the maneuver element so that the shock effect of fire upon the enemy will not be lost.

Fire and Movement

Once the maneuver element meets enemy opposition and can no longer advance under the cover of the base of fire, it employs fire and movement to continue its forward movement to a position from which it can assault the enemy position. Fire and movement is primarily used in the assault where a unit or element advances by bounds or rushes, with subelements alternatively moving and providing covering fire for other moving subelements. Individuals (personnel or vehicles) or units may conduct fire and movement attacks.

Assault

The purpose of the assault is to place violent and intensive firepower on the objective and move rapidly across it to destroy or capture the enemy as quickly as possible. The term assault refers to that phase of an attack when the attacking force actually closes with the enemy. Mech forces can assault the objective mounted or dismounted.

Mounted

The decision to make a mounted assault is based on METT-T. A mounted assault is best used when the enemy is occupying hasty fighting positions, antiarmor fires can be suppressed, and terrain near the objective allows for rapid movement onto and across the objective. The assault must be carried out rapidly. Normally, tanks lead followed closely by AAVs. As the assault force approaches the objective, the AAVs should move closer to the tanks for added protection from enemy short-range antiarmor weapons.

Movement across the objective must be fast and continuous. A heavy volume of suppressive fires is maintained to keep enemy soldiers down in their positions. Stabilized turrets allow tanks to continue moving while conducting fire and movement. AAVs normally stay as close to the tanks as possible to provide protection to the flanks and rear of the tank.

Once the tanks and AAVs reach the far side of the objective, they occupy hull-down positions if possible. From support-by-fire positions, the tanks and AAVs can engage retreating enemy forces, continue the attack or defend against counterattack. If it is necessary to seize the objective, the dismounted infantry is used to clear remaining pockets of enemy resistance and to secure prisoners.

Dismounted

The assault is normally conducted dismounted if the enemy is in well-prepared defensive positions, antiarmor fires cannot be suppressed or the terrain restricts vehicle movement onto the objective. If the attack starts initially mounted, the infantry should be dismounted in a covered and concealed position that is as close to the objective as possible. The base of fire element(s) delivers supporting fires, while the dismounted infantry deploys. The dismounted infantry uses radio, prearranged visual signals (e.g. pyrotechnic), and/or messengers to direct the base of fire element(s) to shift and cease supporting fires. The dismounted infantry then employs fire and movement through the objective. Elements of the base of fire element normally displace to subsequent support-by-fire positions. When the tanks and

AAVs from the base of fire element rejoin the dismounted infantry, the infantry—

- Suppresses any remaining enemy position as the tanks and AAVs move to the objective.
- Reconnoiters initial SFPs and guides tanks and AAVs into the positions when necessary.
- Provides flank and rear security for the AAVs and tanks.

Based on METT-T, tanks may continue through the objective to engage resistance and pursue by fire until the infantry has consolidated the position.

Consolidation and Reorganization

The mech unit should consolidate and reorganize as soon as it takes an objective. An objective is held until the commander orders other action. At times, the attack may be continued with little or no hesitation to exploit success. In this case, only required reorganization is done, and consolidation is unnecessary.

Consolidation consists of actions taken to secure an objective and prepare to repel an enemy counterattack. In the order, the commander normally designates rifle platoon and AA unit positions and actions to be taken. The AA platoon consolidates an objective by—

- Occupying the position designated in the attack order (AAVs are moved into hull-down positions, if available, and assigned specific sectors of fire).

- Establishing local security and mutual support between AAVs and adjacent infantry units.
- Eliminating remaining pockets of enemy resistance and securing enemy prisoners of war.
- Preparing hasty fighting positions as quickly as possible.

Reorganization includes actions stated in the SOP that are taken to prepare to continue fighting.

The AA section leader has the following reorganization responsibilities:

- Replaces key personnel (e.g., vehicle commanders, drivers).
- Assesses damage to AAVs and reports to the AA platoon commander if assistance is needed.
- Conducts vehicle maintenance and ammunition redistribution as required.

The AA platoon commander has the following reorganization responsibilities:

- Replaces key personnel (e.g., platoon sergeant, squad leaders) who were lost.
- Informs the AA company and/or infantry company commander of the platoon's status.
- Oversees evacuation of casualties.
- Requests needed resupply.
- Sends prisoners of war (POWs) under guard to the POW collection point.

SECTION IV. ROLE OF THE RESERVE

See MCDP 1-0, Chapter 6, for definition of reserve.

The mobility of the AAV allows the reserve to react to troubled spots in the area quickly or to exploit an unexpected gap in the enemy's position. The AAV's speed allows it to exploit this gap from greater distances and over rugged terrain that other types of vehicles might not be able to negotiate. In addition, bodies of water that are normally viewed as obstacles are avenues of approach for AA units. The commander can plan the use of the reserve along the avenues that the enemy would not normally expect a unit to maneuver through.

SECTION V. CONDUCT OF PASSAGE OF LINES

See MCDP 1-0, Chapter 9, for definition of passage of lines.

Planning

The time or event at which responsibility for the zone of action transfers from the stationary force to the moving force must be agreed upon by the two commanders or specified by higher headquarters. The passage of lines must facilitate rapid transition to the subsequent missions of the moving and stationary units.

Unit Responsibilities

Upon receipt of a warning order that directs an operation requiring a passage of lines, the commander will make contact as soon as possible with the stationary unit. The passing unit commander's CP should collocate with the stationary unit CP to facilitate a smooth passage. Normally, the stationary unit would designate contact points, passage points, and routes.

Command and Control

Collocated tactical units should—

- Coordinate security measures during the passage.
- Coordinate time or circumstances when responsibility for the control of the area of operations (AO) is transferred.
- Exchange intelligence, tactical plans, and recognition signals.
- Exchange SOPs.
- Arrange for reconnaissance.
- Select passage areas and provide guides.
- Prioritize the use of routes and facilities, including provisions for movement control.
- Coordinate fire and other combat support to be provided by the stationary unit.
- Coordinate service support to be provided by the stationary unit to include medical, maintenance, and recovery assistance.
- Exchange liaison personnel.
- Exchange information on minefields and other obstacles.
- Coordinate command relationships between the passing unit's combat support and CSS assets and the stationary unit.
- Coordinate tactical cover and deception plans.

Rearward Passage of Lines

The rearward passage of lines is conducted to withdraw security forces or to hand the battle over to another unit when a main battle force is withdrawing. The stationary and moving forces coordinate positions forward of the battle hand-over line (BHL) to be occupied by the stationary unit's security force. Fires are planned to support the disengagement of the moving force, to support the obstacle/barrier plan, and to support the deception plan. Fires on the passage points should be planned for after the moving force passes through. Stationary force guides should make contact with the moving force at each passage point. Lanes through obstacles are marked and provisions made to close them quickly. The moving force normally sends the CSS elements first. The stationary force must have positive enemy identification before engaging any target.

CHAPTER 5. DEFENSIVE OPERATIONS

The defense is the employment of means and methods available to prevent, resist or destroy an enemy attack. Compared to the offense, the defense is generally the less decisive form of war. It can deny success to the enemy but rarely can it assure victory. As stated in Marine Corps Doctrinal Publication (MCDP) 1, *"An effective defense must assume an offensive character, striking at the moment of the enemy's greatest vulnerability."*

Defensive operations are conducted to—
- Counter surprise action by the enemy.
- Cause an enemy attack to fail.
- Gain time.
- Concentrate combat power elsewhere.
- Increase the enemy's vulnerability by forcing him to concentrate his forces.
- Attrite or fix the enemy as a prelude to offensive operations.
- Retain decisive terrain or deny a vital area to the enemy.
- Prepare to resume the offensive.

Defense Fundamentals

The basic defense fundamentals that must be considered include maneuver, preparation, concentration of combat power, flexibility, offensive actions, use of terrain, security, mutual support, defense in depth, as well as fire support and obstacle plans.

Maneuver

See MCDP 1-0, Chapter 8. AA units maneuver in depth, taking advantage of terrain and tactical developments, to concentrate, disperse, and occupy positions to bring effective fire on the enemy.

Preparation

See MCDP 1-0, Chapter 8 for explanation.

Concentration of Combat Power

See MCDP 1-0, Chapter 8. The commander may employ AAVs as part of a mech force to reinforce threatened sectors or counterattacks.

Flexibility

The commander's plan must be flexible enough to deal with different enemy courses of action. Flexibility is created by—

- Detailed planning for contingencies.
- Designating supplementary and alternate positions.
- Properly locating, task-organizing, and planning use of the reserve.
- Designing a counterattack plan.
- Preparing to assume the offense.
- Planning on-call fire support.

Offensive Actions

Since the offense is the decisive form of combat, the commander seeks every opportunity to take offensive action while defending. The commander may employ AAVs as part of a mech force to—

- Launch spoiling attacks while the enemy is preparing or assembling for an attack.
- Attack with security forces to harass, distract, deceive, and damage the enemy before he reaches the main battle position (BP).
- Counterattack to destroy or repulse enemy penetrations.

Use of Terrain

When making an estimate of the situation, the defending commander takes account of key terrain and visualizes possible enemy avenues of approach. The defender seeks to defend on terrain that maximizes effective fire, cover, concealment, movement, and surprise.

Security

Using active and passive measures, security forces are assigned screen, cover, and guard missions based on METT-T. The commander may employ AAVs as an element of security forces to exploit the vehicle's mobility and firepower.

Mutual Support

Mutual support is achieved when defensive positions are located so the enemy cannot attack one position without coming under fire from another position. The degree of mutual support obtained depends on the terrain, range of weapons, and visibility. AAVs are usually employed by sections to achieve mutual support.

Defense in Depth

See MCDP 1-0, Chapter 8 for explanation. Defense in depth is necessary to—

- Disrupt the momentum of the attack and prevent a breakthrough.
- Force the enemy into engagement areas (EAs).
- Allow the defender time to determine the enemy's main effort and to counter it.
- Force the enemy to commit his reserves at a nondecisive point.
- Disperse the effects of enemy fires.

Fire Support and Obstacle Plans

Organic direct fires and fires from available supporting arms are integrated with maneuver and obstacle plans. Natural and manmade obstacles enhance the effects of firepower by increasing target acquisition time and creating exploitable vulnerabilities.

Defensive Position Variations

Two defensive position variations are the reverse-slope defense and the perimeter defense.

Reverse-Slope Defense

A reverse-slope defense is organized on that part of a slope that is masked by the topographical crest from enemy direct fire and observation. The defender can deliver surprise fires on the enemy when he crosses the crest of the forward slope or when significant enemy forces are exposed on the reverse slope.

Perimeter Defense

A perimeter defense is designed to defeat attacks from any direction. The majority of the force forms the perimeter and a reserve is established to provide depth. The perimeter consists of a series of mutually supporting positions that take advantage of observation and fields of fire afforded by dominating terrain.

Organization of the Battlespace

An AAV-equipped force can be employed in security, main battle, and rear areas of the battlespace. See MCDP 1-0, Chapter 8 for organization of the battlespace.

Organization of the Force

The commander organizes the force into security, main battle, and rear area forces for defensive operations.

Security Forces

See MCDP 1-0, Chapter 8 for explanation of security forces. Normally, LAR and aviation units are tasked as the security force within a MAGTF; however, mech force units containing AAVs may also be assigned this mission. Leaders post local security to provide early warning. Counterreconnaissance inhibits the enemy's intelligence gathering capabilities and deceives the enemy to the exact location of the main defenses.

Main Battle Forces

See MCDP 1-0, Chapter 8 for explanation of main battle forces. The defender reacts to the enemy's main effort by reinforcing the threatened sector or allowing the enemy's main effort to penetrate into EAs within the main battle area (MBA) to cut him off and destroy him by counterattack. AAVs are suited to transport reinforcements to threatened sectors or conduct a counterattack as part of a mech force.

Rear Area Forces

See MCDP 1-0, Chapter 8 for explanation of rear area forces. Normally, a mech force does not have a rear area mission within the MAGTF. However, the mech force may be assigned offensive missions against penetrations of enemy conventional or unconventional forces.

Types of Missions

In the defense, mech forces are normally assigned to security, defend in sector, defend a BP, defend a strong point, reserve, and counterattack missions.

Security

The screen, guard, and cover security missions are ideally suited to mech force's mobility and firepower. See MCDP 1-0, Appendix D for screen guard and cover discussions.

Screen

See MCDP 1-0, Appendix D.

Guard

See MCDP 1-0, Appendix D.

Cover

See MCDP 1-0, Appendix D.

Defend in Sector

Assignment of defensive sectors to subordinate units provides those commanders with maximum latitude to accomplish assigned tasks. Within the sector, the commander of the mech force may assign subordinate sectors, BPs, strong points or any combination of these. See figure 5-1 on page 5-4. Commanders usually defend in sector when—

- Avenues of approach are not easily defined.
- Dominating terrain is not available.
- AO is wide or large.
- Mutual support is not easily achieved.
- Commander's ability to control is degraded.

Defend a Battle Position

Defense from a BP or blocking position requires the mech force to occupy a general location where it can block an avenue of approach, fire into an assigned area, retain key terrain or perform other tasks. Usually BPs are hastily occupied but continuously improved. A blocking position is a BP suited to deny the enemy access to a given area or prevent his advance in a given direction. Commanders defend in BP and blocking position when—

- Avenues of approach are well defined, and the enemy can be canalized.
- Key terrain dominates avenues of approach.
- AO is narrow or small.
- Mutual support is achievable.
- Commander's ability to control is good.

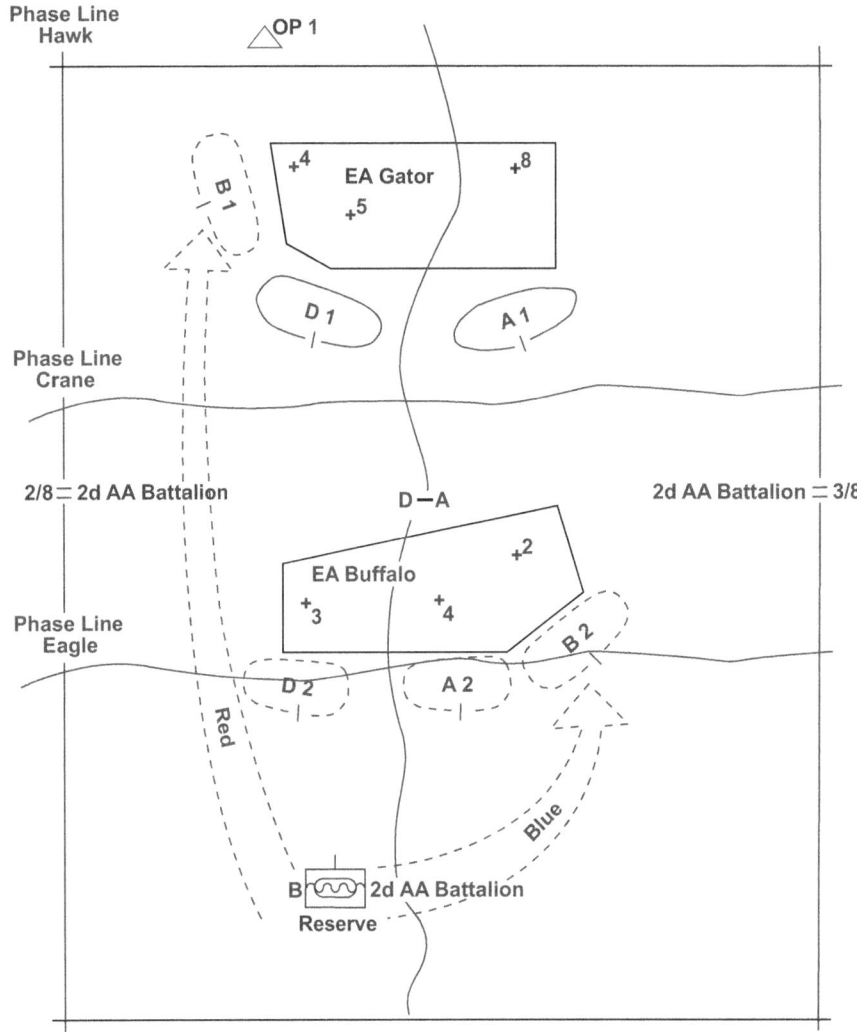

Figure 5-1. Defense-in-Sector Plan.

Defend a Strong Point

Defense from a strong point implies the defense of a heavily fortified position that holds or controls key terrain or blocks an avenue of approach. A key point in a defensive position, a strong point is usually fortified and often designed to defeat enemy armor and mech attacks. Located on a terrain feature that is critical to the overall defense, a strong point is intended for permanent or extended occupation.

Defending a strong point is the most labor-intensive mission a mech force may execute. While the defense is static, there has to be built-in flexibility using direct and indirect fire plans and properly constructed positions.

If infantry is positioned in front of tanks, the infantry should have overhead cover and hearing protection to protect them from blast, over pressure, and discarding sabot from the tanks. If infantry is positioned in front of AAVs, the AA unit leader must ensure that the infantry have a route back to the AAVs while ensuring that the infantry do not get in the UGWS's fields of fire.

Terrain should be used to ensure optimum shots for direct fire weapons systems; dead space and infiltration routes should be minimized or made inaccessible. Mobility within the strong point should be enhanced using terrain and trenches. Innovation must be used to prevent the enemy from anticipating the defender's next move.

When conditions permit, mobile assets like mech infantry may remain outside the defensive perimeter to provide early warning and to delay or confuse the enemy. Once these mobile assets are inside the strong point, the mission becomes holding the defensive perimeter against the enemy. Interlocking direct fires must be planned over the entire strong point along with counterattack by fire positions and external direct-fire control measures.

The enemy will probably not want the strong point unless it is key terrain. If it is, he will throw overwhelming forces against the strong point. Preceding a ground attack may be a massive artillery preparation that will destroy or damage anything that is not protected. Enemy maneuver units will accompany enemy artillery moving toward the strong point. At this point, stay-behind reconnaissance units can call in fires to disrupt the enemy's formations. Aviation assets, naval surface fire support, and artillery should be called in to prevent the enemy from reaching the strong point.

As the enemy nears the strong point, direct fires will engage them in accordance with the fire support and obstacle plan. If the enemy is not stopped at the main EA, the commander must be able to direct fires against enemy penetration. If the enemy manages to make a penetration, forces will have to seal off and isolate this penetration. Repositioning forces to supplementary positions near the penetration will save the unit's reserve for other tasks later.

Reserve

Missions assigned to the reserve normally consist of counterattacks, reinforcement of the main effort, protection for the flanks, and support of committed units by fire. In a reserve mission, the commander holds part of the force to influence the course of the battle at the critical time and place and to exploit opportunities.

Normally the less that is known of the enemy or his intention, the greater the proportion of combat power that must be held in reserve. The reserve is usually located in assembly areas or forward operating bases in the MBA. Once the reserve is committed, a new reserve must be created or obtained. Reserves are organized based on the factors of METT-T. The tactical mobility of mech and helicopterborne forces make them well suited for use as the reserve.

AAVs in Mobile Reserve

While most units assigned to defend from BPs have similar mobility, some task-organized units may not be mounted in AAVs. Some may have been trucked while others lifted by helicopters or MV-22s. In this case, the commander should use AAVs in the mobile reserve role to maximize their inherent mobility and firepower and therefore use the AAVs as a combat multiplier.

Reserve In a Strong Point

In a strong point defense, a reserve must be designated to conduct the following missions:

- Block a threat penetration against the perimeter.
- Reinforce success or a section of the defense.
- Counterattack to restore a portion of the defense.

The reserve could be mounted and/or dismounted, and formed from combat support and CSS units if infantry and armor units are employed. Ideally, the reserve should be near the CP to provide protection and to minimize employment delays. AAVs should be used in this role within a strong point along with tanks to give the commander flexibility and mobility.

The reserve is usually tasked with conducting the counterattack in a strong point defense. Ideally, the reserve force should hit the enemy at a flank, isolate the penetration force, and seal the gap in the position. This action should be rehearsed and synchronized with the fire support and obstacle plan over the main enemy avenue of approach to determine the most probable penetration points.

If the reserve is unable to conduct the counterattack, the commander must use available units to conduct the counterattack against the penetration. The attacker is most vulnerable after he takes the objective and before he consolidates his position. Integration and synchronization with the fire support and obstacle plans are key elements to the success of a hasty counterattack. If possible, the commander should designate combat support and CSS units as a reserve counterattack force.

Normally counterattacks in a strong point will use fire and maneuver to seal the gap created by the enemy. The enemy must be destroyed, and the lines must be restored to maintain the integrity of the position.

Counterattacks

A counterattack is an attack by a defending force against an attacking enemy force. A counterattack is launched to regain ground lost, cut off and destroy enemy advance units, and deny the enemy the attainment of his purpose for attacking. In many cases, the counterattack is the decisive action in defensive operations. A separate counterattack force may be established by the commander to conduct planned counterattacks and can be made up of uncommitted or lightly engaged forces and the reserve. Counterattacks can be made by fire or by fire and maneuver. Counterattack by fire exploits weapons standoff and/or cover to full advantage. All available fires destroy the enemy. Counterattack by fire and maneuver can either seize terrain that the enemy has occupied or destroy the enemy.

Planning

Planning for the defense begins when the commander receives a mission/warning or anticipates a need to defend. Concurrent planning is essential to facilitate preparation. The defensive plan should take advantage of the natural strengths of the terrain and the defending force.

Intelligence

In defensive operations, planners use the intelligence preparation of the battlespace (IPB) to prepare the reconnaissance and surveillance (R&S) plan, deception plans, and key intelligence requirements.

Intelligence Preparation of the Battlespace

The IPB is employed during operations to identify, assess, and reduce the effects of enemy, environment, and terrain uncertainties on friendly and enemy forces. See Army Field Manual (FM) 34-130, *Intelligence Preparation of the Battlefield,* for additional information.

Reconnaissance and Surveillance Plan

The R&S plan must be coordinated with higher headquarters to avoid duplication of efforts, exploit available R&S assets, and reduce risk of potential fratricide (friendly fire) among forces employed in the security area. AAVs can be used as assets in the R&S plan if better suited mobility assets are not available. As the enemy reconnaissance elements are identified and destroyed, the S-2 should start piecing together the enemy's plan to support the commander's defensive and counterattack planning.

Deception Plan

Deception plans take on added importance in positional defenses since the static nature of these defenses lends itself to enemy targeting. AAVs can be used to highlight a deception BP by having them occupy a terrain feature, set up dummy positions, and then leave at night.

Intelligence Requirements

Key intelligence requirements for planning a defense include—

- Enemy avenues of approach (mounted and dismounted) and mobility corridors into the defensive area.
- Location of potential assembly areas and firing positions for enemy supporting arms.
- Size, composition, organization, rate of movement, capabilities, limitations, and tactics of the enemy force.
- Locations of enemy reserves, fire support, and CSS.
- Enemy C2 systems.
- Enemy intelligence capabilities, with emphasis on enemy reconnaissance capabilities.

Maneuver

The scheme of maneuver plan for the defense includes—

- Counterreconnaissance and other force protection measures.
- Initial positions to be occupied, prepared, and reconnoitered.
- Withdrawal routes and passage points for the security force.
- Primary, alternate, and supplementary positions for the main battle forces.
- Counterattack plans.
- Contingency plans to block penetrations or reinforce threatened areas.
- Dummy positions designed to deceive the enemy.
- Obstacles and barriers (integrated with the fire support plan).
- Plans to draw the enemy into EAs.

Fires

The commander must plan to mass fires of available weapons in EAs to contain, delay, disrupt or destroy the enemy. EAs are—

- Used as a tool to concentrate fires and optimize their effects.
- Used most effectively with combined arms.
- Identified by TRPs on the corners of the EA or by easily recognizable terrain features around the EA.

Direct fire

Commanders and staff must plan for direct fire of each AAV and determine the number and type of weapons available to defeat the enemy at a designated EA. The AA unit leader must ensure that the supported commander is aware of the capabilities and limitations of the UGWS, because the commander makes decisions about designating an EA. The following key planning factors must be considered when using AAVs:

- Range to the EA's kill zone.
- Rate of fire.
- Hit/kill probability.

Positioning

When planning positioning, the commander and staff should consider the following:

- Cover and concealment (hide position, hull defilade, and turret defilade).
- Dispersion (laterally and in depth with maneuver space between primary, alternate, and supplementary positions).
- Mutual support (AAVs normally employed by sections).
- Standoff range (minimize exposure time to enemy fires).
- Flank shots available.

Methods of Engagement

The commander and staff should plan for concentric fires and massed surprise fires, which are general methods of antiarmor engagements.

Concentric Fires

This method of engagement involves increasing the volume of fires from heavy, medium, and light antiarmor weapons and supporting arms that engage enemy targets at their maximum effective ranges. Normally employed against large mech formations, concentric fires are planned to destroy enemy mech as far forward of the friendly positions as possible. Major disadvantages of concentric fires are an increased likelihood of early detection of friendly positions and longer exposure to enemy direct and indirect fires.

Massed Surprise Fires

Planning for this method of engagement involves visualizing all direct fire weapons engaging the enemy simultaneously. Massed surprise fires are ideal in the ambush of individual or small mech formations. While this technique will result in more initial kills at much closer range, the mass and momentum of the enemy's attack may carry the force into friendly positions.

Fire Control

The defender engages the enemy with long-range fires as early as possible unless fires are withheld to prevent the loss of surprise. Commanders make maximum use of fire support to destroy and disrupt enemy formations as they approach the MBA. As the enemy closes, he is subjected to an ever-increasing volume of fires from the MBA forces and supporting arms. Obstacles and barriers are located to delay and canalize the enemy and are covered by fire to destroy him while he is halted or slowed and focused on the process of breaching.

Combat power that can be concentrated most quickly, such as offensive air support and artillery is brought to bear while mech forces move into position. The defender reacts to the enemy's main effort by reinforcing the threatened sector or allowing the enemy's main effort to penetrate into EAs within the MBA, then cutting him off and destroying him by counterattack. When the enemy attack has been broken, the commander looks to exploit any advantageous situations.

AA units normally support with fires from their MK-19 40-millimeter grenade launcher and M2 HB .50 caliber machine guns. AAVs can be a considerable distance away from infantry, as long as the AAVs can support the infantry by fire and rapidly rejoin the infantry by covered and concealed routes. AAVs are positioned to provide the best fire on the enemy. For example, AAVs may first be forward of the infantry to engage the approaching enemy. Then, as the enemy closes, AAVs move to alternate positions to support dismounted infantry.

Commanders should plan to position their units to provide the most effective fire without adjusting their locations by considering sectors of fire, TRPs, priority of engagement, methods of initiating engagement, disengagement break lines, the fire support plan, and control procedures.

Sectors of Fire

A sector of fire is an area that is covered by fire by an individual, a weapon or a unit. The commander designates a sector of fire for each unit. Sectors of fire ensure adequate distribution of massed fires within the EA. Assigning primary and secondary sectors of fire enhances mutual support. Primary, alternate, and supplementary positions are normally planned for each weapon system.

Target Reference Points

The commander delineates sector of fire orientations with TRPs. The TRP is an easily recognizable point that is natural or manmade used for identifying enemy targets, controlling fires, and distributing or converging fires.

Priority of Engagement

Commanders should establish the precedence of targets to be attacked. This priority of engagements is general guidance to a unit. For example, this guidance may include the following:

- Tanks fire at enemy tanks.
- AAVs fire at AT weapons, crew-served weapon positions, and enemy troops.
- Individual small arm and crew-served weapons fire at unarmored AT weapons and exposed enemy troops.
- AT weapons fire at tanks, ATs, and fortified positions from concealed overwatch positions.
- Artillery and mortars fire to suppress enemy fires, kill exposed enemy AT crews and exposed troops, and conceal friendly movement with smoke.
- Air defense weapons fire at enemy aircraft.

Methods of Initiating Engagement

On-order fire control and event-oriented fire control are general methods of initiating engagement that may be used with the concentric or massed surprised fires.

On-Order Fire Control. This method of initiating engagement is used when the commander gives the command to begin engaging the enemy. The commander must have reliable communications and be in a position to see the entire EA or sector.

Event-Oriented Fire Control. In this method of initiating engagement, the commander gives gunners guidance about what enemy action or event should occur before firing. The maximum engagement line and trigger point or line are fire control measures related to the methods of initiating engagements. The maximum engagement line is a line where targets can be engaged. This line will normally be the range limit of the sector of fire. Trigger points or lines are selected along identifi-

able terrain that crosses the EA. This ground location is where the enemy comes within the effective range of a given system. An example of event-oriented fire control guidance is "Commence fire after 10 tanks cross the trigger line."

Disengagement

The commander designates disengagement break lines to prevent decisive engagement. Units are told how much damage to inflict in a given EA and the order of weapon system disengagement. If the enemy continues, units can displace/move to subsequent positions with little or no communications based on disengagement break lines and commander-designated or event-oriented criteria (e.g., "Move to secondary positions once three enemy vehicles breach the minefield.")

Fire Support Plan

The fire support plan must support the scheme of maneuver. It is normally designed to place the enemy under increasing volumes of fire as he approaches a defensive position or the fire is withheld initially to allow for massed surprise fires. Fires are planned along expected enemy avenues of approach and in EAs. In addition, fires are integrated with obstacles, barriers, and defensive positions to support delay and counterattack plans. Indirect and aviation-delivered fires are closely integrated with infantry, tank, AAV, and antiarmor direct fire weapons. The FSC normally develops at least a fire support plan for the defense and plan for counterattack.

Control Procedures

When planning for effective fire control, commanders and staff should consider the following procedures:

- Use each weapon in its best role.
- Engage the enemy as rapidly as possible to minimize friendly exposure.
- Expose only those weapons needed to fire.
- Distribute fires to ensure complete coverage of enemy targets.

- Engage the most dangerous threat first.
- Maximize integration of direct and indirect fires with natural and manmade obstacles.
- Fire first. (The weapon that fires first has the advantage.)
- Engage one target with one weapon. (Avoid overkill.)
- Establish simple and complete fire control procedures.
- Centralize the control of antiarmor fires.
- Centralize and mass indirect fires.
- Designate responsibility for an EA to one individual (e.g., commander of the mech company team or MTF).

Preparations for the Defense

When not engaged in the attack, the commander must initiate preparations for the defense. The type of defense depends on preparation time and is considered either deliberate or hasty.

A deliberate defense is normally organized when out of contact with the enemy or when contact with the enemy is imminent and time for organization is available. A deliberate defense includes fortifications, strong points, extensive use of obstacles, and fully integrated fires. The commander is normally free to make a detailed reconnaissance of the sector, select terrain to defend, and decide the best tactical deployment of forces.

A hasty defense is a defense normally organized while in contact with the enemy or when contact with the enemy is imminent and time for organization is limited. Reconnaissance of the sector may or may not be detailed and the defense may be assumed directly from the current positions of units. Depending on the situation, the commander may initiate a hasty attack to seize terrain suitable to the defense. The commander may employ a security force to delay the enemy while deploying the bulk of the force to more suitable defensive terrain. A hasty defense is improved continuously as the situation permits and may eventually become a deliberate defense.

Commands must prepare simultaneously, and priorities of work must be established to comprehensively provide a strong defense. Priority of work for AAV units includes the following:

- Post security (turret watch for AAVs).
- Plan and develop fire control measures (sectors, TRP orientations, EAs). (AA unit leaders ensure that range cards are made and then integrated with the unit fire plan.)
- Designate alternate positions. (Ensure ability to engage the primary avenue of approach.)
- Designate supplementary positions. (Ensure ability to engage the secondary avenue of approach.)
- Designate hide positions. (May be dug in if needed; ensure that resources and time are available.)
- Dig primary fighting positions for anticipated fighting conditions. (AA unit leader must have AAVs dug in before assets are allocated.)
- Achieve mutual support/concentration of fires. (Combine UGWS with mortars, AT weapons, and tanks.)
- Emplace obstacles.
- Clear fields of fire.
- Establish coordination or contact points.
- Emplace wire for communications. (Use gun loop for AAVs if the position will be occupied for more than 30 minutes.)
- Prestock or dig in ammunitions and other supplies. (Ensure batteries are recharged, fuel is topped off, and ammunition is replenished in the AAVs.)
- Designate observation posts (OPs)/listening posts and patrol routes. (Ensure crewmen are aware of the obstacle plan if AAVs will be used for patrols.)
- Mark and prepare routes. (Coordinate with engineers to plan alternate routes if possible.)

- Rehearse movement back to and into the position. (AAVs must practice getting to their firing positions during all visibility conditions with or without ground guides. To prevent accidents, ensure that the infantry does not get in the way.)
- Use back briefs to ensure mission intent is understood.
- Install chemical agent detectors; prepare the appropriate mission-oriented protective posture (MOPP).
- Install intrusion-sensing devices. (Ensure friendly vehicles do not set off devices.)
- Install camouflage and concealment measures continuously.

Engineering

The four functional areas of engineer effort are mobility, countermobility, survivability, and general engineering. While the functional areas may be applicable to the defense effort, survivability and countermobility are the primary engineering tasks associated with the development of the EA. Commanders should involve engineers as early as possible during the planning of the EA, because preparation of fighting positions for large equipment (e.g., AAVs, tanks) or the creation of obstacles (e.g., mines, ditches, hedgehogs) requires lead time and planning for engineers to mobilize equipment, supplies, and personnel to provide support.

Obstacle Employment

Obstacles are employed in depth to support the scheme of maneuver and are integrated with the fire support plan to maximize the effects of fires. AAVs may be used to assist engineers in performing these missions because of their mobility and ability to carry large amounts of demolitions, mines, and engineer materials. The following are some key countermobility measures:

- Prepare obstacles to prevent overrun by enemy tanks.
- Prepare hull down positions for vehicular assets.

- Emplace obstacles at optimum weapons range.
- Construct protected routes between positions.
- Plan and coordinate for scatterable mines.
- Assist in building infantry fighting positions and CPs.
- Prepare and booby trap dummy positions.
- Prepare disabled vehicles for destruction.
- Place sandbags around, on top, and on the side of AAV positions to enhance survivability.

Obstacle Effects

AA unit leaders must consider AAV capabilities and limitations when integrating obstacle effects (i.e., disrupt, turn, fix or block) in fire planning and the obstacle plan.

Disrupt. The disrupt effect is used to break apart an enemy's formation and tempo, interrupt the enemy's timetable, cause premature commitment of enemy forces or force his piecemeal attack. Obstacles are used to disrupt the enemy's march and assault formations, force the enemy to commit breaching assets prematurely, and separate the enemy's forward combat elements from his supply trains.

Turn. A turn effect is used to divert an enemy formation off one avenue of approach to an adjacent avenue of approach or into an EA. Turning obstacles entice or force the enemy to move in a desired direction, splitting his formation, canalizing him or exposing his flank.

Fix. A fix effect is used to slow an attacker in a specified area, normally an EA. In delaying operations, the use of fixed obstacles allows the delaying force time to break contact and disengage or move to subsequent positions.

Block. A block effect is used to stop an attacker on a specified avenue of approach or to prevent an enemy from exiting an EA. Always integrated with fires, blocking obstacles are employed in depth to prevent the enemy from proceeding.

Logistics

When planning for logistics in defensive operations, the commander positions the CSS elements away from locations that will be targeted by the enemy. However, the elements should be close enough to ensure rapid resupply of the mech force's assets. A CSS traffic control plan must be developed to ensure that supplies and personnel are transported and casualties are delivered to the aid station.

Combat trains and contact teams normally plan multiple routes to defensive positions and rehearse their movement to minimize confusion during the actual battle. Defenders often employ preplanned contact teams to conduct emergency resupply or repair as far forward as possible to reduce turnaround time. Prestocked ammunition and other classes of supply reduce reliance on emergency resupply and minimize movement within defensive positions that might be observed by the enemy.

AAVs may be used to supplement the vehicles of the combat trains. AAVs assigned to support CSS units may be used to carry fuel bladders, prepackaged ammunition, and other supplies or as an ambulance when fitted with litter carriers. Because AAVs can travel rough terrain, they are used to provide CSS in a large strong point.

Command and Control

The commander, with key staff, normally fights the defensive battle from the forward tactical echelon. This position allows the commander to remain near major actions or critical events. Located to the rear of the frontline units, the main echelon maintains contact with subordinate units and the tactical echelon. The main echelon focuses on monitoring the progress of the battle, forwarding information and support requests, and coordinating the activity of supporting units. The commander controls forces in the sector through

redundant and secure communications usually from the AAVC7A1.

Types of Defense

Every defense contains a dynamic or mobile element that generates combat power through maneuver and concentration of forces and a static or positional element that is anchored in key terrain. Mobile defense is characterized by offensive action, supplementary positions, shifting of forces, and commitment of the reserves. Positional defense is characterized by the use of BPs, strong points, fortifications, and barriers to halt enemy advance. Marine commanders use mobile and positional type defenses simultaneously and rarely use one type exclusively. Mech units are ideally suited for the mobile defense.

Mobile and Position Defense

See MCDP 1-0, Chapter 8 for discussions.

Deployment Methods in Position Defense

AAVs employed in the defense of a BP can be deployed with infantry mounted, infantry and AAVs on the same BP, and infantry and AAVs on a separate BP.

Infantry Mounted

The infantry mounted method of deploying infantry in defense of BP is used when the BP is only temporarily occupied, and the unit may be required to quickly relocate. Although this technique simplifies the control and coordination between the infantry commander and supporting AAVs and improves the unit's ability to react and move fast, the unit has less firepower than it would if its Marines were dismounted. Normally, this deployment method is used when—

● Enough firepower can be employed from the AAVs.

● Increased local security or observation is not needed.

● A short-notice move may be required.

Infantry and AAVs on the Same Battle Position

Decentralized and centralized control methods are used when the infantry and AA unit deploys on the same BP.

Decentralized Control of AAVs. In this method, some or all of the infantry dismount under control of their platoon commanders who also retain control of their respective AA section. The platoon commander gives orders to the AA section leader, who instructs respective AAV crews. This method is used when the infantry cannot stay mounted but must temporarily occupy a BP and be ready to quickly relocate.

Centralized Control of AAVs. This method of control is used when the mech company must occupy a BP and be prepared to repel an attack. The infantry dismounts and positions away from the AA platoon. The infantry company commander controls the AAVs through the AA platoon commander. This deployment is effective when the company BP has multiple avenues of approach with both long- and short-range fields of fire. Centralized control enables each AAV and infantry element to be positioned on terrain suited to its own capabilities.

The infantry is usually positioned in close terrain that limits vehicle movement and firing positions. The AA sections take up positions on terrain that offers AAV movement and good AAV firing positions with long fields of fire. AAVs may be positioned forward of, flanking or behind the infantry.

The positions of the units must allow the infantry to quickly remount. To do this, the AA platoon commander will plan assembly areas where the AAV sections will rejoin the infantry platoons. In addition, the AA platoon commander will designate routes that allow covered but fast movement to the assembly areas.

Infantry and AAVs on Separate Battle Positions

This deployment is used when the supported infantry commander needs dismounted infantry in one location and AAVs in another. The AA platoon commander will control fires and maneuver as required by the company commander. AAV and infantry units may be separated if the infantry is ordered to occupy positions in heavily wooded or rugged terrain where AAVs cannot go. At this time, the AA unit is located in a concealed assembly area near the infantry or is assigned a BP in suitable terrain.

In the reserve, AAVs may be called upon to conduct a counterattack from BPs. Counterattack planning for defense of a BP is similar to that in defending a sector. Both counterattack by fire and counterattack by fire and maneuver need to be considered and rehearsed. Control measures for maneuver and fire control ensure that the counterattack force does not overrun its fire support and that it does not become a victim of friendly fires. Mech forces should be used for counterattacks because of their inherent mobility. Ideally, the counterattack force is not committed until the commander is certain that the enemy's second-echelon forces have been slowed or stopped by deep fires and/or obstacles. This will ensure that the force does not get trapped between two enemy forces. Obstacles should be used to reduce the enemy's ability to maneuver against the counterattack force.

The counterattack force should recommend and prepare several BPs in case the first BP comes under heavy enemy attacks. Alternate BPs will ensure that the force is not reduced before it is committed in a counterattack. If the counterattack force is pinned down in its BP, the MTF commander may assign the counterattack mission to another force.

CHAPTER 6. LOGISTICS OPERATIONS

Logistics is the science of planning and carrying out the movement and maintenance of forces. At the AA battalion level, logistics is defined as the science of planning and effecting the development, deployment, and sustainability of the battalion's resources in support of the mission. Sustainability is the ability to maintain the necessary level and duration of operational activity to achieve military objectives by providing for and maintaining levels of ready forces, material, and consumables necessary to support the military effort. At the AA battalion level, sustainability means accurately using organic assets and coordinating logistic support with higher combat service support elements (CSSEs) to accomplish the mission.

At the battalion level, logistics are directed by the battalion logistics staff officer (S-4). AA battalion logistics support forward deployed AA units with AAV-unique sustainment of parts, materials, and limited third echelon maintenance. The AA battalion, because of its extensive organic maintenance capability, generally creates maintenance contact teams (MCTs) to operate in DS of forward units. Normally, an MCT supports a company but may be created to support a reinforced platoon operating independently. The battalion should maintain close liaison with the supported unit (regiment) and the supporting CSSE. The AA battalion is the focal point for AAV support and sustainment.

Responsibility for logistical support is dependent on the AAV unit's mission. AAVs can be attached to another MAGTF element or be assigned a DS or GS mission. If attached, the attached unit commander is responsible for the logistics of the supporting AA unit. In the DS role, the responsibility for logistical support rests on the parent unit. The attached unit commander has TACON/OPCON of the supporting AA unit (i.e., the vehicle unit is under the command of its parent unit, but supports another specific unit).

For GS missions, the responsibility for logistical support rests with the AA battalion (i.e., employment of AA assets to support requests from subordinate elements of the force, not assigning priority to any given element, therefore allowing C2 to be maintained by the AA unit).

Logistic Trains

The CSSE provides sustained CSS. Task-organized CSS units will replenish the AAV unit/battalion trains, which will replenish their companies or separate detachments using combat and field trains.

Types of Trains

Regimental, unit, battalion, and company trains provide logistics and link forward tactical elements and the supporting CSSE.

Regimental Trains

The regimental train consists of CSS to sustain the regimental headquarters and organic or attached units under the direct control of the regiment. The regimental commander may choose to consolidate the battalion field trains in one location for security, control, and resource pooling. CSS that is of immediate need to combat units should be allocated to the battalion trains, but CSS not of a time-critical nature can often be consolidated at regimental level. The MCT may collocate with the regimental train.

Unit Trains

Unit trains centralize organic CSS assets of the supported unit in a single location under the direct control of the unit commander. Unit trains are most appropriate in defensive, slow moving or static situations.

Battalion Trains

Battalion trains operate under the control of the battalion S-4 and are normally echeloned into combat and field trains. Battalion trains should provide their own security while effecting simultaneous resupply of each maneuver element. Combat trains must be located far enough forward to remain responsive, normally not more than 3 to 5 kilometers behind the tactical units. Field trains must be readily accessible to the combat service support detachment (CSSD) to improve coordination.

Combat trains are organic assets that usually include—

- Rations, POL, ammunition (classes I, III, and V), and selected medical and maintenance items to last for a specified period (usually not more than 24 hours).
- The forward BAS with supporting ambulance teams.
- MCTs with a limited number of maintenance and recovery vehicles.
- Other anticipated critical CSS.
- Organic or attached firepower for local and antiair/antiarmor security as required (Stinger, TOW, AT-4, and heavy machine guns).

Field trains consist of the organic CSS capability not located in the combat trains. The field trains usually include—

- Remainder of the BAS.
- Supply section, minus organic or attached motor transport (less supply vehicles in the combat train).
- Remaining CSS not in the combat train.

The field trains can also include—

- Nuclear, biological, and chemical (NBC) MOPP exchange/decontamination.
- Ammunition.
- Additional water and fuel.

Company Trains

Company trains consist of the immediate support that the company commander requires in a combat situation to distribute critical supplies or evacuate casualties. These trains include the company recovery vehicle, the company medical section, and attached CSS support. A company operating independently or at some distance from the battalion will have a portion of the battalion's organic CSS attached, including vehicles for resupply. Company trains, normally no more than a few vehicles, move with the company under the control of the company gunnery sergeant or AAV leader, gaining security from its proximity to the platoons. The company trains move one terrain feature in trace of the company. Organic or attached CSS of a less time-critical nature is normally located with the battalion trains.

Command and Control

METT-T, the seven principles of CSS, and the six functional areas of CSS drive the positioning and employment of supply trains through the chain of command.

S-4

The S-4 controls battalion combat trains but must coordinate with the S-3 in selecting train locations. To best control the train, the S-4 travels or operates with an appropriate communications platform that allows monitoring of multiple nets. CSSD trains will normally monitor the battalion tactical radio frequency.

Company Commander or Supply Officer

Normally, the H&S company commander or supply officer controls battalion field trains. The battalion S-4 may direct the field train if it is collocated with the regiment or battalion.

Tactical Logistics Operation Center

The tactical logistics operation center (TLOC) may be collocated with regiment and/or battalion field trains. The TLOC monitors designated nets when coordinating DS missions, i.e., transporting supplies directly to the combat train.

The TLOC should provide liaison to supported units, i.e., regiment and/or battalion. The liaison officer should arrive with communication assets and pass coordinating traffic from the CSSD to the supported unit on the CSS request net. Additionally, the mission may require the AA battalion to request a liaison team from the CSSE.

Battalion Support Area

MCTs and supply trains must be protected to maintain the sustainability of forward units. The location of the battalion support area depends on the situation. MCTs in DS may be collocated in battalion support areas or where most responsive yet survivable. MCTs can be collocated with the battalion field trains or regimental trains except when providing DS to maneuver units.

Positioning Considerations

To satisfy the CSS principles of responsiveness and survivability, the unit/battalion trains or MCTs in DS should be located—

- On defensible terrain and outside enemy artillery range.
- In an area with enough space to permit dispersion of both vehicles and activities.
- Where there is good cover and concealment from air and ground observation.
- On firm ground that supports continuous vehicle traffic.
- Near a suitable helicopter LZ for medical evacuation and helicopter resupply.
- Close to main supply routes (MSRs) forward and rearward.
- Near good communications with forward elements and supporting CSSD.

Security of Positions. Security of the battalion support area is a joint effort between the CSS commander and the AAV units. Security considerations include—

- Using OPs to provide early warning.
- Establishing a perimeter defense if expecting to be stationary for an extended period.
- Establishing reaction teams and assignment of positions and sectors of fire.
- Using vehicles with heavy machine guns to cover likely avenues of approach.
- Establishing internal communications by wire.
- Plotting on-call targets for point defense.
- Seeking positions that offer overhead concealment.
- Positioning near the reserve.

Displacement of Positions. When repositioning the trains, the S-4 or commanding officer selects the displacement technique that best complements the supported unit's concept of operations. The trains may displace as a whole or by echelon. Displacement by echelon permits continuous CSS and enhances survivability.

Replenishment Methods

The service station and tailgate issue methods are the two most common methods used to replenish unit trains.

Service Station Method

When using the service station method (see figure 6-1 on page 6-4) of replenishment—

- Tactical vehicles enter the resupply point following a one-way traffic flow.
- Only those vehicles requiring immediate unit or higher maintenance will stop in the maintenance holding area before conducting resupply.
- Personnel rotate individually to eat, pick up mail and supplies, and refill or exchange water cans.
- Vehicles that complete resupply move to the holding area where precombat inspections are completed.
- AAVs pull out of their positions in rotation, resupply, and return.

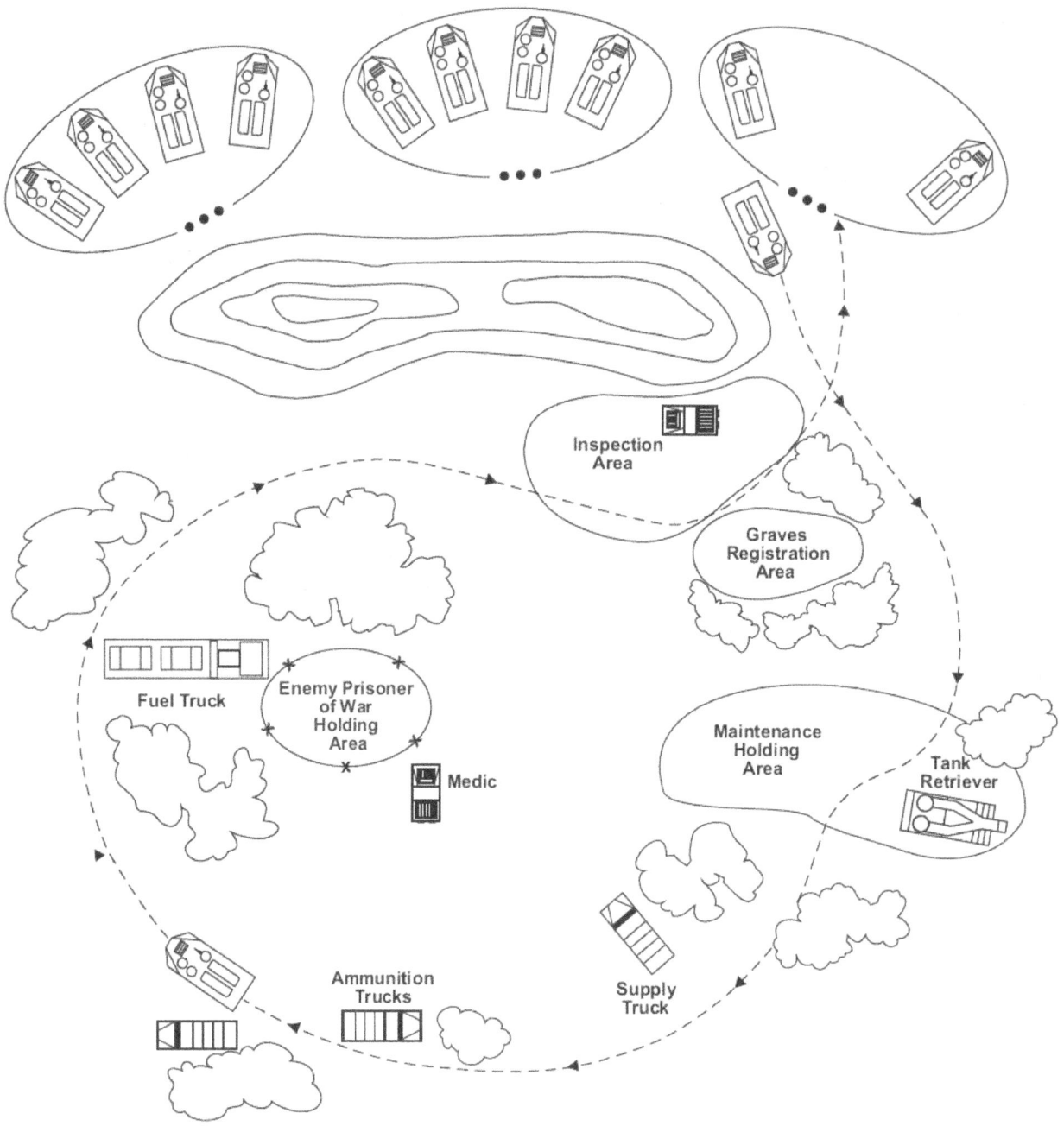

Figure 6-1. Service Station Method.

Tailgate Issue Method

The tailgate issue method (see figure 6-2) is normally conducted only in an assembly area. If it is employed in forward positions, the terrain must mask resupply. This procedure takes much longer than the service station method and places the resupply vehicles at greater risk. When using the tailgate method of replenishment—

● Combat vehicles remain in place while POL and ammunition trucks go to each vehicle position in turn.

● Personnel rotate through the feeding area and pick up supplies, water, and mail individually.

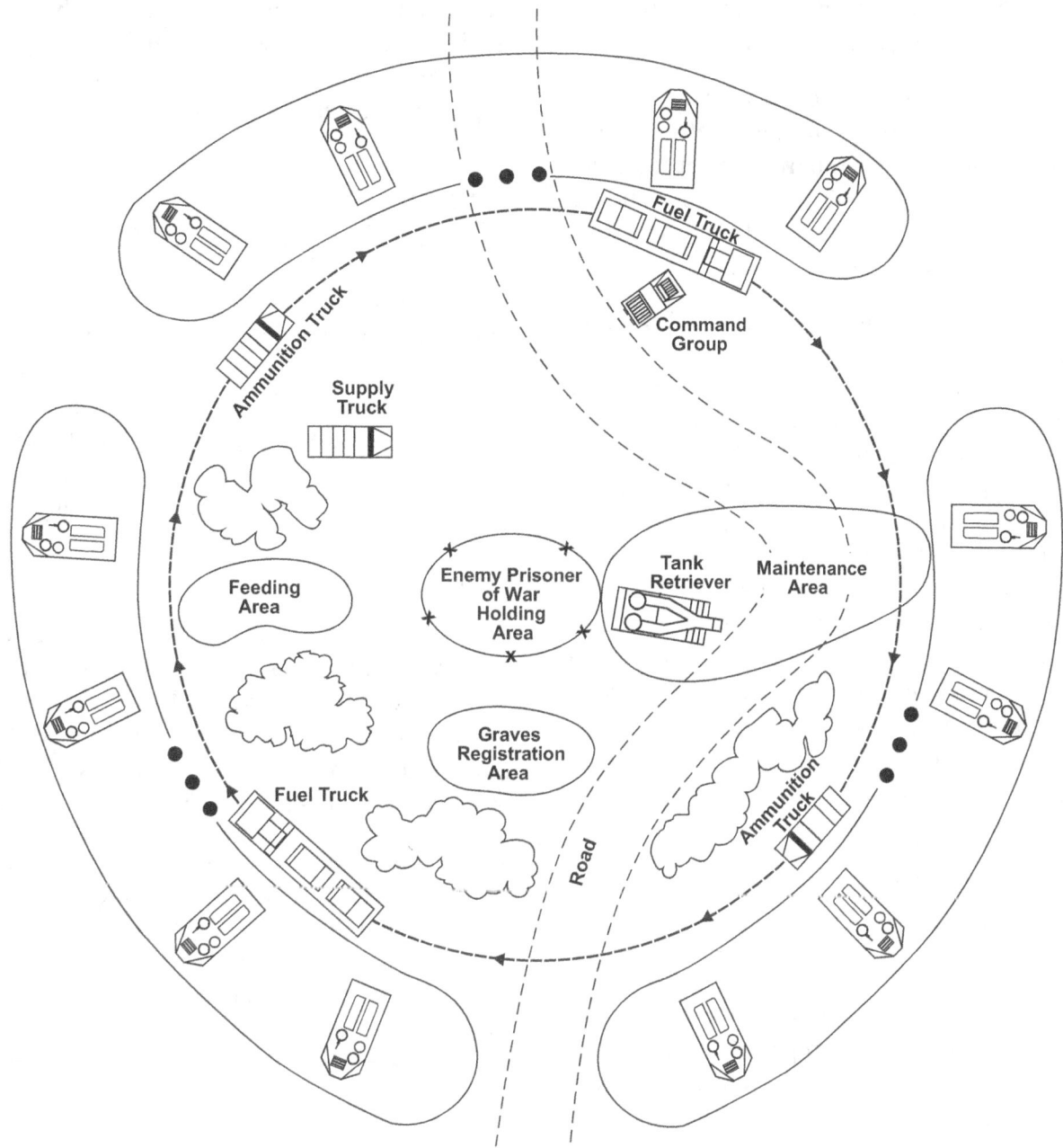

Figure 6-2. Tailgate Issue Method.

- Platoon personnel deliver troops killed in action and personal effects to the holding area.
- Enemy prisoners of war are centralized and guarded.
- Vehicles requiring maintenance are brought to the maintenance area.
- Precombat inspections are completed at each vehicle position.

Recovery and Repair

Recovery and repair are accomplished as far forward as possible, at the lowest capable echelon. When equipment cannot be repaired on site, it is moved only as far as necessary for repair. When the maintenance requirements of the force cannot be met, the commander determines maintenance support priorities for subordinate units based on recommendations of the S-4 and on tactical requirements.

It may be necessary to selectively interchange or cannibalize parts from damaged vehicles that cannot be immediately repaired to return other equipment to combat. The commander should establish guidelines to prevent uncontrolled, selective interchange and cannibalization.

Commanders with organic or attached maintenance sections should task-organize MCTs to inspect, diagnose, assist with recovery, and repair equipment at forward sites. Contact teams typically operate with combat trains. Based on guidance from the commander, the S-4 task-organizes the contact teams to meet each specific requirement. Based on the tactical situation, contact teams determine whether the damaged item is repairable at the recovery site. If the item is repairable, MCTs fix it or obtain parts, additional tools, and personnel from the rear. If the item is not repairable at the recovery site, MCTs supervise evacuation of the equipment to a designated maintenance collection point.

Company maintenance personnel will recover disabled vehicles and attempt to repair them on site. If company personnel cannot repair the vehicle, it is repaired on site by battalion maintenance personnel or moved by company personnel to a unit maintenance collection point to await repairs. If battalion personnel cannot repair the vehicle, it is repaired on site by an MCT (third echelon) from the supporting CSS unit or moved to a repair replenishment point operated by the CSSE.

Based on the situation, crewmen may remain with the vehicle being evacuated to return it or a replacement to the unit. Crewmen's personal equipment, rations, water, ammunition, and other equipment not installed on the vehicle should be transferred to other vehicles before evacuation.

During fast moving operations, rather than establishing specific collection points, the commander may direct that vehicles be towed to the MSR and secured to await maintenance support from MCTs advancing along the MSR. If vehicles cannot be repaired or evacuated quickly during retrograde operations, they must be destroyed in place to prevent their falling into enemy hands.

AA Battalion Organic Logistic Support

The AA battalion has a large organic logistic capability with robust supply and maintenance units. In addition, the battalion has a large transportation unit for transporting its logistic needs and can provide some of its own engineering, health services, and services requirements. These capabilities ensure the battalion can operate continually.

Supply

The AA battalion supply section (located within the H&S company of the battalion) uses a combination of unit distribution and supply point methods to support the battalion and its subordinate units. The battalion supply section is capable of providing organic supply support for the battalion.

The AA company may maintain operating and training repair parts if requested and authorized. The company may also maintain a 30-day stock of mount-out repair parts. The company is organized to handle the internal distribution of supplies and to carry a basic load. Additional supplies are provided by the battalion or supported unit.

The following are the nine classifications of logistical supplies relating to mech operations:

- Class I—Subsistence (food).
- Class II—Clothing, individual equipment, tools, and administrative supplies.
- Class III—POL.
- Class IV—Construction/barrier materials.
- Class V—Ammunition and explosives.
- Class VI—Personal demand items (cigarettes, razor blades, and post exchange items).

- Class VII—Major end items (equipment such as a rifle or a replacement AAV).
- Class VIII—Medical supplies.
- Class IX—Repair parts.

Maintenance

The AA company is capable of organizational (first and second echelon) maintenance on AAVs, assigned table of equipment (T/E) weapons, motor transport assets, and communications-electronics assets. The company is provided with sufficient tools and test equipment to troubleshoot and diagnose mechanical, electrical systems faults to the repairable component level on organic equipment. Limited third echelon maintenance may be authorized by higher headquarters to support mission requirements.

The AA platoon is task-organized by organic assets and personnel. At a minimum, the platoon is capable of first and second echelon maintenance on AAVs. The platoon may be staffed with a company armorer, motor transport mechanics, communications-electronics technicians or a welder. Maintenance capability on other equipment depends on attachment of Marines with the appropriate MOS and equipment. Limited third echelon maintenance may be authorized by higher headquarters to support mission requirements.

Recovery and battle damage assessment and repair (BDAR) are separate subsets of the maintenance effort. The owning unit is responsible for these maintenance efforts to return combat assets to the battlefield as quickly as possible.

Recovery

Recovery is retrieving or freeing immobile, inoperative or abandoned material from its current position and returning it to operation or to a maintenance site for repair. These actions typically involve towing, lifting, and winching.

Towing is typically limited to moving vehicles to the nearest collection point.

Recovery consists of self-recovery, like-recovery, and dedicated-recovery actions. Self-recovery actions use only the equipment's assets. Like-recovery actions involve the assistance of a second, similar vehicle. Dedicated-recovery actions require the assistance of a vehicle that is specifically designed and dedicated to recovery operations. AAV operators are specifically trained in self-recovery and like-recovery actions. Each AA company and each deployed AA platoon, Marine expeditionary unit (special operations capable) (MEU[SOC]), has one AAVR7A1.

Battle Damage Assessment and Repair

BDAR is the procedure used to rapidly return disabled equipment to the operational commander by expediently fixing, bypassing or replacing components. BDAR restores the minimum essential combat capabilities necessary to support a specific combat mission or to enable the equipment to self-recover. Depending on the repairs required and the amount of time available, these repairs are temporary and may or may not restore the vehicle to full mission-capable status. Performed by the crew, maintenance teams, maintenance support teams (MSTs) or recovery teams, BDAR repairs are usually not permanent and should be replaced with permanent repairs as soon as possible. See MCRP 4-11.4A, *Battlefield Damage Assessment and Repair*, for comprehensive recovery and BDAR information.

Transportation

The battalion possesses Logistics Vehicle System container haulers, 5-ton series trucks, and HMMWVs and provides transportation for supported units, equipment, weapons, as well as administrative and logistical functions. Based on METT-T, AA companies can receive a limited number of motor transport vehicles from the AA battalion.

Engineering

The battalion possesses limited quantities of engineering equipment such as generators, decontaminating systems, air conditioners, fuel and water modules, and a rough terrain forklift. These assets are designed to support battalion-level operations and are not generally deployed below that level.

Health Services

The AA battalion possesses a BAS that requires several AAVs with litter kits to mechanize.

Services

Services available at the AA battalion include personnel administration; religious ministry; billeting; financial management; morale, welfare, and recreation; and messing. During combat operations, food service resources may be centralized within the MAGTF.

Logistic Support Requirements

AAV employment at the company and platoon level focuses on the ability to displace and travel quickly. The AA element will only carry minimum levels of consumable POL and supplies. The CSSE must plan to resupply the AA unit element, normally using logistic trains. The AA unit leader must coordinate frequently with the CSSE to identify changes in supply, maintenance, and transportation requirements.

Supply

The CSSE commander establishes issue points for classes of supply. Ideally, repair parts issue points will be located near intermediate mainte-

nance sites. AA commanders should tailor repair part blocks to the anticipated need of the AA unit. Supply point and unit are the two normal methods of distributing supplies. Under these methods, the using unit is responsible for internal distribution.

Supply Point Distribution

In this distribution method, the using unit is issued supplies at a supply point established by the CSSE. The advantage of supply point distribution is that while it requires the use of organic transportation, the AA unit can request a desired time to make the supply run, even if the run is only for a single, critical repair part.

Unit Distribution

Because the CSSE delivers supplies to the using unit, these deliveries will be prioritized based on the MAGTF mission; however, the unit requiring supplies may not receive them at the desired time. The advantage of unit distribution is that AA units do not allocate organic transportation assets except to distribute supplies internally.

Distribution Considerations

While unit distribution is preferred, frequently the commander must use a combination of methods. In most cases, the main and supporting efforts should be on unit distribution, but if that is not possible, the commander should—

- Consider the main effort for unit distribution.
- Ensure that supplies are delivered forward to the combat units to maintain momentum.
- Avoid combat units having to move rearward to be replenished.
- Prioritize engaged units with limited organic transportation first for unit distribution.
- Prioritize units not in contact with the enemy last for unit distribution.
- Provide sufficient trucks and tankers to units for internal resupply.

Combat Load

Because AAVs rely heavily on class III and class V supplies to complete their missions, CLs are prescribed by the AAV commander in concert with the supported unit's SOP and METT-T. The Marine Corps Technical Manual (TM) 09674A-10/3A, *Assault Amphibious Vehicle*, lists the AAV CL. Generally, each AAV will carry the following:

- 200 ready rounds for the M2 (1,000 rounds stowed in 10 ammunition boxes).
- 96 ready rounds for the MK-19 (768 rounds stowed in 24 ammunition boxes).
- 8 smoke grenades loaded in 2 M257 launchers.
- 1 5-gallon can of lubrication oil.
- 2 5-gallon cans of potable water.
- 1 5-gallon can of coolant.
- 4 1-quart cans of hydraulic fluid.

Maintenance

The CSSE is responsible for intermediate (third and fourth echelon) maintenance. The focus of effort is timely repair as far forward as possible. Intermediate maintenance includes diagnosis, adjustment, direct exchange, and technical assistance. CSS intermediate maintenance elements augment the capabilities of MCTs from the AA unit. The CSS MSTs operate in a GS role while the AAV MCTs operate as a function of their organic maintenance responsibility.

MSTs normally work on equipment in the combat service support area (CSSA) until called forward for a specific repair. This permits better use of maintenance and transportation assets and allows the MST to draw and bring needed parts when called forward. The CSS commander may position MSTs forward if enough work is anticipated to justify the move. When moved forward, the MST should carry a repair parts block and only remain forward for as long as the workload demands.

Maintenance During Amphibious Assault

Assault elements of the LF are either in scheduled or on-call waves. AAVs in the assault element land with limited organizational maintenance personnel. Initially, the CSSE of the landing force support party (LFSP) has limited recovery, evacuation, and repair capabilities, with the majority of CSS maintenance capability going ashore in nonscheduled waves. The LFSP replaces components and assemblies rather than repairing them and uses selective interchange and cannibalization as authorized to offset the limited repair parts ashore.

Maintenance During Transition Periods

When the tactical situation ashore has stabilized, nonscheduled units are landed. These include the CSS trains and the remainder of their maintenance capability. Then the CSS expands its intermediate maintenance effort and establishes MSTs.

Maintenance During Subsequent Operations

When the situation ashore stabilizes further, the CSS becomes fully established and the LFSP disbands. At this time, the CSS reaches full capability for providing maintenance and supply support.

Transportation

CSS transportation assets provide support at the proper locations and times to initiate and maintain operations. The AA element should develop a requirements list identifying personnel, supplies, and equipment that must be moved; requirements that can be supported with organic assets; and requirements that must be requested from the CSS transportation element.

AAV-Unique Planning Considerations

Planners must consider unique refueling, preventive maintenance (PM), and environmental factors when employing AAVs in logistic operations.

Refueling

Refueling an AA unit can be a time consuming task and should be planned carefully to avoid unplanned operational pauses. AA units consume a large amount of fuel in combat operations because they have large mech vehicles. Logistic planners should be familiar with normal fuel requirements before the start of operations. AAVs can be refueled while aboard ship, from ground CSS units once ashore or by air-dropped fuel at a predetermined location.

Fuel Requirements

The AA unit fuel cell (AAV7A1) holds 171 gallons of diesel fuel. Nominal range with a full tank is about 300 miles at 25 miles per hour on land or 7 hours at 2,600 RPM in the water. While the AA unit fuel cell (RAM/RS) also holds 171 gallons of diesel fuel, the nominal range with a full tank is about 280 miles at 25 miles per hour on land or 6.5 hours at 2,600 RPM in the water. Water speed and distance traveled in water depends on currents and sea state. For planning purposes, the AAV7A1 will consume 25 gallons per hour on the water and average 1.7 miles per gallon on land. The RAM/RS will consume 26.5 gallons per hour on the water and average 1.6 miles per gallon on land. Refer to Technical Instruction (TI) 10340-15/1D, *Fuel Requirements Authorized Fuels for Engines*, for detailed information regarding AAV fuel types.

Ground

AA units can refuel from various fuel platforms, including fuel modules, fixed-bulk fuel facilities or an AA unit equipped with two 500-gallon fuel bladders. Time-consuming refueling methods are gravity feed, hand pumps or fuel cans.

Shipboard

The ship's crew supervises shipboard fueling operations. AA unit leaders order fuel and prepare spare fuel filters to guard against possible fuel contamination.

Air

AA units are capable of receiving fuel via rapid ground refueling from the KC-130 and CH-53E.

Preventive Maintenance

To prevent corrosion damage, first echelon PM must be performed on AAVs, especially after saltwater operations. The primary concern is corrosion of electrical leads, components, and communication connectors. Approximately 1 hour of supervised PM time should be allocated for every 7 hours of operation under normal conditions. In adverse climates or after water operations, this ratio will decrease slightly.

Environmental Effects

When planning AAV employment in jungle, desert, and cold weather operations, environmental effects must be considered.

Jungle

In jungle operations, the following environmental effects should be considered:

- Troops require more water, placing a greater demand on water purification equipment and transportation.
- Metal parts rust and corrode more quickly.
- Seals deteriorate faster.
- Battery life is shorter than normal.

- Electrical connections corrode more quickly.
- Lenses and dials become fogged because of internal moisture.
- Maintenance requirements, especially first echelon PM, increase.
- Lubrication of working parts must be done daily.
- Onsite maintenance and repair are essential because evacuation is often difficult or impossible.
- Critical repair parts should be positioned as far forward as feasible.

Desert

In desert operations, the following environmental effects should be considered:

- Troops require more water, placing a greater demand on water purification equipment and transportation.
- Dust and sand damage equipment mechanisms.
- Vehicles require more oils and lubricants.
- Batteries do not hold their charge because of the intense heat.
- Blowing sand can damage optical equipment (i.e., vision blocks and sight glass).
- Maintenance requirements and first echelon PM requirements increase.
- Air filter and precleaner must be frequently inspected and cleaned with compressed air.

- Fuel filters must be used when refueling and the fuel inlet should be covered.
- Oil filters will require frequent replacement.
- Oil filler cans and extensions should be cleaned of sand before filling reservoirs.
- Evacuation is usually difficult and onsite maintenance is essential.
- Critical repair parts (e.g., water pumps, belts, hoses, clamps, replacement filter elements) should be positioned forward.

Cold Weather

In cold weather operations, the following environmental effects should be considered:

- Troops require special clothing and higher daily caloric intake.
- Bare hands will stick to cold metal.
- Fuel contacting bare skin will evaporate and result in super cooling.
- Skin and hands can be frozen in a matter of seconds.
- Engines can be much harder to start; warmup time can approach 2 hours at −50 degrees Fahrenheit.
- Batteries can be destroyed if they freeze.
- Mechanical parts are more susceptible to breakage in extreme cold.
- Maintenance can be exceptionally difficult because protective clothing encumbers personnel.

CHAPTER 7. SPECIAL OPERATIONS

AA units are often assigned unique missions classified as special operations. These missions are usually conducted as part of a MEU(SOC). In addition to MEU(SOC) missions, other missions are conducted that may be part of larger offensive or defensive operations. These operations include NBC defense, tactical road marches, breaching operations, and MOOTW.

Marine Expeditionary Unit Operations

The AAV offers the MEU and BLT commanders a rapid and intimidating method of power projection ashore. Amphibious mech company personnel are organized and trained to perform or support MEU(SOC) missions.

Organization

The AA platoon is reinforced with maintenance personnel, communication technicians, and a cook before the platoon is attached to the MEU. The total strength is approximately 1 officer, 50 enlisted, and 1 corpsman to support the platoon while deployed. The platoon will have 13 AAVP7A1s, 1 AAVC7A1, and may have 1 AAVR7A1 attached to it in DS from the MEU service support group. The AA platoon attaches to the BLT and is often placed in DS of the mech company. When attached, the BLT accepts full responsibility for logistical and administrative support and exercises OPCON of the platoon. The AA platoon commander reports to the BLT commander and staff to establish a relationship early and to support the mission of the infantry company.

Training

During the predeployment phase, relationships are more complex and vary from phase to phase. Joint limited technical inspections are conducted

before the AA platoon attaches to the BLT. Normally, 6 months before deployment, the AA platoon attaches to the BLT. Once attached, the platoon uses the following D-day and R-day timeline to conduct training and maintenance:

- D-160—Initial support logistic administrative and personnel inspection.
- D-120—Special operations training group raid week.
- D-70—Final support logistic administrative and personnel inspection.
- D-65—MEU exercise.
- D-40—Special operations capable (SOC) exercise/joint task force exercise.
- D-25 to D-day—Block leave/final inspections.
- R+10—Post support logistic, administrative, and personnel inspection and joint limited technical inspections.
- R+15—Final gear inspection/block leave.
- R+30—Return under AA battalion ADCON and OPCON.

Missions

Shock, firepower, and troop and equipment-lift capabilities enable AAVs to conduct amphibious raid, NEO, FHA, and embassy or airfield security missions. For the majority of SOC missions, the AAV offers similar capabilities and limitations.

Amphibious Raid

The AA platoons are used primarily against heavily defended targets near coastlines.

Capabilities. AAVs and the mech company have superior firepower, armor, and mobility. They also have better immediate sustainability than helicopter and boat companies. In addition, AAVs have a larger troop-carrying capacity than helicopters and boats. AAVs can operate in poor weather conditions that would ground helicopters. The vehicles' psychological and political impact on an opposing force may deter future violence.

Limitations. AAVs are relatively slow in the water. Troop fatigue in the water should be considered as a METT-T limitation. The vehicles are loud and have a large footprint ashore thus reducing the chances of a surprise attack. AAVs may require a major maintenance/logistical effort. In addition, AAVs are vulnerable to AT weapons. The use of AAVs may have a psychological and political impact on the American public and may signal a need for a major commitment of forces.

NEO, FHA, and Embassy or Airfield Security

The versatility of AAVs enables them to sustain these sometimes prolonged missions.

Capabilities. AAVs can serve as static or mobile checkpoints and protect LOC or installations. They also provide a significant logistical and mobility capability for NEOs and FHA missions. In addition, AAVs provide an armored and protective firepower platform for infantry operating out of a mobile bunker.

Infantry can patrol from AAVs by using them as patrol and/or fire bases. The shock and intimidation factor that an AAV possesses can be a force multiplier. AAVs also offer armor protection for noncombatants and troop carrying capacity with immediate sustainability. In an amphibious assault, AAVs can leave last and cover a withdrawal.

Limitations. AAVs can require substantial logistical support for maintenance. AAVs also give a psychological/political impression that may not be consistent with the desires of the commander. For example, AAVs can present a large, intimidating presence when ashore that may have a negative impact on the host country. AAVs have a limited capability to operate in military operations on urbanized terrain (MOUT). Infantry may have trouble fighting from the vehicle because it is not

an IFV. Vulnerable to AT fire, AAVs make good targets if employed improperly.

Nuclear, Biological, and Chemical Defense Operations

In many operations that AA units conduct, there is an increasing possibility that the enemy may employ NBC warfare agents against Marines. NBC employment can have devastating environmental effects. AA unit operations in such an environment require constant training to properly defend against NBC attacks and decontamination procedures to complete the mission assigned.

Organization

From organic resources, each AA company organizes NBC defense teams to fulfill the mission of decontamination, monitoring, and survey. An additional duty NBC officer and NBC NCO head the AA company NBC team.

These personnel will be designated and school trained to operate assigned NBC equipment and to assist during decontamination operations as well as monitoring and survey operations when directed. The NBC officer and NBC NCO are responsible for ensuring company Marines, NBC teams, and other command personnel are trained according to MCWP 3-37, *MAGTF Nuclear, Biological and Chemical Defense Operations.*

The NBC NCO will advise and assist in the NBC defense activities of the company and in training the different NBC teams and operators of NBC defense equipment.

The NBC officer and NBC NCO will advise the commander on NBC defense operations and ensure that aspects of NBC defense are included in operational planning. Along with the company medical personnel, the NBC officer and NCO also advise the commander on operational exposure guidance and decontamination operations. In addition, the NBC officer and NCO coordinate radiological monitoring as well as survey and decontamination operations.

Nuclear, Biological, and Chemical Environmental Effects

An NBC environment can affect offensive and defensive AA operations.

Offensive Operations

The risk of exposing protected infantrymen by dismounting them in contaminated areas may outweigh the risk of attacking mounted. Ultimately, the pattern of contamination, risk, and duration of the combat operation must be considered when making the decision to attack dismounted or mounted.

MOPP 4 degrades the AA crewmen and embarked infantrymen's ability to maintain orientation in the battle by fatiguing crew members due to the heat and limited visibility/communication provided by the M40 field protective masks. Locations of chemical mines as part of enemy obstacles pose a serious threat to infantrymen and force them into MOPP 4. This posture produces the following effects on movement and breaching efforts:

- Movement rates of dismounted infantry are reduced.
- Target acquisition for AAVs and infantry is hindered.
- Synchronization of combat assets on the battlefield is more difficult.
- Platoons move more slowly and less often.
- Combat support arrives later.
- CSS lines become longer and have the added problems of contaminated supplies.

Defensive Operations

Since MOPP gear prevents personnel recognition at a distance and increases the physical effort needed to move from position to position, division of authority is critical. Commanders must anticipate being hit by chemical agents while conducting a defensive mission. To prepare the initial BP, the NBC NCO should analyze the terrain to identify those areas where agents are less likely to accumulate. This information will help identify alternate platoon positions.

Nuclear Defense

The ease with which many countries are able to obtain nuclear materials and production information makes a nuclear threat more likely. A nuclear detonation produces its damaging effects through blast, thermal energy, radiation, and electromagnetic pulse (EMP). The use of armored vehicles for protection of crews and mounted infantry will help minimize these effects.

Electromagnetic Pulse

An EMP is the high-energy, short duration pulse generated by the nuclear detonation. The pulse is similar to a bolt of lightning. As with a close lightning strike, the EMP can affect electronic equipment by inducing a current in an electrical conductor that can disrupt, overload, and damage unprotected equipment (e.g., radios, computers).

Use of Armored Vehicles for Protection

The AAV gives reasonable protection from the effects of a nuclear attack. Though the armor and weight of the vehicle provide the majority of the protection, personnel should take the following steps to enhance protection:

- Get as low as possible inside the AAV. Marines in the vehicle should get to the floor. This includes the driver, gunner, and TC. Assuming a low position on the floor reduces the radiation received by a factor of four.
- Keep hatches shut. An open hatch will unnecessarily expose the crew to blast effects and radiation.
- Secure loose equipment inside the vehicle to prevent injury. The blast wave will throw Marines and unsecured equipment inside the vehicles.

- Dig in AAVs (hull defilade) or place them in trenches or cuts in the road. This will provide limited line of sight radiation protection and considerable blast protection. A hull defilade fighting position or trench that allows half of the vehicle to be covered can reduce gamma radiation by a factor of two.

- Use sandbags as radiation shielding. A single layer of sandbags placed on the top of an AAV provides valuable overhead gamma shielding. Each layer of sandbags reduces gamma radiation by a factor of two. Wetting the sandbags enhances the neutron radiation shielding and protects the sandbags from the heat.

- Place the AAV bow into the blast. This places the mass of the vehicle's engine between the potential radiation source and the crew. This head-on orientation can reduce potential radiation exposure to the crew by half of that of a broadside exposure. In addition, closing the plenums will reduce radiation exposure.

Chemical/Biological Defense

Chemical/biological defense in an AAV is not much more complicated than for the infantry on the ground. The AAV does not have an NBC overpressure capability or any system for protecting those embarked in the passenger compartment. Because the AAV is not airtight, aerosols are a distinct danger. Marines in the AAV during a chemical or biological attack will need to wear their NBC individual protective equipment (i.e., M40 field protective mask and chemical protective overgarment). When closed up, the vehicle will only provide cover from direct contact with liquid agents.

Chemical/biological defense procedures in an AAV are no different than for an individual with the exception that the personnel vent fan on the AAV should be shut off. Transition to various levels of MOPP gear should be determined by the commanding officer based on the threat assessment of possible contamination or attack. When an attack is detected, personnel not in MOPP 4 should don the protective gear as quickly as

possible. The AA unit commander who detected the attack should send an NBC 1 report to higher headquarters. Once the all clear is sounded or the unit has moved into an uncontaminated area, the MOPP gear should be exchanged as quickly as possible. See MCWP 3-37; MCWP 3-37.3, *NBC Decontamination*; and MCRP 3-37A, *NBC Field Handbook*, for additional information on NBC threat assessment, NBC reports, as well as decontamination procedures and MOPP gear exchange.

Decontamination Procedures

Before conducting decontamination procedures, the commander must obtain approval from higher headquarters. Decontamination of AAVs can be easier than other Marine Corps vehicles because AAVs are designed to operate in water and resist water damage. The AA unit commander should ensure AAV decontamination should be completed as quickly as possible after an NBC attack to prevent the spread of contamination by the vehicles. This can occur when troops climb in and out of a contaminated vehicle and spread the agent from the outside to the inside of the AAV and to areas around the AAV. The AA unit has organic NBC decontamination equipment. This equipment can be used to conduct immediate and operational decontamination to continue the mission, or thorough decontamination is conducted away from contaminated areas as part of a reconstitution effort.

Equipment

The M11 decontamination apparatus (DAP), M13 DAP, M17 lightweight decontamination system (LDS), and M100 sorbent decontamination system (SDS) are used for vehicle decontamination.

M11 DAP. The M11 DAP is used to perform spot decontamination on small areas of vehicles (e.g., steering wheels, crew compartments that Marines will have to touch in the accomplishment of the mission) and other large pieces of equipment. See figure 7-1. The M11 DAP is a small container the size of a fire extinguisher. It holds 1 1/3 quarts of decontamination agent (DS2) and a nitrogen

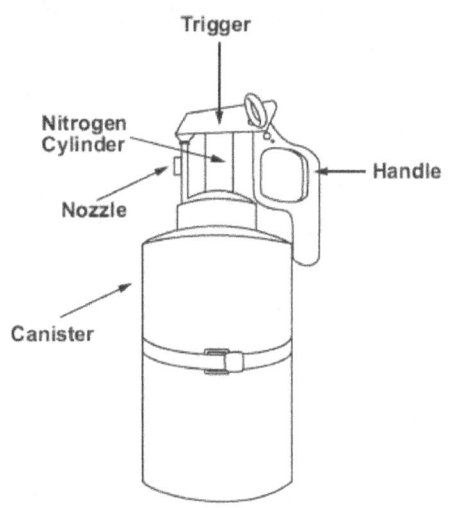

Figure 7-1. M11 DAP.

cylinder that provides pressure. The M11 can decontaminate an area of 135 square feet and spray effectively 6 to 8 feet out. After each use, the M11 DAP is refilled with DS2 and a new nitrogen cylinder. For further information, see

TM 3-4230-204-12&P, *Operator's & Unit Maintenance Manual for Decontaminating Apparatus, Portable, ABC-M11.*

═══ **CAUTION** ═══

When handling DS2, use extreme caution. DS2 can produce chemical burns and severe illness if inhaled. DS2 is highly corrosive and will damage or corrode nonmetals if allowed to sit and soak into the material. Do not use DS2 in areas where super tropical bleach (STB) is also being used. DS2 and STB are highly reactive and produce extreme heat and possibly fire if allowed to mix.

M13 DAP. The M13 DAP is used to decontaminate vehicles and other large equipment. See figure 7-2. The M13 DAP is about the size of a 5-gallon gasoline can and comes prefilled with 14 liters of DS2. The M13 DAP can decontaminate an area of 1,200 square feet. A hose assembly, pump assembly, wand assembly, and brush are attached to the fluid container to apply the

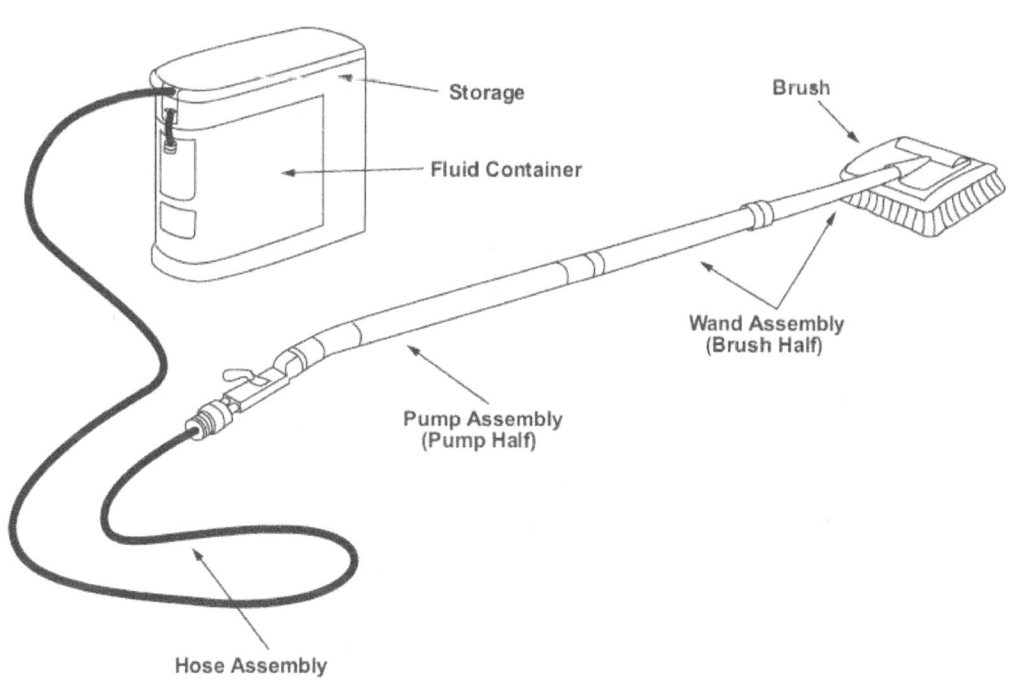

Figure 7-2. M13 DAP.

DS2. The brush allows for removal of thickened agents, mud, grease or other material from the surfaces being decontaminated. For further information, see TM 3-4230-214-12&P, *Decontamination Apparatus, Portable, 14 Liter.*

M17 LDS. The M17 LDS is used to decontaminate vehicles and other large pieces of equipment. See figure 7-3. A battalion NBC section usually stores the M17 LDS. The M17 LDS may be used for company and battalion-sized operational and thorough decontamination operations. A hose and wand assembly is attached to the M17 LDS to release a high-pressure stream of hot water for removal of thickened agents, mud, grease or other material from equipment surfaces. An attachment also allows the operator to add detergents to the

water stream and use hot soapy water in the decontamination effort. For additional information, see TM 3-4230-228-10, *Decontaminating Apparatus: Power Driven, Lightweight, M17.*

M100 SDS. The M100 SDS allows the user to conduct the operator's wipedown portion of immediate decontamination. See figure 7-4. The system consists of one case, two decontamination kits, and two straps. Each decontamination kit contains one applicator mitt and one pack filled with sorbent powder. To conduct the operator's wipedown, the user opens one of the decontamination kits and extracts the mitt and sorbent pack. While wearing the mitt, a user pours a generous portion of the sorbent onto the mitt. The user then rubs the sorbent filled mitt

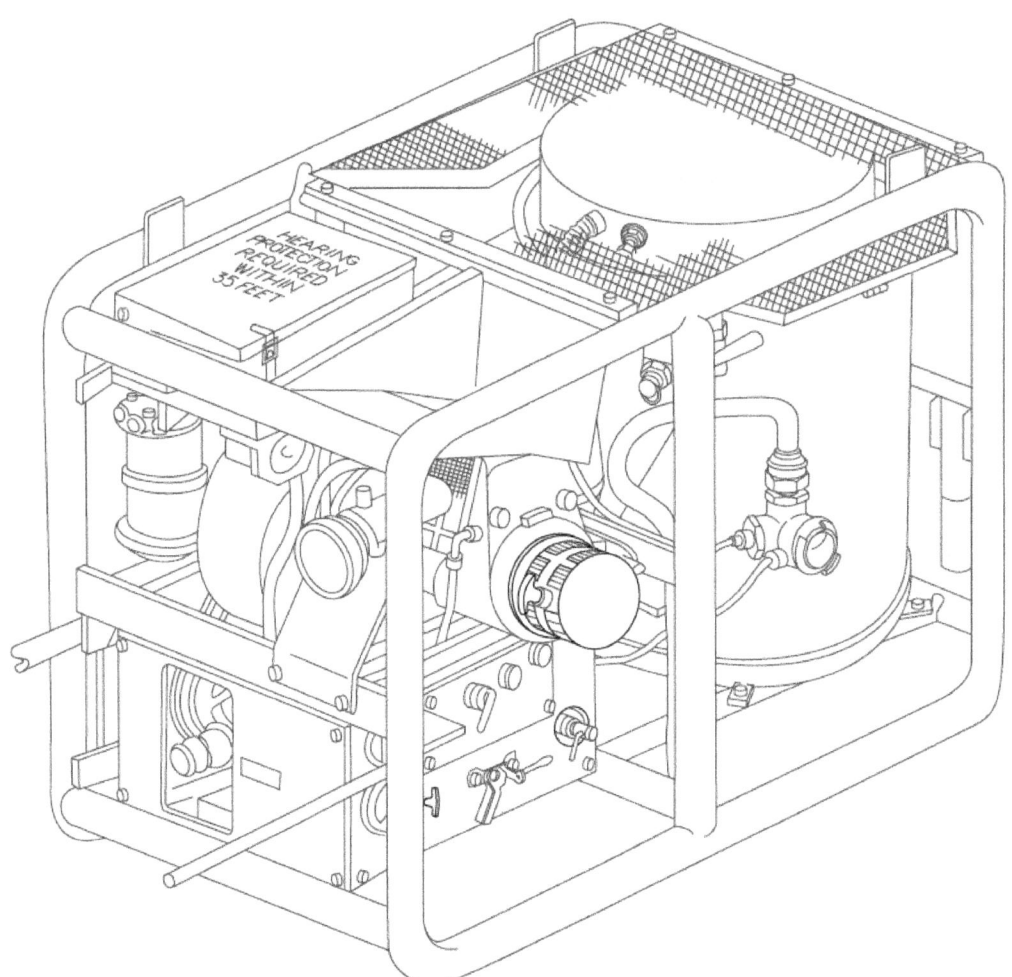

Figure 7-3. M17 LDS.

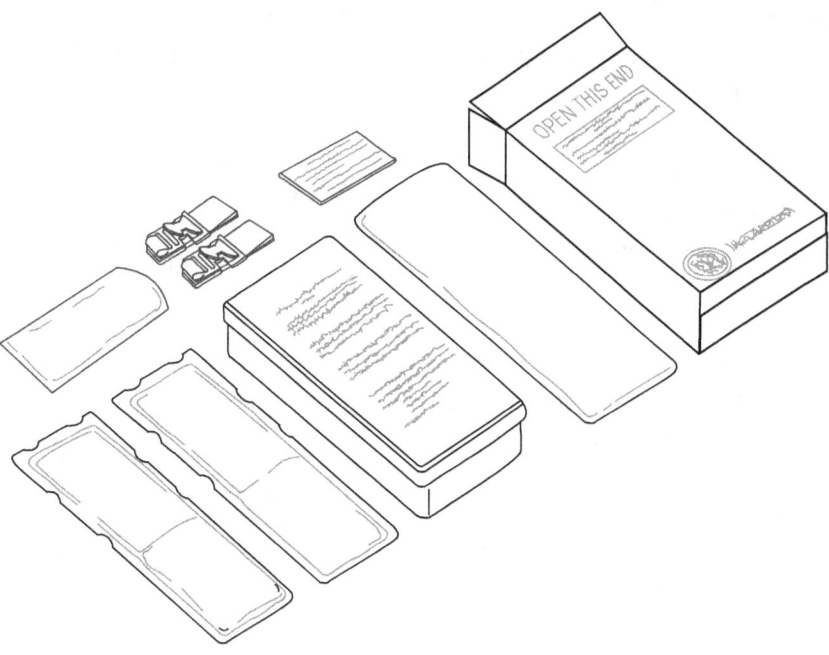

Figure 7-4. M100 SDS.

on the contaminated surface until the surface appears dry. Sorbent powder may be added to the mitt as needed.

Methods

The three levels of decontamination are immediate, operational, and thorough. The AA company will use these doctrinally established methods to decontaminate their vehicles as defined in MCWP 3-37.3. Whenever possible, DS2 and hot soapy water/hot rinse water will be used to decontaminate the vehicles in a chemically or biologically contaminated environment, while hot soapy water and hot rinse water will be used to decontaminate vehicles in a radiologically contaminated environment.

Immediate Decontamination. For vehicles and equipment, immediate decontamination is known as the operator's spraydown/wipedown technique. This method is conducted as soon as possible after an attack and is most effective when

done within 15 minutes of contamination (following completion of personal wipedown).

Chemical—Whenever possible, a chemical agent monitor and/or M8/M9 detector paper is used to determine what surfaces require decontamination. Those surfaces that must be touched on the exterior of the vehicle or mission essential equipment should be decontaminated with the M100 SDS. The M11 DAP/M13 DAP may be used in conjunction with or in lieu of the M100 SDS to decontaminate those surfaces (e.g., crew seats, operator's pedals, steering wheels, door handles). The M100 SDS must be used to decontaminate equipment that DS2 may corrode. When using the M11/M13 DAP, decontamination personnel use the following procedures:

- Spray/brush DS2 on surfaces (do not spray surfaces that DS2 may corrode).
- Allow the DS2 to sit on the surface for approximately 30 minutes (contact time).
- Rinse the surface thoroughly with water.

● Recheck surfaces with a chemical agent monitor and/or M8/M9 paper to ensure equipment is contamination free before operation/use.

Biological—A bleach solution is first used for biological contamination; however, if bleach is not available, hot soapy water may be used. Decontamination personnel use scrub brushes to apply the solution, scrub thoroughly, and rinse completely with water the exterior areas of the vehicle that must be touched or mission essential equipment. In the absence of bleach and hot soapy water, DS2 (M11/M13 DAP) and STB may be used but, due to their corrosive nature, they are not the preferred decontaminates.

Radiological—If vehicles and equipment are contaminated by fallout, decontamination personnel use monitoring equipment (i.e., AN/VDR-2) to locate contamination. Radiological contamination can be removed from areas of vehicles that must be touched and mission essential equipment by brushing or scraping. Water is also effective for flushing away radiological contamination; however, the runoff will be contaminated and must be treated accordingly. Equipment and vehicle parts must be rechecked with monitoring equipment after decontamination and before operation/use.

Operational Decontamination. For equipment and vehicles, operational decontamination limits the spread of contamination and facilitates additional decontamination requirements by speeding up the weathering process, thereby possibly eliminating the need for thorough decontamination of vehicles and equipment. Vehicle washdown is the procedure through which this is accomplished. This procedure is covered in detail in MCWP 3-37.3. The procedure consists of using the M17 LDS and hot soapy water to washdown/decontaminate vehicles and equipment. The following steps apply:

● Step 1: Button up vehicle and equipment—close access doors, hatches windows, and other openings.
● Step 2: Perform washdown—use M17 LDS and hot soapy water to wash vehicles and equipment from top to bottom.

Thorough Decontamination. For equipment and vehicles, thorough decontamination reduces and sometimes eliminates contamination. Normally, this procedure is part of a reconstitution effort and will always require logistical support from elements of the FSSG. AA company NBC-trained personnel will be tasked to augment FSSG personnel in accomplishing thorough decontamination tasks. To perform thorough decontamination, AAVs will move to a detailed equipment decontamination site based on the type of contamination (chemical and biological decontamination is a five-step process, whereas radiological contamination is only a four-step process). See figure 7-5. This procedure is covered in detail in MCWP 3-37.3. The following steps apply:

● Station 1: Primary Wash—Vehicle is washed using the M17 LDS and hot soapy water.
● Station 2: DS2 Application—DS2 is applied from the top to the bottom of the vehicle. (This station is not used for radiological contamination.)
● Station 3: Contact Time/Interior Decontamination—Wait time for DS2 neutralization of contamination is observed; M8/M9 paper (chemical contamination) and the AN/VDR-2 (radiological contamination) are used to locate contamination within the vehicle. The interior of the vehicle is then decontaminated using the M100 SDS or a rag soaked in a high test hypochlorite (HTH) or STB solution. HTH should only be used if STB is not available.

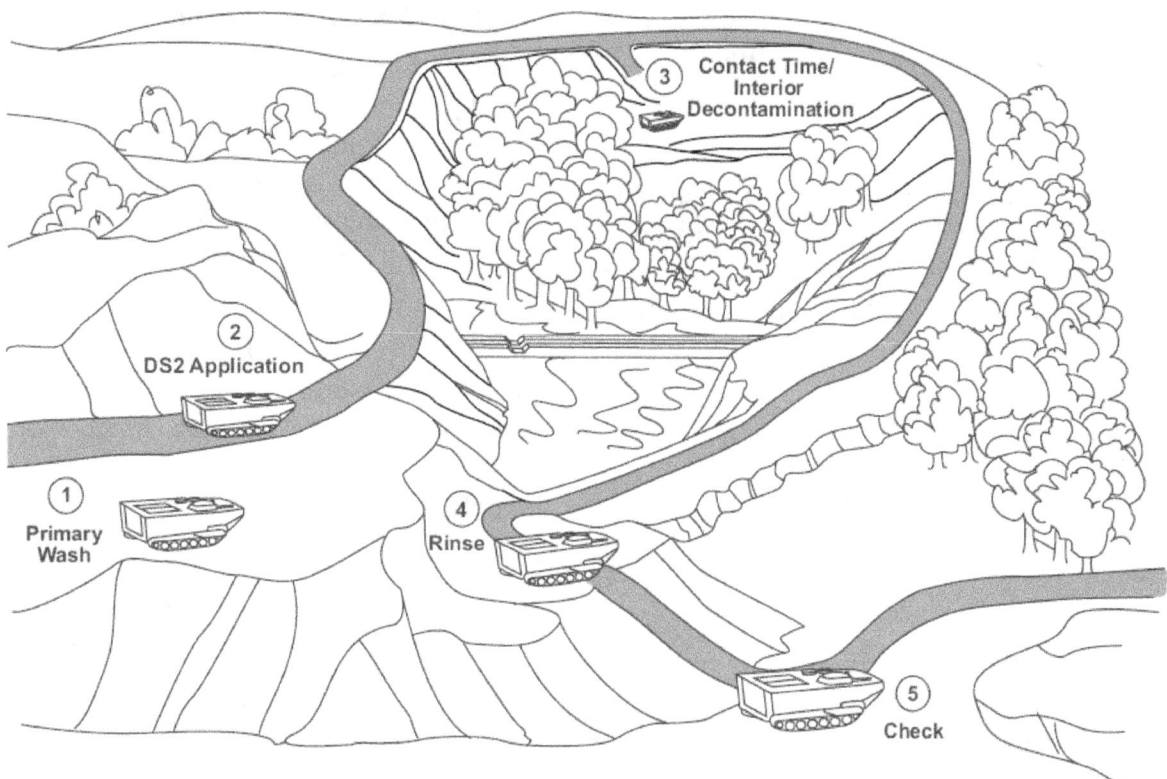

Figure 7-5. Thorough Decontamination Site.

===== **CAUTION** =====

When handling STB or HTH, use extreme caution. STB and HTH can produce chemical burns and severe illness if inhaled. STB mixed with DS2 and HTH mixed with DS2 are highly reactive and produce extreme heat and possibly fire.

- Station 4: Rinse station—DS2 is rinsed off of the vehicle.
- Station 5: Check—Vehicle/equipment is checked for residual contamination.

Road March Operations

When not in enemy contact, the mech company team may have to move long distances to position for future operations. These movements, called road marches, are planned at the battalion, company, and platoon level. The purpose of a road march is relocation, not to gain contact with the enemy. The road march is planned and conducted at a prescribed rate of speed with a prescribed interval maintained between vehicles. The primary consideration for this operation is the rapid movement of units from one area to another. The AA unit leader should plan and control the movement of the unit conducting a road march. The success of a road march depends on the method of movement, organization, understanding of concepts, preparation, and thorough planning. See MCWP 4-11.3, *Convoy Operations*, for detailed discussion of road march operations.

Military Operations Other Than War

See MCDP 1-0, Appendix E. Although the intensity of fighting may be less in many cases, the restrictiveness and variance of MOOTW on mech forces makes the training, planning, and execution infinitely more difficult on the military.

Types

An AA unit may be called upon to support any of the 16 MOOTW missions/operations listed in JP 3-07, *Joint Doctrine for Military Operations Other than War*, but most likely, the unit will be involved in the following:

● Enforcing exclusion zones.
● FHA.
● Military support to civil authorities.
● NEO.
● Peace operations.
● Recovery operations.
● Combating terrorism.
● Enforcing sanctions.
● Strikes and raids.

Employment Advantages

AAVs are employed in MOOTW missions for their distinct logistical capability; mobility, firepower, and armor protection; amphibious capability; and shock/intimidation value.

Logistical Capability

When employed in a logistical role, the AAV provides the following advantages:

● Armor protection—The AAV has a large personnel carrying capacity while providing armor protection. This is especially important when carrying noncombatants, critical supplies or nongovernmental organization workers though potentially hostile terrain.
● Armored ambulance capability—The AAV with a litter kit can transport up to six personnel on stretchers under armor protection.
● Large logistical capacity—The AAV can carry large quantities of food, water or supplies over varied terrain and under armor protection.

Mobility, Firepower, and Armor Protection

When conducting convoy, convoy security, and checkpoint operations, the AAV's mobility, firepower, and armor protection are important. The AAV can provide fire support from the UGWS, armor protection to the embarked infantry, and infantry mobility in diverse and difficult terrain.

Amphibious Capability

The AAV can provide NEOs' or combat operations' logistical support from ship to shore.

Shock/Intimidation Value

When employed in crowd control, patrolling, convoy or checkpoint operations, the AAV's size and appearance can intimidate combatants and noncombatants.

Employment Disadvantages

While the AAV's shock and intimidation value can be useful in MOOTW, it can be a detractor in a volatile situation. The appearance of AAVs or other armored vehicles may incite violence or destabilize a situation. The commander must weigh this consideration. In addition, the commander must plan for the AAV's large logistical requirements.

Breaching Operations

In battle, Marine Corps forces can expect to encounter numerous manmade and natural countermobility obstacles. When such obstacles cannot be bypassed, they must be overcome. The Marine Corps has equipment and forces to deal quickly and efficiently with these obstacles to maintain the momentum and shock of the attack. Within the AA battalion, this mission belongs to the M/CM platoon. The primary mission of the M/CM platoon is to provide support in the clearing of lanes through minefields and other obstacles during amphibious operations and in support of subsequent operations ashore. Because of this specialized mission, the M/CM platoon is considered a division asset and has established a special working relationship with the division combat engineer battalion. Operational proficiency in the employment of M/CM assets requires an understanding of the MK-154 LMC system used to clear obstacles, the organization of M/CM assets, M/CM precepts, and amphibious breaching operations. See MCWP 3-17.3, *MAGTF Breaching Operations,* for an indepth analysis of tactics, techniques, and procedures for breaching operations. For information involving types of breaching equipment, see FM 5-100, *Engineer Operations.* For information involving types of obstacles, see FM 5-100; FM 5-102, *Countermobility*; and FM 20-32, *Mine/Countermine Operations.*

MK-154 Linear Mine Clearing System

The MK-154 LMC system is a special mission kit specifically designed for use on the AAVP7A1. When not installed on the AAV, the kit is stored in its own shipping container. A trained crew can mount the MK-154 in 2 hours. The use of the AAVR7A1 boom or another heavy-lift asset is required to mount the kit on top of the AAVP7A1. See figure 7-6.

The MK-154 ammunition load occupies the entire troop compartment of the AAV. A full reload of the system, three line charges and rockets, requires approximately 45 minutes. Each line charge consists of a rocket, a line charge of 100 meters of C-4 explosive, and 66 meters of safety line. The crew remains inside the AAV when using the hydraulically deployed rocket launcher.

Characteristics

The MK-154 LMC has the following characteristics:

- Launching device weighs 3,040 pounds.
- Container and device weighs 8,790 pounds.
- Container dimensions are 175.75 by 96.88 by 60.5 inches.

The MK-154 ammunition has the following characteristics:

- Linear demolition charge with tub (ML25) weighs 2,550 pounds.

Figure 7-6. MK-154 LMC.

- C-4 charge weighs 1,750 pounds.
- Three MK22 model rockets weigh 115 pounds each.
- Four MK22 model rockets weigh 128 pounds each.
- LMC and combat-equipped AAV with EAAK weigh 65,600 pounds.

Capabilities

- The MK-154 LMC system is specifically designed for defeating manmade obstacles intended to hinder and delay military operations. The following are capabilities of the MK-154 LMC system:
- Can be mounted on any AAVP7A1 hull without additional modification to the AAV.
- Is capable of firing three line charges consecutively without reloading the system.
- Permits the breaching of a minefield up to 260 meters in depth with proper overlap of each charge.
- Creates a line charge explosion blast area 16 meters wide and 100 meters in length that is 95 percent clear of mines (with the exception of double impulse and magnetic impulse mines).
- Reduces wire obstacles and trip wires with the line charge blast.

Limitations

Environmental factors may restrict the ability of the MK-154 LMC system. When the vehicle is on a slope in excess of 53 percent bow up, the MK-154 LMC system is unable to fire using its electrical system. However, the system can be fired manually with the vehicle on a slope up to 60 percent bow up. In addition, waves over 3 feet in the surf zone may swamp the vehicle when the system is raised and preparing to fire.

Employment Techniques

The operational employment techniques for the MK-154 are as follows:

- AAVP7A1 with MK-154 approaches the minefield/obstacle belt.

- AAVP7A1 with MK-154 stops approximately 70 meters before the minefield boundary.
- MK-154 launcher is deployed.
- MK-154 is aimed by pointing the entire vehicle in the direction of intended rocket flight.
- MK-154 is launched. When fired, the rocket pulls the line charge from the troop compartment of the AAVP7A1.
- Rocket reaches the end of the 166-meter line (62.5 meters of safety line and 103.5 meters of explosive), rocket pulls the line charge taut, and line falls to the ground. The 62.5-meter safety line provides the maximum distance between the launch vehicle and the explosion.
- AAV crew detonates the line charge from within the AAV. The explosion creates a lane approximately 100 meters long by 16 meters wide.
- AAV moves to execute additional firings to accomplish the mission if additional lanes are required or if the minefield is of such a depth to require multiple charges.

Organization of Mobility, Countermobility Assets

The M/CM platoon is located in the H&S company, AA battalion, and consists of 24 AAVs with 12 MK-154 line charge kits. Normally, the smallest unit used for breaching operations is the breach team, consisting of four AAVs and two MK-154 kits. Table 7-1 shows the M/CM organization.

Table 7-1. M/CM Organization.

M/CM Unit	Equipment
Platoon	12 AAVP7A1 equipped with 12 MK-154 LMC systems 12 AAVP7A1 support vehicles
Section	6 AAVP7A1 equipped with 6 MK-154 LMC systems 6 AAVP7A1 support vehicles
Breach Team	2 AAVP7A1 equipped with 2 MK-154 LMC systems 2 AAVP7A1 support vehicles
Breach Element	1 AAVP7A1 equipped with 1 MK-154 LMC system 1 AAVP7A1 support vehicle

Mobility, Countermobility Precepts

The commander should consider the following precepts when planning for M/CM platoon employment:

- MK-154 vehicles never operate alone and require the security of the supported unit.
- The smallest M/CM unit to be employed for an operation will be a breach team consisting of two MK-154 vehicles and two AAVP7A1 security vehicles. This is done to maintain 100 percent redundancy that is essential at the breach site. Breaching doctrine anticipates 50 percent losses during obstacle reduction operations.
- Breach AAVs are not amphibious tanks or mine plows and are susceptible to antiarmor weapons and mines.
- High speed underway launches with breach AAVs are similar to AAVP7A1 high speed underway launches.
- MK-154-equipped AAVs are sophisticated ordnance items that should not be used to transport troops or equipment.

Preparations for Amphibious Operations

When planning to employ the MK-154 in amphibious breaching operations, the commander should consider embarkation factors and develop a launch plan.

Embarkation Planning Factors

When planning for embarkation of the MK-154 vehicles, the commander should consider the following factors:

- Because of the size of the MK-154 shipping container and the difficulty of installation, the AAV should embark either pier side or offshore with the MK-154 launcher installed.
- The breaching element equipment should be embarked to ensure the element is in the first assault wave. Extra space is needed for loading ordnance aboard the MK-154 LMC vehicles and at least 10 feet of overhead clearance for elevating of the launcher platform. MK-154 vehicles need to be staged on a flat level surface to conduct operational checks of the MK-154 electrical system. (Ordnance will not be loaded aboard the MK-154 LMC vehicle during operational tests.)
- The vessel must have adequate magazine storage, including ammunition capability issues, for the ordnance. An arming plan must be developed so the MK-154 can be armed onboard ship before deployment.

Launch Plan

Underway launches for the MK-154 LMC vehicles are the same as standard AAVs. When developing the launch plan, the commander must consider that fuel usage of the MK-154 LMC vehicle is approximately twice the rate of the standard AAV in the water and on land.

CHAPTER 8. AAV GUNNERY AND FIRE CONTROL

The AA unit possesses a significant firepower potential that increases the combat power of the supported infantry unit. The UGWS of the AAVP7A1 combines the infantry support capabilities of the M2 HB .50-caliber machine gun and the MK-19, 40-millimeter automatic grenade launcher into a single, nonstabilized turret operated by the vehicle commander. The UGWS was designed for the primary mission of infantry fire support during the conduct of offensive and defensive operations. The secondary mission is for vehicle self-defense, which is the protection of the flanks and rear of mech forces from the fires of AT teams and ATGMs. The third firepower mission is the local air defense of the mech force in extreme circumstances. Additional information and details pertaining to AAV gunnery and fire control can be found in FM 23-27, *MK-19 40 mm Grenade Machine Gun Mod 3*; FM 23-65, *Browning Machine Gun Caliber .50 HB, M2*; and MCWP 3-15.1, *Machine Guns and Machine Gun Gunnery*. The proper employment of the AAV's weapons systems and smoke capabilities greatly increases mission success and enhances the survivability of both the AAVs and the supported infantry.

Weapons System Employment

To employ the AAV's weapons station safely and effectively, the AA unit personnel must have a sound understanding of fire control responsibilities, weapons effectiveness, water gunnery, classes of fire, principles of fire distribution, UGWS capabilities, techniques of employment, and fire control.

Fire Control Responsibilities

Fire control of AAVs includes operations connected with the preparation and application of the selected targets. It implies the ability of the AA unit leader to correctly identify the target, open fire when desired, adjust the unit's fire upon multiple targets, regulate the rate of fire, shift fire from one target to another, coordinate the fire with the movement of dismounted infantry, and cease firing. The ability to exercise correct fire control depends primarily on the discipline, knowledge, and training of the AAV crews and leaders. The AAV UGWS is a nonstabilized platform that requires intensive sustainment training for accurate delivery of fires. Failure to exercise correct fire control results in danger to friendly troops, loss of surprise, premature disclosure of vehicle positions, misapplication of fire on important targets, loss of time in securing target adjustments, and waste of ammunition. The responsibilities for AAV fire control follow the chain of command for the AAV unit. The AA platoon commander, section leader, and crew chief execute fire control.

AA Platoon Commander

The AA platoon commander is responsible to the supported unit commander for the effective employment of AAV firepower in support of combat operations. To maximize fire support and ensure proper control of fires to prevent friendly casualties, the AA platoon commander must clearly understand the location of adjacent unit boundaries to preclude firing outside the unit's zone of action and must maintain positive communications with the supported infantry. Normally, the AA platoon commander—

- Assigns fire missions and firing positions to the section leaders.
- Selects weapon to fire (either .50 caliber or 40 millimeter).
- Designates sectors of fire.
- Makes target assignments.
- Identifies locations of friendly troops that may be endangered by section fire.

AA Section Leader

The AA section leader is responsible for the tactical and technical employment of the section's firepower. When the AA platoon is operating under decentralized control, the AA section leader will receive requests for fire and direction from the supported infantry platoon commander. The AA section leader is responsible for passing information to the AAV crew chief regarding—

- Firing positions.
- Targets to be engaged and estimated range.
- Sector of fire.
- Fire adjustment of the section.

AAV Crew Chief

Responsible for the fire control and tactical employment of the AAV, the crew chief carries out the orders of the AA section leader and platoon commander. The crew chief/gunner also directs the AAV driver to—

- Position the vehicle for maximum effectiveness of its fire.
- Move to assigned firing positions.
- Provide cover during reload. (Together with the third crewman/assistant driver, the crew chief/gunner reloads the turret.)

Classes of Fire

To properly employ the UGWS-mounted machine gun and MK-19, AAV gunners must understand and correctly apply plunging, grazing, frontal, flanking, oblique, and enfilade fires.

Plunging

In a plunging fire, the danger space created by the angle of falling rounds in relation to the ground slope is confined to the shortened beaten zone. Plunging fire is obtained when firing from high ground into low ground, low to high ground, and at long ranges.

Grazing

Grazing fire is fire approximately parallel to ground where the center cone of fire does not rise above 1 meter. When firing over level or uniformly sloping terrain, the maximum extent of grazing fire is approximately 1,000 meters for a .50 caliber machine gun.

Frontal

In a frontal fire, the long axis of the beaten zone is at a right angle to the long axis of the target.

Flanking

This fire is delivered against the flank of a target.

Oblique

In an oblique fire, the long axis of the beaten zone is at an angle, but not a right angle to the long axis of the target.

Enfilade

In an enfilade fire, the long axis of the beaten zone coincides or nearly coincides with the long axis of the target. This class of fire is either frontal or flanking with respect to the target, because it makes maximum use of the beaten zone

Weapons Effectiveness

To properly engage a target, the AA unit leader must understand the weapons' effects of the UGWS. Unit leaders must select the weapon to be fired and decide whether to mass fires. Destruction of point targets will require firing from the halt because the AAV's UGWS is not stabilized. Firing on the move may at best provide area suppression or at worst, waste ammunition. Overhead fire support of dismounted infantry must be fired from the halt and carefully thought out.

Up-Gunned Weapons Station

The UGWS is composed of weapons, sight, and fire controls. The M36E3 sight provides the gunner with a 7-power sight with a reticle calibrated for the M2 and MK-19. The sight is laser protected against enemy lasers. A properly bore-sighted UGWS in the hands of a trained gunner can provide first round hits on targets within maximum effective range. However, the sight does not take into account dynamic cant of the vehicle. That is the off-level attitude of the vehicle that may arise from being on a front, rear or side slope. This is when the art of gunnery is required to manipulate the weapons on target using intuitive adjustment of the reticle in relation to the target.

M2 .50-Caliber, Heavy-Barreled Machine Gun

The M2 .50-caliber machine gun of the AAV normally fires armor piercing incendiary and armor piercing incendiary tracer ammunition at a maximum effective range of 1,830 meters and a maximum range of 6,800 meters. Capable of penetrating 1 inch of rolled homogeneous [steel] armor (RHA) at 200 meters and 0.7 inch of RHA at 600 meters, the M2 can be effectively employed against lightly armored vehicles, material, and infantry. The sabot light armor penetrator (SLAP) round is highly effective against light armor targets out to ranges up to 1,500 meters. At that range, the SLAP round will penetrate ¾-inch steel armor at 0 degrees obliquity. The M2 is not effective against tanks or the frontal armor of the Russian-made, BMP infantry combat vehicle. Compared to the MK-19, the .50-caliber machine gun is the weapon of choice for immediate suppression of ATGM launchers because of its fast flight time and high fire rate. The M2 can also be employed to range targets for the MK-19 using the burst-on target method. The section leader uses the burst-on-target method to effectively mark and suppress the target and pass the correct range for the MK-19.

MK-19 40-Millimeter Grenade Launcher

The MK-19 is an area weapon principally designed for the destruction of infantry, material, and lightly armored vehicles. The AAV-mounted MK-19 normally fires the high explosive dual purpose (HEDP) ammunition that provides excellent fragmentation and blast effect against infantry (up to a 15-meter effective casualty radius), while possessing a shaped charge capable of penetrating 2 inches of RHA. The ballistic qualities of the MK-19 can be characterized as relatively straight trajectory out to 1,000 meters with plunging characteristics past 1,000 meters to its maximum range of 2,200 meters. Table 8-1 shows the time of flight for each of the three MK-19 rounds fired from the UGWS. This table can be used to judge when rounds will impact the target after firing.

Table 8-1. MK-19 Time of Flight Table.

Range (meters)	B542/M430 HEDP (seconds)	B480/M385 HE (seconds)
500	2.40	2.43
1,000	5.63	5.74
1,500	10.17	10.53
2,000	18.97	17.44

As the primary weapon for the destruction or suppression of enemy infantry, the MK-19 can be used to engage troops located in the open, dug-in on reverse slopes or behind hills by employing high-angle fire techniques like a light infantry mortar. When firing the MK-19 from a defilade position, the gunner must be able to communicate with a spotter to make adjustments.

The 40-millimeter HEDP round can penetrate the armor of fielded IFVs. Despite the degree of adjustment at longer ranges and long time of flight, the MK-19 is the AAV's weapon of choice for the frontal engagement of light armored IFVs at ranges up to 1,000 meters. Although not designed as an AT weapon, the MK-19 fire of an

AAV unit can be massed to engage tanks with high-angle plunging fires at ranges exceeding 1,000 meters to achieve penetrations of the turret or engine compartment roof. Under extreme circumstances, the MK-19 may be effective against the rear armor of older tanks. The AAV should only be employed as an AT weapon for its own defense or in extreme circumstances.

Water Gunnery

Water gunnery encompasses a higher level of gunnery skill. To effectively employ the weapons, the AAV gunner must be able to adjust the azimuth, traverse the elevation, and fire the weapon while remaining focused on the target. At the same time, the driver must minimize steerage and maintain a constant speed during firing. Water gunnery requires more ammunition than land gunnery and requires training to familiarize the crews with the intricacies of firing from a moving platform.

Crews with solid land gunnery performance should practice water gunnery skills on a body of water with a smooth surface. After practicing dry firings while looking through the sight, the gunner begins with live fire and builds toward live firing on an amphibious landing. AAV crews familiar with water gunnery skills will be better prepared for amphibious landings or riverine operations.

Amphibious Landings

During an amphibious landing, a multitude of factors can affect the position of the vehicle. Waves and swells create a constant state of various motions to the vehicle. The driver also creates motion by steering in the direction to the beach. These motions have an effect on the gunner's ability to track the target. On average, only one-third of the ammunition fired is near or on target. When firing during an amphibious landing, the gunner must continually range the target while the driver must keep the vehicle headed straight without steering.

Riverine Operations

Gunnery in riverine operations is similar to gunnery in amphibious landings. In riverine operation, most targets will be to the port or starboard side of the vehicle and will require constant azimuth adjustments to the target while firing from a moving vehicle. Currents, tides, and the bottom hydrography will affect the vehicle and the UGWS. The driver must minimize steering and maintain a constant speed while the gunner engages the target.

Range Determination Methods

Methods for determining range include estimating by naked eye, observing the size of targets through a sight, firing the gun for observed impacts when on level ground, measuring from a map, stepping off the distance with a pace count or securing information from other units such as an adjacent vehicle with a laser range finder. Ranges are determined to the nearest 100 meters for machine gun firing. In combat, the most commonly used methods are observing by eye and observing by fire.

Observing by Eye

When determining distance by eye using the 100-meter unit of measure method, the gunner must visualize 100 meters on the ground and determine how many 100-meter units to the target. If the distance is over 500 meters, the gunner should calculate half the distance to the target and multiply that distance by two. Certain conditions affect the appearance of objects when they are observed by eye. Light and terrain can make objects appear closer.

Objects seem closer—
- In bright light.
- When the color of the object contrasts sharply with the background color.
- When observed over water, snow or a uniform surface (e.g., wheat field, flat open desert).
- When observed from a height downward.

- In clear atmosphere at high altitudes.
- When observed over a partially hidden depression.
- When observed straight down a road or railroad track.

Objects seem more distant—

- When observed over a visible depression.
- In poor light or fog.
- When only a small part of the object can be seen.
- When observed from low ground to high ground.

Observing by Fire

The only accurate method of determining range by observing fire is through the M-36 sight when on level ground. When receiving range information from another AAV, the gunner must consider the frontal or downward slope from that vehicle.

Principles of Fire Distribution

Survival of the AA unit often depends on how quickly and effectively its fires can be distributed on the enemy. If the AA unit's fires are not controlled, ammunition will be wasted and targets will not be effectively engaged. SOPs must be established for distributing fires, because the AA unit commander may not have to give subordinates detailed fire missions when fighting in a surprise meeting engagement. The following fire distribution principles and the initiative of the AAV section leaders and crew chiefs must be relied on during the first minutes of contact.

Cover Enemy Targets

Fires from each AA section should be distributed so that enemy targets are completely covered. Proper distribution saves ammunition and increases the number of kills by AAV gunnery.

Avoid Target Overkill

A unit fighting outnumbered or at close quarters cannot afford killing a target more than once. Each AAV should strive to engage a single target unless the mass fire of the section is required to ensure the destruction of large targets or more heavily armored vehicles.

Fire First and Fast

Firing first with accurate fire greatly increases chances of winning the engagement. If the initial burst misses, the first to fire can probably shoot again and hit the target before receiving return fire. If surprised by the enemy and unable to fire first, the AA unit should return fire as quickly as possible. The AA unit should continue to engage the enemy as fast as possible, because fire placed in the enemy's area will lessen his effectiveness and give friendly weapons time to adjust. A wasted opportunity to engage a target may never be regained.

Optimize Each Weapon

AA unit commanders must be able to effectively coordinate available firepower to maximize fire support for the supported infantry. The effective use of each weapon will depend on their capabilities, limitations, and availability. When a mix of weapons (MK-19 and M2) is desired, the AA unit commander should designate which AAV within the section should employ what gun. Accuracy decreases as range increases, so it may be necessary to mass fires on a distant target. Normally, the section leader suppresses, marks, and confirms range with the M2 as the rest of the section kills with the MK-19. When engaging IFVs, two AAVs of a section should mass their fires on one enemy vehicle while the third AAV destroys its dismounted infantry or ranges and/or suppresses the next vehicle for section engagement. This technique should be used in long-range engagements, normally past 1,000 meters, where the accuracy and lethality of the AAV's UGWS may not allow effective one-on-one engagements.

Destroy Dangerous Targets

Target danger varies with range, terrain, and target type. For example, at a range of 600 meters, an APC may be more dangerous with its dismounted infantry than tanks at a greater range. A target should be destroyed based on the degree of danger it presents.

Most Dangerous. An enemy weapon that can destroy a friendly element and is engaging or preparing to engage is classified as most dangerous and should be engaged first. If there is more than one such target, the closest is engaged first.

Dangerous. A dangerous target is an enemy weapon that could engage and destroy a friendly element but has not seen friendly units yet. This target is engaged after the most dangerous targets are destroyed.

Least Dangerous. The least dangerous enemy target cannot engage or is not powerful enough to destroy a friendly element, but the target can report the friendly element's location to another enemy unit capable of engagement. This target is engaged after the most dangerous and dangerous targets are destroyed.

Redistribute Fires

If needed, fires can be redistributed when time permits.

Fire Control Techniques

In the offense and during the conduct of a mobile defense, there is usually little time for planning AAV fire control and distribution. Often the initial area of coverage is hurriedly assigned to an AA section. Infantry and AA unit commanders must use simple fire control measures that can be clearly understood by leaders and crews. Fire control measures must be used routinely, without detailed instruction. The TRP, nearest-half, sector of fire, and EA techniques can be used to control fires.

Target Reference Point

The TRP is used for identifying enemy targets and for controlling fires. The TRP can be an easily recognizable natural object (e.g., rock outcrop, unique tree) or a manmade object (e.g., engineer stake, chemical light behind a tree). TRPs can be used to designate targets for the infantry company, AA platoon, section or individual AAV. In addition, TRPs can designate the center of an area where a com-

mander plans to distribute or converge fires in a surprise engagement.

The supported company commander or AA platoon commander usually designates TRPs. The TRPs should be planned on likely avenues of approach during defensive operations and in likely enemy locations during offensive operations. Compass points (e.g., north, east) are used when giving directions centered on a TRP because AAVs will be engaging from different directions.

Nearest-Half

The nearest-half technique is a method for rapid distribution of initial fire and coordination of the initial volley. Each section leader estimates how much of a target can be seen and then directs fires into the closest half of the target area. The section leader distributes fires in half of the target area using variations of the frontal fire, crossfire, and depth fire engagement patterns.

Frontal Fire. The frontal fire engagement pattern is used when targets present themselves laterally and friendly weapons can fire to the front. Each gunner engages targets directly to the front and then shifts to the inside of the target area. The center gunner engages the center target and then shifts to either side.

Crossfire. The crossfire pattern is also used when targets present themselves laterally. Each gunner engages targets on the enemy flank diagonally and then shifts to the inside. This technique is effective against armored fighting vehicles because it enables target engagement on vulnerable side armor.

Depth Fire. The depth-fire engagement pattern is used when targets present themselves in depth. One section engages close targets while another section engages deep targets.

Sector of Fire

In this fire control technique, a specific area is assigned to a unit or an AAV to cover by fire. Sectors of fire are assigned to ensure adequate target coverage by fire and observation not to restrict a section to firing only in its assigned section. Each section or AAV should be assigned one primary and one secondary sector of fire. If no targets appear in the primary sector, the AAV is free to engage targets in the secondary sector.

Engagement Area

An EA is an area where the supported unit commander intends to contain and destroy an enemy force with combined arms and massed fires of available weapons. The EA may also be divided into sectors to concentrate fire and to optimize fire distribution on the battlefield. EAs can be identified by multiple TRPs, depending on the size and complexity of the EA.

Range Cards

A range card is a rough sketch or drawing that serves as a record of firing data and a document for defensive fire planning. No matter how long an AA unit plans to occupy a position, it immediately prepares a complete range card for primary positions and a partially complete range card for alternate or supplementary positions. Each AAV makes a range card in duplicate using the available standard range card modified for AAVs and the UGWS. One copy is passed up the chain of command to the AA section leader for organizing the defense and preparing a fire plan sketch. The other copy stays with the AAV. The gunner uses the card to recall the data to fire at predetermined targets and as an aid in estimating ranges to other targets. When making a range card, the gunner should include as much information as necessary for another gunner to man the turret. A third card may be necessary if the AAV is directly supporting an infantry squad. Revisions and improvements are made on the range card when necessary. Each AAV crewman should understand the range card and should know the location of the range card. MCWP 3-15.1, FM 23-27, and FM 23-65 contain details on the construction of range cards.

Orientation

The range card provides spaces for the vehicle's tactical number, section, and platoon, supported unit, the GPS grid for the AAV, and the magnetic vehicle azimuth of the AAV. The dot represents the AAV. These cards are clearly marked indicating primary, alternate or supplementary position. The elevations for the .50-caliber M2 and 40-millimeter MK-19 are separated to allow the gunner to place the range from the sight in each block and to place the range from the AAV to the target in the range block. For example, an AAV that is in a defilade position may be positioned with its nose canted at 10 degrees. This creates dynamic cant in an upward angle and provides an additional angle of elevation for the UGWS.

Figure 8-1 on page 8-8, the sample range card, depicts an AAV with 10 degrees nose-up cant. The target at TRP 1 is physically 1,000 meters from the vehicle. Because of the added angle to the AAV and the UGWS, the range to the target when looking through the reticle of the sight for the M2 is 800 meters to the target. If the AAV gunner looks through the sight and elevates to 1,000 meters on the reticle, the gunner would shoot over the target. From experience and training, the AAV gunner can look at the elevation of the barrel and see that it is too high to hit the target. However, since the ballistics are different for the MK-19, the gunner sets the MK-19 on 950 meters on the range memory drum. If the gunner fires at these targets, the gunner would see the exact range.

Experience and training give the AAV gunner the knowledge required to estimate the angle of the barrel relative to the target and to calculate the trajectory of the round. When targets of greater or lesser elevation are engaged, the AAV gunner should shoot low on a target, because low rounds can be observed and walked on target. High rounds are more commonly not seen and therefore cannot be adjusted quickly.

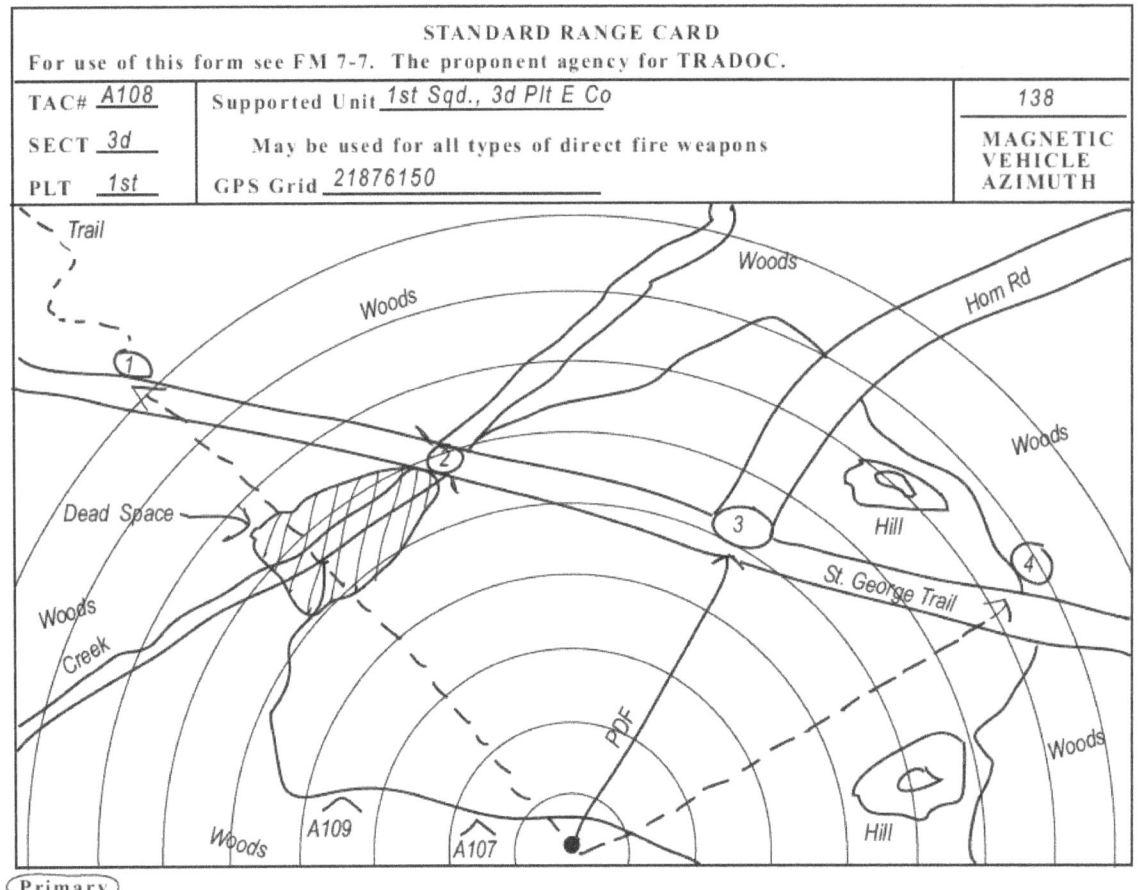

STANDARD RANGE CARD

For use of this form see FM 7-7. The proponent agency for TRADOC.

TAC# _A108_	Supported Unit _1st Sqd., 3d Plt E Co_	_138_
SECT _3d_	May be used for all types of direct fire weapons	**MAGNETIC VEHICLE AZIMUTH**
PLT _1st_	GPS Grid _21876150_	

Primary
Alternate
Supplementary

DATA SECTION						
POSITION IDENTIFICATION Primary BP-12			**DATE** 15 Feb 2002			
WEAPON M2/MK-19 UGWS			**EACH CIRCLE EQUALS** _100_ **METERS**			
TRP/TARGET	**TURRET AZIMUTH**	**MAGNETIC AZIMUTH**	**ELEVATION** .50	**ELEVATION** 40mm	**RANGE**	**DESCRIPTION**
TRP 1	310°	88°	800	950	1000	Intersection Road/Trail
2	325°	103°	550	650	650	Bridge
3	17°	155°	500	550	550	Intersection PDF
4	53°	191°	700	800	850	Intersection Road/Woods
REMARKS AAV is on a 10° degree nose up cant behind a small berm.						

DA Form 5517-R, Feb 96 (Revised for use with AAV UGWS)

Figure 8-1. Range Card Example.

Recording Information

The vehicle commander records firing data on the range card to include the final protective line (FPL) or the principal direction of fire (PDF). This is the single most important piece of information of concern to superiors.

FPL. When choosing an AAV position and making a range card, the commander should consider the following principles:

- FPLs should provide as much grazing fire as possible.
- Terrain and obstacles should be used to force enemy formations into positions where the fires of the FPL will be flanking and enfilade.
- FPLs should be interlocking, which adds to the effectiveness of the fire plan by eliminating gaps in the FPLs and maximizing the coverage by fire across as much of the frontage as possible.
- Machine gun FPLs are usually fired at a rapid rate for the first 2 minutes and a sustained rate thereafter.

An FPL is drawn as a heavy line, shaded to signify grazing fire with the M2. Gaps are left in the heavy line to indicate dead space that can be covered by the MK-19. The range is recorded to the near and far ends of the dead space and to the maximum extent of graze along the FPL. The firing data needed to engage the target is recorded on the range card. Firing data is taken from the turret ring azimuth indicator and memory range drum of the UGWS. A magnetic azimuth reading should also be placed on the card so unit leaders will know the direction from the position.

PDF. The PDF is drawn as a solid line with an arrow, and the range is recorded to the near end of the avenue of approach. The firing data and magnetic azimuth are also recorded on the data section at the bottom of the form. Dashed lines designate sector limits. The data for these are recorded on the range card sketch. Other targets of tactical significance are predetermined, sketched, and recorded on the range card sketch. The targets are numbered consecutively from the

FPL. The FPL is always target number 1. When a PDF is assigned, targets are numbered starting from either side.

Fire Commands

Within the AA platoon, fire control is exercised by using fire commands that are instructions issued to the AAV gunners, which enable them to properly engage the desired targets. The AA platoon commander or section leader will determine which elements to include in the fire command. Although the fire command should be as brief as clarity will permit, some targets may require all elements. The fire command elements can be remembered by using the brevity code for alert, direction, description, range, assignment, and control (ADDRAC). The following are examples of fire command elements:

- **A**lert—"First section fire mission."
- **D**irection—"Left front."
- **D**escription—"BRDM."
- **R**ange—"1100."
- **A**ssignment—"A101 and 103 use MK-19. I will mark and suppress with M2."
- **C**ontrol—"Fire."

Initial Fire Commands

Fire commands must be as brief and concise as possible, but initial fire commands must at least contain the elements of **A**lert, **R**ange, and **C**ontrol.

Subsequent Fire Commands

During and upon conclusion of firing, the AAV unit commander must maintain control over the engagement and cease fire or shift fire once targets are destroyed. When dismounted infantry are closing upon an objective engaged with supporting fire, the AAV unit commander ensures that fires are being shifted correctly. The AAV unit commander should not assume that the gunners in a section have the same vision of the battlefield as other sections. When adjusting fire, the AAV unit commander should give the deflection of fire first.

Infantry Calls for Fire

One of the primary missions of the AA unit is to provide fires in support of its embarked infantry. AA unit commanders should plan and coordinate the employment of their weapons with the supported infantry commander before the conduct of operations. Aspects of fire control and support, in conjunction with the overall concept of operations, are important to the effective planning and execution of the mission. SOPs should be established to coordinate and control AAV fires with the dismounted infantry to maximize effect and ensure safety.

Infantry calls for fire are generally made over the infantry company tactical net or the AAV command net. When AA sections are operating in support of infantry platoons under decentralized control, the AA section leader may monitor the infantry platoon net for calls for fire. However, under most circumstances, calls for fire should be made to the AA platoon commander to ensure proper control and distribution of fires.

Antiaircraft Gunnery

Individual M2 .50-caliber machine guns can provide AA units with a self-defense capability against hostile, low flying, low performance aircraft. These guns are employed in the air defense role as part of the unit's local defense. Although machine guns are not components of an integrated and coordinated air defense system, they should be used to engage hostile aircraft within maximum effective range of the gun unless otherwise directed. Surveillance, reconnaissance, and liaison aircraft; troop carriers; helicopters; and drones are typical targets. See FM 44-80, *Visual Aircraft Recognition,* for aircraft recognition and identification information.

Engagement Rules

Normally the following rules for engagement apply:

- Attack aircraft identified as hostile.
- Attack aircraft committing a hostile act.

Requirements for a Hit

To engage enemy aircraft effectively, the AAV gunner must accurately estimate the future position of the target and point the gun in such a manner that the fired rounds and the aircraft will arrive at the estimated point at the same time. The gunner must fulfill the following requirements to hit the target:

- The line requirement demands that the gunner cause the round to intersect at the target course line. (The vertical size of the target provides the gunner a small angle of tolerance.)
- The lead requirement demands that the gunner cause the round to intersect the target. (The length of the aircraft provides some angular error.)

Smoke Generation

Smoke generation aboard AAVs is one of the primary methods to mask tactical movements of AAVs or supported infantry from being observed by the enemy. When smoke is being used to designate targets for CAS or other fire support coordination, the AA platoon commander must coordinate through the same fire control procedures as gunnery to obtain authorization before using smoke on a battlefield. The use of smoke must be carefully planned and should be used as part of defensive efforts against ATGMs. The AAVP7A1 is capable of generating smoke for obscuration through either an onboard engine generating system or by using the M-257 smoke grenade launchers.

Engine Generating System

The AAV has the capability to generate white smoke for visual obscuration. The vehicle injects raw fuel onto the hot exhaust manifolds producing smoke from the vehicle's top exhaust. Usually this requires the engine to be operated at high RPM to produce a reasonable volume of smoke. Wind direction is a key factor in using vehicle-generated smoke. For example, if the smoke is used for an amphibious landing, the wind should be blowing towards land. In a land environment with no wind, the smoke will plume over the vehicle.

M-257 Smoke Grenade Launcher

Located on the back of the turret, the M-257 smoke grenade launcher has a left bank and a right bank of four grenade tubes each. The grenades can be fired as a left bank of four, a right bank of four or both banks simultaneously. The turret should be facing the threat so the grenades will provide 105 degrees of coverage for the AAV. The grenades are propelled into the air, detonate at approximately 30 feet, and provide coverage 20 to 50 feet from the AAV.

A critical element in firing the smoke grenades, wind will affect the burst distance from the vehicle, persistence of the screening agent, direction of travel of the screen, and adverse effects of the screening agent on the vehicle. For example, the L8 red phosphorous grenade will produce a smoke screen that persists for several minutes in very light wind. However, a wind coming towards the AAV can blow red phosphorous particles on the AAV, which can be dangerous to personnel. For this reason, hatches must be closed before firing. The M-257 can fire several different types of grenades, to include those fired by the M1A1 tank. The type of grenade load depends upon the threat environment. Table 8-2 provides capabilities of available AAV M-257 grenades.

Table 8-2. Grenades for the AAV M-257 Grenade Launcher.

Grenade	Spectrum Screened	Fill Material	Time to Effective Cloud	Obscuration Duration
L8A3	Visual	Red phosphorous	8 seconds	3 to 4 minutes
M76	Visual plus IR	Brass flake	2 seconds	45 seconds
M82 (training)	Visual	Titanium dioxide (smoke agent)	2 seconds	45 seconds
M81	IR plus radar	Brass flake and graphite	2 seconds	20 seconds

CHAPTER 9. OPERATIONS IN SPECIAL TERRAIN

Special terrain is geography or an environment (e.g., jungle, riverine, river crossing, urban, desert, mountain areas, and cold weather) that requires peculiar or unique operational and logistical considerations. In planning for operations in special terrain, the commander must consider the mobility limitations and maintenance requirements when employing the AAV. This chapter will focus on these special requirements and offer ways to compensate for expected limitations.

Jungle Operations

Jungle operations limit the mobility of AAVs and other armor assets. The terrain and topography of jungle areas can radically change from flat rice paddies to a steep-sided, triple-canopy jungle in only a few miles. Many jungles have rivers and tributaries that are the primary means of transportation for much of the population. These avenues of approach are a major consideration in tactical operations and are a viable mission for AAVs. Jungle areas traditionally have two wet seasons throughout the year. During these periods, vehicular mobility may be constrained if roads and trails wash out. During the dry seasons, armor will be confined to established roads and trails or armor-created paths. These changes in the jungle environment provide intelligence, CSS, tactical planning, fire support, engineer, and communications challenges to the AAV unit.

Intelligence

The AA battalion S-2 will provide the following information to the commanding officer, S-3, and S-4 for planning operations in a jungle environment:

- Weather, type of vegetation, and topography in the operational area.
- Avenues of approach and their trafficability during wet and dry seasons.

- Enemy's ATGM and recoilless rifle capability. (Wire-guided missiles are generally ineffective in a jungle, but rocket-propelled grenades and recoilless rifles can be devastating when armor contact ranges are 15 to 25 meters.)
- Enemy's engineering capability. (Mines, particularly command-detonated and off-road, can halt an operation in areas where roads/trails are only one-vehicle wide.)
- Additional stocks of maps. (One map of the area of operation should be maintained in each vehicle.)

Combat Service Support

Units moving in a jungle environment present to the supporting unit staff numerous CSS challenges that include but are not limited to the following:

- The AA battalion S-4, in conjunction with the battalion motor transport officer, should formulate plans to push supplies forward as rapidly as possible because class III/V/IX resupply is essential to maintaining combat momentum. Concurrent plans should be made, to include the transfer of supplies from wheeled vehicles to tracked vehicles when terrain becomes impassable during the wet season.
- The AA battalion S-4 makes plans based on availability of aerial resupply for supported units and trained personnel to operate LZs.
- The AA battalion S-4, working with supported unit commanders and the AA H&S company commanding officer, should plan for all-around security for supply columns sent forward to conduct resupply and recovery of disabled vehicles.
- The AA battalion S-4 develops criteria for the destruction of battle-damaged equipment due to restriction on battlefield vehicle evacuation from the jungle.
- The AA battalion commander and S-4 place special emphasis on equipment and weapons maintenance.

Tactical Planning

Due to the close nature of jungle operations, AAVs and their embarked infantry should modify their tactics and equipment to facilitate close combat. Generally, AA units will be cross-attached to support sustained infantry operations at the platoon and company levels. The following tactical considerations should be addressed when planning for jungle operations:

- Issue additional hand-held munitions (AT-4, hand grenades) as well as M-203s to vehicle crews and embarked personnel.
- Ensure embarked personnel maintain watches from open cargo hatches and the open rear personnel door of a moving AAV, which will allow for 360-degree security. The open rear personnel door and cargo hatches will also limit the effects of high explosive antitank warheads/mine blast if the vehicle is hit.
- Use mounted infantry patrols where the shock and mobility of the AAV can be used to close with known or suspected enemy positions before dismounting embarked infantry.
- Close vehicle intervals to allow for the massing of vehicle and embarked infantry fires.
- Use the inherent weight of the AAV to overrun and crush enemy bunkers and trench systems.
- Equip augmented AA units with additional night vision devices. Be aware that high humidity and rainfall in jungles may reduce the effectiveness of IR and thermal capabilities.
- Employ dismounted patrols and OPs when halted, ensuring that enemy infiltration routes are targeted.
- Prepare to use infantry where the enemy situation is unclear.
- Employ early warning sensors to provide a more integrated defense.
- Do not use AAVs in a static position for an extended length of time. This will be an invitation to infiltrating enemy infantry to single out the AAV(s) for attack/destruction.

Fire Support

For fire support coordination within a jungle environment, the embarked FO and the forward air controller (FAC)/FAC (airborne) should consider the following aspects of their mission:

- Using creeping fires to support the unit's mission.
- Adjusting fire by sound.
- Following a white phosphorous first round with an HE delayed fuse.
- During CAS sorties, ensuring that pyrotechnic marking criteria for the enemy does not duplicate marking criteria for friendly units.

Engineer

Engineers attached to an AA unit in a jungle environment are an invaluable asset to offensive, defensive, and support operations. If properly equipped, engineers will be able to improve existing roads and trails and construct or improve LZs to support operations. While the jungle traditionally provides excellent concealment, engineers will enhance that concealment by creating semipermanent and permanent covered positions (e.g., bunkers, trench works) for the AA unit.

Communications

Communications in a jungle environment will vary depending on the terrain in the AO. The AA battalion communications officer must accomplish the following before conducting operations in a jungle area:

- Secure additional GPS/PLRS assets to support units that may be widely separated.
- Prepare to operate, man, and support communication retransmission sites within the operational area.
- Elevate antennas above the jungle canopy or use directional antennas if possible.

Riverine Operations

Riverine operations are conducted to control the military aspects of an area dominated by inland bodies of water. These military aspects include communications, traffic, and commerce. The objective of riverine operations is to prevent an opposing force from using the river for its own purposes while permitting the use of the river by friendly forces.

Although it applies in varying degrees to operations conducted in mid- and high-intensity warfare, this section is principally written toward the conduct of operations against guerrilla-type forces in a low intensity warfare environment. Many of the techniques applicable to amphibious assault operations are applicable to the riverine environment. Forces to conduct riverine operations may be introduced through an amphibious assault. Riverine operations may be initiated from amphibious ships or be conducted as an adjunct to amphibious operations. The tactics and techniques set forth in this section apply to riverine operations conducted under any circumstances. Riverine operations require a tailored organizational structure and selection of equipment particularly suited for the environment. Riverine operations may be conducted in conjunction with other Service forces or as combined operations with allied forces.

The basic tactics and techniques governing riverine operations are set forth in MCWP 3-35.4, *Doctrine For Navy/Marine Corps Joint Riverine Operations;* JP 3-02, *Joint Doctrine for Amphibious Operations;* and JP 3-02.1, *Joint Doctrine for Landing Force Operations.* This section supplements these publications by emphasizing the unique capabilities of AAV employment in support of MAGTF riverine operations.

Environment

The general and physical environment assumes vital importance in planning and conducting riverine operations, because sharply contrasting riverine environments are found throughout the world, and their impact on riverine ground force techniques varies. Major drainage areas that can affect riverine operations are generally divided into three longitudinal sectors.

Longitudinal Sectors

These three longitudinal sectors are the upper sector or headwaters, the middle sector or central valley, and the lower sector or delta.

Upper Sector or Headwaters. The upper sector or headwaters is often a mountainous region drained by numerous large and small tributaries that merge to form a river system. Navigation is difficult or impossible, because headwaters are characterized by waterfalls, rapids, high banks, steep gradients, and local variations in water depth that complicate the design of watercraft for use in this sector.

Middle Sector or Central Valley. The middle sector or central valley is generally a broad river valley fed by numerous smaller tributaries. The middle sector is wider and slower than the upper sector and is often interspersed with obstacles.

In the upper part of the middle sector, the erosion process is dominant, but downstream the deposition process becomes progressively more active. Navigation is influenced in the upper part by river-bedrock formations and often approaches conditions similar to those of the headwaters.

In some parts of the middle sector, braiding or multiple channeling can occur, making successful navigation dependant on determining the principal channel. Deep channels are usually scarce in braided middle sectors; consequently, navigation is often a severe problem. In addition, braided channels constantly change their course and characteristics.

In the meandering part of the middle sector, river channels change gradually and are more predictable than channels in braided streams. At low to average river stages, the location of maximum water depth is usually close to the location of the maximum current.

Lower Sector or Delta. The lower sector is generally the widest of the sectors, and the speed of the current may change or even reverse with the tide. The lower sector is usually navigable by ships in natural or manmade channels. When a delta is formed, it is usually characterized by a flat deposition plain formed by a number of river tributaries disbursing sediment and water into a gulf, bay or ocean. When planning riverine operations, the commander should consider the following delta characteristics:

- Dominant watercourses in the delta are relatively straight tributaries, assisting in the identification of navigable channels.
- Bottoms of tributaries normally slope up to a crest at river mouths and form a critical dimension that requires the use of high tides for watercraft of marginal drafts.
- Water depth throughout the delta area is often predictable at various river and tidal stages.
- Tidal activity can influence velocity and direction of currents radically. Tidal activity frequently results in saline invasion, so that the water in rivers and canals is too brackish for human consumption. This saline invasion may extend inland up to 30 miles or more from the seacoast.
- Delta areas located in favorable climates are extremely productive agricultural areas. Natural levees, river flood plains, flat terrace land, and distributary levees are converted to productive cropland in many of the world's major river deltas. In addition, large areas of land are reclaimed from natural swamp or marsh conditions and converted into productive wet and dry crop fields.

Classification

Because of the broad spectrum of environmental conditions, a classification of riverine environments is necessary to provide a basis for planning operations and facilitating discussion. The spectrum has been divided into Type I, Type II, and Type III environment categories. These environments generally affect the extent of waterborne operations in riverine operations, with waterborne operations increasing in significance as the categories progress from Type I to Type III.

Type I. This is the least significant type of riverine environment. Operations are conducted according to established procedures with only minor modifications. To obtain intelligence and deny the enemy use of the waterways, watercraft will be required for extensive patrolling of rivers.

Waterways—A Type I environment contains only minor rivers, usually not navigable by medium or deep draft boats except in their lower reaches, but too deep to be forded without difficulty. As a result, the waterways are primarily obstacles as opposed to LOC.

Watercraft—Only small, shallow draft boats can be used in the Type I environment. The rigid raiding craft and combat rubber raiding craft organic to the MEU(SOC) are ideal boats for use in this environment. The MAGTF's AAVs can be used extensively where conditions permit. In addition, small boats can be procured locally for use in this environment.

Type II. Riverine operations will be essentially normal, but the waterways will be exploited significantly. Waterborne operations will augment or support land operations whenever advantageous. Major waterways permit the use of larger watercraft that can be employed in tactical and logistical operations. Sufficient dry land areas exist to permit normal siting of ground force installations.

Waterways—A Type II environment contains one or more major rivers and may have numerous smaller streams, canals, and paddies. These waterways may present serious obstacles, but may also be useful as LOC.

Watercraft—This environment permits extensive use of AAVs. Typically, amphibious landing craft and modified local craft that are larger than craft organic to the MAGTF are used for operational support. Normally, these boats will not be manned by Marines, but will require crews and support from the Navy or indigenous sources.

Type III. This environment will affect MAGTF operations significantly. Waterways must be exploited to exercise control over the area of responsibility. Extensive support by Navy elements will be required. The unavailability of land sites for installations and the possible limitations of wheeled and tracked vehicles are major considerations in planning operations in this environment. Facilities for C2, combat support, and CSS must be waterborne. Helicopters will play a major role in transport of personnel and logistics.

Waterways—A Type III environment is dominated by water. There may be several major waterways in the area in addition to an extensive network of lesser waterways, canals, and irrigation ditches. In tropical and subtropical areas, the banks may be covered with a dense growth that precludes visibility inland from the water. The generally flat terrain and lush vegetation severely limit ground observation. Waterways are the predominant LOC and usable roads are scarce. Cross-country mobility is drastically curtailed, and suitable land area for command, control, fire support, logistics, and air installations frequently is not available.

Watercraft—This environment will accommodate watercraft from small local craft to ships the size of an LSD or LST. Barges can be used as floating helicopter pads. AAVs can be used selectively; however, they are not suited to long-distance water movement against the currents and have limited mobility through soft paddies and swamps.

Effects on Operations

Each riverine area is different. Even within a given riverine area, the effect of the environment on operations will vary with seasonal changes in rainfall, temperature, and other climatic conditions. An area trafficable to tracked and even wheeled vehicles in the dry season may be nearly impassable to foot troops in the wet season. Tactics to be employed will vary according to the nature, armament, and effectiveness of the enemy. Nevertheless, the C2, command relationships, intelligence, logistics, and mobility principles for the conduct of successful riverine operations will remain valid in all riverine areas.

Command and Control. Maximum use of ship-based command facilities and AAV command vehicles will be essential in a riverine environment. The lack of adequate hardstand and the general absence of roads will limit the use of wheeled vehicles containing CP equipment and communications facilities. CP displacements will normally be by helicopter or boat. Ground OPs will be of little use and FACs, NGF spotters, and artillery FOs will frequently be unable to control fire missions from the ground because flat terrain and lush vegetation will severely restrict ground observation. Commanders at battalion level and above must consider the employment of alternative platforms to observe and control maneuver and employment of supporting arms.

Command Relationships. Task organization within the MAGTF for riverine operations will emphasize the use of attachment and DS.

Intelligence. Waterways assume great importance in intelligence planning. Since the enemy will normally use the waterways as natural highways and LOC, the study of waterway traffic patterns will frequently reveal enemy troop movements, logistic routes and installations, and communications systems. In areas subject to saline invasion, the location of fresh water springs becomes important. Accurate intelligence of hydrographic conditions must include—

- Width and depth of waterways at high and low tides.
- Shape and composition of river and canal banks.
- Direction and velocity of currents and effects of tide on currents.
- Presence of sandbars or manmade obstacles in waterways.

- Under-bridge clearance for boat traffic at high and low tides.
- Points of ingress and egress suitable for use by AAVs.
- Accurate tidetables.

Logistics. Land suitable for logistic installations will be virtually nonexistent, because the civil populace will normally use such dry land as exists. Because of the constraints on positioning logistic support forward, maximum use of ship-based logistic installations and/or helicopter support may be mandatory to minimize the adverse effects of environment on the sustainability of the MAGTF. The lack of adequate road networks will require dependence on a combination of helicopter and watercraft transportation for most logistic movements. While transportation over waterways will normally be more economical and efficient for movement of large quantities of supplies, helicopter support must be maintained for support of units operating in areas difficult to reach by watercraft. These challenges must be adequately addressed since AAVs are maintenance and supply intensive assets that will not operate effectively for long periods without the required logistic support.

Mobility. Foot mobility is impeded by the unstable soils, the generally soggy nature of the terrain, and the presence of numerous waterways that are obstacles to infantry. In addition, high temperatures and humidity can limit the load-carrying capability of the individual Marine and cause slow movement rates. The lack of an adequate road network and the poor trafficability of soils also severely limit the use of wheeled and tracked vehicles. AAVs will be less susceptible to running aground than conventional watercraft. Sandbars and shallow water with a firm bottom may enable AAVs to move along the riverbed at relatively high speed.

Concept of Operations

Operations in a riverine environment require the employment of tactics and techniques that depart from standard operating procedures. The concept of operations for riverine operations are derived from joint doctrine for riverine operations, consideration of environmental effects, and lessons learned from combat experience. AAVs provide the mission commander with an excellent platform to conduct riverine operations. Because the AAV is amphibious, it provides flexibility and mobility in the riverine environment.

Flexibility

The AAV provides the MAGTF with an organic, armor-protected vehicle capable of a protracted riverine operation. The design characteristics allow the vehicle's effective operation on the open sea, in rough surf, and in riverine environments. The AAV provides the commander the flexibility to exploit the water or land. By moving the vehicle from solid land, to the riverbed, to the channel and back, the AAV can operate in a range of terrain, optimize speed, and increase endurance.

Mobility

The track, water-jet drive, and armor of the AAV are less vulnerable to underwater obstructions and debris than the traditional propellers, rudders, and light construction of most watercraft. The AAV's speed and range are significantly affected by the river current, water depth, and condition of the riverbed. Speed and range will increase when the AAV is swimming with the current but decrease when swimming against the current. In shallow water, the AAV may be able to operate at high speed in the water-tracks mode, which increases the vehicle's range of operation.

Missions

Depending on the elements of METT-T, AA units may conduct assault troop movement; direct fire support; riverine control, waterway patrol, interdiction, and surveillance; blocking force; resupply and evacuation; C2 support; and obstacle and mine clearance missions.

Assault Troop Movement

To ensure surprise, assault troop movements should be conducted at night and should take advantage of trafficable riverbeds and road networks along the axis of advance to maximize speed and shock and to conserve fuel. Vehicle ingress/egress points, potential obstacles, and mines along the river should be identified. If suitable exits from the river cannot be located, the embarked Marines can be off loaded along the bank in shallow water or over the bow onto the bank if conditions permit.

Direct Fire Support

The firepower of the AAV's MK-19 and M2 machine guns, along with its smoke-generating capabilities and low silhouette in the water, enable AAV units to provide effective direct fire in support of assault operations ashore, other elements of the MAGTF or riverine assault squadron afloat. The MK-19 is extremely effective against ground forces. The MK-19 provides an excellent overhead burst effect in forested areas around rivers. However, close coordination of supporting fires is critical to preclude friendly casualties, because visibility on the shore can be severely limited due to vegetation.

Riverine Control, Waterway Patrol, Interdiction, and Surveillance

AA units operating with or without supporting infantry may be employed to destroy enemy naval and land forces operating in their assigned zone of action. Working in cooperation with air/land forces and the riverine assault squadron, AA units can suppress enemy commerce, protect vital

river and sea LOC, and assist in establishing local military or civil authority. AAVs can be effectively employed from ships and shore patrol bases and can actively participate in the security and defense of land and floating bases.

Blocking Force

AAVs operating afloat in shallow water or ashore may provide a significant capability to prevent the escape of hostile forces along waterways. AAVs may be employed as a blocking force in waters too narrow or shallow for the employment of naval craft.

Resupply and Evacuation

With the AAVP7A1's 10,000-pound cargo capacity or ability to carry two 500-gallon fuel bladders and associated pump and hoses, AA units can support many of the MAGTF's CSS efforts. Outfitted with the litter kit, the AAV can transport six litter cases and a corpsman. AAVR7A1s can recover mired AAVs, other wheeled and track vehicles, and beached or grounded watercraft.

Command and Control Support

The AAVC7Al is capable of providing a highly mobile C2 asset in support of the MAGTF. The vehicle, along with other AAVs, can provide direct communication and retransmit capabilities.

Obstacles and Mine Clearance

The AAVP7Al, equipped with the MK-154 line charge, is the primary asset organic to the AA battalion for mine clearance ashore and afloat. AAVs can also support the removal of obstacles using grappling hooks, towropes or the recovery winch on the AAVR7A1.

Command Relationships

When Navy and Marine forces conduct riverine operations, a mobile riverine force will be formed. When riverine forces are introduced into an operating area through an amphibious operation or when riverine operations are conducted as an adjunct to an amphibious operation, the command relationships established in JP 3-02 will apply until termination of the amphibious operation. The CATF will normally establish a mobile riverine force (MRF) as a subordinate element of the ATF to provide for unity of command of riverine operations.

Mobile Riverine Force

At a minimum, an MRF will include a commander, a MAGTF, and a Navy force. The MAGTF, whether a MEF, MEU or special purpose MAGTF will include a balanced force of maneuver and support elements, including aviation elements. The riverine Navy force will normally include landing craft or watercraft organized into one or more riverine assault squadrons, ships, and craft comprising a riverine base element, as well as Navy aviation units and CSSEs. The commander of the MRF, designated in the initiating directive, will form an integrated staff based on the composition of the forces and the character of the mission assigned. If also serving as commander of a component force, the MRF commander may form a staff by designating members of the staffs of component commands.

Unity of Command

To unify the command in riverine operations, the MRF commander exercises OPCON of assigned forces through subordinate commanders and/or through the commanders formed for specific operations. The AA unit commander performs duties as a special staff officer to the MRF commander.

Subordinate Task Organizations

If only a segment of the MRF is required to accomplish a specific operation, the MRF commander may elect to form a subordinate organization. The MRF commander will designate a commander of the subordinate task organization, assign Marine Corps and Navy forces, prescribe responsibility for combat support and logistic support, and assign specific missions to the force. The commander of the subordinate task organization will exercise OPCON of assigned forces.

Organization Fundamentals

Preferably, a section of three AAVs is the smallest unit capable of independent riverine operations. Operating from a centrally located AA platoon BP, the AA section can support a variety of missions over a greater area. When an AA company is in support of the MAGTF, the AA company may be assigned an AO. In this situation, the AA company commander will conduct and coordinate operations among the AA platoon BPs and patrol areas. In addition, the AA company commander will coordinate the required unit resupply, recovery, maintenance, and refueling of with the CSSE.

Plan of Attack

The plan of attack for a riverine assault operation includes a scheme of maneuver, landing/assault plan, and a fire support plan. The landing assault plan is developed to support the scheme of maneuver and the fire support plan. Waterborne and helicopter borne movement plans are developed to support the landing/assault plan.

Control Measures

For riverine operations, the following control measures will be useful:

- Routes of advance should be named and prescribed for waterborne movements.
- Start point (SP) and checkpoints should be at easily identifiable locations along the waterways to help control and report progress of waterborne movements.

- H-hour for landing of the first waterborne wave should be designated to simplify coordination of scheduled fire support and to regulate waterborne movement.
- River landing sites should be identified by color; river-landing points within a site should be numbered.

A reference system for identifying terrain locations (e.g., checkpoint, thrust line) should be employed. To be effective, identical reference systems must be used by Marine Corps and Navy units, and the meaning of such reference points must be intelligible to participating fire support and air agencies. The generally flat terrain may require that waterway junctions or other terrain features identifiable from air and ground be used as the principal reference points.

Movement Techniques

AAVs should be positioned to cover strategic locations along waterways during the conduct of riverine operations, waterway patrols, as well as interdiction and surveillance operations. Because of its low water speed, the AAV should be position to allow maximum travel with the current. When this is not possible, a review of the river's hydrography may indicate areas where the AAV may travel in the track mode. Areas of shallow water with less than 68 inches depth should be identified and charted in trafficability analysis studies. Positions should allow good fields of fire and natural or manmade obstacles to channelize the enemy into kill zones. AAVs should be camouflaged along the riverbanks or on sandbars to conserve fuel and provide a stable platform for employing the AAV's weapon system. Natural camouflage should be used because it will help mask the vehicle's thermal signature at night. Night vision goggles and sensors/ground surveillance radar should be used to enhance the early detection of enemy activity. Once contact is made, illumination may be requested or the vehicle's searchlights used to illuminate suspicious watercraft for boarding and/or destruction.

Tactics

It is best to employ AAV units at night in conjunction with observation craft or helicopters equipped with forward-looking IR. AAVs will generally operate with two elements. The first element or point usually consists of one-third of the force. For a section, the point is usually one AAV; for a platoon, the point is a section of three AAVs. The point generally travels 200 to 500 meters forward of the second element or main body that consists of the remaining two-thirds of the force. Since the main body comprises the bulk of the combat power, the main body must be close enough to support the lead element by fire but not close enough to become decisively engaged or ambushed.

The primary mission of the point is to provide security and identify the best route along the axis of advance. The point will search for signs of the enemy and will identify obstacles to navigation. In the event of enemy contact, the point will develop the situation. The main body will support the point by reinforcing landing infantry to envelop the enemy or suppress the enemy by fire to allow the point to disengage. In the event the point becomes mired, the main body can assist in a recovery effort. When operating along a wide waterway, units may travel along opposite shorelines. See figure 9-1 on page 9-10. Each unit will use a point and main body on its assigned shoreline during movement. At the same time, these units will be prepared to support by fire across the river if required.

Combat Service Support Employment

The principles and fundamentals of logistics, operational logistics, and CSS remain valid in the riverine environment. However, the nature of the terrain and the type and duration of operations being supported will place greater demands on organic CSS capabilities of MAGTF elements and the CSSE. AAV units can help alleviate the MAGTF's CSS burden in Type I and II riverine environments. However, AAVs in the Type III

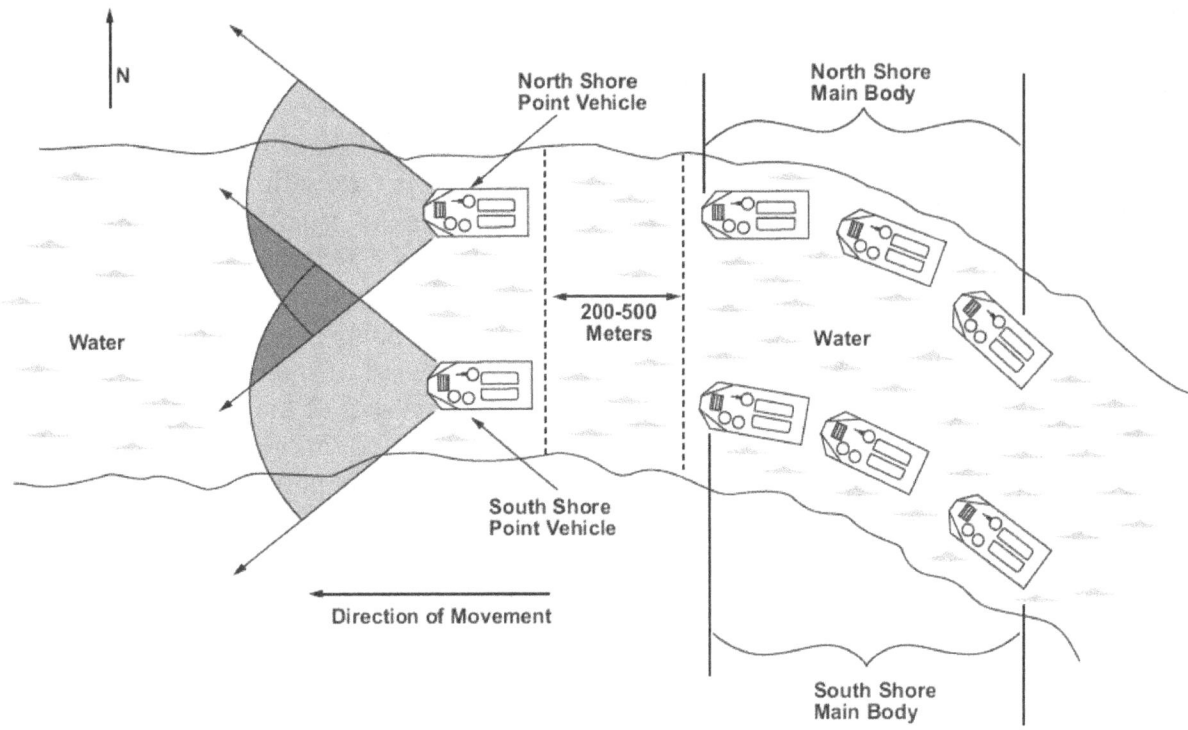

Figure 9-1. AAVs Moving on Opposite Shorelines.

environment require the widest variation from normal CSS supply and maintenance techniques because of strong river currents, marshy areas, and AAVs' unsuitability to transit long distances in the water.

Variations in Techniques

Storage and maintenance space will be at a premium, whether the riverine base is on land or afloat. Space in the shallow-draft ships and craft used to form mobile riverine bases is always limited and must be used with maximum efficiency. The MAGTF, including the AA unit and supporting Navy boat elements deployed in forward areas, will require resupply of many common items such as ammunition, rations, and water. For these reasons, logistics/CSS operations of the MAGTF and Navy components of the riverine force must be coordinated and integrated to an unusual degree. The following situations require

variations in logistic/CSS techniques for AAVs in riverine operations:

● Increased decentralization in execution of CSS tasks, requiring a greater degree of task-organization and attachment of specific CSSE assets to the supported units for specific missions.
● Lack of suitable sites for logistic/CSS installations.
● Increased maintenance demand required by the effects of climate and terrain (e.g., mud, sand, vegetation, salt water in lower delta areas).
● Absence of roads and the lack of suitable land sites for logistic/CSS installations.

Supply

Careful planning can minimize the supply challenges for embarked Marines and AAVs in riverine operations by ensuring prescribed loads, storage sites, distribution, and supplies are mission-based.

Prescribed Loads. The prescribed load for the individual Marine is a concern in a riverine environment because of the difficulty with foot mobility. To keep the prescribed load to the absolute minimum necessary to accomplish the mission, the infantry unit commander will often plan to have extra ammunition, rations, and water carried on the AAVs operating in the forward areas or have helicopters resupply as necessary. The AA unit commanders can expect to be tasked in a combat and CSS role for the same mission

Storage Sites. In a Type III environment, MAGTF supplies will likely be maintained aboard support ships. One ship might be capable of providing support to more than one area of responsibility by moving from place to place.

Distribution. Unit distribution is the preferred technique for units deployed on waterways. Normally, helicopters are used for this task when units are operating away from the waterways, but boats should be used for routine resupply missions along waterways. AA units will normally be the recipients of resupply and not the supplier, but will be used to transport supplies if necessary.

Class III Supply. Aboard ships, storage of class III POL will be required in helicopter-transportable containers that are suitable for use ashore. However, other means are available, such as the 500-gallon collapsible rubber drum and the 900-gallon six containers together (modular system) for transport by landing craft and helicopter or the 500-gallon version for transport by the AAV. The AAVP7Al can transport two 500-gallon bladders with hose and pump unit. Required greases, lubricants, and preservatives can be stored in their standard packages. Measures must be taken to reduce spillage of class III supplies and decrease the danger of fire.

Maintenance

Organizational and intermediate maintenance performed by AAV crews and organic MCTs requires unique techniques in a riverine environment.

Organizational Maintenance. Maintenance performed at the first and second echelon will be vital because the severe climate and likelihood of frequent immersion of equipment demand the execution of a rigorous PM program. Maintenance support beyond the organic capabilities of the AA unit is complicated by limited mobility and the isolation of deployed units from CSS installations and maintenance facilities.

Intermediate Maintenance. Organic MCTs should be employed to replace components on inoperable AAVs. When land-based, field maintenance units will use T/E tools and equipment. When based on ships, T/E equipment must be adapted to the establishment of integrated floating workshops on well decks.

Transportation

AAVs offer commanders a greater degree of flexibility by being the single transportation mode with the greatest utility or versatility. AAV crews can expect to be employed in a variety of transportation tasks, to include retrieval. The AAV's towing capability will likely be used extensively to retrieve grounded or inoperable water and land vehicles. AAV MCT may require the use of Navy/Marine boat assets to reach disabled AAVs and to support maintenance and logistical requirements.

River Crossing Operations

The purpose of a river crossing operation is to project combat power across a water obstacle to accomplish a mission. The river crossing permits the force to overcome an obstacle quickly and continue advancing to destroy the enemy. Specific procedures and equipment required to cross the water obstacle that prevents normal ground maneuver will be based on the size and composition of the obstacle and the enemy situation. Although mech infantry is mounted in AAVs and possesses an amphibious capability, the mech force will require engineering assistance to cross rivers. River crossing procedures are covered in detail in MCWP 3-17.1, *River Crossing Operations*.

Planning Factors

River crossings are difficult to plan and require an intimate knowledge by MAGTF planners and AA unit commanders to execute. In addition to knowing riverine crossing factors, units conducting this operation must plan and rehearse, because units can become vulnerable when engaged in river crossings.

Bridgehead Establishment

A bridgehead is the area on the hostile side of the river that is seized and secured by the assault elements of the LF. The area should accommodate and facilitate maneuver of the crossing forces without congestion, provide protection for the crossing of the remainder of the force, and provide a base for future LF operations. Concurrent with the development of a scheme of maneuver, the commander should consider the extent of the bridgehead on the far shore. In many ways, the planning considerations encountered during this phase (and therefore the operating procedures by AAV crews) parallel those in planning and executing the seizure of a beachhead in an amphibious operation. However, there is one major difference. The beachhead usually includes the force objectives, and the amphibious operation may be terminated when the beachhead has been secured. In a river crossing, however, it would be a coincidence if the force objectives were within the bridgehead.

The crossing is a means to continue the attack. A crossing area is that portion along a river that contains bridge and raft sites, the assault crossing sites required to secure the bridge and raft sites, and the surrounding terrain that is subject to the effects of enemy fires concentrated at the crossing sites. A crossing front is the length of the river line in a unit's zone of action. Crossing sites are the locations where bridge, raft, and assault crossings can be made within a crossing front.

Reconnaissance

The AA unit commander or a designated representative should be assigned to the reconnaissance party that conducts a physical reconnaissance of potential crossing sites. Based on an analysis of the enemy situation, a separate security element may be assigned to the reconnaissance party. If the likelihood of enemy contact is significant, the security element may precede the reconnaissance party and remain at the site(s) until the main party arrives.

The following resources can be used to narrow the choice of potential sites before the final selection is made through an onsite visit:

- Maps, nautical charts, and/or aerial photography.
- Aerial reconnaissance (helicopter preferred if not too risky).
- Information from indigenous personnel.

Assembly Areas

The assembly area is used to conduct prewater operations checks before the river crossing to minimize congestion and delays at the entry points. Time spent in the assembly area should be minimized for security purposes. When selecting an assembly area, the AA unit commander should determine if the area—

- Is large enough to allow for tactical dispersion.
- Offers concealment.
- Is close enough to the crossing site to allow for responsive reaction in case of a surprise attack on the crossing elements, but far enough away to be safe from indirect fire on the crossing site.

Approaches to the River

As many approaches as practicable should be considered based on the standard METT-T criteria. By approaching from many avenues, the mech force commander is better able to conceal the exact point (or points) of crossing from the enemy for as long as possible. This technique also gives the commander the opportunity to deceive the enemy by a feint river crossing to draw the enemy away from the intended point(s) of crossing. The commander can also disperse the force and maintain the flexibility of selecting from a multiple of potential crossing sites.

Entry/Exit Points

AA unit commanders will advise the mech force commander on the suitability of entry and exit points when AAVs will be used to traverse the river. The unit commander must consider the degree of slope and soil composition of the riverbanks because unsuitable bank conditions can restrict river crossings.

Hydrography

The navigability of many rivers can be estimated based on existing charts; however, the only way to determine for sure is from onsite examination. Hydrographic information can be obtained from a combination of sources ranging from aerial over flights to underwater swimmers' reports. Composition of the river bottom is essential hydrographical information for planning AAV crossings to determine if the bottom is firm enough to prevent the vehicles from getting mired.

Current

The effects of the current become key planning factors when the water depth is great enough to cause the vehicles to float, a floating bridge is an option or a precise landing site is essential to the success of the mission. Greater care is needed in calculating the speed and angle of travel when the river is wider and current is stronger. A strong current may necessitate changing the entry point

to a site upstream from the chosen landing site. MCWP 3-17.1 provides detailed guidance on calculating drift due to current and determining offset angles for crossing swift flowing rivers.

Fire Support

Planned fire support during a river crossing provides cover for the mech force during the vulnerable period while it has elements in the water. Fire support planning also compensates for the fact that the river will split the mech force so elements on each side will not be able to reinforce one another in case of a counterattack.

Fire support should be planned and directed to limit damage to exit points from the river. The use of heavy ordnance (i.e., 500-pound bombs from aircraft) should be used inland away from the landing sites.

Extensive use of helicopters or other aircraft as aerial observation platforms for FOs, FACs, and NGF spotters should also be planned because flat terrain and dense vegetation associated with rivers frequently restrict ground observation.

Ground Security

Because a unit crossing a river is extremely vulnerable, prudent security precautions must be taken to protect the unit. The far side must be secured. Until troops and equipment are actually on the far side to provide security for the crossing force, supporting arms will be the primary means of achieving security and isolating the crossing sites. AAV7A1s serve as key elements in the initial security force for the far side of the river.

Formation and Speed

While the planning strategy should be to cross at as many points as terrain, enemy situation, and equipment availability will allow, often river crossings will be more toward the column formation because of the limitations of suitable crossing sites. The vehicles should hastily resume their land movement formation once the far shore is reached. Speed should be as fast as conditions will permit, but the same interval should be maintained between vehicles as on land for security purposes. If practical, river crossings should be conducted with the AA platoon on line.

Smoke

Smoke should be planned to provide concealment from an enemy observation and attack. Skillful use of smoke serves to confuse the enemy and may cause him to shift his fires to unimportant targets and to commit his reserves away from the main crossing. The highest responsible commander of the operation must control the use of area smoke. The area covered by the smoke should exceed that actually required for the preparation of the assault. Covering too small an area with smoke permits the enemy to mass air and artillery fires on likely crossing sites. The area covered by smoke should include several potential crossing sites, likely assembly sites, and suitable access roads. When wind conditions permit, AAVs may use their inherent smoke generation capabilities to intensify smoke density and effects at the crossing sites just before they land.

Types of Crossings

Hasty, deliberate, and retrograde are types of river crossing operations.

Hasty

To maintain the momentum of the attack, the attacker makes a hasty crossing whenever the situation permits. A hasty crossing, which is the preferred method of river crossing, uses readily available crossing means without pausing to make elaborate preparations. Planning for the execution of a hasty river crossing is minimal.

Planning. A hasty river crossing is a decentralized operation. Predominantly, SOPs will guide units in preparing for a hasty crossing. The

commander should seize intact crossing sites or a crossing of opportunity.

Execution. After the commander determines that a river crossing will be required, the following sequence of events may transpire:

- Appropriate bridging or rafting assets are attached or placed under OPCON of the assaulting unit.
- The plan for the river crossing is included in the OPORD to preclude the requirement to stop and issue a separate order and a potential loss of momentum. If the situation changes, a fragmentary order is issued during the attack.
- Situation permitting, the commander may employ light armored infantry or helicopter-borne forces to secure crossing sites until the main body arrives. AA units may establish overwatch positions on the near side of the river to cover the crossing by infantry in AAVs.
- Infantry organic antiarmor weapons remain with the infantry to provide an antiarmor capability in the event of an enemy counterattack after objectives on the far side of the river are secured.
- Infantry in AAVs conduct a river crossing on as broad front as possible, which is usually dependent on the characteristics of the exit bank.
- As the assault wave crosses the river, bridging or rafting assets are employed to get tank and AT units across the river as soon as possible.
- As initial objectives are seized and the crossing site is protected from enemy direct fire, the remainder of the force crosses.
- The attack continues.

Deliberate

A deliberate crossing is required when a hasty crossing is not feasible, has failed or when offensive operations must be renewed at a river line.

Planning for the execution of a deliberate crossing requires detailed preparations.

Planning. Centralized command of the operation insures coordination of support and assault forces. Positive control of crossing elements increases the probability for success; however, there must be sufficient flexibility to permit adjustments in the plan and changes during execution. While AAVs are an excellent means for transporting assault forces across a river obstacle, tank and other wheeled units generally require bridges or ferries. When possible, tanks support the crossing by fire until bridging is available. Consideration should be given to crossing at night if security is a high-risk concern. A deception plan should also be considered to prevent the enemy from determining the actual crossing site. In addition to Marine Corps bridging assets, additional assets may be required from the US Army or allied nations. Limited bridging assets may be found in tank battalions and combat engineer battalions, with larger bridges found in the bridge company, engineer support battalion.

Detailed planning is required to ensure that forces are aligned properly when crossing begins. Planning must also include traffic control measures, assembly areas for bridging assets, and dispersed holding areas for forces waiting to cross. Exit point objectives are planned for the mech force. RPs across the river are selected, as are bridgehead objectives (areas on the hostile side of the river to be seized and secured by LF assault elements). In addition, sites for artillery, mortars, LAAD, and CSS units must be selected. Higher headquarters will inform the AA unit commander of the friendly forces' location on the far side of the river.

Execution. The deliberate river crossing is conducted in the following phases:

- Advance to the river—The advance to the river can begin at varying distances from the river and is normally started beyond the beginning of the crossing area. Ideally, the movement into the crossing area and the handoff of the control to the crossing force commander should be conducted rapidly to deny the enemy time to determine the location of the crossing sites. The attack will normally be led by tanks, which will move into overwatching positions along with long-range antiarmor weapons. Mech infantry forces will conduct the assault crossing, rapidly followed by bridging or rafting units. The MTF commander must establish a control group to coordinate the arrival, movement, and departure of units at the crossing sites.

- Assault crossing—For AA units the actual assault is conducted in a manner identical, or at least similar, to the hasty crossing. The actions taken by the AAVs resemble an amphibious landing with tanks, long-range antiarmor weapons, and/or heavy machine guns providing support from overwatch positions. Tanks, other combat support forces, and then the CSS units rapidly follow the mech infantry.

- Advance from the exit bank—The advance from the exit bank phase extends from the RP/line to the bridgehead objectives. This phase resembles a normal attack and may be characterized by movement to contact techniques, hasty attacks, and deliberate attacks on intermediate objectives.

- Securing the bridgehead—This action will also mirror other land offensive operations in terms of how AAVs are employed. Assaulting forces will lead the attack and continue beyond the RP to seize bridgehead objectives and intermediate objectives en route, following forces will provide overwatch direct and indirect fires, and CSS units will regroup to perform their normal support functions.

Retrograde

Retrograde river crossings are conducted when a force is to be employed elsewhere, the operation no longer promises success, or the purpose of the ongoing operation has been achieved. In many cases, retrograde operations will be conducted under enemy pressure.

The following are common characteristics of a retrograde crossing situation:

- Existing bridges or other crossing sites will be intact and available to the retrograde force to speed the crossing.
- Relative combat power will favor the enemy.
- Enemy commander will have a maneuver advantage.
- C2 will be more difficult for the crossing force.

Enemy Actions. Normally, the enemy's offensive operations will force a retrograde crossing. The enemy usually has a significant river crossing capability and may attempt hasty crossings to envelop the retrograding force. When the enemy knows the location of existing crossing sites and the vulnerability of the retrograding forces during the crossing, he can also conduct artillery strikes on the entry side and air strikes on the crossing sites.

Planning Considerations. RPs are used on both sides of the river. The retrograde is conducted as a delay; however, in the final phase of the crossing, mech infantry will control the final delay positions while rafts and bridging assets are withdrawn and tanks and TOWs occupy overwatching positions on the exit side of the river. When the mech infantry withdraws and swims the river, overwatching forces cover them with indirect and direct fires. LAR units may provide a screen and cross the river last.

Urbanized Terrain Operations

MOUT are conducted in areas such as cities, towns, villages, and concentrations of industrial installations. Because these areas are increasing in number and size throughout the world, tactics and techniques of fighting in urbanized areas are becoming increasingly important.

When planning MOUT, the attacking commander must assess the effect of operations on the civilian population.

Urbanized areas limit fields of fire and observation but afford dismounted infantry excellent cover and concealment in combat. Furthermore, urbanized terrain yields restrictions on maneuver but increases opportunities for infiltration and bypassing. Close quarter fighting often increases vulnerability of vehicles to attack at short range. That, coupled with the presence and concern for civilian population, may significantly restrict tactical operations. In addition, fratricide is of greater risk due to the close proximity of friendly forces. C2 and decentralized actions are often limited by range in urbanized areas. Combat operations will likely be fought in three dimensions: at street level; on rooftops or in buildings; and underground in subways, basements, and sewer systems.

Built-up structures make strong defensive positions. Additionally, the operational tempo is slow and the attacker requires a disproportionately high number of combat forces. An obstacle to movement, the built-up areas cannot be bypassed easily but can delay operations, forcing the attacker into a time-consuming attack. The rubble and debris caused by fires can make the area impassable and separate units.

Types of Urbanized Terrain

While mech forces have been successfully employed in strip areas and small villages, towns and large cities may require dismounted forces in a support-by-fire role. The following types of urban terrain present challenges and tactical opportunities:

- Strip areas are primarily urbanized areas along thoroughfares or depressions.
- Small villages are built-up areas with a population base of 1,000 to 3,000.

- Towns or small cities are built-up areas with a population base of 3,000 to 100,000.
- Large cities are areas with extensive structures and a population base greater than 100,000.

Hub Phenomenon

The hub phenomenon or built-up area is present in the four types of urban terrain. When in the defense, the hub may serve as the operational nerve center or strong point of enemy forces. If terrain, cover, and concealment permit, the hub should be bypassed. When bypassing the hub, mech forces must not expose their vulnerable flanks. Attacking and defeating the hub, which can be time consuming and risky, may be the only course of action when a suitable bypass route is not present. In this instance, the hub should be treated as an enemy center of gravity or strong point.

Offense

When conditions are not favorable for bypassing the hub, dismounted forces will be committed to attack, and AAV units will be tasked to support the mission.

Phases of Attack

The three phases of attack in a MOUT offensive are: isolate the enemy; seize a foothold; and advance and clearing.

Isolate the Enemy. The attacker isolates the point of attack by using supporting arms, seizing terrain features, and dominating the high probability avenues of approach. Enemy defensive tactics (e.g., obstacle plan) may prevent complete isolation. The attacker must secure positions to provide support for the assaulting forces. Feints and demonstrations can be conducted by using mech and dismounted troops to prevent the enemy from reinforcing the point of attack.

Seize a Foothold. The attacker must advance to the edge of a built-up area and seize a foothold. This position must deny the enemy observation and direct fire on the attacker's approaches to the town. While a flank attack or envelopment is preferred, a penetration may be required. Mobility, shock, and massed firepower are required to secure a foothold and rupture the defense.

Advance and Clearing. Dismounted forces must conduct the attack in a systematic building-by-building, block-by-block advance through the city. Tanks and AAVs can provide direct fire support, reduce enemy strong points, neutralize barricades, and suppress enemy positions. Within built-up areas, tanks and AAVs may be restricted because their main guns may not have the elevation or depression required to engage the enemy, and their mobility may be decreased. In addition, AAVs are more vulnerable than tanks to small arms fire and ATGMs.

Use of AAVs

Even with the same mobility restrictions as tanks in built-up areas, AAVs can provide valuable combat support and/or CSS roles for supported infantry. The AAV's mobility affords the infantry rapid movement across open areas during the seizure of a foothold when covered and concealed routes are not available. During the seizure of a foothold, AAVs can also provide direct fire from an overwatch position or act as a mobile command echelon. Mech infantry can provide rapid movement in cleared areas for reserve forces or serve as evacuation platforms for EPWs or civilians. In the CSS role, AAVs are easily equipped for medical evacuations. Additionally, the AAV can supply concentrated sustained direct fires in a combat support role.

Defense

In general, urbanized terrain favors the defender. Mech forces may use strip areas and small towns to create defensive strong points to block enemy advances. If preservation of a built-up area is required, the defense may assume the characteristics of a position defense organized in depth and supported by strong mobile forces. More commonly, AAVs and mech forces will be deployed outside the built-up area in reserve or to serve in a counterattack role.

Types

The defense is oriented around a strongly constructed building or groups of structures in key locations making up a strong point.

In Depth. Defense in depth is essential along with mutually supporting fortified positions. If forced from one position, the defender merely falls back to another.

Reserve. When defending in urbanized areas, success usually means having a centrally located reserve facilitated for easy movement to threatened areas.

Counterattack. Mech forces may be employed to counterattack the enemy on the outskirts of the urbanized area as he attempts to gain a foothold.

Mobile. A mobile defense could also be employed. Maneuver is used with organized fires along with terrain to seize the initiative from the enemy. Light forces in the MBA characterize a mobile defense, while the bulk of the force's combat power is held in reserve for a defensive counterattack. In addition, a mobile defense may be employed if the depth of the MBA is sufficient to draw in the enemy and maneuver against him.

Use of AAVs

AAVs will ordinarily be a vital part of the commander's defensive plan but not part of the security area that is established well forward of the built-up area. The MBA will likely contain the built-up area and will probably be critical to defending the urbanized area. Armored kill zones will be established forward, to the flanks, and within the MBA. Units will be assigned sectors, strong points, BPs or a combination of the three. In the MOUT defense, AAVs provide direct fire support from covered positions and rapid mobility for reaction forces or reinforcements to counter enemy preparations. Commanders should

use the direct fire capability without exposing the AAVs to antiarmor fire.

Desert Operations

When the character of the desert permits, the speed, firepower, and shock action of mech forces make them especially effective in desert operations. Desert terrain is usually advantageous for wide, rapid envelopments. Most desert terrain allows the commander broad freedom in developing a scheme of maneuver. Desert operations present maintenance challenges and unique tactical employment of AAV units.

Maintenance Considerations

While dust and sand are probably the greatest danger to the functions of the AAV in the desert, the following factors should also be considered:

- Lubrication must be the correct viscosity for the temperature, and exposed or semiexposed parts must be kept to a minimum.
- Track and suspension should be checked frequently.
- Air cleaners and precleaners must be inspected frequently and cleaned with compressed air because an AAV's engine depends on clean air for efficient operation.
- Filters must be used when refueling and the fuel inlet should be covered because sand can block a fuel line.
- Oil filters will require frequent replacement and spare oil cans and filler cans should be cleaned of sand before use because sand mixed with oil forms an abrasive paste.
- Cables should be protected with tape before insulation becomes worn because wind-blown sand will damage electrical harnesses over time.
- Radios should be cleaned frequently because sand and dust may affect communications equipment.
- Weapons should be cleaned frequently and excess lubrication minimized.

● Optics should be protected from blowing sand or abrasive wear.

Tactical Considerations

The following basic tactical considerations are applicable to mech forces:

● Desert operations are normally characterized by freedom of maneuver, long-range observation, and fires (often out to maximum effective range of direct-fire weapons, wide envelopments, extensive use of mines, and rapidly shifting fronts).

● Infantry often supports mech vehicles by providing local security, reducing mines and obstacles, engaging in close combat, and defending when the terrain permits.

● Sparse vegetation will offer minimal natural camouflage, resulting in an increased importance on techniques to counter poor overhead concealment.

● Heavy dust signature often compromises rapid vehicular movement and may decrease visibility within a column.

● Potential rapid and deep envelopments increase the necessity of all-around security for units, including those in rear areas.

● Good observation and limited natural camouflage improve the effectiveness of direct-fire weapons, but mirages or heat shimmer may lessen their accuracy.

Mountain and Cold Weather Operations

Mountain combat may involve operations in areas of high altitudes subject to extreme changes in weather, snow-covered slopes, few roads (most are narrow and twisting), and few communication centers. In general, operations in mountainous terrain retard or restrict maneuver, reduce the rate of effective fire, and make communications and resupply of armored units difficult. The employment of AAVs in mountain operations is limited by the vehicle's weight and bulk as well as the difficulty of supporting AAVs logistically in mountainous areas where roads are limited.

AAVs possess the ability to ascend grades of 60 percent; when combat-loaded, AAVs can negotiate 40 percent side slopes. However, these characteristics are intended to enable the vehicle to negotiate obstacles and climb hills close inshore. Limited employment of AAVs in mountain operations is possible to transport troops and equipment if care is exercised to ensure that the roads are passable. AAV brakes are not built to support rapid or frequent stops. To alleviate the problem of stalled vehicles on narrow roads that prohibit passage or turnaround of other vehicles, the commander should choose multiple routes and position maintenance personnel and recovery vehicles throughout the column. When conducting deep snow and extreme cold weather operations, the commander must consider mobility, logistics, and vehicular modifications to offset the characteristics of the environment when employing AAVs.

Mobility

The commander must consider mobility when employing AAVs in operations during deep snows, springtime, freezes, and ice crossings. These conditions can severely limit the use of mech forces to accomplish the mission and present both operational and/or safety challenges.

Deep Snow Operation

When employing AAVs in deep snow, the commander must consider the following:

● Generally, 3.5 pounds per square inch is the accepted ground pressure to assure floatation on deep snow. The ground pressure of a tank is 11.3 pounds per square inch, and the AAV's ground pressure is 7.5 pounds per square inch.

● Establishing definite rules for deep-snow operations is difficult because conditions vary. While experience in the various conditions is necessary to accurately predict snow trafficability, reconnaissance must be conducted to determine snow conditions.

- Most tracked vehicles are slowed by 24 to 29 inches of wet snow. Heavy tracked vehicles may negotiate fine, dry snow of 3- to 6-foot depths. The AAV can negotiate snow depths up to 35 inches with little difficulty.
- Normal speeds may be maintained after a packed snow trail has been formed by the passage of several vehicles, but proper driving techniques must be used to prevent vehicles from tracking and eventually becoming mired.
- Wet clinging snow has a tendency to accumulate on the tracks, suspension idler wheels, and sprockets, and may require occasional halts for removal.

Springtime

When employing AAVs in the springtime, commanders must consider the following:

- AAVs should be parked on high dry ground, unthawed snow, or brush/logs to prevent freezing. Vehicles mired in deep frozen mud or ice require special recovery techniques.
- Traction is poor when the active frost layer begins to melt and the ground becomes soft and marshy, but AAVs can penetrate the mud and find footing on the frost layer below.
- AAVs may sink deeper into the mud, become immobile or turn over as the season progresses and the frost layer thaws. To provide greater mobility under these conditions, vehicles should not follow in the tracks of preceding vehicles.
- Movement is possible in areas where permafrost is near the surface (i.e., on the shaded side of woods, on ground with a good moss cover, and on the shaded slopes of hills).
- Limited operation may be possible on crests where drainage is best when the valleys become impassable.

Freezes

Freezes frequently follow thaws and produce glare ice that makes roads practically impassable to tracked vehicles, particularly on slopes of 35 percent or greater. Proper driving techniques must be emphasized, because vehicles should follow in the same path of the lead vehicle. When employing AAVs during freezing conditions, commanders must consider the following:

- Conditions during the early freeze are much the same as those that occur in the spring.
- Ground thaws in the daytime and freezes at night.
- AAVs can experience high mobility when the frost comes to the surface and the ground is completely frozen.
- The frozen ground offers good traction and shallow snow does not effectively reduce the speed of the AAV.
- Frozen ruts are a hazard especially during early fall.
- Stream and lake ice cannot be used for crossing; however, AAVs can ford or swim across by breaking through the thin ice.
- Late freeze season offers the best opportunity for AAV employment in areas with few streams.

Ice Crossing

In addition to the guidance in MCRP 3-35.1A, *Small Unit Leader's Guide to Cold Weather Operations*, the commander must consider the following factors when employing AAVs for ice crossing:

- Lakes and streams may be crossed on the ice during the winter months if ice is of sufficient thickness and reasonable precaution is exercised.
- Crossing sites must be inspected for cracks, pressure ridges, and thin spots before placing vehicles on the ice.
- Extreme caution is necessary in crossing large streams and lakes early and late in the cold season. Table 9-1 lists the acceptable freshwater ice layer thickness for the AAVP7, AAVC7, and AAVR7. It also gives the safe minimum distance allowed between vehicles under those conditions. Measurements have been rounded off to the nearest one half. Risk ice measurements can be used for individual crossings with safety. The normal ice measurements are for repeated loadings.

Table 9-1. Freshwater Ice Crossing.

Load Units	Risk		Normal		Distance Between	
	centimeters	inches	centimeters	inches	meters	yards
AAVP7	45	17.20	65	25.50	70	76.50
AAVC7	40	15.50	49	19	39	43
AAVR7	40	13	48	19	30	33

Logistic Considerations

Weather conditions and terrain in arctic regions can make resupply and maintenance of AAVs difficult. Frequent operations checks, proper winterization of vehicles and an aggressive PM program will minimize breakdowns. AAVs deploying to the arctic must be winterized with the proper coolant, POL, and appropriate arctic grade fuel to be operational when they arrived.

When planning logistic support for cold weather operations, commanders should consider the following:

- Additional coolant, POL, and repair parts should be mobile-loaded with the AAV company combat train and travel with the lead elements. Additionally, bulk fuel in 500-gallon bladders may be carried inside AAVs or flown in by helicopter to minimize reliance on wheeled assets that may not be able to keep up with the assault elements.
- Normal and higher echelon maintenance can take five times longer than normal when temperatures fall to -40 degrees Fahrenheit, because equipment must be allowed to warm up before repairs can be accomplished.
- Bare hands performing maintenance in extreme cold will stick to cold metal. In a matter of seconds, hands in contact with fuel can be frozen because of super cooling due to evaporation.
- Vehicle starting and warmup time may take 2 hours in temperatures of -50 degrees Fahrenheit.

- Supplies of hot rations, water, clothing, lubricants, and oils are required for troops in arctic regions; warming tents are required to keep water and oil cans in a usable state.

Vehicular Considerations

When planning to operate amphibian vehicles in arctic conditions, the commander must consider the vehicle's suspension system, carbon monoxide hazard, main engine, batteries, winterization kit, winter visor kit, and fuel cells.

Suspension System

Wet snow and ice may become packed in the water jets and deflectors of amphibian vehicles, temporarily restricting or immobilizing them. Salt water does freeze and may cause problems with plenum operation or water jets if not exercised before and preceding water operation. Tracks may freeze to the ground in moderately cold weather, to the extent that tools may be required to extricate the vehicles if dunnage is not employed.

Carbon Monoxide Hazard

Intense cold, strong winds, and heavy snowfalls will require personnel to seek whatever shelter is available in arctic regions. The interior of the AAV offers warmth and protection from the elements when heaters are operational. Care should be exercised to ensure that persons seeking this shelter do not suffer carbon monoxide poisoning. The vehicle does not offer protection from the elements when the heaters cannot be operated. Personnel should avoid using the vehicle under these conditions as the vehicle interior can become colder than the outside temperature.

Main Engine

The greatest problem inherent in cold weather engine operation is lack of engine lubrication. Cold weather starting considerations for the AAV is as follows:

● A vehicle's engine should be properly lubricated and exercised frequently to prevent the power train from freezing.

● Towing attempts to start extremely cold vehicles easily damages frozen power trains and engines.

● Metal tow cables, final drives or push bars become brittle in extreme cold and may fail under shock loads.

Batteries

Battery power decreases rapidly during cold weather and batteries cannot be satisfactorily charged once the electrolyte temperature is less than 0 degrees Fahrenheit. Extended hours of darkness and low temperatures create increased demands on batteries and electrical systems. Batteries should be serviced and cleaned frequently and must be heated before recharge and use during cold weather.

Winterization Kit

The AAV winterization kit is designed to supply large quantities of fresh heated air to the personnel, cargo, and engine compartments. The kit may be used to heat a vehicle that has been idle for a long period or to maintain compartment temperature during periods when engines are not in operation.

Winter Visor Kit

The AAV visor kit is designed to protect the AAV driver from extended exposure to the cold.

The kit has a windshield wiper and a defroster. This kit is not to be used for water operations.

Fuel Cells

Fuel cells should be topped off with fuel regularly to avoid condensation in the cells. Frozen water in the fuel system, particularly the fuel filters, will cause fuel starvation.

Tactical Employment Considerations

Although the principles of tactics remain the same, they are affected by conditions peculiar to cold climates. The conditions require that the commander use techniques and procedures which may be considered inappropriate in temperate climates. AA units may be tasked with varied missions in response to the situations created by cold weather conditions.

Waterways in cold weather contingency areas provide excellent avenues of approach for AAVs but formidable obstacles for other units. These waterways must be secured for use by friendly forces, and the use of these waterways must be denied to enemy amphibious forces. Assigning these waterways to AAV units as a sector of defense or zone of action may be the best option available to commanders because the AAV's UGWS is an ideal weapons platform for this purpose. Adjacent land areas, such as narrow strips of the coast, could be included in the AAVs assigned sector/zone. ATGMs, infantry or other type units are representative of those that could be attached to the AAV unit for the assigned mission.

Since the movement of AAVs in cold weather contingency areas is generally restricted to roads and prepared surfaces by the mountainous terrain, the employment of AAVs in the assault is more restricted and therefore less desirable than in other environments. An AAV moving on a narrow plowed road within range of enemy antiarmor weapons is a target that is hard to protect. To avoid stalled vehicles on narrow roads that prohibit passage or turnaround of other vehicles, the commander should choose multiple routes and designate maintenance collection points off the road along the route of march. Terrain and trafficability studies may help minimize trafficability problems when employing AAVs.

If the terrain or enemy situation does not permit mech assault employment, the AAV can be assigned a mission to support the extensive logistic effort required to operate in cold weather. The AAVs can move supplies, ammunition, and equipment along prepared routes from rear logistic areas to unit supply points where specialized over-snow vehicles can handle transportation requirements for the infantry units.

Individual Equipment Considerations

The bulkiness of certain cold weather equipment can take up much of the interior space of AAVs and should be carried external to the AAV. The following equipment should be included for AAV crewmen operating in cold weather environments:

- Squad stove.
- Anticontact gloves.
- Insulated water can covers.
- Specialized clothing to include face masks.

CHAPTER 10. COMMUNICATIONS

Maintaining C2 of AAVs requires an effective means of communication within AA units and with supported and supporting organizations to send and receive instructions, control and coordinate movement and supporting fires, request CSS, and gather and distribute information. The AAV crew achieves these goals through various forms of communications.

Forms of Communications

Visual signals, radio, wire, and messenger methods of communications are available to AAV crews.

Visual Signals

Predominantly used by AAVs at the platoon and section level, visual signals can be hand and arm, flags, flashing light or pyrotechnics. These signals are particularly useful in the ship-to-shore movement. Section leaders transmit orders or information to the individual vehicles using hand and arm signals. Transmitting information by the hand and arm signals—

- Provides instantaneous transmission of commands to units within visual range.
- Does not emit an electronic signature.
- Does not impede net transmissions.

Radio

When visual communications cannot adequately support the mission, the primary method of communications is by internal and external radio transmissions.

Internal

AA units depend on voice radio to control their vehicles when the vehicles are closed up. In normal operations, the AA platoon uses the broadcast technique to pass orders to section leaders and other AAVs. In addition, the platoon and section leaders use the AA platoon command net to transmit fire commands to the unit. Vehicle commanders must limit their transmissions to the reporting of unusual situations. Radio discipline to limit transmissions must be strictly enforced because of the number of stations on the net and because the opposing forces may possess radio intercept and jamming capability. The AA battalion activates battalion command, battalion logistic, company command, platoon command, and other nets to provide administration and logistic requirements of each unit.

Battalion Command Net. The AA battalion commander uses the battalion command net for control. The battalion command net is guarded by the battalion command echelons, company commanders, the AA platoon commanders of H&S company, and the battalion logistic and recovery trains, when required.

Battalion Logistic Net. The battalion logistic net may be established for coordinating and reporting administration and logistic requests and reports.

Company Command Net. The AA company commander uses the company command net as a means of coordinating support and control of subordinate AA units. The company CP, platoon commanders, and AAV maintenance and recovery elements attached to or in support of the company normally enter this net.

Platoon Command Net. The platoon commander uses the platoon command net to direct the employment of AA sections. Vehicles within the platoon and units/elements attached or under the OPCON of the platoon commander activate and enter the platoon command net. With a minimum of 12 AAVs per platoon, radio discipline must be maintained to ensure that the net is available to support the mission.

Additional Nets. In addition to the command and logistic nets, AAV crews monitor their higher headquarters' command/tactical net and the net of the supported unit. If the platoon is attached to an infantry battalion and has been placed in DS of a company, the AAV platoon commander monitors the infantry battalion and supported rifle company tactical nets. In this situation the section leader monitors the AAV platoon command net and rifle platoon tactical net. Other nets to be monitored will be specified in unit SOPs or in the OPORD.

External

Radio communication requirements of the AA battalion, when operating subordinate to a MEF or a division, are dictated in the guard chart located in annex K of the higher command's OPORD. The S-6 officer is responsible for insuring that the battalion command and letter companies have the proper frequencies, net encryption keys, and battalion guard chart. External communication requirements are discussed in MCWP 3-40.3, *Communications and Information Systems.*

Wire

Wire provides a means of unsecured communication that does not radiate energy, which can be used by the enemy to determine a unit's location. However, wire only works in static situations and is time consuming to install and maintain. Extra care must be taken to ensure that tracked vehicles moving into and out of positions do not break wires.

Wire is used predominately in an AA battalion within the battalion CP to provide local telephone service. When the situation is sufficiently static, wire lines to higher headquarters and subordinate units will be installed. At the platoon and section level, wire may be used when the supported unit is in a static situation such as a defense or when movement has been halted for an extended period. In these situations, a net or loop circuit would connect the supporting vehicles on a single circuit. Dismounted infantry can also enter this circuit

Messenger

Messengers may be used in lieu of other means of communication or to supplement existing capabilities. Higher headquarters will direct external messenger service. Normally in static situations, internal messenger service is established to transit routine administration or logistic reports or requests. See MCWP 3-40.3 for additional information.

AAV Assets

Each variant of the AAV has specific communication assets. The AAVP7 communication assets are primarily for TACON of the AAV unit. The AAVC7 provides communications required for a headquarters unit.

AAVP7A1

Each AAVP7A1 comes equipped with two AN/VRC-89D SINCGARS radio suites. The AN/VRC-89D consists of two RT-1523 VHF radios. Each AN/VRC-89D is capable of transmitting one high power and one low power radio signal for a total of four radio nets per AAVP7A1. The SINCGARS family of radios has single-channel and frequency-hopping modes. In addition, it is capable of storing encryption-keying material internally.

The senior embarked Marine on each vehicle occupies the TC hatch located behind the driver's station. A combat vehicle commander (CVC) helmet permits the remote operation of radios and provides communications with crew members via an intercom. By using the remote box mounted next to the TC position, the operator can change frequencies rapidly to communicate over the four radio nets.

AAVC7A1

The primary headquarters communication asset the AA battalion possesses is the AAVC7A1. Equipped with VHF, HF, and UHF radios, the AAVC7A1 can be used as a mobile CP or an FSCC. These AAVs are maintained by the units within the AA battalion to ensure that the vehicles are operational and the communications systems will be ready for the using unit. The communications system in the AAVC7A1 contains the following radios:

- One AN/VRC-89D (consists one long-range radio and one short-range radio).
- One AN/PRC-104 radio set for HF communications.
- One AN/VRC-83 radio set for UHF communications.
- Two AN/VRC-92D SINCGARS VHF radio sets (each set consists of two long-range radios).

This communications suite provides the embarked unit with eight radios. The AAV crew is provided with an additional AN/VRC-89D for its communications needs.

AAVC7A1 Internal Layout

The AAVC7A1 is a highly capable C2 platform. Its communication system allows for tactical radio communications while remaining self-contained and highly mobile. The internal arrangement allows for seating of five radio operators to monitor nets and five staff personnel, as shown in figure 10-1.

The AAVC7A1 communications suite was designed to integrate the radios with the MIQ-115 intercom system. This intercom system, designed to work with the AAVC7A1 radio suite, allows the staff officers to communicate over any radio within the AAVC7A1 and with the AAV crewmen.

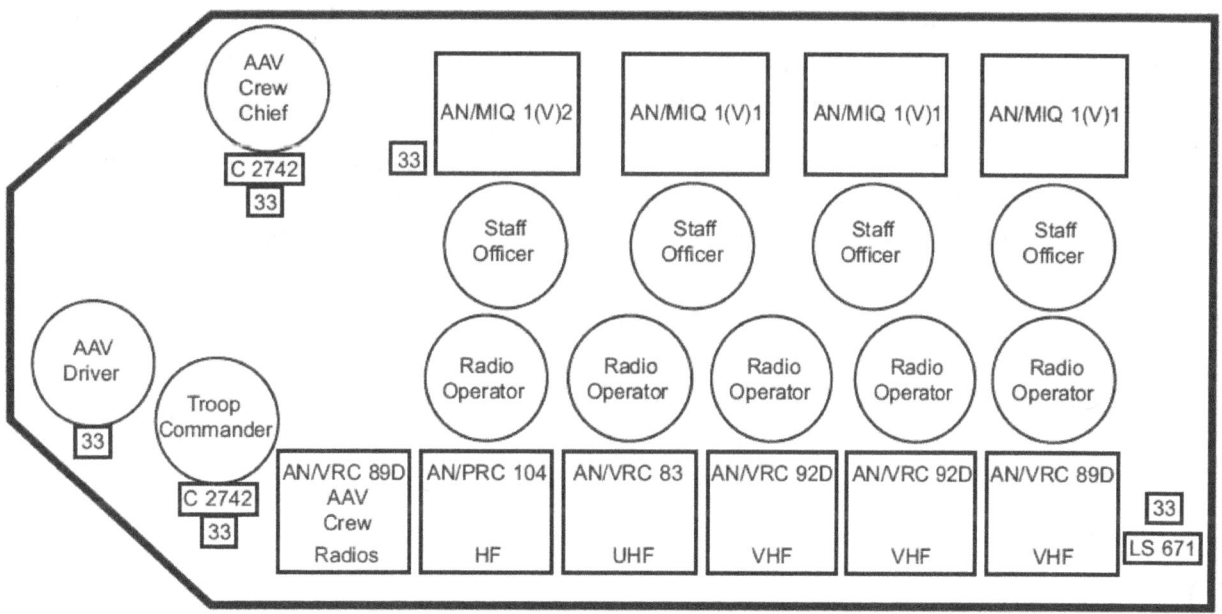

Figure 10-1. AAVC7A1 Layout.

NOTE: When operating in the SINCGARS radio single-channel mode, the intercom works normally; however, difficulties with the intercom may be experienced while operating at high power in the SINCGARS radio frequency-hopping mode.

AAVC7A1 Configured as a Combat Operations Center

When the AAVC7A1 is deployed as a combat operations center (COC) for an infantry unit, the communications and staff personnel of the using unit will use the radios. The AAVC7A1 will always be accompanied by an AAVP7A1 for support. The AAVC7A1 and AAVP7A1 comprise one command section. The crew of the AAVP7A1 has the ability to monitor the AA battalion nets with the vehicle's AN/VRC-89Ds.

When a stop is anticipated, the AAVC7A1 and AAVP7A1 can be configured to create a COC. For example, an AAVC7A1 and AAVP7A1 can be backed up to one another. The vehicles' ramps can be lowered, and a fly tent or covering can be thrown over the area in between the vehicles. This configuration will give the staff increased space, provide light discipline at night, and allow for a rapid displacement of the COC.

A battalion and higher-sized unit command should have two command sections for their use.

The unit using the AAVC7A1 may be required to monitor more radio nets than the AAVC7 and AAVP7 (section) is capable of monitoring. Several options will satisfy this requirement. As an option, one of the command sections can be used as a tactical echelon, and the second command section can be used as a main echelon. With the use of both echelon sections, less critical nets can be monitored from the main echelon. The main echelon can then pass only the necessary traffic to the tactical echelon.

As a second option, the using unit can use its organic communications assets in the mobile radio component vehicles to cover extra nets. Once the AAVC7A1 and AAVP7A1 are static, the nets from the MRC vehicles can be remoted into the COC. Adding extra radios to the AAVC7A1 is not recommended because the enemy can use the increased electromagnetic signature to detect the COC, and the extra signals can interfere with the radio signals already transmitting.

There is no standard utilization of radios or monitored nets in the AAVC7A1. The using unit will determine nets to monitor, personnel to man the nets, and staff in the AAVC7A1. The AAVC7 vehicle commander should conduct indepth coordination with the using unit to ensure successful deployment on the battlefield.

CHAPTER 11. SAFETY GUIDELINES

Effective safety requires trained and skilled AA crews, properly oriented passengers, and well-maintained vehicles. Many mishaps can be directly attributed to not following proper procedures and safety guidelines.

General Safety

The combination of heavy equipment, high mobility, limited observation, and waterborne maneuvers creates conditions that require strict adherence to instructions and SOPs concerning AA operations. Carelessness, recklessness, shortcuts, and inattention can result in serious injuries to personnel and damage to equipment. Personnel must be instructed, inspected, reminded, and corrected on a continuous basis about following proper procedures.

Responsibilities

Safety is the responsibility of all Marines. However, the troop leaders embarked on AAVs and AA unit leaders share specific responsibilities to ensure safe operations.

Embarked Troop Leaders

While aboard AAVs, the senior troop leader present is responsible for briefing embarked personnel on their responsibilities as passengers aboard AAVs. The senior AA representative present has the final decision if the safety of the AAV, crew or passengers is in question.

AA Unit Leaders

When AAVs are employed, the safety of embarked personnel and proper operation of vehicles falls on the senior AA representative present. This AA unit leader establishes effective C2 procedures and ensures the safety of personnel on and around the vehicles. The AA unit leader should be the primary advisor to supported infantry units on safety aspects of AA operations and mechanical operability of AAVs.

Crewmen

The crew chief is responsible for the performance of the AAV and the safety of its passengers and crew. The third crewman advises the crew chief of the situation and physical welfare of embarked troops. In an emergency, the third crewman is responsible for quelling panic and assisting troops in an orderly evacuation of the vehicle.

Vehicle Employment

The safety of crew and passengers embarked in amphibious vehicles is protected through strict adherence to the following guidelines:

- Smoking is not allowed on or in AAVs.
- Embarked troops must wear helmets and not ride topside.
- Troops on foot should give an AAV a wide berth, because the field of vision from a closed-up AAV is limited.
- Open personnel hatches must be secured with restraints when the AAV is moving, because unsecured open hatches can inadvertently close on a person's hands and head. Personnel riding in the AAV open-hatch area will not ride in the vehicle with chests extending above the hatch opening.
- Hatches must be closed and locked while the AAV is transiting through the surf zone.
- Front and rear ground guides must be used when vehicles are backing up or moving in congested areas, while troops are on the deck or during periods of reduced visibility.
- Personnel must stand clear of the ramp area when the ramp is being raised or lowered. In other than tactical situations, the vehicle's horn must be sounded three times before the ramp is raised or lowered. An inoperable ramp will be

held with a ramp jack, a sign indicating "ramp held by jack" will be placed on the back and inside of the vehicle, and a tow cable will be attached from the mooring cleats to the tow shackle.

- Plenums will be raised and lowered by a minimum of two personnel; if the plenum springs are bad, at least three personnel will raise and lower them. Personnel must ensure their fingers and toes are clear and that no personnel are inside the engine compartment before lowering the plenums.
- AAVs must never operate alone on land or in the water; a minimum of two vehicles will operate together.
- AAV must not be left with the engine running without an operator in the driver's seat.

Preventive Maintenance

AAVs require time for preventive and corrective maintenance. Preoperational, prewater, and post-operational checks and services are required at halt. Generally, a minimum of 1 hour of PM should be planned for every 7 hours of operation in the field. While performing PM, crewmen should be careful when dealing with hazardous material, handling engine and drivetrain covers, and moving on top of the vehicle.

Hazardous Materials

Personnel must take extra precautions or wear the correct personal protective equipment when dealing with hazardous materials (e.g., POL, hot radiator fluid, battery acid). Opening radiator caps when the fluid is hot can cause the fluid to spray, resulting in severe burns to personnel. Spilling or splashing battery acid can cause severe burns to skin and eyes.

Engine and Drivetrain Covers

Covers must be properly installed before AAVs are operated. Unsuspecting crew and passengers around uncovered lateral drive shafts or engines with missing panels can be severely injured.

Moving on Top of Vehicle

While working and moving around on top of vehicles, personnel must remain situationally aware, because many Marines have slipped or fallen off vehicles.

Operational Briefs

Before an operation, the senior AA unit leader will ensure AAV leaders, vehicle crew chiefs, and crewmen receive an operational briefing to include concept of operations, anticipated water/terrain conditions, a review of emergency and immediate action procedures, and safety precautions.

Passenger Orientation

At the beginning of each operation, the AAV vehicle commander will ensure that safety orientation classes are conducted for embarking units. The orientation should include vehicle employment and capabilities, emergency procedures, and specific training considerations.

Waterborne Safety

Safety in AAV water operations is paramount. Often embarked troops will have only limited experience in waterborne operations. AAV Marines conducting these operations must have a clear understanding of required equipment, operational requirements, safety criteria, water operating speeds and distances, emergency signals, and embarked troops' safety procedures. In addition, embarked troops must have a clear understanding of what their safety roles and responsibilities are when on AAVs in the water.

Required Equipment

Each AAV has personal and vehicle equipment that ensure safe operations while conducting water operations.

Personal

The AAV passengers and crew must be properly outfitted with their lifejackets, helmets, flak jackets, and weapons before the AA vehicle commander orders launch into the water.

Lifejackets. Lifejackets must receive an operational check before being worn, to include a serviceable carbon dioxide cartridge, light or chemical light, and whistle. Before launching, the AAV vehicle commander ensures embarked personnel wear lifejackets and secure them around the waist. Embarked personnel and crew will blow three puffs of air into their lifejacket before launching. AAV crewmen required to come topside while waterborne for line handling, transfer operations or rescue procedures will blow an additional two puffs of air into their lifejackets.

Helmet. While embarked in operating AAVs, personnel must wear their helmets (i.e., CVC or Kevlar).

Flak Jackets and 782 Gear. Embarked troops will wear the lifejacket under their flak jackets and 782 gear that will be worn loose enough to jettison without delay if required. Upon touching down, lifejackets can be removed and equipment fastened.

Weapons. During training and combat operations, troops will invert and put their weapons in condition 3 (i.e., magazine inserted, weapon on **safe**, and bolt forward on an empty chamber). When exiting the vehicle, troops will change their weapons to a condition 1.

Vehicle

Vehicles must have the following equipment on board before launching:

- One November flag.
- Two red and two white flares for night water operation.
- Two 50-foot towropes with spliced eyelets.
- Two serviceable boat hooks.
- First aid kit.

- Two chemical lights mounted on starboard cargo hatch handles.
- Ax mounted on the turret.
- Battle lantern or searchlight.

Operational Requirements

The following reports, checklists, and training must be completed before launching vehicles:

- Prewater operational checklists must be completed before vehicles enter water deep enough to float the vehicle.
- SUROBs must be completed before launching AAVs in the ocean to determine if surf conditions meet the minimum safety criteria.
- Waterborne vehicle orientation must be briefed to embarked personnel before the vehicle enters the water. The brief will include the proper use of the lifejacket, wearing of equipment, and weapons considerations. In addition, emergency procedures (e.g., transfer of troops, vehicle abandonment, man overboard, actions for sinking vehicles) will be explained and practiced.
- Personnel manifest of passengers and crewmen must be prepared before the AAV is launched. The manifest will include each embarked person's name, rank, and Social Security number. Passengers listed on the manifest must remain on board until the crew chief authorizes debarkation.
- Launch team inspections must be conducted before the AAV is launched. Supervised by a designated AA unit leader, the launch team ensures bilge pumps are operational and the AAV is watertight. In addition, the team inspects the vehicle's ramp and ensures the personnel hatch remains secured until the AAV reaches land.
- Swim qualifications for crewmen participating in AA water operations must be at least at the combat water survival 2 level.
- Surf survival training and qualification should be conducted on an annual basis.

Rescue Teams

The rescue teams (RTs) will be designated before splash; the RT vehicle number and location will be made known to all hands. This vehicle is the primary rescue vehicle if an AAV becomes disabled, although every vehicle is a potential rescue vehicle. The RT vehicle must be capable of receiving personnel from a disabled AAV, and will have a corpsman embarked.

Safety Criteria

AA unit leaders must have a good working knowledge of the AA safety criteria. The criteria reflect different standards for general training and combat conditions. Acceptable surf for general training is a combination of the factors of vehicle load, surf height, wave types, and breaker interval. The three load conditions are CL 10,000 lbs, TL 5,600 lbs, and CE no load. Refer to chapter 3, table 3-2 for maximum safe surf conditions.

Water Operating Speeds and Distances

AAV operations in the water can be especially challenging when many vehicles are operating at the same time in close proximity and/or in periods of limited visibility. Safe distances and speeds between AAVs must be observed. In addition, AAV crewmen must know the signals for AAVs in distress should their vehicle begin sinking or require assistance.

Speed Afloat

Maximum AAV speed afloat is 8.2 knots per hour at 2,800 RPM in calm conditions. Factors such as sea state, wind, current, and vehicle load greatly affect water speed. During daylight with unrestricted visibility, 50 meters or five AAV lengths should be kept between vehicles. During restricted visibility and at night, 50 meters or less should be kept between vehicles, depending on the limit of visibility.

Emergency Signals

The VHF radio is the primary method of emergency communications, but secondary methods of communications are also used for disabled and sinking vehicles.

Disabled Vehicles

During daylight, the November flag should be displayed from a vertical boat hook. At night, a searchlight or battle lantern should be turned on and pointed vertically. If the night signal fails, one white flare should be fired into the air.

Sinking Vehicles

During daylight, the November flag should be waved continuously or a red flare should be fired into the air. At night, a searchlight or battle lantern should be turned on and pointed vertically or a red flare should be fired into the air.

Embarked Troops

The time AAVs with embarked troops are waterborne should be limited because of the combined effect of heat, noise, fumes, seasickness, and claustrophobia. Ventilation in the troop compartment may prevent troop discomfort and sickness.

Land Safety

Once on land, collisions with other AAVs or vehicles often result in serious injuries or deaths. In addition, AAVs are not air-conditioned and can cause heat injury to crews or embarked troops if the right precautions are not followed. Safe operations of AAVs on land depend largely on the environment in which they are operating and crews' ability to adjust.

Crew Composition

A minimum of two qualified crewmen will be on board for land operations.

Operating Speeds

The AAV's safe operating speed over land is influenced by the following conditions:

- During daylight with unrestricted visibility in a congested area, near troops, equipment or AAV parks, the AAV should not exceed 5 miles per hour with ground guides.
- During daylight with unrestricted visibility in an uncongested area, the AAV should not exceed 35 miles per hour.
- When visibility is restricted by dust, fog, wooded areas, buildings or other AAVs, the AAV should operate at a speed slow enough to permit the vehicle to stop and move safely.

Operating Distances

The AAV's safe operating distance between vehicles is influenced by the following conditions:

- During daylight with unrestricted visibility, AAVs should maintain 50 meters or five lengths between vehicles.
- During restricted visibility and at night, AAVs should maintain 50 meters or the limit of visibility, whichever is less between vehicles.

Road Crossings

When AAVs cross hard surface roads (highways) during training exercises or administrative road marches, road guards must be positioned on both sides of the crossing site at a minimum of 100 yards on 55-mile per hour roads and 50 yards on 35-mile per hour roads. Road guards should wear reflective vests, carry flashlights or flares at night, and position themselves to safely stop traffic for the crossing AAVs.

Operational Environments

The AAV's safe operations over land can be influenced by unfamiliar climates and terrain.

Hot Weather

Because heat injuries are probable in closed vehicles, personnel must have proper ventilation and constant hydration in hot weather. Water cans should be filled at every opportunity, and vehicles must be frequently checked for leaks and overheating.

Desert

In addition to hot weather conditions, high dust conditions can reduce visibility significantly and affect AAV operations in desert terrain. Vehicle speeds and distances must be adjusted, because reduced visibility can cause drivers to misjudge distances between vehicles and increase the potential for vehicle collisions.

Jungle

In a jungle environment, obstacles can limit AAV movement to existing trails and roads.

Heavily Wooded

The AAV's visibility and maneuverability can be reduced in heavily wooded areas.

Mountainous

Steep inclines and declines in mountainous terrain can reduce speeds and maneuverability of vehicles. AAV drivers must keep the engine's RPM up to ensure that the hydraulic steering is not reduced.

Cold Weather/Arctic

AAVs must be properly ventilated during cold weather conditions because the use of vehicle heaters poses a risk of carbon monoxide poisoning to personnel inside the vehicles. Marines working with all-metal vehicles are at risk of hypothermia. In addition, AAVs can slide on icy surfaces, causing great risk to other vehicles and personnel on the ground.

Limited Visibility

During night operations when night vision devices are used, operating speeds and distances must be adjusted to compensate for reduced visibility. Rest time must be allotted for personnel using these devices, because night vision devices cause vision to quickly fatigue.

Other Safety Considerations

AAV vehicle commanders and embarked troop leaders must be aware of safety concerns in regards to weather, NBC operations, medical evacuation, lasers, UGWS, LMC, and onboard vehicle fires. AAVs have unique safety guidelines in these areas that should be reviewed.

Weather

Lightning, high winds, and heavy rains can pose hazards to personnel.

Lightning

During periods of lightning, personnel should stay off the vehicle top and away from antennas.

High Winds

Unsecured hatches are subject to closing or slamming rapidly during high wind conditions.

Heavy Rains

During and after heavy rains, the ground can become unstable and cause vehicles to slide, roll or get stuck.

Nuclear, Biological, and Chemical Operations

During NBC operations, AAV crewmen and embarked troops can experience reduced visibility and heat injuries.

Reduced Visibility

The wearing of the field protective mask reduces the crew and driver's visibility and makes communications more difficult. This may require operating the AAV at slower speeds.

Heat Injuries

The MOPP suit with the field protective mask increases the risk of heat injuries. If the AAV must operate with hatches closed, leaders must watch personnel closely for signs of heat exhaustion or heat stroke. Temperatures can become extremely hot inside the AAV for personnel in MOPP suits.

Medical Evacuation

Personnel should know the procedures for requesting emergency medical evacuation and preset the medical evacuation frequency on one radio in each vehicle before operations. A corpsman should always be present during any AAV operation.

Lasers

While conducting mech operations, personnel must be advised of the eye hazards associated with the use of lasers. Common sources of lasers are tanks, LAVs, and aircraft providing CAS.

Up-Gunned Weapon Station

Strict adherence to operational procedures must be followed when dealing with the UGWS. The greatest risk to personnel is from a supposedly unloaded weapon. Every weapon will be treated as if it were loaded. Personnel must know the proper procedures for immediate action and clearing of the MK-19 and M2 .50-caliber machine guns. Weapons should be doublechecked by a section leader after live fire exercises. Personnel should be aware of the hazards of white phosphorus in the smoke grenades.

Linear Mine Clearing

AAV crews, in addition to engineer detachments, must be trained and certified in LMC operations. During line-charge operations, only authorized personnel should clear ranges. These personnel should be kept to a minimum number.

If the line charge is burning from the rocket during the launch or a piece of it does not detonate and is burning, the potential for the line to detonate on its own is great.

Onboard Vehicle Fires

AAV crewmen should know immediate actions for onboard fires to include location of the portable fire extinguisher, fire system activation levers, and evacuation procedures.

APPENDIX A. AAVP7A1 DATA

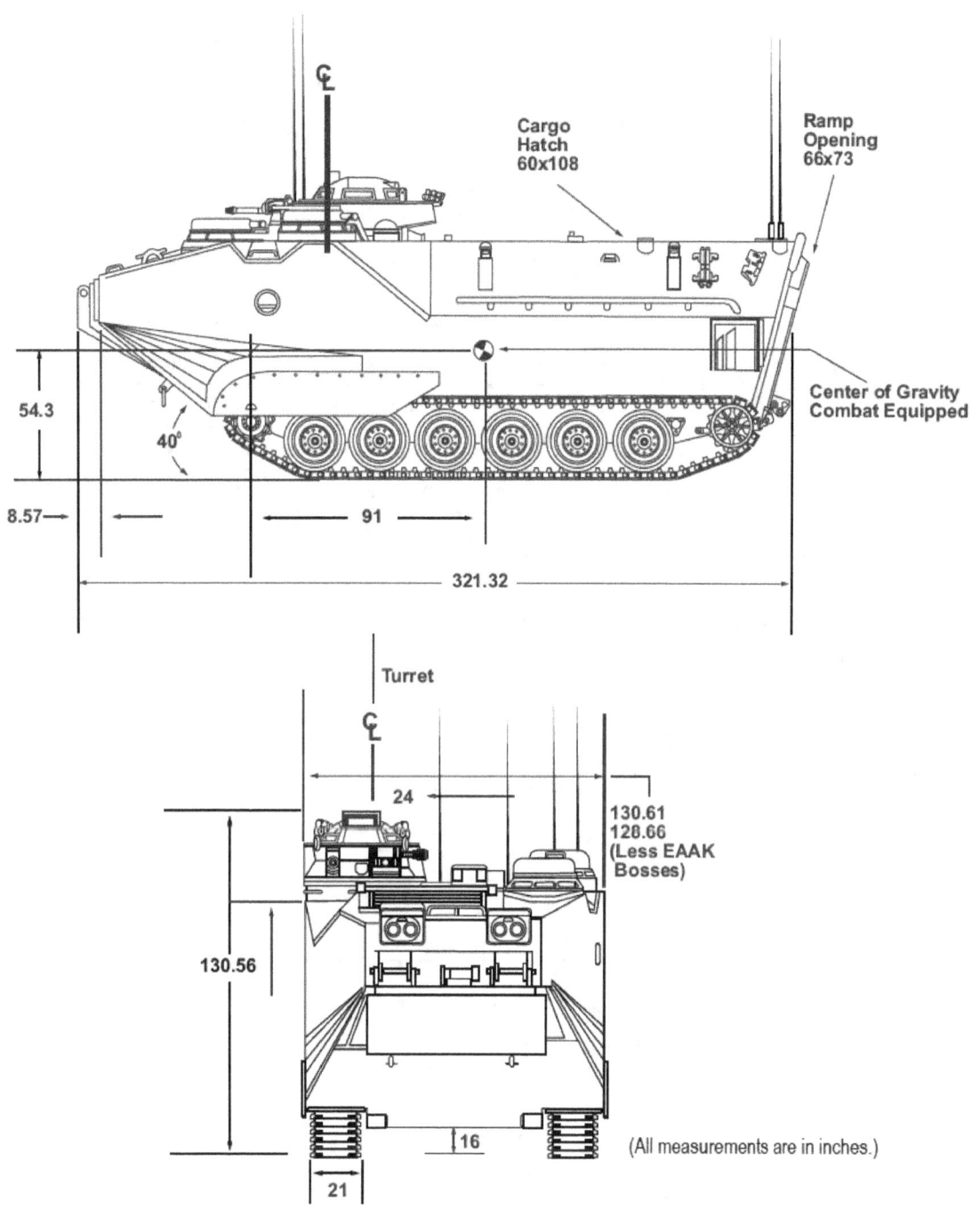

Figure A-1. AAVP7A1.

General	
Crew	3
Weight	Unloaded: 46,314 pounds (with enhanced appliqué armor kit [EAAK], less crew, fuel, on-equipment material [OEM], and ammunition)
	Combat-equipped: 50,758 pounds (EAAK, crew, fuel, OEM, and ammunition)
	Troop-loaded: 56,743 pounds (combat-equipped with troops)
	Cargo-loaded: 60,758 pounds (combat-equipped with cargo)
	Mine clearance kit: 61,158 pounds (combat-equipped with MK1 model 0 mine clearance system
Load capacity	21 combat-equipped troops (at 285 pounds each) or 10,000 pounds of cargo
Center of gravity	Unloaded: 52.8 inches above ground, 84.4 inches from station 100.0
	Combat-equipped: 54.3 inches above ground, 91.0 inches from station 100.0
	Troop-loaded: 53.6 inches above ground, 97.0 inches from station 100.0
	Cargo-loaded: 52.8 inches above ground, 100.3 inches from station 100.0
	Mine clearance kit: 54.4 inches above ground, 103.2 inches from station 100.0
Mean seawater draft (cargo-loaded)	75.2 inches
Freeboard at bow (station 34)	18.9 inches
Freeboard at stern (station 346)	10.8 inches
Unit ground pressure (cargo-loaded, zero penetration)	9.1 pounds per square inch
Fuel capacity	171 gallons
Performance	
Gross horsepower to weight ratio (cargo-loaded)	13.2 horsepower per ton
Net horsepower to weight ratio (cargo-loaded)	8.8 horsepower per ton
Drawbar pull (maximum at stall tractive effort)	42,644 pounds on level, firm terrain
Cruising range	Land at 25 miles per hour: 300 miles
	Water at 2,600 rotations per minute: 7 hours
Cruising speed	Land: 20 to 30 miles per hour
	Water: 6 miles per hour
Maximum speed forward	Land: 45 miles per hour
	Water: 8.2 miles per hour
Maximum speed reverse	Land: 12 miles per hour
	Water: 4.5 miles per hour
Obstacle ability	8-foot trench span, 3-foot vertical wall

Maximum forward grade (cargo -loaded)	60 percent
Maximum side slope (cargo-loaded)	40 percent
Ground clearance (cargo-loaded)	16 inches
Minimum turning radius	Land: pivot
	Water: pivot
Surf ability	Negotiate 6-foot plunging surf, cargo-loaded and survive 10-foot plunging surf without sustaining mission failure
Engine	
Make	Cummins
Model	VT400
Type	4-cycle, 8-cylinder, 90-degree V, water-cooled, turbocharged
Bore	5.5 inches
Stroke	4.75 inches
Displacement	903 cubic inches
Compression ratio	15.5:1
Fuel	Multifuel
Rated horsepower	400 plus 5 percent at 2,800 rotations per minute with diesel fuel-2 (DF-2)
Rated torque	825 foot-pounds plus 5 percent at 2,050 rotations per minute with DF-2
Oil capacity (dry)	6.5 gallons
Oil capacity (wet)	4.5 gallons
Coolant system capacity	30 gallons
Power Train	
Transmission	Naval sea (NAVSEA) HS-400-3A1
Type	Hydraulic torque converter, parallel shaft gear arrangement
Maximum converter torque multiplication	2.83:1
Gear ratios forward	First speed: 8.27:1
	Second speed: 4.63:1
	Third speed: 2.25:1
	Fourth speed: 1.27:1 (Reverse uses first and second speed ratios)
Final drive ratio	3.06:1
Overall maximum torque ratio (engine to sprocket)	70.8:1
Transmission oil capacity	23 gallons (with oil coolers, filters, lines)

Running Gear	
Type	Torsion bar and tube suspension, front sprocket, raised rear idler
Wheels	6 rubber-tired, dual per side, 26-inch diameter
Return idlers	1 per side, 20-inch diameter wheels
Sprocket	Teeth: 11
	Feet per revolution: 5.5
Shock absorbers	3 per side
Track	Steel, single pin, rubber bushed, with replaceable pads
Blocks	85 maximum per side
	Pitch: 6 inches
	Weight per block: 34 pounds maximum
	Weight per side: 2,890 pounds maximum
Water Propulsion	
Water jet pumps	Capacity: 14,000 gallons per minute
	Thrust: 3,025 pounds static
	Quantity: 2
	Location: port, starboard, and aft
Steering and reverse	Jet deflectors
Electrical	
Nominal voltage	24 volts, direct current
Generator	300 ampere
Battery	Volts: 12
	Type: 6-cell, terminal, lead
	Quantity: 4
Communication	
Control monitor C-11291	2
Radio frequency amplifier AM-7238	2
Vehicular amplifier adapter AM-7239	2
Mount MT-6353	2
Loudspeaker LS-671	1
Receiver-transmitter RT-1523	4
Antennas AS-3916	4
Audio frequency amplifier AM-7162	1
Intercom control box C-11133	4
Intercom control box C-11135	1

Armor	
Permanent hull	Aluminum armor plate
Ramp outer	1.000 inch
Ramp inner	.500 inch
Sides	1.750, 1.395 and 1.222 inches
Top	1.185 inches
Bottom	1.185 inches
Stern	1.395 inches
EAAK	Protection for vehicle side and slope, troop compartment overhead, and slope rack kit for sponson stowage of OEM
	Attachment: boss and joint offset method
	Material: homogeneous harden steel, rubber, mild steel composite
	Boss offset from hull (no armor): 0.75 inch per side
	Maximum offset from hull: 8.50 inches per side
Fire Extinguishers	
Automatic fire sensing and suppression system:	
Cylinders	3
Locations	Aft engine compartment bulkhead, and forward starboard stanchion
Capacity	7 pounds each, Halon 1301
Sensors	4
Portable	Cylinders: 1
	Location: starboard, aft
	Capacity: 5 pounds carbon dioxide
Manual fire suppression system:	
Troop compartment	Cylinders: 1
	Location: port sponson
	Capacity: 17 pounds Halon 1301
Engine Compartment	Cylinders: 2
	Location: one in driver's compartment and one in aft engine compartment
Bulkhead capacity	7 pounds each, Halon 1301
Vision and Sighting Equipment	
Driver's station:	
Direct vision blocks	7
Driver's night vision device	AN/VVS-2(V)1A: 1
	AN/VAS-5A(V)6: 1 (Note: Device AN/VAS-5A(V)6 is currently being fielded.)
Commander's station:	
Direct vision blocks	7

Periscope, M27	1
Device AN/VAS-5A(V)6	1 (Note: Device is slaved to drivers night vision device.)
Weapon station:	
Direct vision blocks	7
Gunner's sight	M36E2 (projected reticle)
Daylight	1X or 7X power
Night	7.1X power (passive vision assembly)
Ramp, direct vision blocks	1
Cargo Compartment	
Length	13.5 feet
Width	6.0 feet
Height	5.5 feet
Volume	445.5 cubic feet
Capacity	21 combat-equipped troops
Armament and Ammunition	
Upgunned weapons station, improved:	
Weight	2,365 pounds
Starboard overhang	1.14 Inches
Traverse	360 degrees
Elevation	Plus 45 degrees
Depression	- 8 degrees
Power control system	Electric-manual
Weapons:	
M2 heavy-barrel caliber .50 machine gun	Rate of fire (cyclic): 450 to 550 rounds per minute
	Muzzle velocity: 3,050 feet per second
	Maximum effective range: 2,000 yards (1,830 meters)
MK-19 model 3 40-millimeter machine gun	Rate of fire (cyclic): 325 to 375 rounds per minute
	Muzzle velocity: 790 feet per second
	Maximum effective range: 1,640 yards (1,500 meters)
Ammunition	Caliber .50: 200 ready rounds, 1,000 rounds stowed in 10 ammunition boxes
	40 millimeters: 96 ready rounds, 768 rounds stowed in 16 ammunition boxes
M257 smoke grenade launchers	Quantity: 2 assembly
	Total: 8 UKL8A1 or UKL8A3 grenades
M16 A2, 5.56-millimeter rifle	Quantify: 3 (troop issue)
Infantry weapons mount kit	2 MK 16 gun stands on vehicle rear deck

Navigation Equipment	
(Note: None integrated/organic to the AAV7A1.)	
Bilge Pumps	
Electric (minimum each pump)	100 gallons per minute
Hydraulic (minimum each pump)	115 gallons per minute
Other	
Capability enhancements	Bow plane assembly NAVSEA part number (P/N) 6227757
	Chemical agent resistant coatings
Special mission kits	Visor kit, NAVSEA P/N 2587015
	Litter kit, NAVSEA P/N 5428676
	Winterization kit, NAVSEA P/N 2600063
	MK 1 model 0 mine clearance system, weight: 10,400 pounds (fully loaded)
Production	FMC Corporation
	Date first prototype: 1979
	Date first production vehicle: 1983

APPENDIX B. AAVP7A1 (RAM/RS) DATA

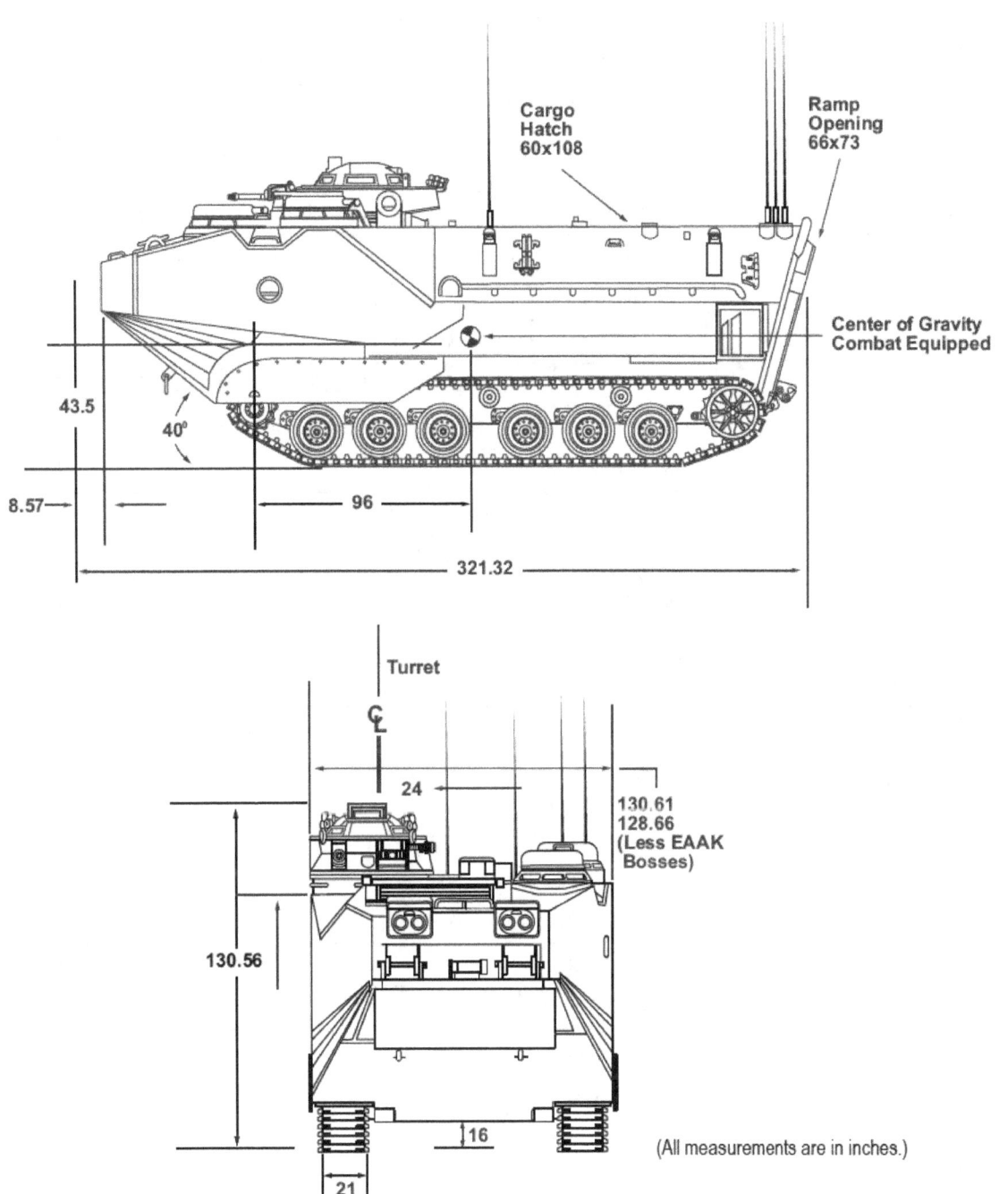

Figure B-1. AAVP7A1 (RAM/RS).

General	
Crew	3
Weight	Unloaded: 48,060 pounds (with EAAK, less crew, fuel, OEM, and ammunition)
	Combat-equipped: 52,120 pounds (EAAK, crew, fuel, OEM, and ammunition)
	Troop-loaded: 58,105 pounds (combat-equipped with troops)
	Cargo-loaded: 62,120 pounds (combat-equipped with cargo)
	Mine clearance kit: 63,620 pounds (combat-equipped with MK1 model 0 mine clearance system)
Load capacity	21 combat-equipped troops (at 285 pounds each) or 10,000 pounds of cargo
Center of gravity	Unloaded: 49.75 inches above ground, 88 inches from station 100.0
	Combat-equipped: 43.5 inches above ground, 96 inches from station 100.0
	Troop-loaded: 42.8 inches above ground, 102 inches from station 100.0
	Cargo-loaded: 50.4 inches above ground, 105.3 inches from station 100.0
Mine clearance kit	52 inches above ground, 95.75 inches from station 100.0
Mean seawater draft (cargo-loaded)	81.8 inches
	Freeboard at bow (station 34): 25.5 inches
	Freeboard at stern (station 346): 11.5 inches
	Unit ground pressure (cargo-loaded): 9.7 pounds per square inch
	Fuel capacity: 171 gallons
Performance	
Gross horsepower to weight ratio (cargo-loaded)	16.9 horsepower per ton
Net horsepower to weight ratio (cargo-loaded)	11.3 horsepower per ton
Drawbar pull (maximum at stall tractive effort)	38,500 pounds on level, firm terrain
Cruising range	Land at 25 miles per hour: 200 miles
	Water at 2,600 rotations per minute: 7 hours
Cruising speed	Land: 20 to 30 miles per hour
	Water: 6 miles per hour
Maximum speed forward	Land: 45 miles per hour
	Water: 8.2 miles per hour
Maximum speed reverse	Land: 12 miles per hour
	Water: 4.5 miles per hour
Obstacle ability	8-foot trench span, 3-foot vertical wall
Maximum forward grade (cargo-loaded)	60 percent
Maximum side slope (cargo-loaded)	40 percent

Ground clearance (cargo-loaded)	16 inches
Minimum turning radius	Land: pivot
	Water: pivot
Surf ability	Negotiate 6-foot plunging surf, cargo-loaded and survive 10-foot plunging surf without sustaining mission failure
Engine	
Make	Cummins
Model	VTA 903 T 525
Type	4-cycle, 8-cylinder, 90-degree V, water-cooled, turbocharged, aftercooled
Bore	5.5 inches
Stroke	4.75 inches
Displacement	903 cubic inches
Compression ratio	15.5:1
Fuel	Multifuel
Rated horsepower	525 plus 25 percent at 2,800 rotations per minute with DF-2
Rated torque	1,127 foot-pounds plus 5 percent at 2,200 rotations per minute with DF-2
Oil capacity (dry)	10 gallons
Oil capacity (wet)	8 gallons
Coolant system capacity	30 gallons
Power Train	
Transmission	NAVSEA HS-525
Type	Hydraulic torque converter, parallel shaft gear arrangement
Maximum converter torque multiplication	2.83:1
Gear ratios forward	First speed: 8.27:1
	Second speed: 4.63:1
	Third speed: 2.25:1
	Fourth speed: 1.27:1 (Reverse uses first and second speed ratios.)
Final drive ratio	3.06:1
Overall maximum torque ratio (engine to sprocket)	70.8:1
Transmission oil capacity	23 gallons (with oil coolers, filters, lines)
Improved transmission upgrade for torque converter and speed change assembly	
Running Gear	
Type	torsion bar suspension, front sprocket, raised rear idler
Wheels	6-rubber tired, dual per side, 24-inch diameter
Return idlers	1 per side, 20-inch diameter wheels

Support rollers	2 single and 1 double per side, 20-inch diameter rollers
Sprocket	Teeth: 11
	Feet per revolution: 5.5
Shock absorbers	4 per side
Track	Steel, single-pin, rubber-bushed, with replaceable pads
Blocks	85 maximum per side
	Pitch: 6 inches
	Weight per block: 35.4 pounds maximum
	Weight per side: 3,009 pounds maximum
Water Propulsion	
Water Jet Pumps	Capacity: 14,000 gallons per minute
	Thrust: 3,025 pounds static
	Quantity: 2
	Location: port and starboard, aft
Steering and reverse	Jet deflectors
Electrical	
Nominal voltage	24 volts, direct current
Generator	300 ampere, 28 volts, direct current
Battery	Volts: 12
	Quantity: 4
Communication	
Vehicle system	AN/VIC-2 (V)
Radio	AN/VRC-89A radio set: 2
Communications security equipment	(integrated into the RT-1523)
AN/VIC-2(V) intercom system	5 stations
Control monitor C-11291	2
Radio frequency amplifier AM-7238	2
Vehicular amplifier adapter AM-7239	2
Mount MT-6353	2
Loudspeaker LS-671	1
Receiver-transmitter RT-1523	4
Antennas AS-3916	4
Audio frequency amplifier AM-7162	1
Intercom control box C-11133	4
Intercom control box C-11135	1

Armor	
Permanent hull	Aluminum armor plate
Ramp outer	1.000 inch
Ramp inner	.500 inch
Sides	1.750, 1.395 and 1.222 inches
Top	1.185 inches
Bottom	1.185 inches
Stern	1.395 inches
EAAK	Protection for vehicle side and slope, troop compartment overhead, and slope rack kit for sponson stowage of OEM.
	Attachment: boss and joint offset method
	Material: homogeneous harden steel, rubber, mild steel composite
	Boss offset from hull (no armor): 0.75 inch per side
	Maximum offset from hull: 8.50 inches per side
Fire Extinguishers	
Automatic fire sensing and suppression system:	
Cylinders	3
Locations	Aft engine compartment bulkhead, and forward starboard stanchion
Capacity	7 pounds each, Halon 1301
Sensors	4
Portable	Cylinders: 1
	Location: starboard, aft
	Capacity: 5 pounds carbon dioxide
Manual fire suppression system:	
Troop compartment	Cylinders: 1
	Location: port sponson
	Capacity: 17 pounds each, Halon 1301
Engine compartment	Cylinders: 2
	Location: driver's compartment and aft engine compartment
Bulkhead capacity	7 pounds each, Halon 1301
Vision and Sighting Equipment	
Driver's station:	
Direct vision blocks	7
Driver's night vision device	AN/VVS-2(V)1A: 1
	Or AN/VAS-5A(V)6: 1 (Note: Device AN/VAS-5A(V)6 is currently being fielded.)
Commander's station:	
Direct vision blocks	7

Periscope, M27	1
Device AN/VAS-5A(V)6	1 (Note: Device is slaved to the driver's night vision.)
Weapon Station:	
Direct vision blocks	7
Gunner's sight	M36E2 (projected reticle)
Daylight	1X or 7X power
Night	7.1X power (passive vision assembly)
Ramp, direct vision blocks	1
Cargo Compartment	
Length	13.5 feet
Width	6.0 feet
Height	5.5 feet
Volume	445.5 cubic feet
Capacity	21 combat-equipped troops
Armament and Ammunition	
Upgunned weapons station, improved:	
Weight	2,365 pounds
Starboard overhang	1.14 inches
Traverse	360 degrees
Elevation	Plus 45 degrees
Depression	8 degrees
Power control system	Electric-manual
Weapons:	
M2 heavy-barrel, caliber .50 machine gun	Rate of fire (cyclic): 450-550 rounds per minute
	Muzzle velocity: 3,050 feet per second
	Maximum effective range: 2,000 yards (1,830 meters)
MK-19 model 3 40-millimeter machine gun	Rate of fire (cyclic): 325-375 rounds per minute
	Muzzle velocity: 790 feet per second
	Maximum effective range: 1,640 yards (1,500 meters)
Ammunition	Caliber .50: 200 ready rounds, 1,000 rounds stowed in 10 ammunition boxes
	40 millimeters: 96 ready rounds, 768 rounds stowed in 16 ammunition boxes

M257 Smoke grenade launchers	Quantity: 2 assembly
	Total: 8 UKL8A1 or UKL8A3 grenades
M16 A2, 5.56-millimeter rifle	Quantity: 3 (troop issue)
Infantry weapons mount kit	2 MK 16 gun stands on vehicle rear deck
Navigation Equipment	
Precision lightweight global positioning system receiver	P/N 822-0077-002
Tactical navigation digital compass system light	1
Position location reporting system	AN/VSQ-1
Bilge Pumps	
Electric (minimum each pump)	100 gallons per minute
Hydraulic (minimum each pump)	115 gallons per minute
Other	
Capability enhancements	Bow plane assembly, NAVSEA P/N 6227757
	Chemical agent resistant coatings
Special mission kits	Visor kit, NAVSEA P/N 2587015
	Litter kit, NAVSEA P/N 5428676
	Winterization kit, NAVSEA P/N 2600063
	MK 1 model 0 mine clearance system, weight: 10,400 pounds (fully loaded)
Production	United Defense Limited Partnership Corporation
	Date first prototype: 1995
	Date first production vehicle: 1998

APPENDIX C. AAVC7A1 DATA

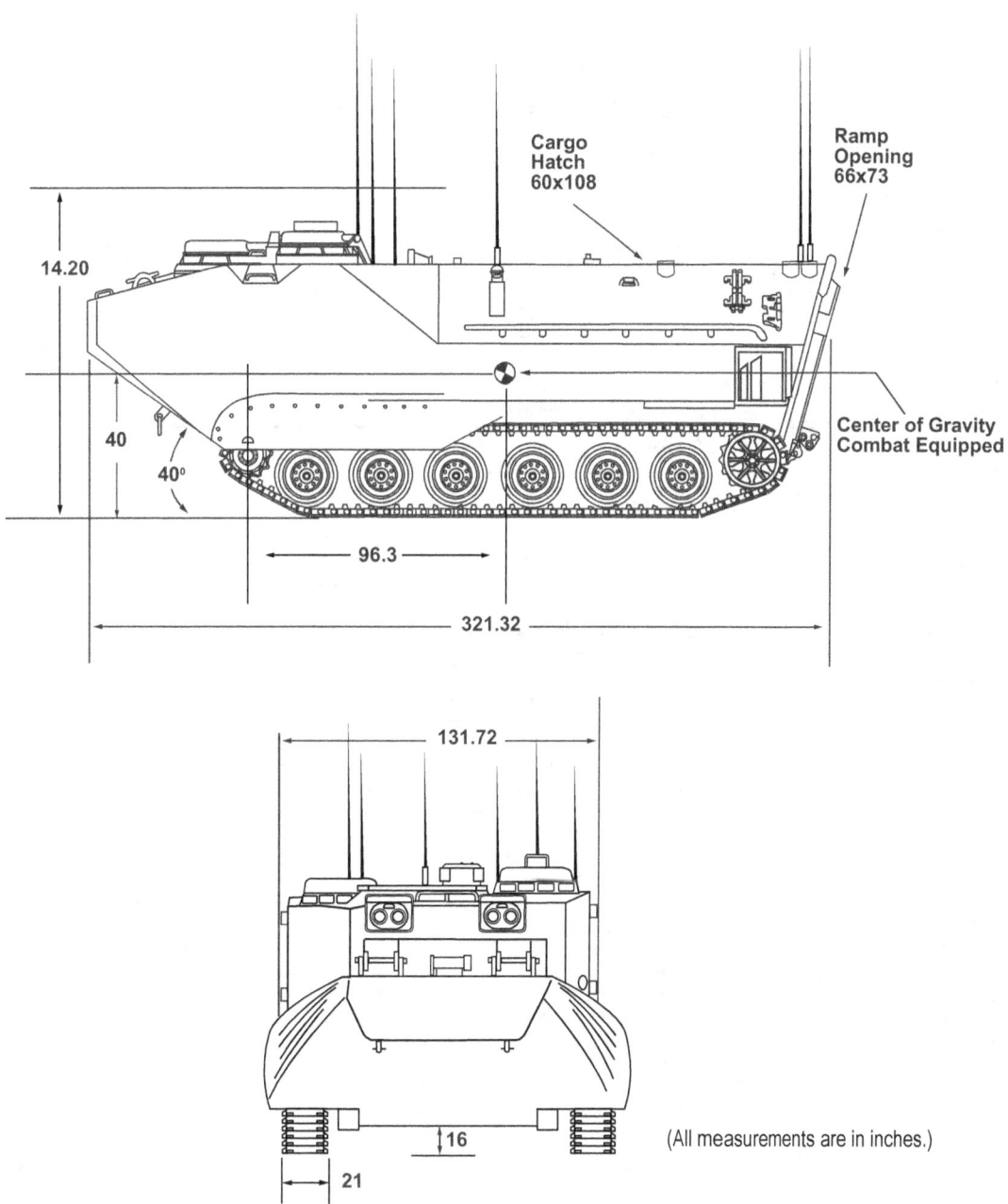

Figure C-1. AAVC7A1.

General	
Crew	3
Weight	Unloaded: 49,614 pounds (with EAAK, less crew, fuel, OEM, and ammunition)
	Combat-equipped: 53,019 pounds (with EAAK, crew, fuel, OEM, and ammunition)
Center of gravity	Unloaded: 49.4 inches above ground, 94.4 inches from station 100.0
	Combat-equipped: 51.3 inches above ground, 95.5 inches from station 100.0
Mean seawater draft (combat-equipped)	Approximately 69.0 inches
Freeboard at bow (station 34)	Approximately 20.2 inches
Freeboard at stern (station 346)	Approximately 21.9 inches
Unit ground pressure (combat-equipped, zero penetration)	7.9 pounds per square inch
Fuel capacity	171 gallons
Performance	
Gross horsepower to weight ratio (combat-equipped)	15.2 horsepower per ton
Net horsepower to weight ratio (combat-equipped)	10.1 horsepower per ton
Drawbar pull (maximum at stall tractive effort)	38,934 pounds on level, firm terrain
Cruising range	Land at 25 miles per hour: 300 miles
	Water at 2,600 rotations per minute: 7 hours
Cruising speed	Land: 20 to 30 miles per hour
	Water: 6 miles per hour
Maximum speed forward	Land: 45 miles per hour
	Water: 8.2 miles per hour
Maximum speed reverse	Land: 12 miles per hour
	Water: 4.5 miles per hour
Obstacle ability	8-foot trench span, 3-foot vertical wall
Maximum forward grade (combat-equipped)	60 percent
Maximum side slope (combat-equipped)	40 percent
Ground clearance (combat-equipped)	16 inches
Minimum turning radius	Land: pivot
	Water: pivot
Surf ability	Negotiate 6-foot plunging surf, combat-equipped and survive 10-foot plunging surf without sustaining mission failure

Engine	
Make	Cummins
Model	VT400
Type	4-cycle, 8-cylinder, 90-degree V, water-cooled, turbocharged
Bore	5.5 inches
Stroke	4.75 inches
Displacement	903 cubic inches
Compression ratio	15.5:1
Fuel	Multifuel
Rated horsepower	400 plus 5 percent at 2,800 rotations per minute with DF-2
Rated torque	825 foot-pounds 5 percent at 2,050 rotations per minute with DF-2
Oil capacity (dry)	6.5 gallons
Oil capacity (wet)	4.5 gallons
Coolant system capacity	30 gallons
Power Train	
Transmission	NAVSEA HS-400-3A1
Type	Hydraulic torque converter, parallel shaft gear arrangement
Maximum converter torque multiplication	2.83:1
Gear ratios forward	First speed: 8.27:1
	Second speed: 4.63:1
	Third speed: 2.25:1
	Fourth speed: 1.27:1 (Reverse uses first and second speed ratios)
Final drive ratio	3.06:1
Overall maximum torque ratio (engine to sprocket)	70.8:1
Transmission oil capacity	23 gallons (with oil coolers, filters, lines)
Improved transmission upgrade for torque converter, steer and brake assembly gears, and oil filter	
Running Gear	
Type	Torsion bar and tube suspension, front sprocket, raised rear idler
Wheels	6 rubber-tired, dual per side, 26-inch diameter
Return idlers	1 per side, 20-inch diameter wheels
Sprocket	Teeth: 11
	Feet per revolution: 5.5
Shock absorbers	3 per side
Track	Steel, single-pin, rubber-bushed, with replaceable pads

Blocks	85 maximum per side
Pitch	6 inches
Weight per block	34 pounds maximum
Weight per side	2,890 pounds maximum
Water Propulsion	
Water jet pumps	Capacity: 14,000 gallons per minute
	Thrust: 3,025 pounds static
	Quantity: 2
	Location: port and starboard, aft
	Steering and reverse: jet deflectors
Electrical	
Nominal voltage	24 volts, direct current
Generator	300 ampere, 28 volts, direct current
Battery	Volts: 12
	Type: 6 cell, terminal, lead
	Quantity: 4
Communication Vehicle System	
Control monitor C-11291	2
Radio frequency amplifier AM-7238	4
Amplifier adapter AM-7239	6
Mount MT-6352	4
Mount MT-6353	2
Loudspeaker LS-671	1
Receiver-transmitter RT-1523	8
Antenna AS-3900	8
Audio amplifier AM-7162	1
Intercom control box C-11133	4
Intercom control box C-11135	1
Communication control box MIQ-1(V)-3	5
Communication control box MIQ-1(V)-2	2
Communication control box MIQ-1(V)-1	3
Communication system controller C-10879/MSQ-115	1
Current regulator CN-1549	5

Receiver-transmitter RT-1319/ VRC-83	1
Receiver-transmitter RT-1209/ PRC-104	1
Armor	
Permanent hull	Aluminum armor plate
Ramp outer	1.000 inch
Ramp inner	.500 inch
Sides	1.750, 1.395, and 1.222 inches
Top	1.185 inches
Bottom	1.185 inches
Stern	1.395 inches
EAAK	Protection for vehicle side and slope, troop compartment overhead: and slope rack kit for sponson stowage of OEM
Attachment	Boss and joint offset method
Material	Homogeneous harden steel, rubber, mild steel composite
Boss offset from hull (no armor)	0.75 inch per side
Maximum offset from hull	8.50 inches per side
Fire Extinguishers	
Automatic fire sensing and suppression system:	
Cylinders	3
Location	Aft engine compartment bulkhead, and forward starboard stanchion
Capacity	7 pounds each, Halon 1301
Sensors	4
Portable:	
Cylinders	1
Location	Starboard, aft
Capacity	5 pounds carbon dioxide
Manual fire suppression system:	
Troop compartment	Cylinders: 1
	Location: port sponson
	Capacity: 17 pounds each, Halon 1301
Engine compartment	Cylinders: 2
	Location: driver's compartment and aft engine compartment bulkhead
	Capacity: 7 pounds each, Halon 1301 each
Vision and Sighting Equipment	
Driver's Station	Direct vision blocks: 7
	Driver's night vision viewer AN/VAS-5A(V)6: 1

Master Station	Direct vision blocks: 7
	Periscope, M27: 1
Vehicle commander's station, direct vision blocks	9
Ramp, direct vision blocks	1
Personnel Complement	
Crew (vehicle commander, driver, assistant driver)	3
Radio operators	5
Unit commander and staff	5
Armament and Ammunition	
M240G, machine gun, pintle-mounted	1
Ammunition	7.62 millimeters; 1,000 rounds stowed
M16 A2 5.56-millimeter rifle, quantity	3 (crew issue)
Navigation Equipment	
(None is integrated/organic to the AAV7A1.)	
Bilge Pumps	
Electric (minimum each pump)	100 gallons per minute
Hydraulic (minimum each pump)	120 gallons per minute
Other	
Capability enhancements	Bow plane assembly, NAVSEA P/N 6227757
	Chemical agent resistant coatings
Special mission kits	Visor kit, NAVSEA P/N 2587015
	Winterization kit, NAVSEA P/N 2600063
Production	FMC Corporation
	Date first prototype: 1979
	Date first production vehicle: 1983

APPENDIX D. AAVR7A1 DATA

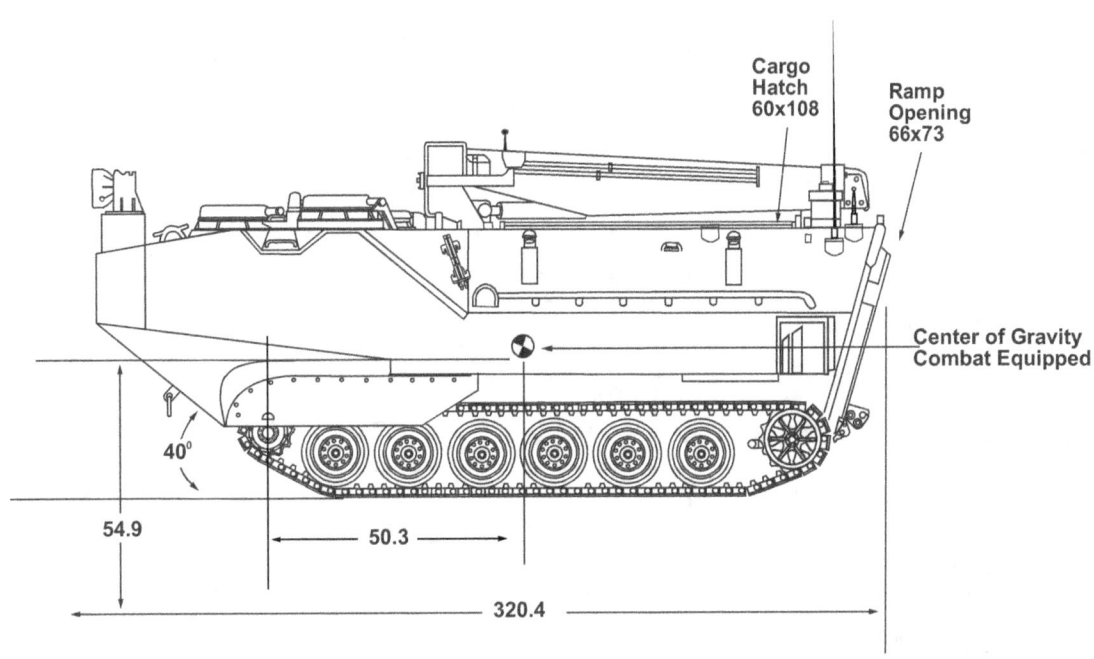

Cargo
Hatch
60x108

Ramp
Opening
66x73

Center of Gravity
Combat Equipped

40°

54.9

50.3

320.4

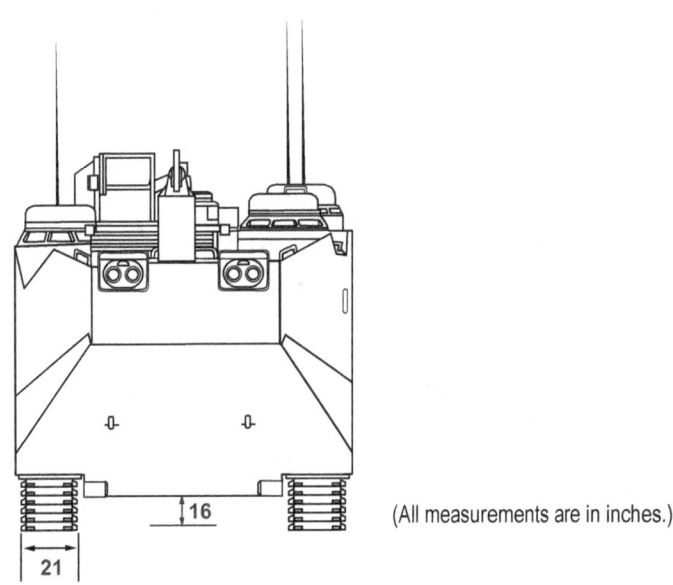

16

21

(All measurements are in inches.)

Figure D-1. AAVR7A1.

General	
Crew	5
Weight	Unloaded: 50,113 pounds (less crew, fuel, and ammunition)
	Combat-equipped: 52,123 pounds (crew, fuel, OEM, and ammunition)
Center of Gravity	Unloaded: 54.0 inches above ground, 90.4 inches from station 100.0
	Combat-equipped: 54.9 inches above ground, 90.8 inches from station 100.0
Maximum seawater draft (combat-equipped)	approximately 68.0 inches
	Freeboard to driver's hatch coaming: approximately 37.3 inches
	Freeboard to inlet of aspirator valve: approximately 39.0 inches
Unit ground pressure (combat-equipped, zero penetration)	7.8 pounds per square inch
Fuel capacity	171 gallons
Performance	
Gross horsepower to weight ratio (combat-equipped)	15.3 horsepower per ton
Net horsepower to weight ratio (combat-equipped)	10.2 horsepower per ton
Drawbar pull (maximum at stall tractive effort)	42,036 pounds on level firm terrain
Cruising range	Land at 25 miles per hour: 300 miles
	Water at 2,600 rotations per minute: 7 hours
Cruising speed	Land: 20 to 30 miles per hour
	Water: 6 miles per hour
Maximum speed forward	Land: 45 miles per hour
	Water: 8.2 miles per hour
Maximum speed reverse	Land: 12 miles per hour
	Water: 4.5 miles per hour
Obstacle ability	8-foot trench span, 3-foot vertical wall
Maximum forward grade (combat-equipped)	60 percent
Maximum side slope (combat-equipped)	40 percent
Ground clearance (combat-equipped)	16 inches
Minimum turning radius	Land: pivot
	Water: pivot
Surf ability	Negotiate 6-foot plunging surf, combat-equipped and survive 10-foot plunging surf without sustaining mission failure
Engine	
Make	Cummins
Model	VT400

Type	4-cycle, 8-cylinder, 90-degree V, water-cooled, turbocharged
Bore	5.5 inches
Stroke	4.75 inches
Displacement	903 cubic inches
Compression Ratio	15.5:1
Fuel	Multifuel
Rated horsepower	400 plus 5 percent at 2,800 rotations per minute with DF-2
Rated torque	825 foot-pounds plus 5 percent at 2,050 rotations per minute with DF-2
Oil capacity (dry)	6.5 gallons
Oil capacity (wet)	4.5 gallons
Coolant system capacity	30 gallons
Power Train	
Transmission	NAVSEA HS-400-341
Type	Hydraulic torque converter, parallel shaft gear arrangement
Maximum converter torque multiplication	2.83:1
Gear ratios forward	First speed: 8.27:1
	Second speed: 4.63:1
	Third speed: 2.25:1
	Fourth speed: 1.27:1 (Reverse uses first and second speed ratios)
Final drive ratio	3.06:1
Overall maximum torque ratio (engine to sprocket)	70.8:1
Transmission oil capacity	23 gallons (with oil coolers, filters, lines)
Improved transmission upgrade for torque converter, steer and brake assembly gears, and oil filter	
Running Gear	
Type	Torsion bar and tube suspension, front sprocket, raised rear idler
Wheels	6 rubber, tired dual per side, 26-inch diameter
Return Idlers	1 per side, 20-inch diameter wheels
Sprocket	Teeth: 11
	Feet per revolution: 5.5
Shock Absorbers	3 per side
Track	Steel, single-pin, rubber-bushed, with replaceable pads
Blocks	85 maximum per side
Pitch	6 inches
Weight per block	34 pounds maximum
Weight per side	2,890 pounds maximum

Water Propulsion	
Water Jet Pumps	Capacity: 14,000 gallons per minute
	Thrust: 3,025 pounds static
	Quantity: 2
	Location: port and starboard, aft
Steering and reverse	Jet deflectors
Electrical	
Nominal voltage	24 volts, direct current
Generator	300 ampere, 28 volts, direct current battery:
	Volts: 12
	Type: 6 cell, terminal, lead
	Quantity: 4
Communication	
Control monitor C-11291	2
Radio frequency amplifier AM-7238	1
Vehicular amplifier adapter AM7239	1
Mount MT-6352	1
Loudspeaker LS-671	2
Receiver-transmitter RT-1523	2 (AN/VRC-89)
Antennas AS-3916	2
Audio frequency amplifier AM-7162	1
Intercom control box C-11133	4
Armament and Ammunition	
M60D machine gun, pintle-mounted	Ammunition: 7.62 millimeters; 400 rounds
M16 A2, 5.56-millimeter rifle, quantity	5 (troop issue)
Armor	
Permanent hull	Aluminum armor plate
	Ramp outer: 1.000 inch
	Ramp inner: 0.500 inch
	Sides: 1.750, 1.395, and 1.222 inches
	Top: 1.185 inches
	Bottom: 1.185 inches
	Stern: 1.395 inches

Fire Extinguishers	
Automatic fire sensing suppression system:	
Cylinders	3
Location	Aft engine compartment bulkhead and forward starboard stanchion
Capacity	7 pounds each, Halon 1301
Sensors	4
Portable:	
Cylinders	1
Location	Starboard, aft
Capacity	5 pounds carbon dioxide
Manual Fire Suppression System:	
Troop Compartment	Cylinders: 1
	Location: port sponson
	Capacity: 17 pounds each, Halon 1301
Engine Compartment	Cylinders: 2
	Location: driver's compartment and aft engine compartment bulkhead
	Capacity: 7 pounds each, Halon 1301 each
Vision and Sighting Equipment	
Driver's Station:	
Direct vision blocks	7
Driver's night vision device	AN/VVS-2(V)1A: 1 or AN/VAS-5A(V)6: 1
Commander's station:	
Direct vision blocks	7
Periscope, M27	1
Auxiliary station, direct vision blocks	9
Ramp, direct vision block	1
Recovery Equipment	
Electrical power source: Generator (engine driven)	
Rating	12.5 kilovolt amperes, 0.8 power factor, 60-cycle, three-phase, four-wire
Output	120 volts alternating current single-phase and 220 VAC three-phase
Speed	3,600 rotations per minute
Hydraulic power source: Pump (engine driven)	
Pressure	2,200 pounds per square inch
Delivery rate at 1,800 engine rotations per minute and 1,680 pump rotations per minute	Section 1: 32.0 gallons per minute
	Sections 2 and 3: 20.0 gallons per minute
	Section 4: 9.0 gallons per minute

Air compressor (two-stage reciprocating):	
Piston displacement	14.4 cubic feet per minute
Operating pressure	145 to 175 pounds per square inch gauge
Speed	720 rotations per minute
Welder power supply: Miller Maxtron 300	
Input voltage (single/three phase)	230 - 460 volt alternating current
Voltage range in constant voltage mode (metal inert gas)	10 - 36 volts, direct current
Amperage range in constant current mode (tungsten inert gas/stick)	For single-phase: 3 - 375 ampere
	Open-circuit voltage in constant current mode: 80 volts, direct current (maximum)
Hydraulic crane:	
Horizontal reach maximum boom load capacity	6,000 pounds
Boom working angle	0 to 65 degrees
Crane swing-moment capacity	14,000 foot-pounds
Crane moment rating	129,000 foot-pounds
Crane swing speed (azimuth rotational speed)	1.5 rotations per minute
Crane winch:	
Single-Line Rating	6,000 pounds
Line speed	First layer: 25.6 feet per minute
	Second layer: 31.2 feet per minute
	Third layer: 36.7 feet per minute
Wire rope	Diameter and classification: 1/2 inch, 6 by 19 wire
	Breaking strength: 23,000 pounds
	Length: 85 feet
Recovery winch:	
Line pull, low speed	Bare drum: 30,000 pounds
	Full drum: 18,200 pounds
Line pull, high speed	Bare drum: 6, 830 pounds
	Full drum: 4,140 pounds
Line speed, low speed	Bare drum: 22 feet per minute
	Full drum: 36 feet per minute
Line speed, high speed	Bare drum: 97 feet per minute
	Full drum: 160 feet per minute

Wire rope	Diameter and classification: 3/4 inch, 6 by 37 wire
	Breaking Strength: 48,600 pounds
	Length: 278 feet
Navigation Equipment	
(None is integrated/organic to the AAV7A1.)	
Other	
Capability enhancements, chemical agent resistant coatings	
Special mission kits	Visor kit, NAVSEA P/N 2587015
	Winterization kit, NAVSEA P/N 5433242
Production	FMC Corporation
	Date first prototype: 1979
	Date first production vehicle: 1983

APPENDIX E. RESCUE PROCEDURES FOR DISABLED AAVs

In any rescue or retrieval operation, the protection of the lives of personnel takes priority over the salvage of disabled vehicles. Vehicles disabled in the surf zone fall under the cognizance and control of the AA unit leader in charge of the operation. Detailed rescue responsibilities are designated in unit SOPs and/or the OPORD. While waterborne AAV rescue procedures cannot be established for all circumstances, this appendix includes emergency signals, rescue teams, transfer of passengers, retrieval of man overboard, towing, special safety considerations, sinking AAV procedures, and crewmen's responsibilities. The following factors may influence the rescue of waterborne AAVs:

- Urgency of the situation aboard the vehicle.
- Condition of the sea.
- Number and experience of the passengers embarked.
- Skill of the AAV crew.
- Availability of rescue means or craft.

Emergency Signals

Radio communications concerning disabled, waterborne AAVs will take precedence over other communications. If the radio is inoperable, the disabled vehicle will use the following visual distress signals:

- Inoperable (day)—Display November flag attached to a vertical boat hook.
- Sinking (day)—Wave November flag continuously. Fire red flare into the air.
- Inoperable (night)—Turn on and point searchlight or battle lantern vertically. If signal fails, fire one white flare into the air.
- Sinking (night)—Turn on and point searchlight or battle lantern vertically. Fire red flares into the air.

Rescue Teams

Waterborne operations will be conducted with a designated rescue team (RT). The RT can be a part of the waterborne operation; the RT is not a separate entity required to remain on the beach. Regardless of the size of the unit, the unit commander will specifically assign at least one AAV for the RT. Its tactical number and location will be specified in the OPORD. The embarked RT should have two first class swimmers and a corpsman. The AAV designated for the RT should not carry a full load of embarked personnel or cargo, because it must be capable of receiving personnel transferring from the disabled vehicle. The RT equipment should include a matched set of nylon towing lines (with spliced eyelets) and one ring buoy with 50 feet of line attached to mark the disabled vehicle in case it sinks. If a ring buoy is not available, an empty water can or life jacket is suitable with the equivalent length of rope to attach to the disabled vehicle.

During waterborne operations, each AAV is a potential safety vehicle and can assist and tow the closest disabled vehicle. The initial aim of the rescuing vehicle is the safety and recovery of embarked passengers and crew. Embarked personnel will be loaded into the designated RT vehicle before recovery of the disabled vehicle is attempted. Vehicles will not be towed with embarked troops on board unless a greater physical hazard would be posed by the sea condition or tactical situation in the transfer of embarked personnel to another vehicle.

Transfer of Passengers at Sea

The greatest hazard to AAV crew and passenger safety at sea is the danger of a vehicle sinking. If a vehicle's watertight integrity becomes questionable, the embarked passengers should be immediately evacuated. Bow-to-bow, side-to-side, and rough sea transfer methods are used to transfer troops.

Bow-to-Bow Transfer

The bow-to-bow transfer is the preferred method of troop transfer from a disabled AAV. See figure E-1. Before approach, the safety vehicle's bow planes must be lowered and fender material placed in a position to prevent bow damage. Both vehicles will open starboard cargo hatches, which will allow embarking/debarking troops to stand on the port cargo hatch and use the radio grill to climb up or down. After approach, the AAVs will be held in position by crewmen using boat hooks or hand-held lines until troop transfer is complete.

Side-to-Side Transfer

An alternate method of troop transfer is the side-to-side transfer. See figure E-2. This method can be used with either an AAV or a Navy safety boat. The rescuing vehicle will come along the leeward side of the disabled AAV. The AAVs will dock port side to port side using fender material secured to the side of the AAVs. Personnel will exit the disabled vehicle by climbing up the radio grill and stepping across the center bar to the port cargo hatch and then onto the receiving vehicle.

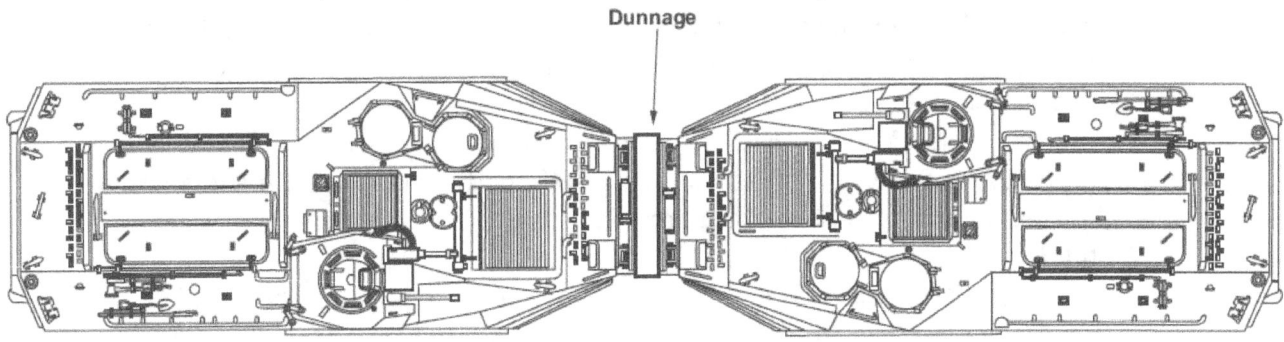

Figure E-1. Bow-to-Bow Transfer Diagram.

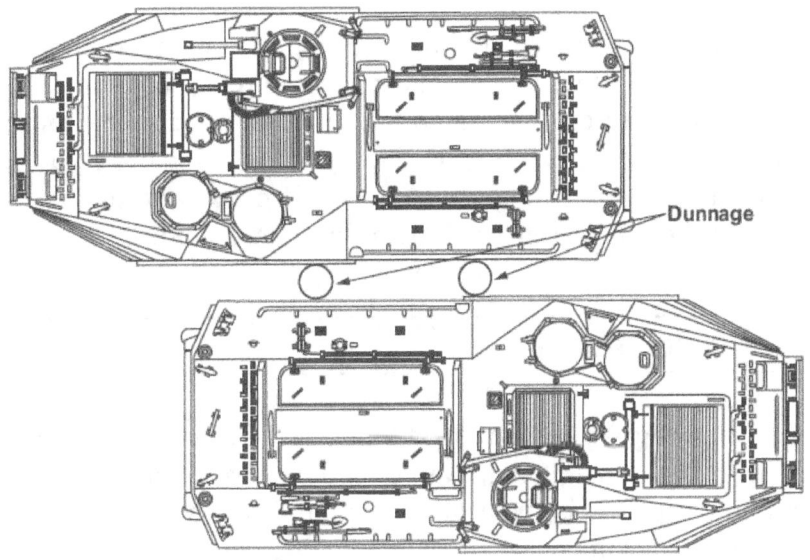

Figure E-2. Side-by-Side Transfer Diagram.

Rough Sea Transfer

Direct transfers should not be attempted in high swells or within the surf zone. In such cases, personnel will enter the water in pairs and swim to the safety vehicle. During transfer operations, the vehicle commander ensures AAVs are in neutral and water-jets are not used. The following rescue procedures are used in rough seas:

- Personnel will exit through the starboard cargo hatch, move to the other side of the AAV, and prepare to swim to the safety vehicle.

- Safety vehicle will be positioned between 25 and 50 meters away from the disabled vehicle on the windward side (wind blows from the safety vehicle toward the disabled vehicle). This prevents the disabled AAV from coming down on personnel as they swim to the safety vehicle.

- Troops embarked on the disabled vehicle will inflate lifejackets, jump (not dive) into the water, stay with their assigned buddy, and swim or paddle to the safety vehicle. The vehicle crew chief will dispatch personnel in an orderly manner.

- Personnel will use the port and starboard cargo hatches to exit if the disabled vehicle is in danger of sinking. They will move quickly to topside and transfer to the safety vehicle. If a safety vehicle is not available, personnel must swim away from the disabled AAV.

Retrieval of Man Overboard

Rescue personnel will use a boat hook, life ring or towline to retrieve a man overboard. Only as a last resort should a man from the safety vehicle enter the water. If required, the rescuer will jump with arms and legs spread wide to keep head above water and eyes on the man. The vehicle, with tracks secured, should be maneuvered close to the man in the water. If necessary, mouth-to-mouth resuscitation will commence as the victim is brought aboard.

Towing a Floating AAV

To prepare for towing, the crew of the disabled AAV sets an operable engine at 1,800 RPMs. Hatches and plenums are closed, watertight integrity is insured, the transmission is placed in the neutral position, and the mode selector switch is set in the water/track mode. If the hydraulic bilge pumps are not functioning due to an engine failure, the master switch is left on and the electric bilge pumps are activated. Before towing of the disabled AAV commences, the crew on the disabled vehicle attempts repairs, and if unsuccessful, the AAV is taken under tow. The preferred method of towing an AAV is stern to bow, and those procedures are as follows:

- The safety vehicle should be positioned with the stern to the bow of the vehicle being towed. An alternative method involving docking the sterns of both vehicles can be used when the integrity of the disabled vehicle's plenums is questioned.

- The disabled vehicle provides the towlines. One end of each of the two 50-foot towlines are passed through the eyes of the aft mooring bits of the towing vehicle and secured to the quick release mechanism.

- The port towline is attached through the starboard mooring bit, and the starboard towline is attached through the port mooring bit. In this way, the towlines are crossed, affording great control over the disabled vehicle once it is under tow. Once the two lines are connected, care must be taken to avoid possible backlash injury.

- The crew of the disabled vehicle secures hatches. The crew of the towing vehicle positions its hatches as follows:
  o The driver's hatch is locked at the combat lock.
  o The troop commander's hatch is closed.
  o The crew chief positions the turret to face aft and secures the hatch.
- The towing vehicle crew chief places the vehicle ax in the turret for ready use to disconnect towlines should the quick release mechanism fail.
- The crew chief of the towing vehicle looks aft from inside the turret to watch the condition of the disabled vehicle. The third crewman is stationed inside at the rear of the towing vehicle to observe the proceedings from the vision block. Crewmen should be evacuated from disabled AAVs that are without electrical power and have lost watertight integrity.
- Hatches should be kept closed on both vehicles until the AAV is towed through the surf zone to the high watermark on the beach and there is slack in the lines.

In addition to the above policy, when towing a disabled AAV with another AAV, the appropriate naval authority will determine the final course of action. Disabled AAVs should be towed to the nearest safe haven (amphibious ship or beach).

Wet-well ships are the preferred platform of amphibious ship. See appendix I for recovery procedures. Disabled AAVs will be towed through the surf at a 90-degree angle to the surf line and to a point on the beach where—

- Neither vehicle has tracks in the water.
- Collision between the vehicles is impossible.
- Disabled AAV will not roll back.

When the point on the beach has been reached, tow cables can then replace towlines. The rescuing vehicle may attempt to tow the disabled vehicle through the surf zone and to the high watermark of the beach, thereby eliminating the necessity of hooking up land towing lines in the surf zone. If the beach gradient is steep or surf conditions permit, the vehicle may stop before the high watermark and connect tow cables.

Special Safety Considerations

The following special safety measures should be considered for water operations:

- When conducting AAV water operations, the third crewman must ride in the troop compartment of the AAV to constantly monitor watertight integrity.

● Planning for water operations should include alternate plans and timed evacuation drills.

● When planning for water operations in an emergency, water temperature, sea state, and available safety vehicles/vessels must be considered to determine the best type of evacuation to employ; brief the evacuation method; and practice these drills.

● When evacuation of troops and crew is required in a combat environment, the crew chief, with advice from the troop commander, must quickly decide whether to retain gear/weapons.

● After the command is given to evacuate the AAV, crewmen will not remain in a disabled AAV that is sinking and without power.

● Only the most experienced AAV crews should attempt the recovery of an AAVR7A1 because of its unique weight and balance considerations.

Sinking AAV Procedures

Although the current series of AAVs is the most seaworthy, rapid vehicle sinking may occur, making it impossible to evacuate embarked personnel before the vehicle slips under the surface of the water. Crew and passengers should stay with the sunken vehicle if it remains buoyant because of wave action in the surf zone and await recovery by another AAV. If the vehicle settles in the surf zone and is completely grounded where the water depth and wave action do not create a buoyant effect, crew and passengers should—

● Seek air pockets formed in the troop compartment.
● Open hatches after internal and external pressures have equalized.
● Abandon the vehicle in pairs over the side in a direction that is parallel to the beach, but not leeward of the vehicle.
● Inflate life preservers after leaving the vehicle.

Crewmen's Responsibilities

Based on the status of the disabled AAV, the crew of the disabled vehicle will have the responsibilities outlined in table E-1.

Table E-1. Crewmen's Responsibilities.

Status of Disabled AAV	Crew Chief	Troop Commander	Driver	Crewman
Dead engine (with battery power)	Display November flag during the day or fire white flare and display vertical light beam in the air at night. Inform platoon commander of the situation by radio. Troubleshoot the AAV systems to attempt to regain power. Inform troop commander of the situation and steps being taken. Check operation of electric bilge pumps. Keep hatches closed to prevent taking in excess water. Prepare to receive tow or transfer troops. Supervise transfer of troops to safety vehicle.	Obey crew chief's commands. Give a warning order to the troops to prepare for evacuation as directed by the crew chief. Assist crew in maintaining discipline.	Keep master switch on. Keep electric bilge pumps on. Shift to neutral. Check fuel shutoff lever to ensure it is in an upright position. Check fuel shutoff valve on deck behind driver. Attempt to restart engine. Continue attempts to restart engine (conserve electricity). Disconnect hydrostatic steer unit if the engine will not start, and prepare for tow and/or transfer of troops.	Check constantly for watertight integrity, and report compromises immediately to the crew chief. Help maintain discipline in the troop compartment. Assist topside with troop transfer.
Dead engine (without battery power)	Display November flag during the day or fire white flare and use battle lantern to display vertical light beam in the air at night. Troubleshoot the AAV systems and attempt to regain power. Inform the troop commander of the situation and steps being taken. Keep hatches closed to prevent taking in excess water. Prepare to receive tow and to transfer troops. Supervise the transfer of troops to safety vehicle or the water.	Obey crew chief's commands. Inform troops of the situation, and prepare for troop transfer or vehicle evacuation. Assist crew in maintaining discipline.	Shift engine throttle to neutral. Troubleshoot the AAV systems to attempt to regain power. Disconnect the hydrostatic steer unit, and prepare for tow and transfer of troops.	Check constantly for watertight integrity, and report leaks immediately to the crew chief. Help maintain discipline in the troop compartment. Assist topside with troop transfer.
Sinking (with power)	Wave the November flag during the day or fire red star distress signal in the air over the vehicle, and direct the beam of the battle lantern vertically at night. Notify the platoon commander by radio. Open cargo hatches with assistance from crewman. Order evacuation of embarked troops/execute evacuation procedures. Order crew to abandon vehicle. Debark the vehicle after personnel have been evacuated.	Obey crew chief's commands. Assist crew in maintaining discipline.	Keep engine, electric bilge pumps, and headlights on. Lower the seat and evacuate the vehicle through the driver's hatch when ordered by the crew chief.	Check constantly for watertight integrity, and report compromises immediately to the crew chief. Help maintain discipline in the troop compartment. Assist crew chief in opening cargo hatches. Assist passengers topside. Notify the crew chief when embarked troops have been evacuated. Evacuate the vehicle when ordered by the crew chief.
Sinking (without power) constitutes an emergency	Wave the November flag during the day, and fire red star distress signal in the air over the vehicle and display vertical light beam in the air at night. Notify platoon commander of the situation via voice or flashing light. Order preparations for evacuation of embarked troops. Open cargo hatches with assistance from crewman. Execute evacuation procedures. Order crew to abandon vehicle. Debark the vehicle after personnel have been evacuated.	Obey crew chief's commands. Assist crew in maintaining discipline.	Keep master switch on. Shift engine throttle to neutral. Troubleshoot the AAV system and attempt to regain power. Lower the seat and evacuate the vehicle through the driver's hatch when ordered by the crew chief.	Check constantly for watertight integrity and report compromises immediately to the crew chief. Help maintain discipline in the troop compartment. Assist crew chief in opening cargo hatches. Assist passengers topside. Notify the crew chief when embarked troops have been evacuated. Evacuate the vehicle when ordered by the crew chief.

APPENDIX F. LANDING DOCUMENTS

MCWP 5-1, *Marine Corps Planning Process*, and NWP 3-02.1, *Ship-To-Shore Movement*, contain instructions for the preparation of landing documents. The documents in this appendix are specific to AA units.

Documents   **Page**

Landing Diagram F-2
Landing Craft and Amphibious Vehicle Assignment Table F-3
Serial Assignment Table F-4
Landing Sequence Table F-5
Assault Schedule F-6
Amphibious Vehicle Availability Table F-7
Amphibious Vehicle Employment Plan F-8

Landing Diagram

The landing diagram is the graphic means of illustrating the plan for ship-to-shore movement of the scheduled waves of an assault unit. The landing formation and type of landing craft or vehicles comprising the wave are normally determined by the commander, amphibious task force (CATF), and the commander, landing force (CLF), based on naval capabilities for supporting the plan and upon recommendations from the AAV unit leader and AAV availability. AAVs depicted in the landing diagram portray the boat teams embarked on AAVs numbered from left to right in each wave. For example, number 5-5 would be the fifth vehicle from the left in the fifth wave. For planning purposes, the landing diagram should allow dispersion of at least 25 (day)/50 (night) meters between AAVs, at least 3 minutes between AAV waves, and at least 10 minutes between boated waves, unless landing in column. This provides room for AAVs to move off the beach before the next wave and for boated waves to extract from the beach to the boat return lane.

Beach Red 1 H-hour 0530 local							
Scheduled Waves	Wave Composition						
Wave 0	01	02	03	04			
H-3 minutes	X^L	X	X^L	X			
Wave 1	1st and 2d Platoons, Company G, BLT 2/5						
H-hour	1-1	1-2	1-3	1-4	1-5	1-6	1-7
	X	X	X	(X)	X	X	X
Wave 2	3rd Platoon and Mortars, Company G, BLT 2/5 Command Group						
H+3 minutes	2-1	2-2	2-3	2-4	2-5	2-6	2-7	2-8
	X	X	X	X	(X)	X	C	R
Wave 3	Weapons Company, BLT 2/5						
H+6	3-6	3-4	3-2	3-1	3-3	3-5	
	U	U	U	(U)	U	U	
X = AAVP7 X^L = AAVP7 W/MK-154 C = AAVC7	R = AAVR7 U = LCU (X) = wave commander						

Landing Craft and Amphibious Vehicle Assignment Table

The landing craft and amphibious vehicle assignment table shows the breakdown of troop units into boat teams and the assignment of boat teams to waves or to a serialized element of an nonscheduled unit. This table and the debarkation schedule furnish ship commanding officers with information for the debarkation of troops. AA commanders advise supported commanders and staffs with respect to vehicle capacity and methods of employment.

Craft Number	Personnel and Material	Boat Spaces	Beach Red 1 Formation
1-1 AAVP7	Company Commander, Company G	1	
	Messenger Radio Operator	1	
	81-millimeter FO Team with 1 Radio Operator	2	Column
	FAC with 1 Radio Operator	2	
	Weapons Platoon Commander, Company G	1	X 1-1
	Company 1st Sergeant, Company G	1	
		8	
1-2 AAVP7	Platoon Commander, 1st Platoon, Company G	1	
	Messenger Radio Operator	13	
	1st Squad, 1st Platoon, Company G	1	X 1-2
	Corpsman	2	
		17	
1-3 AAVP7	Platoon Guide, 1st Platoon, Company G	1	
	2d Squad, 1st Platoon, Company G	13	
	Corpsman	1	X 1-3
	1st Machine Gun Team, Weapons Platoon, Company G	3	
		18	
1-4 AAVP7	Platoon Sergeant, 1st Platoon, Company G	1	X 1-4
	3d Squad, 1st Platoon, Company G	12	
	Corpsman	1	
	1st Assault Team, Weapons Platoon, Company G	2	
		16	
1-14 AAVC7	BLT 2/5 Commander	1	
	S-3	1	
	S-2	1	
	NGF Liaison Officer	1	
	Air Officer	1	
	Company Commander, Weapons Company (FSC)	1	C 1-14
	Artillery Liaison Officer	1	
	Radio Operators	1	
	Communications Technician	3	
		11	
X = AAVP7	C = AAVC7		R = AAVR7

Serial Assignment Table

A serial is a group of troop units, supporting units, and their equipment embarked in the same ship that will be landed on the same beach at the same time. AAVs may be used to transport a serial.

The table is prepared and issued at LF level. AA unit personnel advise as to capacities of AAVs and potential problems with loading AAVs aboard ships.

Serial Number	Unit	Number of Personnel	Material Equipment Vehicles	Number and Type of Craft	Parent Ship	Remarks
A Company (Rein), 1st Battalion, 4th Marines (1401-1402)						
1401	Co A (-)	140		7 AAVP7 1 AAVC7	LST-1179	1st Wave Beach Red 1
1402	3d Platoon (Rein) Company C	126	2 81-mm mortars	7 AAVP7	LST-1179	2d Wave Beach Red 1
B Company, 1st Battalion, 4th Marines (1403-1404)						
1403	Company B (-)	133		7 AAVP7	LSD-49	1st Wave Beach Blue 1
1404	3d Platoon, Company B	120		7AAVP7 1 AAVR7	LSD-36	2d Wave Beach Blue 1

Landing Sequence Table

Detailed plans for the ship-to-shore movement of nonscheduled units are set forth in the landing sequence table. The LF and naval agencies use this table as the principal document in executing and controlling the movement of non-scheduled units. The completed table is prepared at LF level, and subordinate units extract applicable portions. AA commanders advise as to which vehicle best meets this LF requirement, where it would be best embarked, and other considerations pertaining to AAV employment.

Unit	Element	Serial Number	Carrier Number	Ship Type	Beach	Remarks
G Company (-), 2/5	3d Platoon	910	3	AAV	LSD-36	Red
A Company (-), 2d Tank Battalion	3d Platoon	911	3	LCU	LSD-36	Red
B Company, 2d Tank Battalion	1st and 2d Platoons	909	3	LCU	LSD-37	Blue
B Company (-), 2d Tank Battalion	3d Platoon	908	3	LCU	LSD-37	Blue
1/10	A Battery	1013	7	LCM	LPD-5	Red
1/10	B Battery	1014	7	LCM	LPD-5	Red
	C Battery	1015	7	LCM	LPD-1	Red
1/10	Headquarters Battery	1016	3	LCM	LPD-5	Red
	D Battery	1023	8	LCM	LPD-4	Blue
Division Tactical CP		401	4	LCM	LHA-1	Blue
A Company (-), 2d Engineer.	1st Platoon	105	3	AAV	LSD-28	Red

Assault Schedule

An assault schedule is prepared and issued to prescribe the composition and timing of waves landing over designated beaches. The schedule is prepared at LF level, and subordinate units extract applicable portions. The schedule shows each scheduled wave number, the time that landing craft or AAVs are scheduled to land, the craft/vehicle serial numbers, and the units landing.

| | | Beach | | | |
| | | Red 1 | | Red 2 | |
Wave	Time	Craft/Vehicle Serial Number	Unit	Craft/Vehicle Serial Number	Unit
1	H-Hour	12 AAVP7 1426	Company A 1/7	12 AAVP7 1426	Company E 2/7
2	H+5	12 AAVP7 1427	Company B 1/7	12 AAVP7 1477	Company F 2/7
3	H+10	6 AAVP7 1430	Company C 1/7 1st and 2d Platoons	6 AAVP7 1480	Company G 2/7 1st and 2d Platoons
4	H+15	6 AAVP7 1431	Company C (-) 1/7 3d Platoon	5 AAVP7 1481	Company G (-) 2/7 3d Platoon
5	H+20	3 LCU 2351	Company A (Rein) 3d Tank Battalion	4 LCM-8 1482/1484	Weapons Company 2/7
6	H+27	8 LCVP 1432-1434	Weapons Company 1/7	8 LCVP 1483/1485	H&S Company (-) 2/7
On-Call Waves					
Report to PCS at H+40		1 LCM-8 2 LCM-6 1 LCVP 2305/2306	Shore Party Team 1	1 LCM-8 2 LCM-8 1 LCVP 2307/2308	Shore Party Team 2
Report to PCS at H+45		2 LCVP	Floating Dumps	2 LCVP	Floating Dumps

Amphibious Vehicle Availability Table

The amphibious vehicle availability table is a list of AAV numbers and types available to the LF. The LF prepares the amphibious vehicle availability table using data derived from consultation with the AAV commander. The table includes the number and type of vehicles embarked in each ship and identifies the AA unit involved.

Ship	AAV Unit	Number and Type of AAV			Remarks
		AAVP7	AAVC7	AAVR7	
LST-1179	3d Platoon, Company B, 3d AA Battalion	13	1	1	
LSD-36	1st Platoon, Company A, 3d AA Battalion 2d Battalion, Company A, 3d AA Battalion 2d Platoon, Company D, 3d AA Battalion	13 12 16	1 1 1	1	2 MK-154 LMC Kits
LSD-37	Company C, 3d AA Battalion	43	3	1	
LPD-1	1st Platoon, Company D, 3d AA Battalion	16	1	1	2MK-154 LMC Kits
Total		113	8	4	

Amphibious Vehicle Employment Plan

The amphibious vehicle employment plan shows the planned employment of amphibious vehicles, including their employment after landing. The CLF's staff prepares the amphibious vehicle employment plan when shipping availability is confirmed and after the assault schedule is completed. The AA commander should be intimately involved in the completion of this document, as it controls AAV employment. The plan includes identification of ships in which vehicles are embarked, number and type of amphibious vehicles employed, wave in which the vehicles will land, and destination of vehicles.

Origin	Number and Type of Amphibious Vehicle				Wave	Destination	Remarks
	AAVP7	AAVC7	AAVR7	LARC			
LSD-36	7				1	Red 1	1st and 2d Platoons Company A 1/7
LSD-36	6	1	1		2	Red 1	3d Platoon Company A 1/7
LSD-38	7				3	Red 1	1st and 2d Platoons Company B 1/7
LSD-38	6	1	1		4	Red 1	3d Platoon Company B 1/7
Second Trip							
3d Platoon, Company B, 3d AA Battalion	12					LHA-1	Transport Company C 1/7 to Red 1
2d Platoon, Company B, 3d AA Battalion	12					LPD-1	To land artillery ammunition as needed

APPENDIX G. GRID REFERENCE SYSTEM

The Navy uses the grid reference system to control the ship-to-shore movement of landing craft. Composed of a time/space overlay known as a boat lane diagram and a series of standard radio transmissions known as grid position messages, the system enables a wave of landing craft [AAVs] to—

- Navigate the boat lane and land in the correct position.
- Land ashore at the proper time as specified by the landing timeline.

Boat Lane Diagram

The boat lane diagram is an approximate picture of the boat lane from the launch area or in the case of an underway launch, from the line of departure (LD) to the beach. Longitudinal lines in the diagram divide the lane into three sections: left (L), center (C), and right (R). Left and right sections are each 40 percent of the total width; the center section is 20 percent of the total width. Lane positions are described by L, C or R followed by a one- or two-digit number. A double letter such as RR or LL indicates positions outside the lane. The boat control team has the gridiron boat lanes plotted to scale in the combat information center (CIC).

The Navy tracks grid positions, which are the locations of the center of waves, by using the boat lane diagram. By using radar to track the landing craft, the Navy can track the wave. As the wave changes course and speed, Navy personnel plot these changes as a series of dots representing the center of the wave on the boat lane diagram laid out in the CIC. The wave's position in the boat lane is based on the distance from the shore and the location relative to the center of the lane.

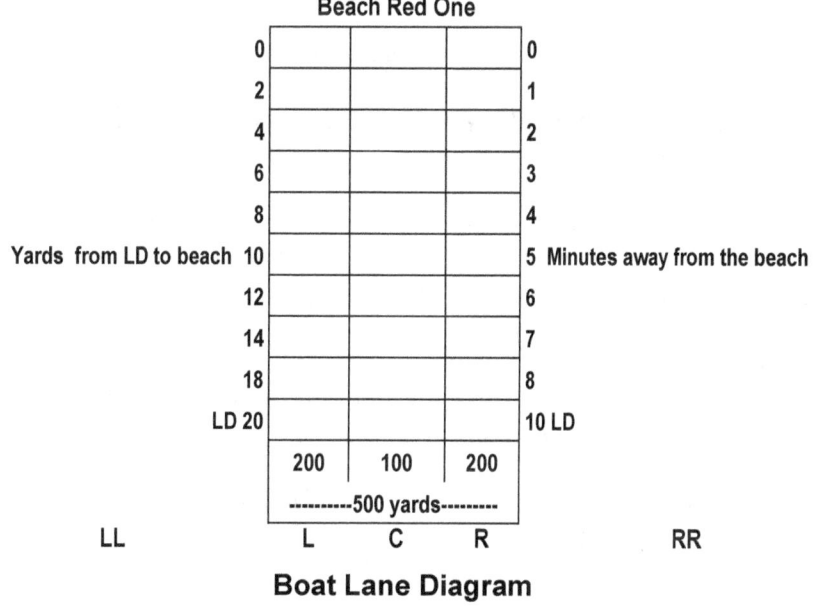

Boat Lane Diagram

Grid Position Messages

To guide the landing craft waves ashore, the Navy has devised a series of short standardized radio transmissions.

Message Parts

Each transmission has six parts, and they follow each other in sequence.

Wave Call Sign

The call sign of the wave consists of the wave number and the designated beach for that wave. The following example refers to the first wave going to Beach Red One:

One Red One.

Message Identifier

The message identifier is the ship's call sign and the words Grid Posit (short for grid position). For example:

One Red One, this is Red Catskill, Grid Posit.

Location of Center Vehicle in the Boat Lane

The location of the center vehicle in the boat lane is the wave's physical location as it is plotted in the CIC. The orientation to the center of the wave is given first. The following example indicates a wave centered in the left side of the boat lane:

One Red One, this is Red Catskill, Grid Posit, Lima.

The following message indicates a wave centered outside and to the left of the boat lane:

One Red One, Grid Posit, Lima Lima.

Distance of the Wave from the Beach

The distance the center vehicle is from the beach will be reported as a number following the location. The following example indicates a wave that is centered in the boat lane 1,600 yards from the beach:

One Red One, this is Red Catskill, Grid Posit, Charlie, 16.

Time in Relation to the Landing Schedule

This is how the wave is proceeding in respect to the timeline for the movement. On time, early or late are the three key phrases used to express time in relation to the landing schedule. This portion is followed by a time in minutes. The following example indicates a wave that is right of center in the boat lane, 1,200 yards from the beach, and 2 minutes behind schedule or late:

> One Red One, this is Red Catskill, Grid Posit, Romeo, 12, Late 2.

Corrections

This is direction from the Navy on how to correct the heading of the wave. These corrections should be transmitted immediately to the wave so it may correct its position. Usually, late time corrections are given only if the wave is more than 1 minute late. Corrections can take several forms. Examples would be:

> Vector Right 10 Degrees, Speed Up.

> Vector Left 5 Degrees, Slow Down.

Assembled Message

Once the parts are assembled into one grid position message, it will tell the wave commander exactly where the wave is in the boat lane and whether or not it needs to correct its heading. The following example indicates Wave One going to Beach Red One is in the center of the boat lane, 1,600 yards from the beach, and they are behind schedule 1 minute:

> One Red One, this is Red Catskill, Grid Posit, Charlie, 16, Late 1, Out.

The following example indicates Wave Two going to Beach Red One is centered in the left side of the boat lane, 1,400 yards from the beach, and they are late 2 minutes. They are directed to vector right 5 degrees and speed up.

> Two Red One, this is Red Catskill, Grid Posit, Lima, 14, Late 2,
> Vector Right 5 Degree, Speed Up, Over.

Procedures

During amphibious operations, the primary control ship (PCS) and AAV waves must track the grids for units involved. The following procedures ensure situational awareness and that the waves land at the correct location on the shore as scheduled:

● Upon launching from the ship, the wave will check in with the PCS on Boat Bravo. Boat Bravo is used to control waves from the time it leaves the ship until it crosses the LD. Since AAVs are normally launched at or in close proximity to the LD, Boat Bravo will probably not be used for long.

- Once the wave crosses the LD, AAVs will switch to Boat Alpha to receive grid positions from the PCS.
- The PCS tracks the wave and fixes the position of each wave on the boat lane diagram in CIC.
- The boat control team then transmits to the AAV wave commander the AAV's position in the prescribed format.
- After receiving a grid position message that indicates the wave is not in the center of the lane and or is not progressing along the lane according to schedule, the wave guide officer (WGO) corrects the position and movement of the wave.
- Control officers will supplement grid positions with vectors and early or late wave-timing information as necessary.
- Normally, grid positions are transmitted every minute from the LD to 20 yards from the beach unless corrective action is required, in which case they are transmitted more frequently. In low visibility, positions will be provided once per minute from the LD to the beach.
- The last 1,000 yards to the beach is run at full (battle) speed.
- To obtain full benefit from the grid, AAV wave commanders may plot their position each time the controlling station transmits it to obtain a track of the wave's progress. The effects of wind and sea and/or taking incorrect headings can be determined and corrected on the next launch.
- Once firm radio communications are established, grid positions are transmitted without requiring wave commanders to receipt. However, vectors should be receipted. If the wave commander fails to receipt for orders by radio, the PCS will continue to transmit and request visual acknowledgment.
- When the AAV wave commander's vehicle contacts the bottom, the WGO will transmit "Touchdown, touchdown, touchdown." This notifies the PCS that the vehicles have landed ashore.

APPENDIX H. AMPHIBIOUS SHIP AAV CAPACITIES

Ships of the amphibious fleet have varying internal characteristics that affect their AAV carrying capacities. The AAV carrying capacities listed below are approximate maximum capacities for the classes of ships. For detailed planning, the ship's characteristics pamphlet must be consulted to determine the true capacity.

Ship Type and Class	AAV Capacity
LSD-28/Thomaston Class: Well Deck	48
LSD-36/Anchorage Class: Well Deck	47
LSD-41/Whidbey Island Class: Well Deck	64
LSD-49/Harpers Ferry Class: Well Deck	27
LPD-1/Raleigh Class: Upper Vehicle Load Well Deck	14 20
LPD-4/Austin Class: Upper Vehicle Load Well Deck	16 20
LPD-17 Class: Well Deck	38
LST-1179/Newport Class: Tank Deck	23
LHA-1/Tarawa Class: Well Deck	79
LHD-1/Wasp Class: Well Deck	52

APPENDIX I. EMBARKATION AND DEBARKATION PROCEDURES

Embarkation and debarkation of US Navy amphibious ships follow similar procedures to safely conduct operations. The landing ship dock (LSD), landing helicopter dock (LHD), landing platform dock (LPD), and general purpose amphibious assault ship (LHA) can conduct embarkation and debarkation operations by flooding their well decks (wet loading), or they can conduct AAV operations with a dry well deck (dry loading). The landing ship, tank (LST) has different procedures due to its older design and capabilities. Although few LSTs are still commissioned, AAV crews may have to conduct operations on LSTs if operating with another nation's navy. AAV crews should be familiar with each ship's method of debarkation and embarkation, safety criteria, and recovery procedures for disabled AAVs.

Methods

The following are methods of LSD, LHD, LPD, LHA, and LST embarkation and debarkation:

- Ship at anchor.
- Ship lying to or with bare steerageway (screws and rudders used only to maintain ships head into the swells). This is the least desirable method of embarkation of AAVs. Such an embarkation should not be attempted when less than optimum conditions exist.
- By ramp while the ship is moored at pier.
- Ship is underway (debarkation only).
- When married to a pontoon causeway (for LSTs).

Safety Criteria

The following chart covers the various safety criteria LSD, LHD, LPD, and LHA ships must follow to safely embark and debark AAVs.

	Stern Gate Position	Vent Fans	Ballast	Water Depth at Sill	Maximum Ship Speed
Debark	0 to –3 degrees[1]	on[2]	N/A	6 inches to 1 foot	21.5 knots
Embark	lowered	on[2]	steep wedge	4 to 6 feet[3]	0

[1] LSD, LHD, LPD, and LHA stern gates should be lowered to an angle level with the well. If depressed greater than 10 degrees, it can interfere with AAV abilities to break free from the ship's wake once launched.

[2] LSD-41 class ships do not have vent fans.

[3] The optimal depth for recovery is approximately 4 feet of water at the sill. Ships should ballast to 8 feet to recover a disabled AAV that is being towed by another AAV or when ships positioning or steadying lines will be used.

The following chart covers the various safety criteria the LST ships must follow to embark and debark AAVs.

	Stern Gate Position	Vent Fans	Ballast	Water Depth at Sill	Maximum Ship Speed	Turntable Position	Stern Anchor
Debark	lowered, locked[1]	on	0	0	16 knots[2]	locked	N/A
Embark	lowered, locked[1]	on	19 feet 6 inches	0	0	free	lowered to 10 feet

[1] Stern gate wires must be sacked and secured to stern of ship to prevent them from fouling AAV tracks.

[2] LSTs should only attempt 16-knot launches if the stern gate lock ship alteration has been performed. If this modification has not been performed, the maximum launch speed is 6 knots.

Embarkation Procedures

Embarking AAVs aboard an amphibious ship can be challenging and dangerous, especially in higher sea states. The following steps should minimize risk:

- The AA unit should maintain an interval of 50 to 75 meters between vehicles in column to facilitate loading. For LSTs, ensure VIC-12 AAV antennas are tied down before embarking.
- Before the signal to load, the first AAV should position approximately 100 meters from the stern, depending upon operational conditions and schedules.
- Just before receiving the signal to load, the first AAV driver will retract the bow plane.
- Upon receiving the loading signal (i.e., green flag or green light) from the ship's crew, the AAV will approach the well bow on. The approach to the ship should be made from directly astern in water-jets mode at 1,500 to 1,800 RPM.
- The AAV driver will receive guidance, via hand signals, from well-deck guides.
- Approximately 30 meters before entering the well, the driver should place the vehicle in first gear to engage the tracks.
- As the AAV approaches the sill, the driver will slow down and proceed until the tracks touch down.
- Once in solid contact with the deck, the driver will be ground-guided to pivot the vehicle 180 degrees.
- Directed by the ground guide, the driver will back the vehicle into its parking space. Although less desirable, AAVs may pivot when waterborne using their water-jets and be ground-guided back into their parking spaces.
- For LSTs, AAVs should not be turned when moving up the stern gate because the ramp will damage the AAV track. A driver failing to negotiate the LST ramp should ease back into the water, reposition in water-jet mode, and try again. Upon reaching the crest of the ramp, the driver will stop and go to land mode. The driver will be ground-guided to the aft turntable. The driver sets the AAV parking brake, and the turntable will rotate the vehicle. Ground guides will guide the vehicle for parking.

- To prevent confusion and mishaps, embarked personnel will remain aboard the AAVs until all vehicles are embarked and stopped.
- Select AAV personnel may disembark to begin preparations to secure the vehicles.
- When directed by the well-deck supervisor or petty officer in charge (POIC), troops and other crewmen may disembark. Troops proceed to assigned berthing, and AAV crews secure their vehicles.
- The procedure is repeated for the remaining AAVs to embark.

Recovery of Disabled AAVs

If conditions necessitate a disabled AAV being brought aboard amphibious ships, recovery safety considerations and procedures must be followed to avoid serious mishaps.

Safety

The decision to load AAVs in rough seas or in foul weather rests with the AA unit leader and ship's captain. Personnel safety will be the primary consideration when retrieving a disabled AAV. Other factors to consider include—

- Crew experience.
- Equipment ability to recover the disabled AAV.
- Action of waves within the well and upon the vehicle to be recovered.

Procedures

The disabled AAV will be towed by another AAV astern the LSD, LHD, LPD or LHA to a distance considered safe under the prevailing conditions. SOPs for towing disabled AAVs in the water will apply. In preparation to recover a disabled AAV, LSDs, LHDs, LPDs or LHAs should ballast to 8 feet of water at the sill. This will provide the towed AAV sufficient room to move into the well before excessive tension is placed on the AAV's towropes/ship's positioning lines. Although the ship's SOP will contain specific embarking details, the following are general procedures for embarking a disabled AAV aboard an LSD, LHD, LPD or LHA:

- When signaled, the towing vehicle will pull the disabled AAV as far into the well deck as possible without causing the towropes to separate.
- Once the disabled AAV is grounded in the well, the towing vehicle will slowly back up, releasing the tension on the towropes. Care should be taken to not foul the towing vehicle's tracks with the towropes.
- After the towropes are removed, positioning lines may be attached to maintain the disabled AAV's safe position in the well. Positioning lines may also be used to turn the AAV for backing into position.

- Once the disabled AAV is secured with lines, the towing AAV will move close enough to the disabled vehicle for AAV personnel to attach a tow bar or tow cables. The towing vehicle will then continue to pull the disabled AAV out of the way of the operation.
- If the AAV cannot be towed into the well to a point where it can be recovered using tow cables or bars, it will be secured to the well deck using positioning or steadying lines, fenders, and/or dunnage. Once the ship has a dry well deck, the disabled AAV can then be recovered using tow cables or a tow bar.

For LSTs, there is a different procedure for receiving disabled AAVs. The disabled AAV will be towed to the area astern of the LST by another AAV to a distance considered safe under prevailing conditions. SOPs for towing a disabled AAV in the water will apply. A disabled AAV will be the second vehicle embarked if possible. Although the ship's SOP will contain specific embarking details, figure I-1 depicts the following procedures for embarking a disabled AAV:

- Two painted (one white and one red) positioning lines (4a and 4b) will be thrown to the AAV (1) and attached to the topside mooring cleats (2).
- To ensure the lines cross, the red one will be attached to the starboard cleat and the white to the port cleat.
- The AAV crewman will secure the positioning lines and attach a section of rope to the tow cable (3) so that it can be lowered from within the driver's hatch to ensure the crewmen are not exposed to lines or cables that may snap during recovery.
- The line handlers aboard the LST will heave to the AAV so that the tracks rest securely on the edge of the ramp.
- Once the AAV has been properly positioned on the LST ramp and upon signal from the tank deck POIC, the AAV driver will lower the tow cable so a ship's crewman can attach the snaking line (6).
- The AAV will be pulled aboard the ship using a series of blocks and the ship's winch.
- Once the AAV is centered upon the aft turntable, the driver will shift the transmission into neutral, set the parking brake, and the vehicle will be turned 180 degrees.

Debarkation Procedures

Debarkation of AAVs can be difficult and complicated. Failure to follow procedures may cause injury or death or cause serious delays that affect the mission. The following are recommended procedures for debarkation:

- AAV crews will proceed to the well deck 1 to 1 1/2 hours before launch.
- The POIC, ship's first lieutenant, and/or AA unit leader will direct the AAV crews to remove and stow gripes.

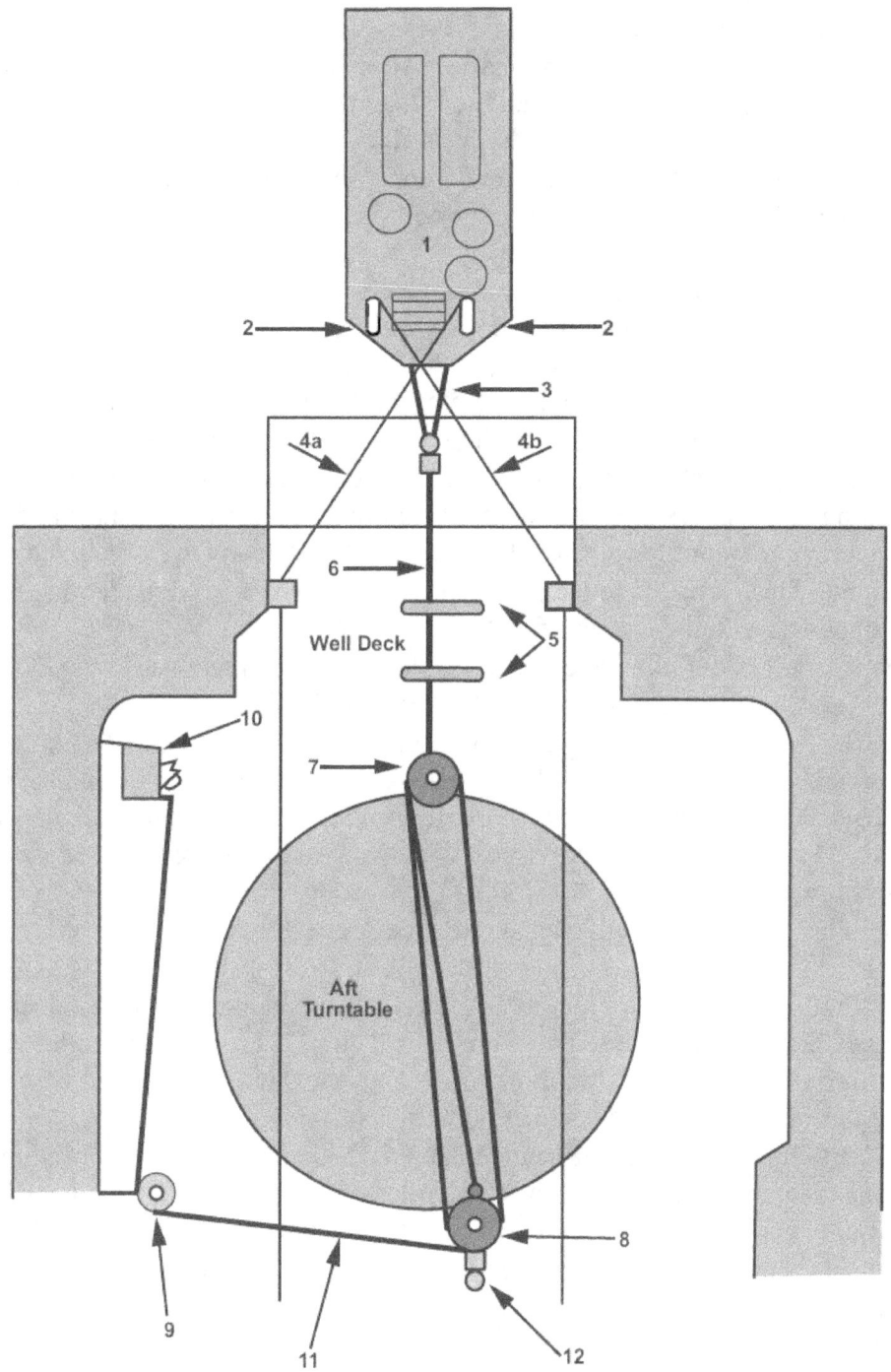

Well Deck

Aft
Turntable

1.	AAV	7.	Traveling Block
2.	AAV Mooring Cleats	8.	Standing Block
3.	Tow Cable	9.	Fairlead Block
4a.	White Positioning Line	10.	Snaking Winch
4b.	Red Positioning Line	11.	6 Nylon Line
5.	Portable Bitts	12.	Baxter Bolt
6.	Snaking Line		

Figure I-1. LST Recovery Diagram.

● The ship's personnel must turn on the well-deck blowers or vent fans to high before the AAVs are started.

● The AAV crews conduct preliminary AAV warmups at least 1 hour before launch. Warmups in groups of not more than three AAVs at one time ensure engine exhaust fumes remain within well-deck blower capacity.

● AAV crews will stand by to embark troops after AAVs have been warmed up, checked, and shut down. Vehicles will only be restarted with permission of the AA unit leader or well-deck debark control.

● Troops should embark aboard their respective AAV no later than 30 to 45 minutes before launch and after the AAV engines are shut down. To reduce confusion and prevent injuries, only AAV personnel and necessary ship's crew should move in and among vehicles until time to load troops.

● Personnel may be required to load through the rear personnel hatch or through topside cargo hatches if tight spacing between AAVs prevents ramps from opening. The debarkation schedule must allow time for such delays and for inexperienced troops to receive safety briefs and find their way to their vehicle.

● The individual vehicle crew chiefs will manifest or verify premade manifests of all personnel to be embarked in their vehicles.

● The AA unit leader will collect, check, and give these manifests to the POIC.

● AAV crews will properly mark AAVs before debarkation during night operations. During night training launches, only blue or red chemical lights will be attached to one of each AAV's antennas. Green will not be used, as it is a signal or marker for a man overboard. If used in combat, chemical lights will be taped so that only the rear portion is showing to minimize enemy observation from shore.

● The ship's personnel will signal the first wave of AAVs to restart their engines.

● The first AAV will then proceed as directed to the launch line that is located approximately one AAV length from the sill (for LSTs, it is a white line just forward of the stern gate traction bars). The AAV will be stopped by a red flag during the day or red wand at night.

● AAVs will be staged in consecutive pairs at the launch line with a minimum 3-foot clearance between vehicles, regardless of whether AAVs are launched in a single column or in pairs. LSTs can only launch AAVs singly in column.

● The ship's personnel will use flags to launch the AAVs, which are normally launched singly.

● Each succeeding AAV, or pair of AAVs, will launch when the preceding AAV is clear and the ship's personnel give the signal. The next AAV will automatically move up to the launch line as each lead AAV launches. The signal to launch is a rapid waving of the green flag during the day or rapid waving of the green wand at night.

● AAVs of the follow-on waves will not restart their engines until signaled to do so by the ship's personnel. Normally, this signal is given 5 minutes before launch of that wave.

Appendix J. Standard Flags, Lights, and Markers Used to Control AAVs

The illustrations in this appendix include flags, lights, and markers that are employed at sea and ashore in the control of AAVs. These devices are also standard to landing craft and landing ships. Appendix C to MCWP 3-31.5 contains more illustrations of control means. The following symbols are used in the illustrations in this appendix:

- Steady light = ◯

- Blinking light = ◎

	Page
Beach Markers (from Seaward)	
Beach Red One	J-3
Beach Red Two	J-3
Oceanographic Markers (from Seaward)	
Rocks, Shoals, and Obstruction	J-4
Port	J-4
Starboard	J-4
Fairway of Channel	J-4
Miscellaneous Beach Signs	
One Way	J-5
Dump Direction Sign	J-5
Dud Flag	J-5
Dump Flag	J-5
Medical Evacuation Station	J-5
Mine Cleared Area	J-5
Unloading Point Markers	
Ammunition	J-6
Rations	J-6
Tracked Vehicles	J-6
Medical Supplies Casualty Evacuation	J-6
Wheeled Vehicles	J-6
Oil and Gas	J-6
Miscellaneous Supplies	J-7
Beaching Point for LST	J-7
Causeway Range Markers	J-7

Miscellaneous Flags and Identification Insignia

Boat Group Commander J-8
Assistant Boat Group Commander J-8
Channel Control Boat. J-8
AAV Emergency Flag J-8
Amphibious Vehicle Pool Control Officer J-8
Transfer Line Control Officer J-8
Self-Propelled Vehicle Embarked J-9
Bulk Cargo Requiring Personnel or Crane to Unload J-9
Cargo Requiring Assistance of Prime Mover to Unload J-9
Boats Assigned to Floating Dumps J-9
Bowser Boat. J-9
Casualty Receiving Treatment Ship. J-9
Salvage Boat J-9
Boat Team Paddle (third boat, second wave) J-10
Serial Paddle for On-Call and Nonscheduled Waves J-10
Beach Red One Flag J-10
Beach Red Two Flag J-10
Medical Boat J-11
Senior Beachmaster J-11

Beach Markers (From Seaward)

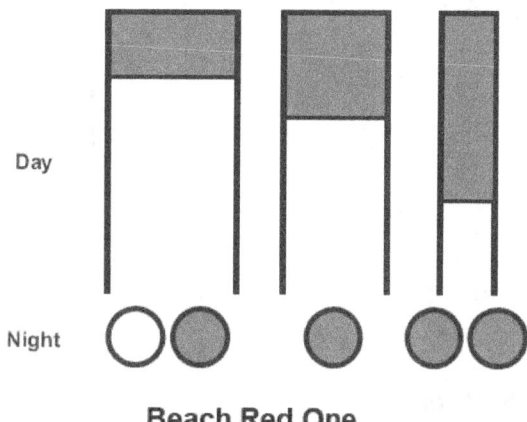

Beach Red One

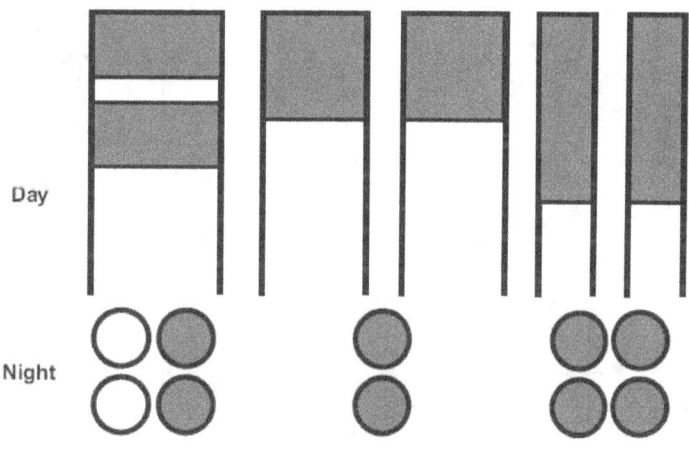

Beach Red Two

Oceanographic Markers (From Seaward)

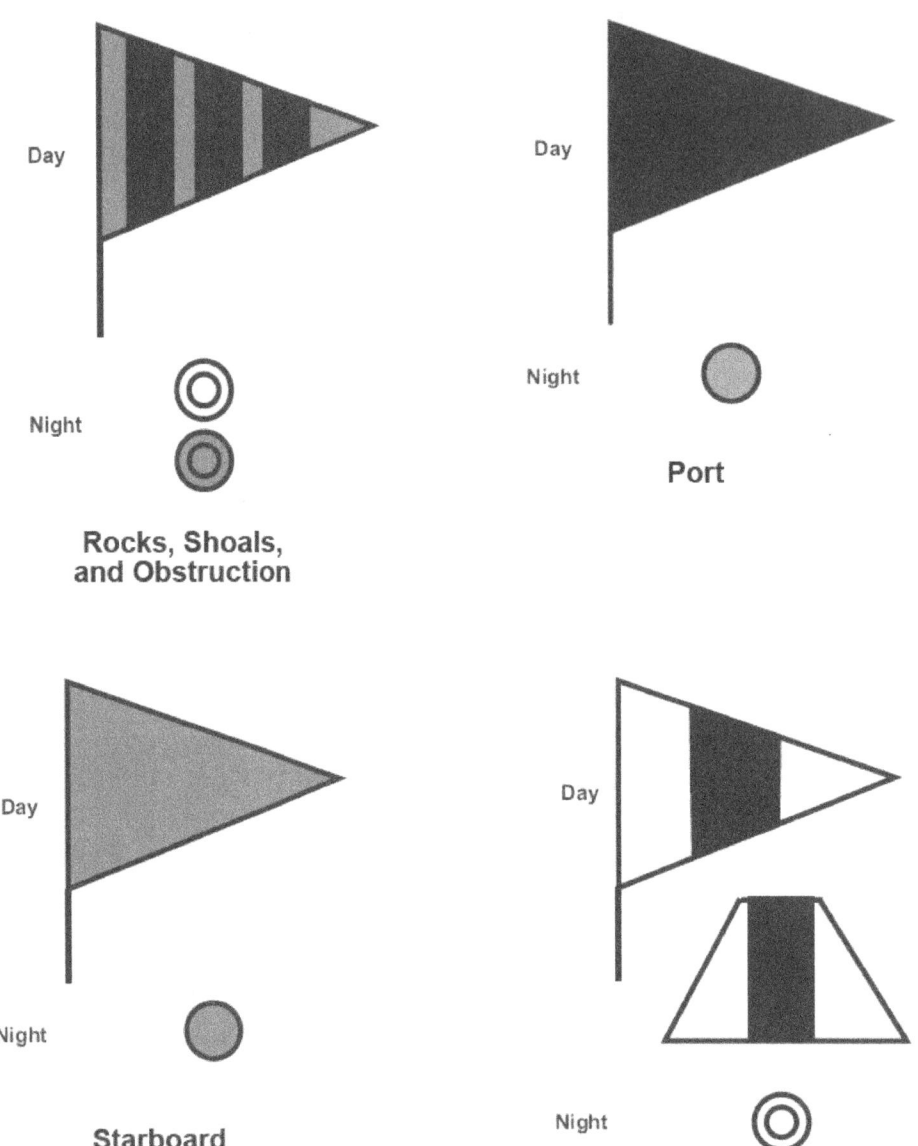

Rocks, Shoals,
and Obstruction

Port

Starboard

Fairway of Channel

Miscellaneous Beach Signs

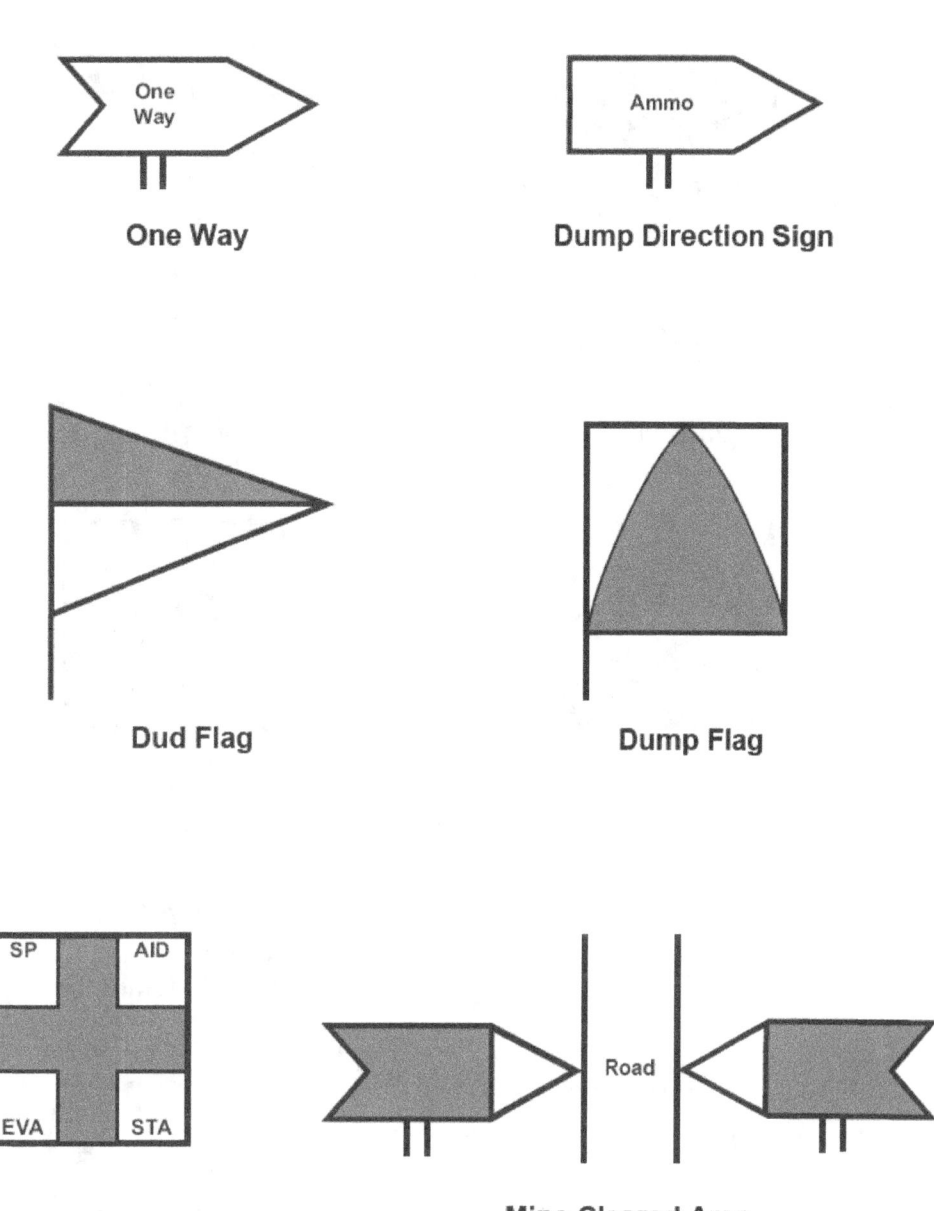

One Way

Dump Direction Sign

Dud Flag

Dump Flag

Medical
Evacuation Station

Mine Cleared Area

Unloading Point Markers

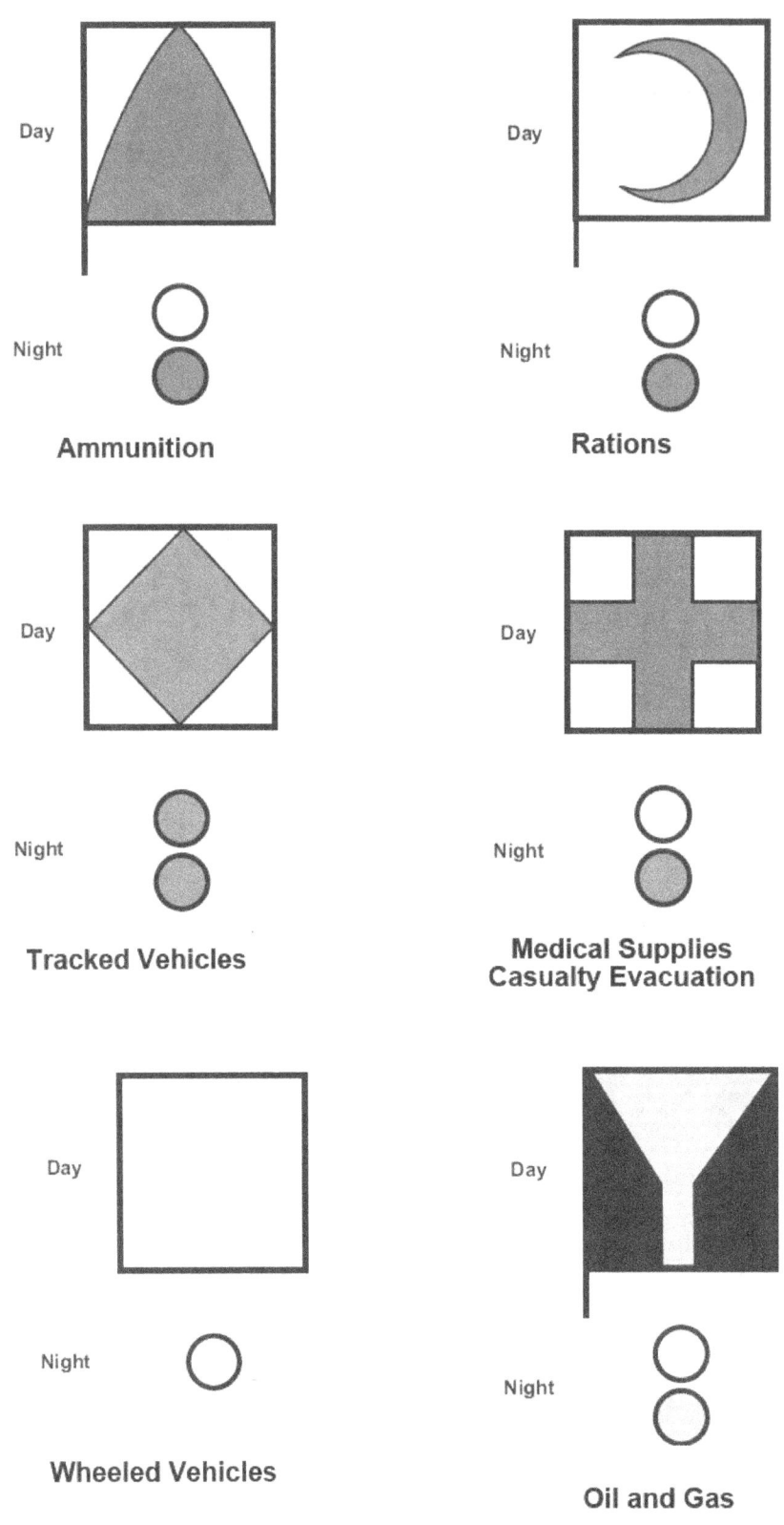

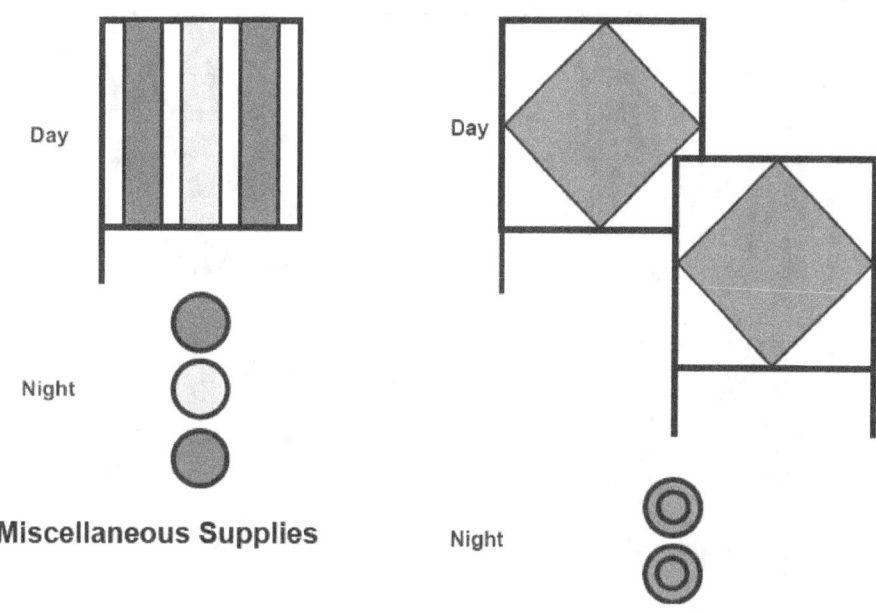

Day

Night

Miscellaneous Supplies

Day

Night

Beaching Point for LST

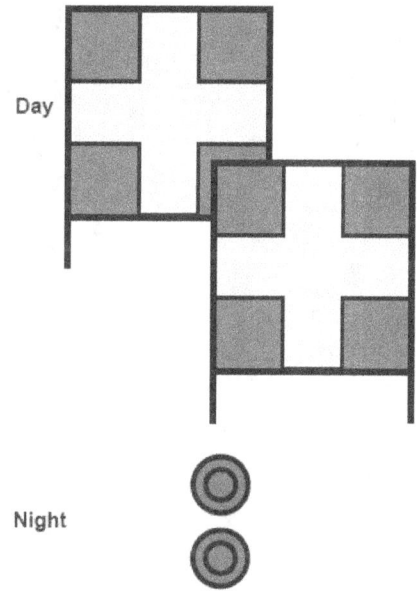

Day

Night

Causeway Range Markers

Miscellaneous Flags and Identification Insignia

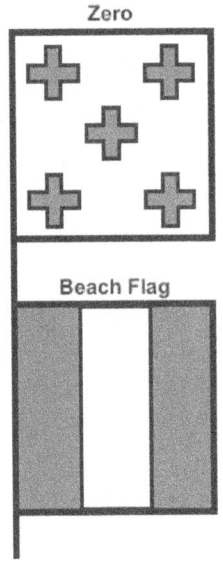

Boat Group Commander

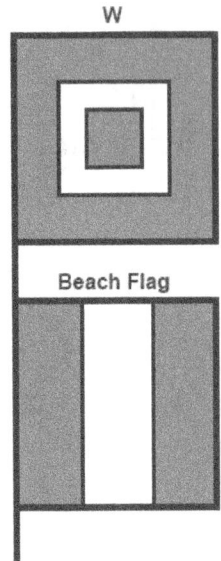

**Assistant Boat
Group Commander**

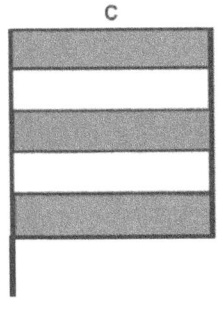

Channel Control Boat

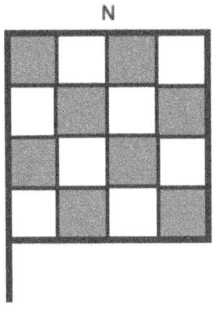

AAV Emergency Flag

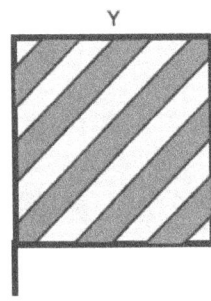

**Amphibious Vehicle
Pool Control Officer**

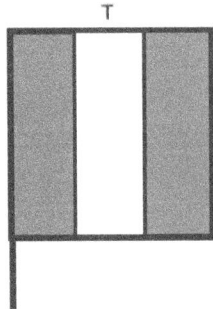

**Transfer Line
Control Officer**

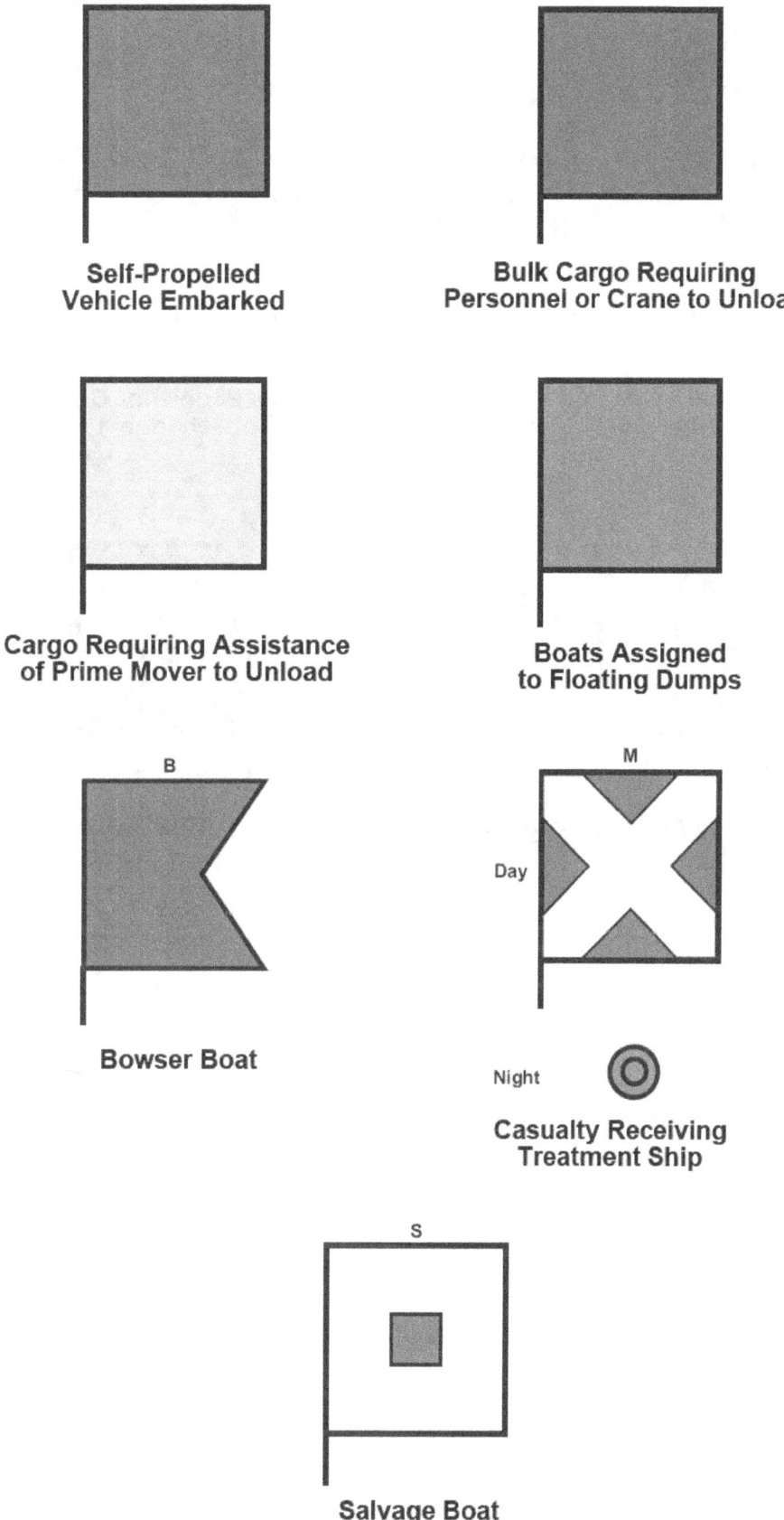

Self-Propelled
Vehicle Embarked

Bulk Cargo Requiring
Personnel or Crane to Unload

Cargo Requiring Assistance
of Prime Mover to Unload

Boats Assigned
to Floating Dumps

Bowser Boat

Casualty Receiving
Treatment Ship

Salvage Boat

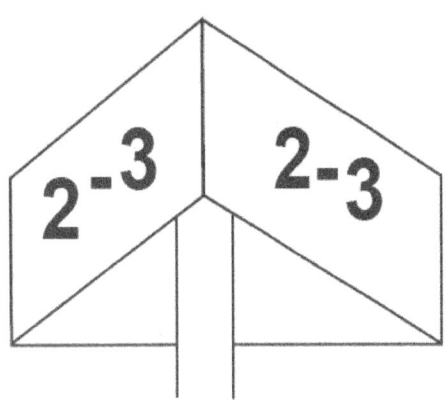

**Boat Team Paddle
(third boat, second wave)**

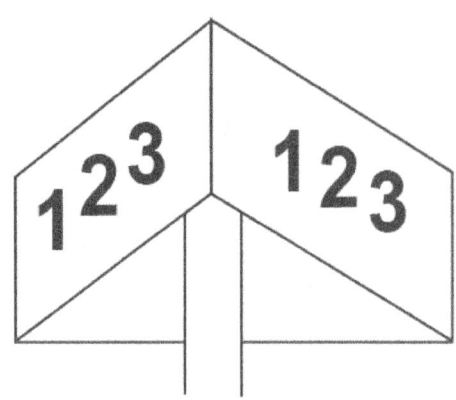

**Serial Paddle for On-Call
and Nonscheduled Waves**

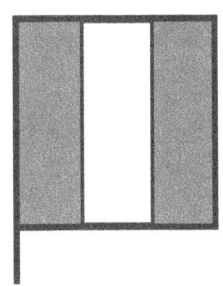

Beach Red One Flag

Beach Red Two Flag

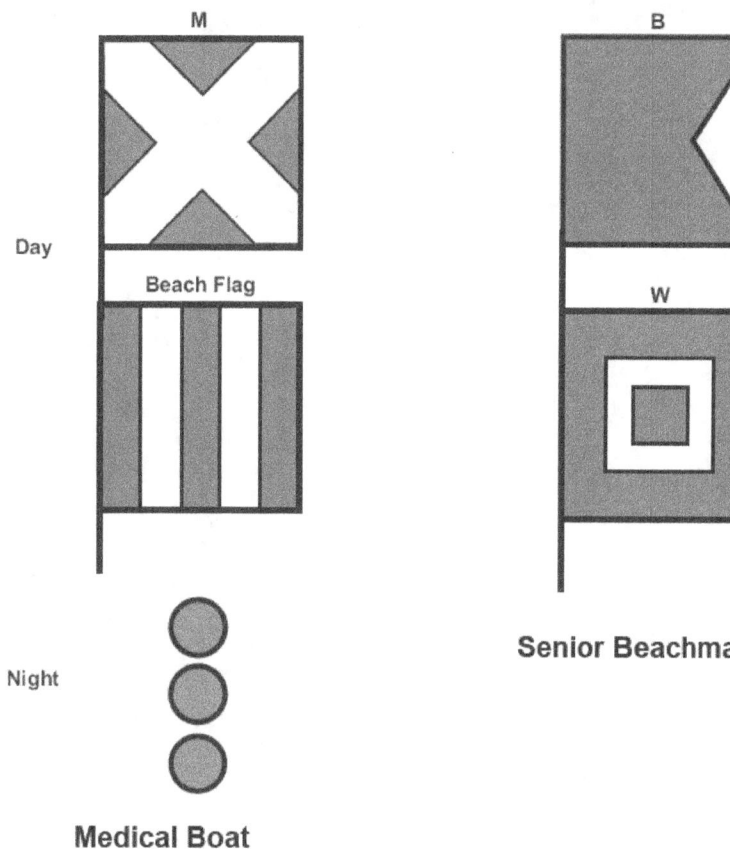

Day

M

Beach Flag

Night

Medical Boat

B

W

Senior Beachmaster

Appendix K. Hand and Arm Signals for Control of AAVs

The use of hand and arm signals aboard AAVs helps to safely control the movement of individual AAVs or AAV units. This appendix presents AAV crews with a uniform, standardized set of signals for conducting day and night operations. AAV crewmen, particularly drivers, should understand the listed hand and arm signals to ensure safe and effective operations during training and combat.

	Page
Assemble or Pass Towline	K-2
Attention	K-2
Cease Fire	K-3
Close Up	K-3
I Do Not Understand	K-4
Column Right (Left)	K-4
Commence Firing	K-5
Decrease Speed (Vehicles) Quick Time (Dismounted Troops)	K-5
Disperse	K-6
Dismount, Down, Take Cover	K-6
Echelon Right (Left)	K-7
Disregard Previous Command—As You Were	K-7
Form Column	K-8
Advance or Move Out	K-8
Halt, Stop, Stop Towing	K-9
Increase Speed, Doubletime	K-9
Line Formation, Deploy into Line Abreast, as Skirmishers	K-10
Man Overboard	K-10
Mount	K-11
Open Up, Extend	K-11
By the Right (Left) Flank	K-12
Start Engines, Prepare to Move	K-12
Stop Engine, Cut Engine	K-13
V Formation	K-13
Wedge Formation	K-14
Breakdown	K-14
Commence Towing	K-15
Cast Off Towline	K-15
Air Attack	K-16
Nuclear Warning	K-16
Ramp Up and Dogged	K-17
Ramp Down	K-17
Vector Left (Right)	K-17
Pivot Right	K-18
Pivot Left	K-18
Right Turn	K-19
Left Turn	K-19
Move Forward	K-20
Move in Reverse	K-20
Vehicle Halt	K-21

Assemble or Pass Towline

Day

Night

Small circle, palm out.

Turn light on when right arm is extended overhead; execute large horizontal circle. Turn light off before lowering arm. Repeat as necessary.

Attention

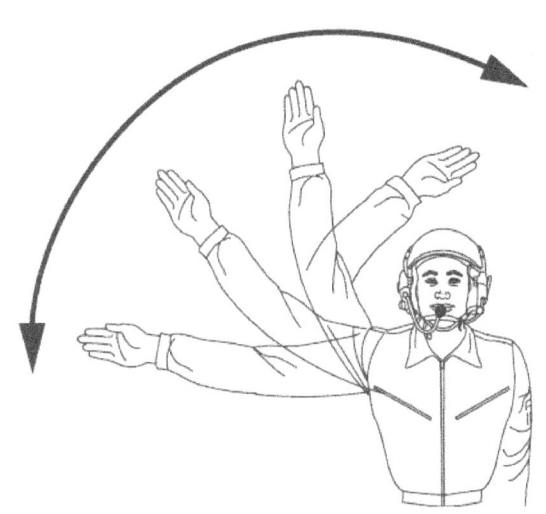

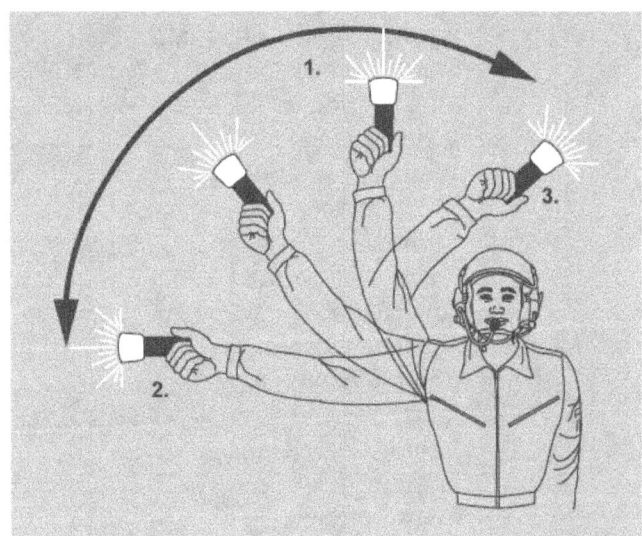

Turn light on when arm is in the starting position. Turn light off when signal is completed. Repeat as necessary.

Cease Fire

Day

Night

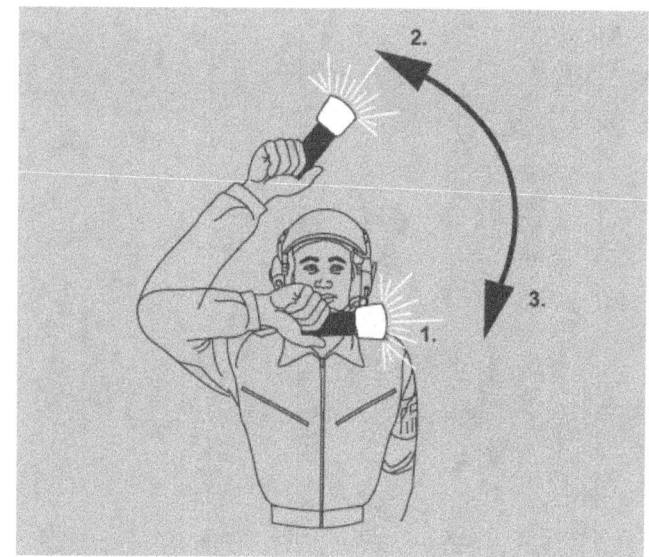

Turn light on when arm is in the starting position. Turn light off when signal is completed. Repeat as necessary.

Close Up

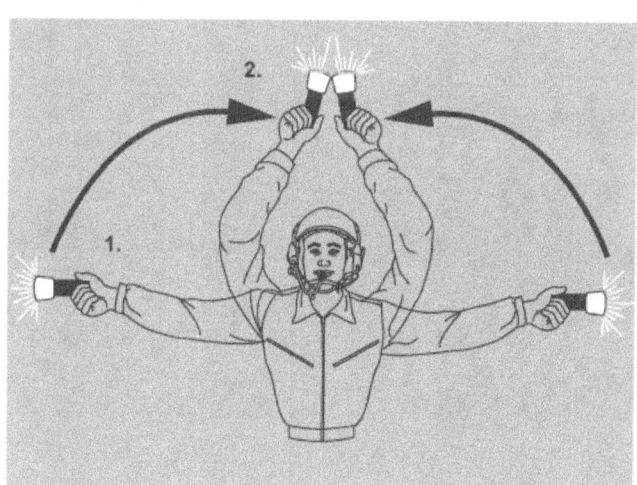

Turn light on when arms are in the starting position; execute signal, turning light off when hands touch overhead. Repeat as necessary.

I Do Not Understand

Day

Night

Turn lights on as hands are brought down across the face; hold in position, parallel, horizontal, until acknowledged. Turn lights off while they are still in front of the face.

Column Right (Left)

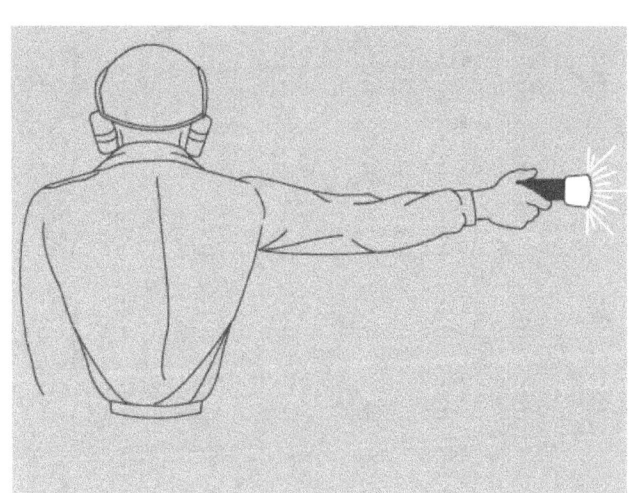

Turn light on as arm is extended; hold in position until understood or acknowledged or the maneuver is executed. Turn light off while arm is still extended. Repeat as necessary.

Commence Firing

Day

Night

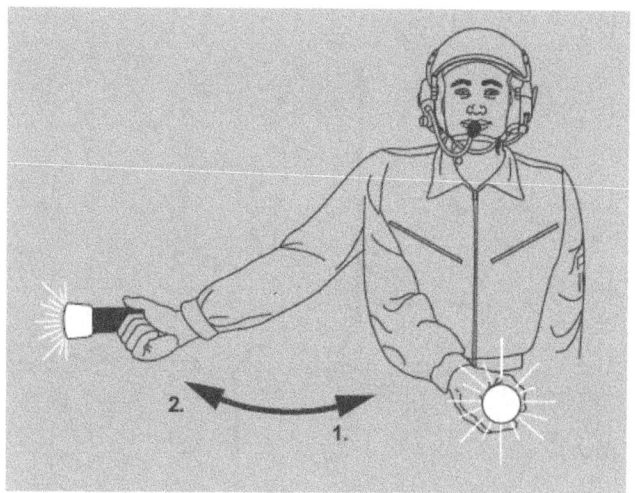

Turn light on when arm is in the starting position. Turn light off when signal is completed. Repeat as necessary.

Decrease Speed (Vehicles)
Quick Time (Dismounted Troops)

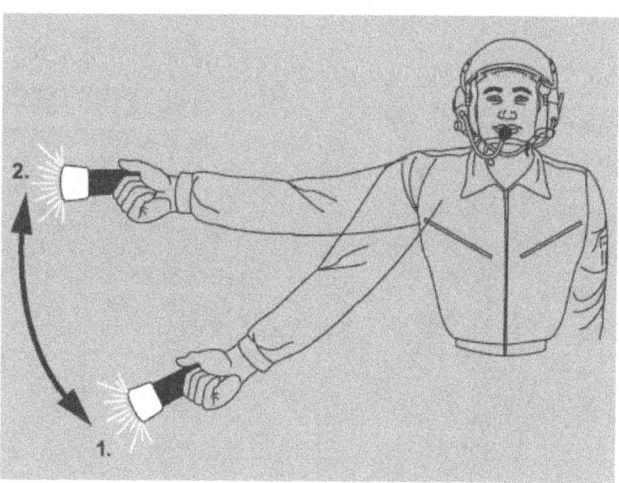

Turn light on when arm is in the starting position. Turn light off when signal is completed. Arm does not move above the horizontal position. Repeat as necessary.

Disperse

Day

Night

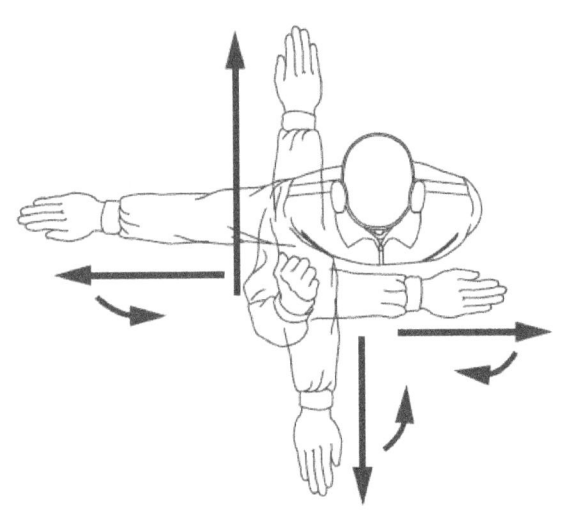

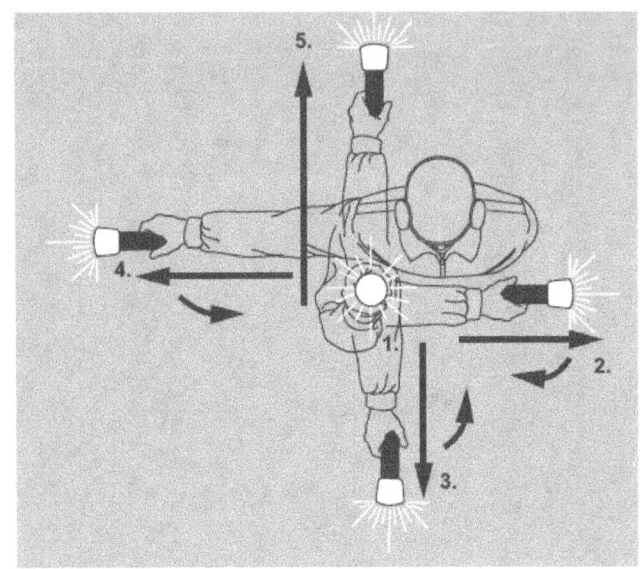

Turn light on when arm is in starting position. Return arm to starting position after each movement in a given direction. Turn light off after arm has been moved to the rear.

Dismount, Down, Take Cover

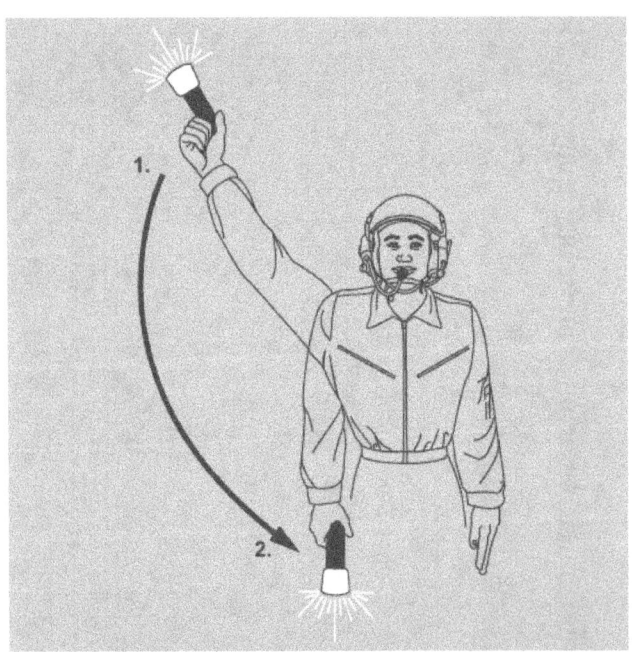

Turn light on when arm is in the starting position. Turn light off when arm is down at the side. Repeat as necessary.

Echelon Right (Left)

Day

Night

Turn lights on when arms are in correct positions. Turn lights off before taking arms from the signal position. Repeat as necessary.

Disregard Previous Command—As You Were

Wands are crossed instead of the hands. Turn lights on when wands are in position overhead. Turn lights off when signal is understood or acknowledged.

Form Column

Day

Night

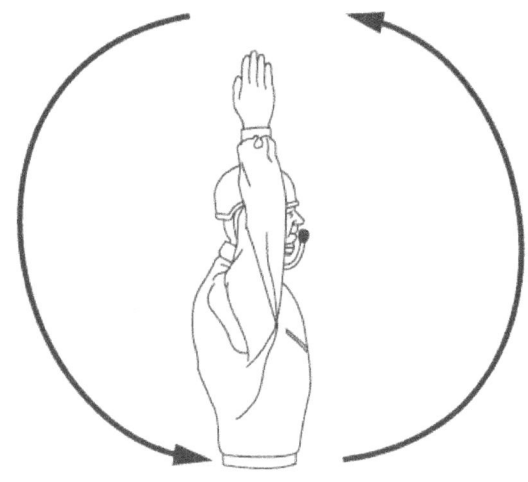

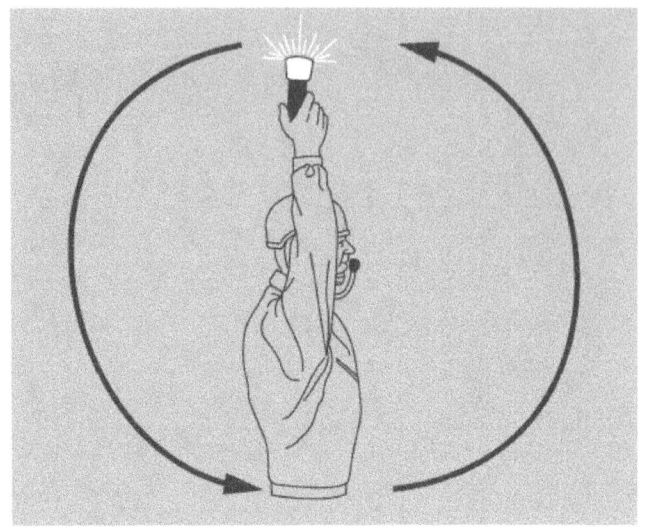

Turn light on when arm movement for signal is started. Turn light off when completed. Repeat as necessary.

Advance or Move Out

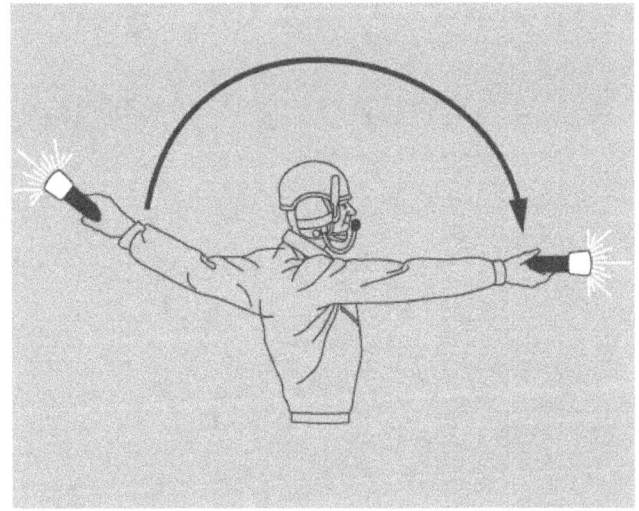

Face the desired direction of movement; turn light on when arm is extended to the rear; swing arm overhead and forward in the direction of desired movement. Turn light off when arm is in horizontal position. Repeat as necessary.

Halt, Stop, Stop Towing

Day

Night

Hand raised, palm out.

Turn light on when arm is in the signal position; blink light several times. Turn light off before lowering arm.

Increase Speed, Doubletime

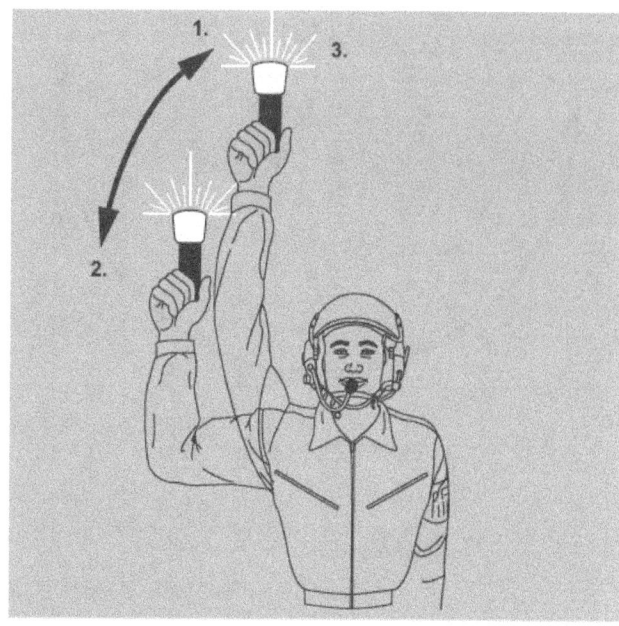

Turn light on when arm is in the starting position. Turn light off when signal is completed. Repeat as necessary.

Line Formation, Deploy into Line Abreast, as Skirmishers

Day	Night

Turn lights on as arms are extended; hold in position until signal is understood or acknowledged or the maneuver is executed. Turn lights off while arms are still in signal position. Repeat as necessary.

Man Overboard

Turn light on when arm is in vertical position; execute complete circle while blinking the light. Turn light off when arm is returned to the vertical position. Repeat as necessary.

Mount

Day

Night

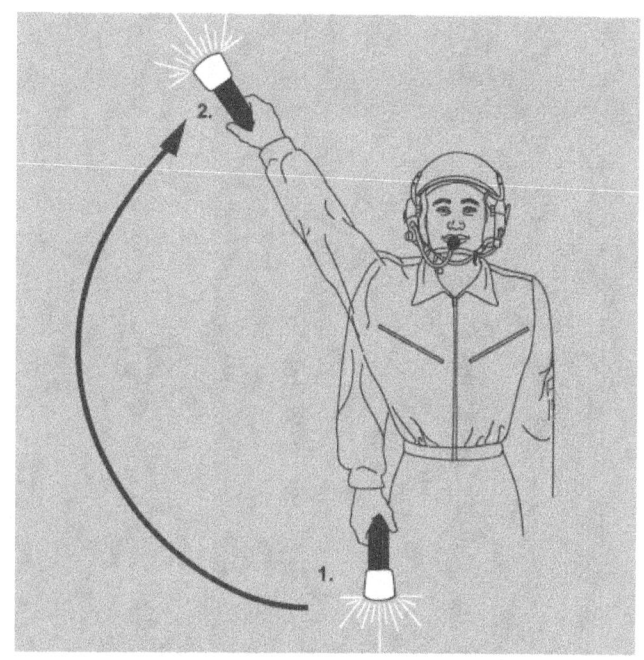

Turn light on in starting position. Turn light off when arm is 45 degrees above horizontal position. Repeat as necessary.

Open Up, Extend

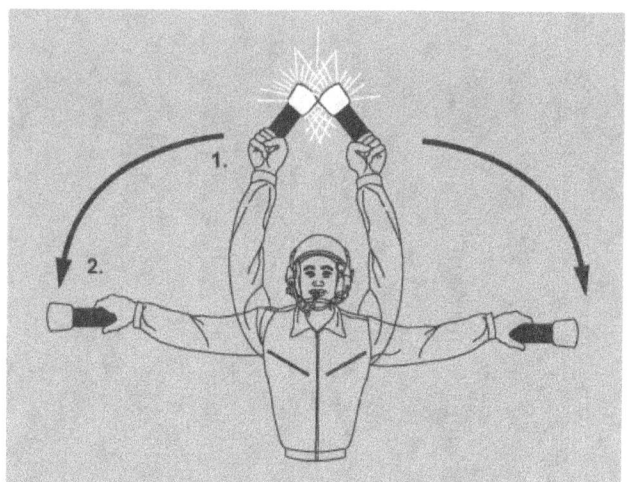

Turn lights on when arms are in starting position. Turn lights off when arms are in horizontal position. Repeat as necessary.

By the Right (Left) Flank

Day

Night

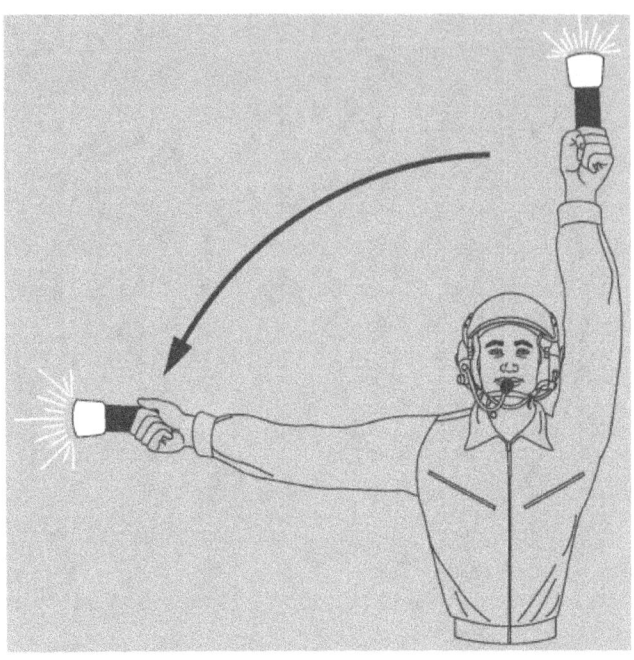

Extend the right (left) arm parallel to the deck and hold the left (right) arm above the head so that both arms are at a 90-degree angle to each other. At the point of execution, move the left (right) arm across the body as if to clap hands together.

Start Engines, Prepare to Move

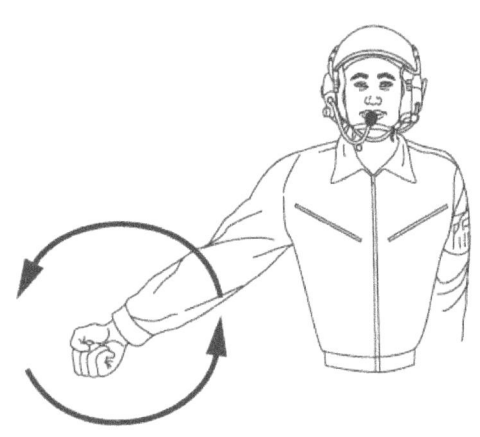

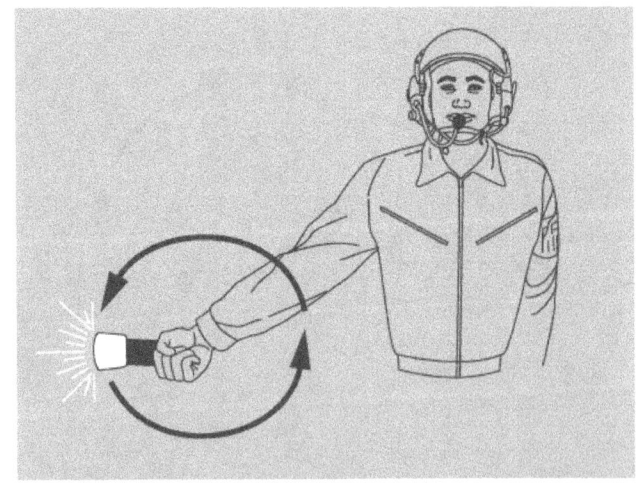

Turn light on when arm is in starting position. Turn light off when signal is completed.

Stop Engine, Cut Engine

Day

Night

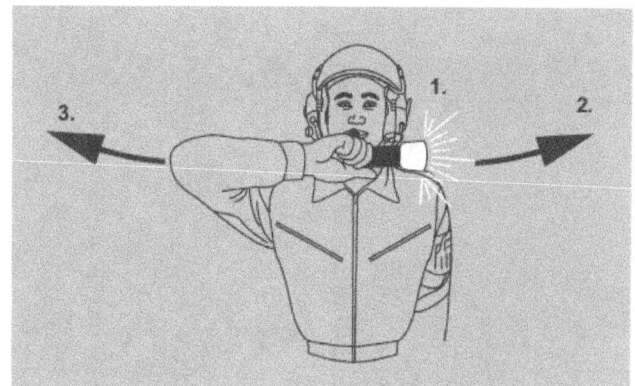

CAUTION: This signal should not be used for waterborne AAVs.

Turn light on when arm is in starting position. Turn light off when signal is completed.

V Formation

Turn lights on as arms are extended; hold in position until signal is understood or acknowledged or the maneuver is executed. Turn lights off while arms are still in signal positions. Repeat as necessary.

Wedge Formation

Day

Night

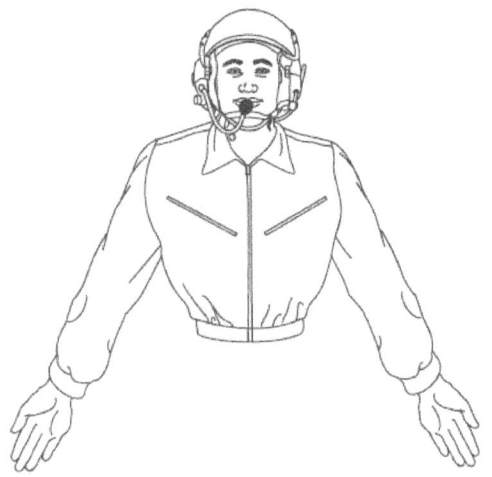

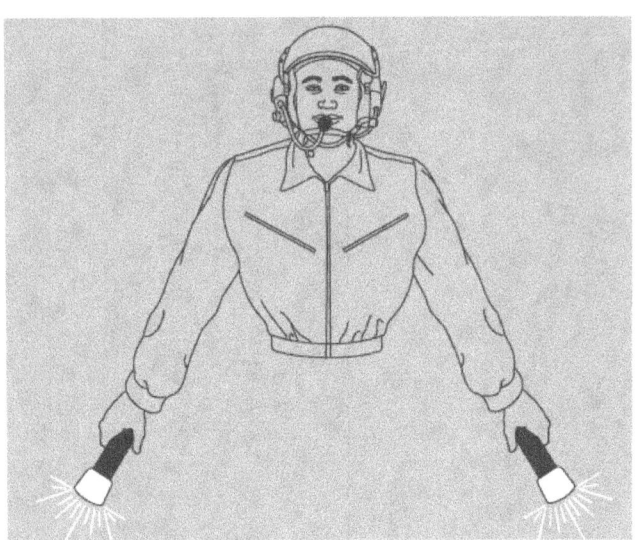

Turn lights on as arms are extended; hold in position until signal is understood or acknowledged or the maneuver is executed.. Turn lights off while arms are still in signal position. Repeat as necessary.

Breakdown

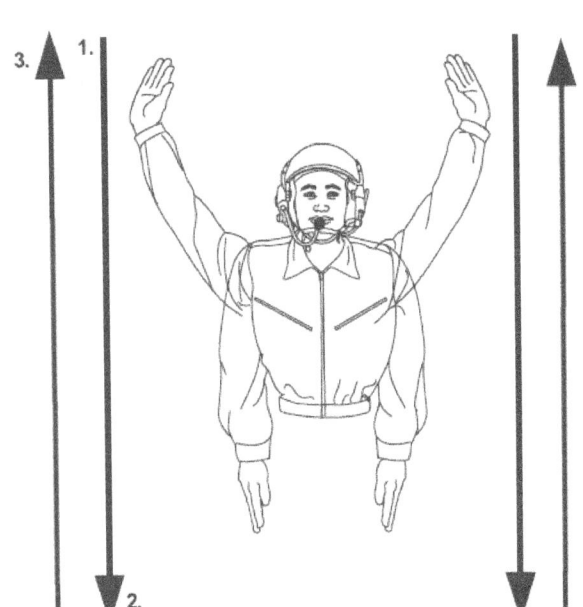

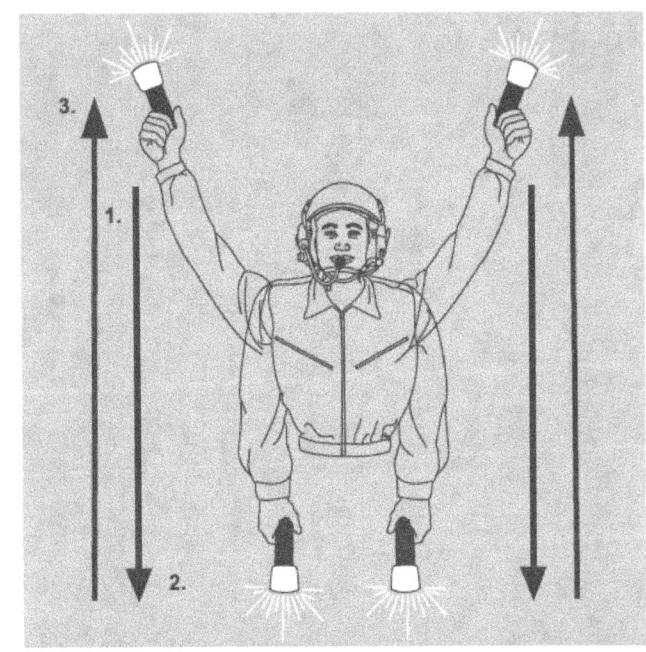

Turn lights on with arms extended overhead. Swing arms forward and down to knees. Swing arms forward and upward from knees to overhead. Continue motion until signal is understood.

Commence Towing

Day

Night

Turn light on when arm is in the extended starting position. Move arm in semicircle from right horizontal position downward to left horizontal position. Turn off light when signal is complete. Repeat as necessary.

Cast Off Towline

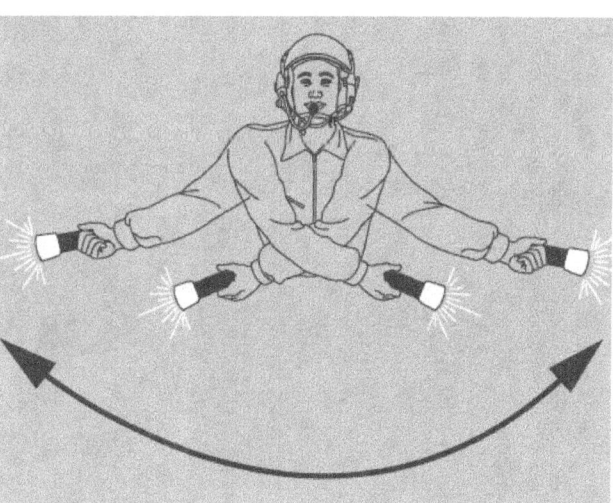

Turn on lights. Cross arms in front of body several times, using swing motion with wand in each hand.

Air Attack

Day

Night

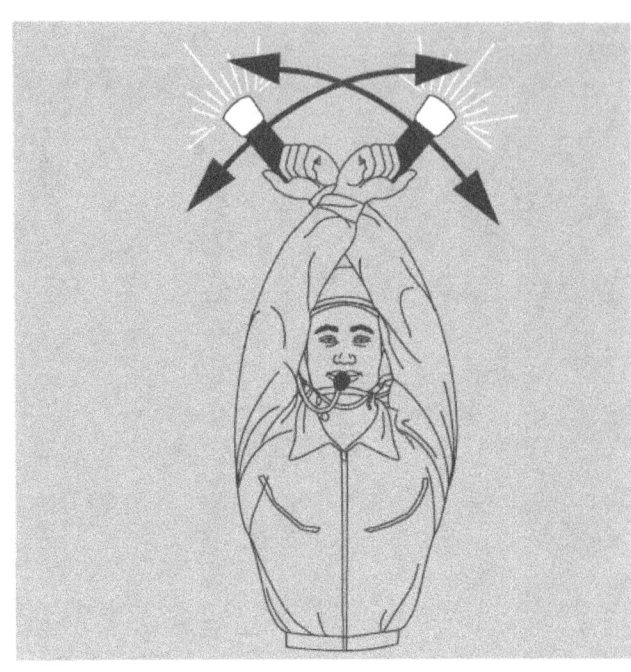

Turn on lights. Rapidly cross and uncross arms fully extended above the head with wand in each hand.

Nuclear Warning

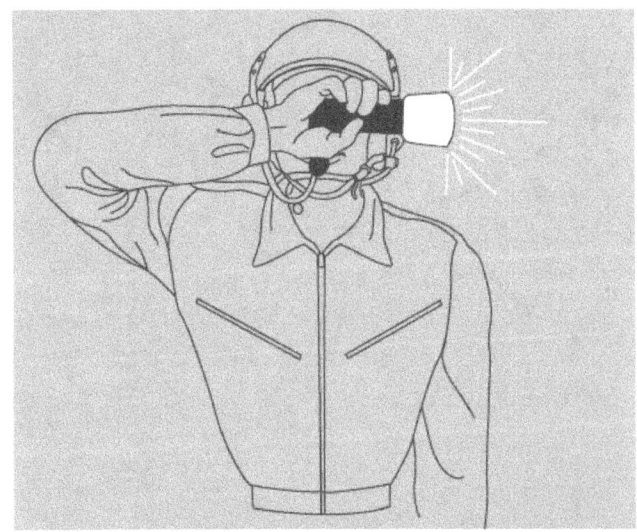

Turn on light. Cover both eyes with wand held in right hand to warn exposed troops to take cover before the detonation of nuclear weapon.

Ramp Up and Dogged

Day

Night

Arms held out parallel to deck with hands held open and pointed up. (Coxswains acknowledge with same signal to inform traffic controlman that the ramp is up and dogged.)

Turn on lights. Arms held out parallel to deck with wands pointed straight up. (Coxswains acknowledge with same signal to inform traffic controlman ramp is up and dogged.)

Ramp Down

Arms held out parallel to deck with hands held open and pointed down. (Coxswains acknowledge with same signal.)

Turn on lights. Arms held out parallel to deck with wands pointed straight down. (Coxswains acknowledge with same signal.)

Vector Left (Right)

Signalman faces beach with one arm straight out to side pointing in direction of the turn, other arm raised straight up, palm forward.

Turn on lights. Light wand in each hand; one straight out to side pointing in direction of the turn, other straight up.

Pivot Right

Day

Night

Hold one hand, fingers together, palm facing inboard in front of the chest in vertical position. Hold other hand with fingers joined, palm facing down, in horizontal position against vertical hand, in direction vehicle is to travel.

Same as day, except with use of light wands.

Pivot Left

One hand is in front of chest in a vertical position, fingers joined, palm facing perpendicular to the chest. Hold other hand with fingers joined, palm facing down, in horizontal position against vertical hand, in direction vehicle is to travel.

Same as day, except with use of light wands.

Right Turn

Day

Night

Form clenched fist on arm in direction of turn is to be made; make beckoning motion with other arm to bring vehicle forward; for reverse, make a pushing motion.

Same as day except point light wand in the direction of the turn.

Left Turn

Form clenched fist on arm in direction of turn is to be made; make beckoning motion with other arm to bring vehicle forward; for reverse, make a pushing motion.

Same as day except point light wand in the direction of the turn.

Move Forward

Day

Night

Move the hands and forearms backward and forward with palms toward the chest as if pulling the vehicle.

Same as day except with the use of light wands.

Move in Reverse

Move the hands and forearms backward and forward with palms toward the vehicle as if pushing the vehicle.

Same as day except with the use of light wands.

Vehicle Halt

Day

Night

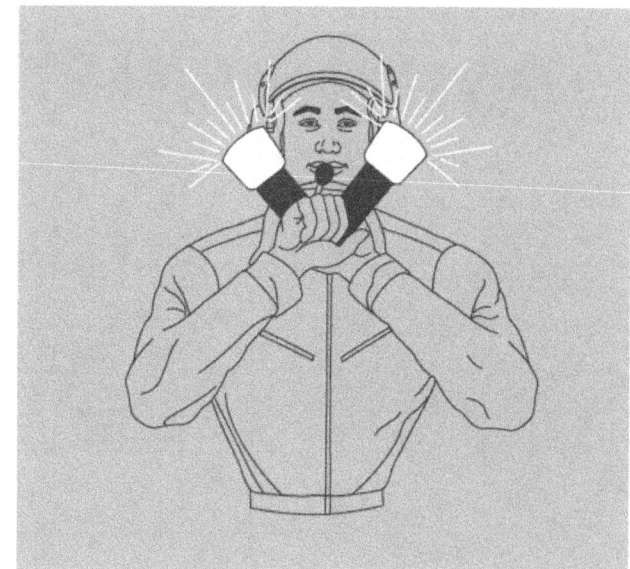

Clasp hands together, palms facing each other at throat level.

Cross light wands in front of throat.

APPENDIX L. SAMPLE TIME SCHEDULE FOR SHIP-TO-SHORE MOVEMENT OF AAVS

Time schedules for the launching of AAVs vary with operational requirements. The following is a sample format for use in planning estimates.

Time	Event
H-90	Ship sets condition 1-A. Station ballast and sea and anchor details.
H-85	Time check.
H-85	AAV crews man vehicles, ungripe the AAVs, and conduct communications checks.
H-80	Start ship exhaust system or tank deck blowers.
H-75	Start and warm AAVs, preoperational checks. Spot AAVs. Boats to the rails.
H-75	Launch boats. Conduct radio checks with boats.
H-70	Boats take station.
H-45	Ship underway.
H-43	Troops load AAVs.
H-18	5-minute standby to launch wave one. Wave one starts engines.
H-17	Number one flag at the dip.
H-16	5-minute standby to launch wave two. Wave two starts engines.
H-15	AAV close topside hatches, switch vehicles to water mode
H-14	Number one flag close up.
H-13	Launch wave one. 2-minute standby to launch wave two.
H-12	Wave one crosses LD. Number one flag hauled down.
H-11	Launch wave two.
H-9	Number two flag close up.
H-7	Wave two crosses LD. Number two flag hauled down.
H-Hour	Wave one touch down on shore.
H+5	Wave two touch down on shore.

Appendix M. Amphibious Ship Launch Tracks

The approach a ship uses when conducting underway launches will affect the launch and landing of the AAV unit. The most common types of underway launch tracks that the Navy employs are parallel, turn away, angled, parallel U-turn, and angled U-turn.

Parallel

In a parallel launch track, the ship approaches the beach at 30 to 45 degrees, turns either left or right parallel to the shore (90 degrees) on or near the LD, launches the waves in column, and turns quickly out to sea. The AAVs continue in a column until they are inside the boat lane where they flank and begin to move toward the beach. This is a popular launching technique because the ship is exposed broadside to the shore for only a short time, the AAV unit is dropped off on or near the LD, and the swim time is short. A disadvantage of using this method is the extra travel time required for the second wave to make it to the boat lane. See figure M-1.

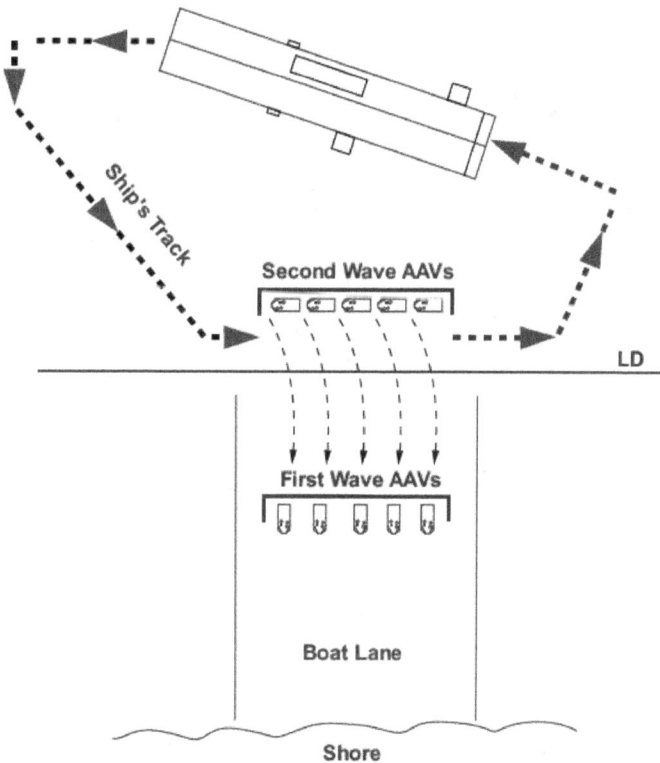

Figure M-1. Parallel Launch of the First and Second Waves.

Turn Away

In a turn-away launch track, the ship approaches the beach at approximately 0 degrees, conducts a U-turn at the LD, and launches AAVs in a column headed directly towards the beach. See figure M-2. This pattern minimizes the ship's exposure to the shoreline and launches the wave in column. Although highly effective at disembarking a wave in column toward the beach, this maneuver may result in a long approach for the last vehicle launched.

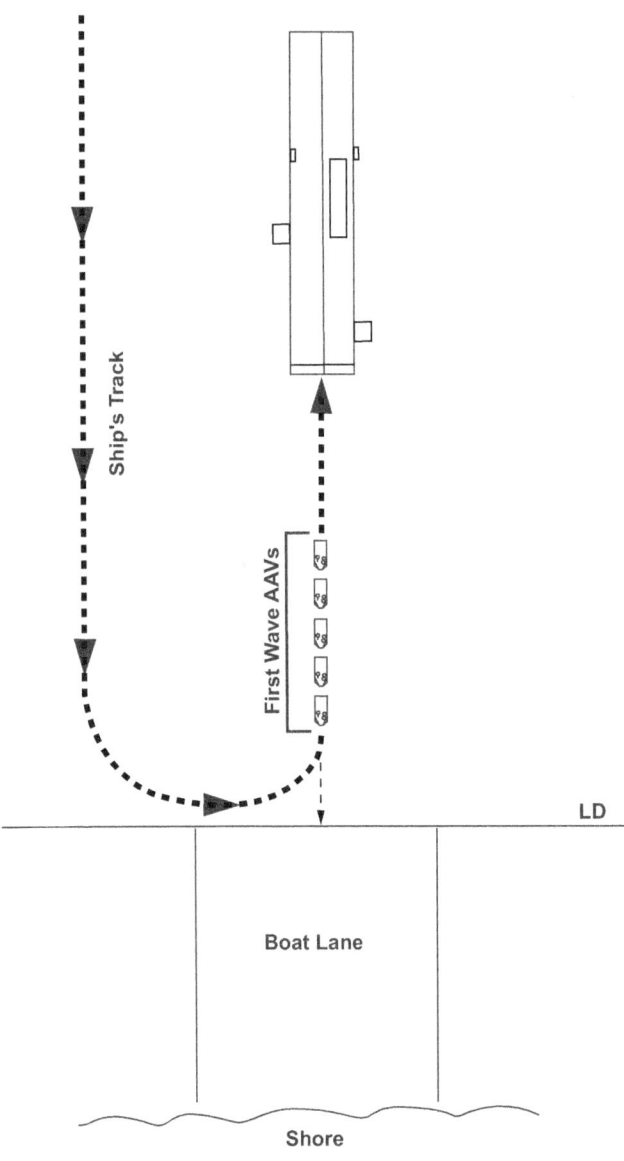

Figure M-2. Turn-Away Launch.

Angled

In the angled launch pattern, the ship approaches the shore at a 45-degree angle and begins to launch AAVs even with the edge of the boat lane. When waterborne, AAVs turn toward the shore and approach the LD. See figure M-3.

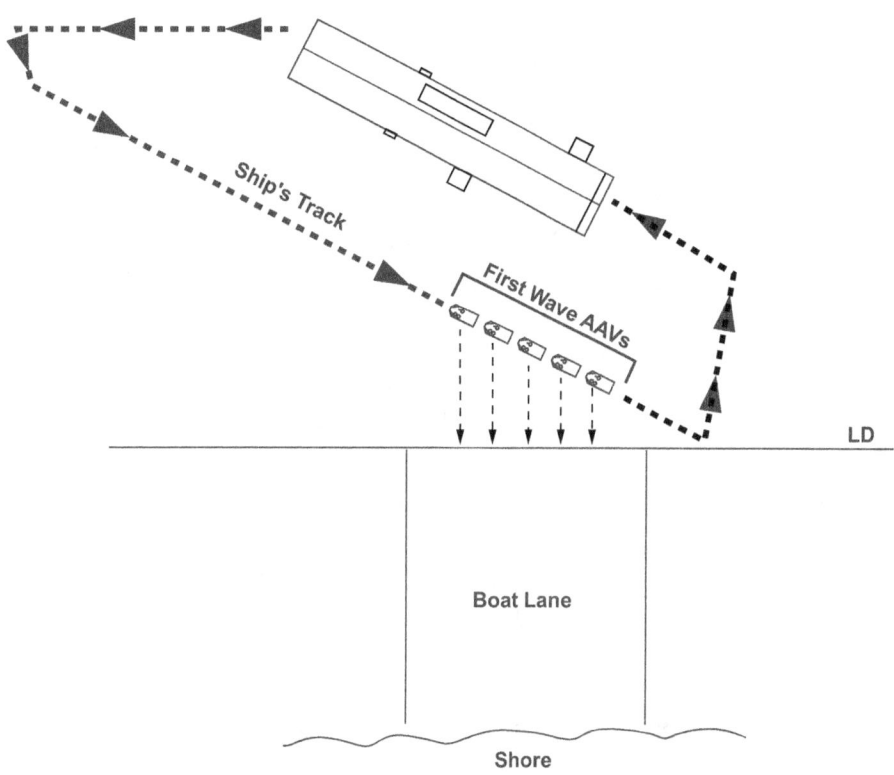

Figure M-3. Angled Launch of the First Wave.

As the ship launches the vehicles closer to the LD, the vehicles form on line and cross the LD. The ship can then turn away and begin a similar approach on the same boat lane for the second wave. See figure M-4. Vehicles turn immediately toward the shore and begin to assault. This launch track minimizes static time spent maneuvering in the water.

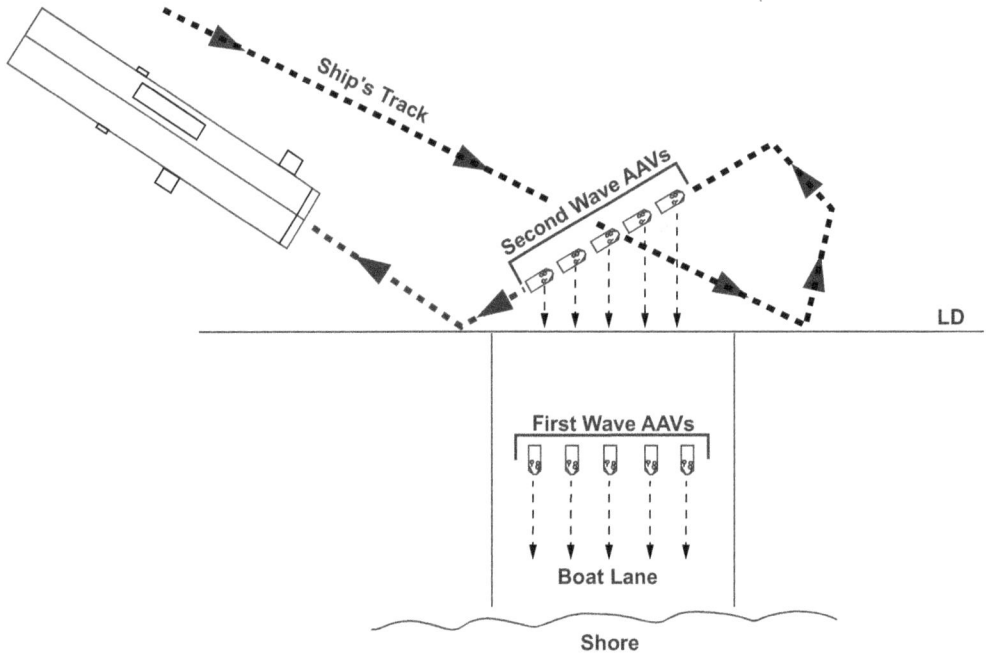

Figure M-4. Angled Launch of the Second Wave.

Parallel U-Turn

The parallel U-turn maneuver combines the parallel launch with the basic turn-away launch. The ship approaches the shore parallel and launches AAVs at the edge of the boat lane. Then the ship conducts a U-turn away from the shore, begins launching the second wave at the opposite edge of the boat lane, and completes the maneuver by turning away from the shore. See figure M-5. This maneuver exposes the ship to the shoreline for the longest period.

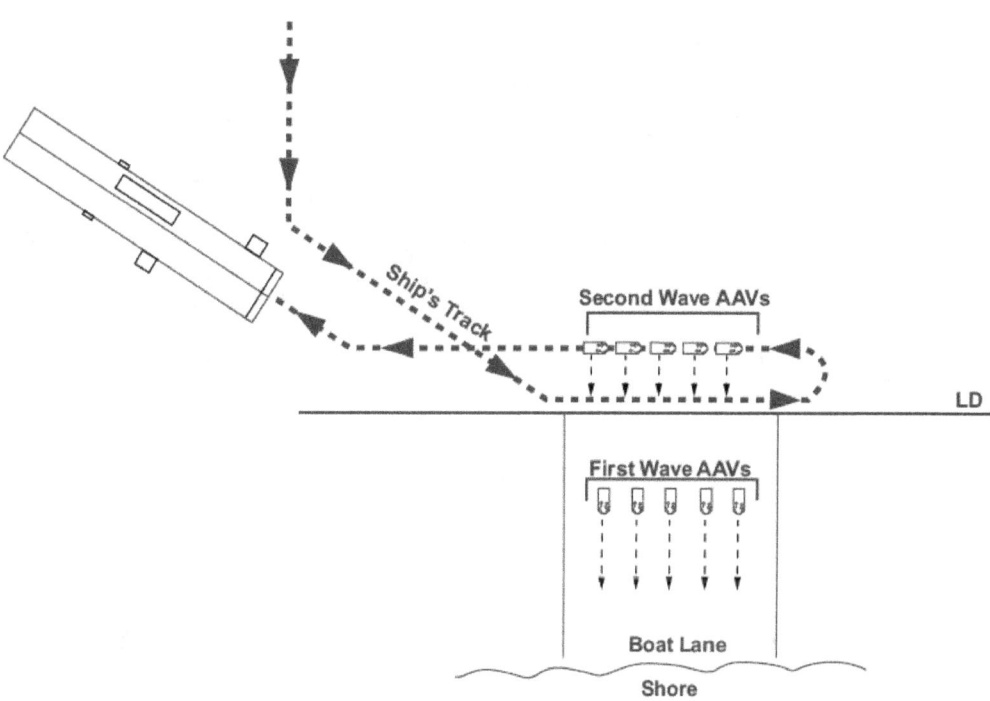

Figure M-5. Parallel U-Turn Launch.

Angled U-Turn

The angled U-turn maneuver combines the turn-away and the angled approach paths. The ship initially conducts an angled launch, executes a tight U-turn, and conducts a parallel launch of the second wave. This maneuver exposes the ship to the shoreline for a slightly shorter period than the parallel U-turn launch track. See figure M-6.

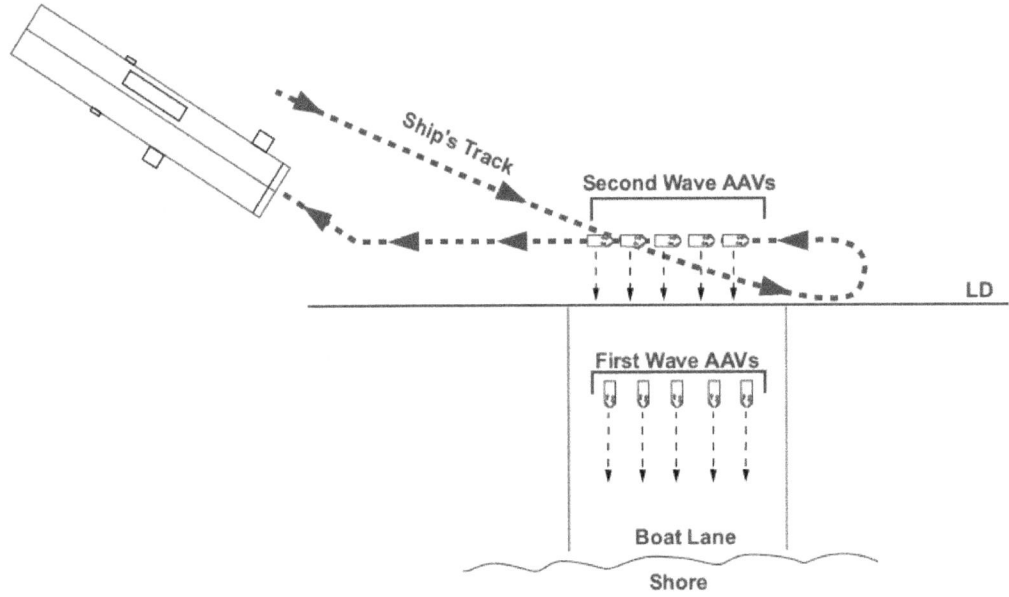

Figure M-6. Angled U-Turn Launch of the First and Second Waves.

APPENDIX N. GLOSSARY

Section I. Acronyms

AA . . . . assault amphibian [unit]
AAV . . . . amphibious assault vehicle
ADDRAC . . . . alert, direction, description,
range, assignment, control
ADCON . . . . administrative control
AF . . . . amphibious force
AO . . . . area of operations
AOA . . . . amphibious objective area
AP . . . . attack position
APC . . . . armored personnel carrier
AT . . . . antitank
ATF . . . . amphibious task force
ATGM . . . . antitank guided munition

BAS . . . . battalion aid station
BDAR . . . . battle damage assessment
and repair
BGC . . . . boat group commander
BHL . . . . battle handover line
BLT . . . . battalion landing team
BP . . . . battle position

C2 . . . . command and control
CAS . . . . close air support
CATF . . . . commander, amphibious
task force
CCO . . . . central control officer
CE . . . . combat equipped
CIC . . . . combat information center
CL . . . . combat load
CLF . . . . commander, landing force
COC . . . . combat operations center
CP . . . . command post
CSS . . . . combat service support
CSSA . . . . combat service support area
CSSD . . . . combat service support
detachment
CSSE . . . . combat service support element
CVC . . . . combat vehicle commander

DAP . . . . decontamination apparatus
D-day . . . . unnamed day on which
operations commence or
are scheduled to commence
DF . . . . diesel fuel

DP . . . . dismount point
DPICM . . . . dual purpose improved
conventional munitions
DS . . . . direct support
DS2 . . . . decontamination agent

EA . . . . engagement area
EAAK . . . . enhanced appliqué armor kit
EMP . . . . electromagnetic pulse

FAC . . . . forward air controller
FEBA . . . . forward edge of the battle area
FHA . . . . foreign humanitarian assistance
FM . . . . field manual (Army)
FO . . . . forward observer
FPL . . . . final protective line
FSC . . . . fire support coordinator
FSCC . . . . fire support coordination center
FSSG . . . . force service support group

GCE . . . . ground combat element
GPS . . . . global positioning system
GS . . . . general support

H&S . . . . headquarters and service
HB . . . . heavy barreled
HE . . . . high explosive
HEDP . . . . high explosive dual purpose
HF . . . . high frequency
H-hour . . . . specific time an operation
or exercise begins
HMMWV . . . . high mobility multipurpose
wheeled vehicle
HTH . . . . high test hypochlorite

IFV . . . . infantry fighting vehicle
IPB . . . . intelligence preparation of
the battlespace
IR . . . . infrared

JP . . . . joint publication

LAAD . . . . low altitude air defense
LAR . . . . light armored reconnaissance
LARC . . . . lighter, amphibious resupply,
cargo
LAV . . . . light armored vehicle

LCAC . . . . .landing craft air cushion
LCM . . . . landing craft, mechanized
LCU . . . . landing craft, utility
LCVP . . . . landing craft, vehicle, personnel
LD. . . . . .line of departure
LDS. . . . . . lightweight decontamination system
LF . . . . landing force
LFSP . . . . landing force support party
LHA . . . . general purpose amphibious
assault ship
LHD . . . . landing helicopter dock
LMC . . . . linear mine clearing
LOA . . . . limit of advance
LOC . . . . lines of communications
LPD. . . . . landing platform dock
LSD. . . . . landing ship dock
LST . . . . landing ship, tank
LZ . . . . .landing zone

MAGTF . . . . Marine air-ground task force
MBA . . . . main battle area
MCDP. . . . . .Marine Corps doctrinal publication
M/CM . . . . mobility, countermobility
MCRP . . . . .Marine Corps reference publication
MCT . . . . maintenance contact team
MCWP . . . . Marine Corps warfighting
publication
mech . . . . mechanized
MEF . . . . Marine expeditionary force
METT-T . . . . mission, enemy, terrain
and weather, troops and
support available—
time available
MEU . . . . Marine expeditionary unit
MEU(SOC) . . . . Marine expeditionary unit
(special operations capable)
MOOTW. . . . .military operations other than war
MOPP . . . . . .mission-oriented protective posture
MOS . . . . military occupational specialty
MOUT. . . . . military operations on
urbanized terrain
MRF . . . . mobile riverine force
MSR . . . . .main supply route
MST . . . . maintenance support team
MTF . . . . mechanized task force

N-2 . . . . Navy component intelligence
staff officer
N-3 . . . . Navy component operations
staff officer
NAVSEA . . . . .naval sea

NBC . . . . .nuclear, biological, and chemical
NCG . . . . naval control group
NCO . . . . .noncommissioned officer
NEO . . . . . .noncombatant evacuation operation
NGF . . . . naval gunfire
NWP . . . . .naval warfare publication

OEM . . . . on-equipment material
OP. . . . . observation post
OPCON. . . . . operational control
OPORD. . . . . .operation order
OTH . . . . over the horizon

PCO. . . . . .primary control officer
PCS . . . . .primary control ship
PDF. . . . . principal direction of fire
PLD. . . . . probable line of deployment
PLGRS . . . . precision lightweight
global positioning system (GPS)
receiver system
PLRS. . . . . . . .position location reporting system
PM. . . . . preventive maintenance
P/N . . . . part number
POIC . . . . petty officer in charge
POL. . . . . .petroleum, oils, and lubricants
POW .prisoner of war

QLP. . . . . quiet landing procedure

R-day. . . . . .redeployment day
RAM/RS . . . . reliability, availability, and
maintainability/rebuild
to standard
rein . . . . reinforcing
RHA . . . . rolled homogenous armor
RLT. . . . . .regimental landing team
RP . . . . .release point
RPM . . . . revolutions per minute
R&S . . . . reconnaissance and surveillance
RT. . . . . .rescue team

S-1. . . . . .manpower staff officer
S-2. . . . . .intelligence staff officer
S-3. . . . . .operations staff officer
S-4. . . . . logistics staff officer
S-6. . . . . communications and information
systems officer (units and
organizations below the
major subordinate
command level)
SCS . . . . secondary control ship
SDS . . . . sorbent decontamination system

SFP . . . . support by fire position

SINCGARS. . . . . single-channel ground and airborne radio system

SLAP. . . . . sabot light armor penetrator

SOC. . . . . special operations capable

SOP . . . . standing operating procedure

SP . . . . start point

STB . . . . super tropical bleach

SUROB . . . . surf observation report

TACON. . . . . tactical control

TC . . . . troop commander

T/E . . . . table of equipment

TI. . . . . technical instruction

TL . . . . troop load

TLOC . . . . tactical logistics operations center

TM . . . . Marine Corps technical manual

TOW . . . . tube-launched, optically-tracked, wire-command link guided missile

TRP . . . . target reference point

UGWS. . . . . up-gunned weapons station

UHF . . . . ultrahigh frequency

US . . . . United States

VHF . . . . very high frequency

WGO. . . . . wave guide officer

Section II. Definitions

amphibious force—An amphibious task force and a landing force together with other forces that are trained, organized, and equipped for amphibious operations. Also called **AF**. (JP 1-02)

amphibious operation—A military operation launched from the sea by an amphibious force, embarked in ships or craft with the primary purpose of introducing a landing force ashore to accomplish the assigned mission. (JP 1-02)

amphibious task force—A Navy task organization formed to conduct amphibious operations. The amphibious task force, together with the landing force and other forces, constitutes the amphibious force. Also called **ATF**. (JP 1-02)

amphibious vehicle availability table—A tabulation of the type and number of amphibious vehicles available primarily for assault landings and for support of other elements of the operation. (JP 1-02)

amphibious vehicle employment plan—A plan showing in tabular form the planned employment of amphibious vehicles in landing operations, including their employment after the initial movement to the beach. (JP 1-02)

approach lane—An extension of a boat lane from the line of departure toward the transport area. (JP 1-02)

approach march—Advance of a combat unit when direct contact with the enemy is imminent. Troops are fully or partially deployed. The approach march ends when ground contact with the enemy is made or when the attack position is occupied. (JP 1-02)

armored personnel carrier—A lightly armored, highly mobile, full-tracked vehicle, amphibious and air-droppable, used primarily for transporting personnel and their individual equipment during tactical operations. Production modifica-

tions or application of special kits permit use as a mortar carrier, command post, flame thrower, antiaircraft artillery chassis, or limited recovery vehicle. Also called **APC**. (JP 1-02)

assault schedule—See **landing schedule**. (JP 1-02)

assault wave—See **wave**. (JP 1-02)

backshore—The area of a beach extending from the limit of high water foam lines to dunes or extreme inland limit of the beach. (JP 1-02)

base of fire—Fire placed on an enemy force or position to reduce or eliminate the enemy's capability to interfere by fire and/or movement with friendly maneuver element(s). It may be provided by a single weapon or a grouping of weapons systems. (MCRP 5-12C)

battle damage repair—Essential repair, which may be improvised, carried out rapidly in a battle environment in order to return damaged or disabled equipment to temporary service. (JP 1-02)

beaten zone—The area on the ground upon which the cone of fire falls. (JP 1-02)

boat group—The basic organization of landing craft. One boat group is organized for each battalion landing team (or equivalent) to be landed in the first trip of landing craft or amphibious vehicles. (JP 1-02)

boat lane—A lane for amphibious assault landing craft, which extends seaward from the landing beaches to the line of departure. The width of a boat lane is determined by the length of the corresponding beach. (JP 1-02)

central control officer—The officer designated by the amphibious task force commander for the overall coordination of the waterborne ship-to-shore movement. The central control officer is embarked in the central control ship. Also called **CCO**. (JP 1-02)

centralized control—In military operations, a mode of battlespace management in which one echelon of command exercises total authority and direction of all aspects of one or more warfighting functions. It is a method of control where detailed orders are issued and total unity of action is the overriding consideration. See also **decentralized control**. (MCRP 5-12C)

close air support—Air action by fixed- and rotary-wing aircraft against hostile targets that are in close proximity to friendly forces and that require detailed integration of each air mission with the fire and movement of those forces. Also called **CAS**. (JP 1-02)

combat air patrol—An aircraft patrol provided over an objective area, the force protected, the critical area of a combat zone, or in an air defense area, for the purpose of intercepting and destroying hostile aircraft before they reach their targets. (JP 1-02)

counterattack—Attack by part or all of a defending force against an enemy attacking force, for such specific purposes as regaining ground lost or cutting off or destroying enemy advance units, and with the general objective of denying to the enemy the attainment of the enemy's purpose in attacking. In sustained defensive operations, it is undertaken to restore the battle position and is directed at limited objectives. (JP 1-02)

covering force—**1**. A force operating apart from the main force for the purpose of intercepting, engaging, delaying, disorganizing, and deceiving the enemy before the enemy can attack the force covered. **2**. Any body or detachment of troops which provides security for a larger force by observation, reconnaissance, attack, or defense,

or by any combination of these methods. (JP 1-02)

cross-attachment—The exchange of subordinate units between units for a temporary period. (MCRP 5-12C)

current, offshore—Deep water movements caused by tides or seasonal changes in ocean water level. (JP 1-02)

decentralized control—In military operations, a mode of battlespace management in which a command echelon may delegate some or all authority and direction for warfighting functions to subordinates. It requires careful and clear articulation of mission, intent, and main effort to unify efforts of subordinate leaders. See also **centralized control**. (MCRP 5-12C)

demonstration—**1**. An attack or show of force on a front where a decision is not sought, made with the aim of deceiving the enemy. **2**. (DOD only) In military deception, a show of force in an area where a decision is not sought made to deceive an adversary. It is similar to a feint but no actual contact with the adversary is intended. (JP 1-02)

electromagnetic pulse—The electromagnetic radiation from a strong electronic pulse, most commonly caused by a nuclear explosion that may couple with electrical or electronic systems to produce damaging current and voltage surges. Also called **EMP**. (JP 1-02)

envelopment—An offensive maneuver in which the main attacking force passes around or over the enemy's principal defensive positions to secure objectives to the enemy's rear. See also **turning movement**. (JP 1-02)

exploitation—**1**. Taking full advantage of success in military operations, following up initial gains, and making permanent the temporary effects already achieved. **2**. Taking full advantage of any information that has come to hand for tactical, operational, or strategic purposes. **3**. An offensive operation that usually follows a successful attack and is designed to disorganize the enemy in depth. See also **pursuit**. (JP 1-02)

feint—In military deception, an offensive action involving contact with the adversary conducted for the purpose of deceiving the adversary as to the location and/or time of the actual main offensive action. (JP 1-02)

flanking attack—An offensive maneuver directed at the flank of an enemy. See also **frontal attack**. (JP 1-02)

foreshore—That portion of a beach extending from the low water (datum) shoreline to the limit of normal high water wave wash. (JP 1-02)

forward arming and refueling point—A temporary facility—organized, equipped, and deployed by an aviation commander, and normally located in the main battle area closer to the area where operations are being conducted than the aviation unit's combat service area—to provide fuel and ammunition necessary for the employment of aviation maneuver units in combat. The forward arming and refueling point permits combat aircraft to rapidly refuel and rearm simultaneously. (JP 1-02)

forward edge of the battle area—The foremost limits of a series of areas in which ground combat units are deployed, excluding the areas in which the covering or screening forces are operating, designated to coordinate fire support, the positioning of forces, or the maneuver of units. Also called **FEBA**. (JP 1-02)

frontal attack—**1**. An offensive maneuver in which the main action is directed against the front of the enemy forces. **2**. In air intercept, an attack by an interceptor aircraft that terminates with a heading crossing angle greater than 135 degrees. (JP 1-02)

global positioning system—A satellite constellation that provides highly accurate position, velocity, and time navigation information to users. Also called **GPS**. (JP 1-02)

guard—**1**. A form of security operation whose primary task is to protect the main force by fighting to gain time while also observing and reporting information, and to prevent enemy ground observation of and direct fire against the main body by reconnoitering, attacking, defending, and delaying. A guard force normally operates within the range of the main body's indirect fire weapons. **2**. A radio frequency that is normally used for emergency transmissions and is continuously monitored. UHF band: 243.0 MHZ; VHF band: 121.5 MHZ. See also **screen**. **3**. A military or civilian individual assigned to protect personnel, equipment, or installations, or to oversee a prisoner. (JP 1-02)

hinterland, near—The area of land within an operational area of a specific beach or terminal operation—usually within 5 miles. (JP 1-02)

hydrography—The science which deals with the measurements and description of the physical features of the oceans, seas, lakes, rivers, and their adjoining coastal areas, with particular reference to their use for navigational purposes. (JP 1-02)

infiltration—**1**. The movement through or into an area or territory occupied by either friendly or enemy troops or organizations. The movement is made, either by small groups or by individuals, at extended or irregular intervals. When used in connection with the enemy, it infers that contact is avoided. **2**. In intelligence usage, placing an agent or other person in a target area in hostile territory. Usually involves crossing a frontier or other guarded line. Methods of infiltration are:

black (clandestine); grey (through legal crossing point but under false documentation); and white (legal). (JP 1-02)

inner transport area—In amphibious operations, an area as close to the landing beach as depth of water, navigational hazards, boat traffic, and enemy action permit, to which transports may move to expedite unloading. (JP 1-02)

landing beach—That portion of a shoreline usually required for the landing of a battalion landing team. However, it may also be that portion of a shoreline constituting a tactical locality (such as the shore of a bay) over which a force larger or smaller than a battalion landing team may be landed. (JP 1-02)

landing craft and amphibious vehicle assignment table—A table showing the assignment of personnel and materiel to each landing craft and amphibious vehicle and the assignment of the landing craft and amphibious vehicles to waves for the ship-to-shore movement. (JP 1-02)

landing diagram—A graphic means of illustrating the plan for the ship-to-shore movement. (JP 1-02)

landing force—A Marine Corps or Army task organization formed to conduct amphibious operations. The landing force, together with the amphibious task force and other forces, constitute the amphibious force. Also called **LF**. (JP 1-02)

landing force support party—A temporary landing force organization composed of Navy and landing force elements, that facilitates the ship-to-shore movement and provides initial combat support and combat service support to the landing force. The landing force support party is brought into existence by a formal activation order issued by the commander, landing force. Also called **LFSP**. (JP 1-02)

landing plan—1. In amphibious operations, a collective term referring to all individually prepared naval and landing force documents that, taken together, present in detail all instructions for execution of the ship-to-shore movement. **2.** In airlift operations, the sequence, method of delivery, and place of arrival of troops and materiel. (JP 1-02)

landing schedule—In an amphibious operation, a schedule that shows the beach, hour, and priorities of landing of assault units, and which coordinates the movements of landing craft from the transports to the beach in order to execute the scheme of maneuver ashore. (JP 1-02)

landing sequence table—A document that incorporates the detailed plans for ship-to-shore movement of nonscheduled units. (JP 1-02)

line of departure—1. In land warfare, a line designated to coordinate the departure of attack elements. **2.** In amphibious warfare, a suitably marked offshore coordinating line to assist assault craft to land on designated beaches at scheduled times. Also called **LD**. (JP 1-02)

main battle area—That portion of the battlefield in which the decisive battle is fought to defeat the enemy. For any particular command, the main battle area extends rearward from the forward edge of the battle area to the rear boundary of the command's subordinate units. (JP 1-02)

Marine air-ground task force—The Marine Corps principal organization for all missions across the range of military operations, composed of forces task-organized under a single commander capable of responding rapidly to a contingency anywhere in the world. The types of forces in the Marine air-ground task force (MAGTF) are functionally grouped into four core elements: a command element, an aviation combat element, a ground combat element, and a combat service support element. The four core elements are categories of forces, not formal commands. The basic structure of the MAGTF never varies, though the number, size, and type of Marine Corps units comprising each of its four elements will always be mission dependent. The flexibility of the organizational structure allows for one or more subordinate MAGTFs to be assigned. Also called **MAGTF**. (JP 1-02)

mechanized operations—Tactical operations designed to maximize the ground mobility, protection, shock action, and firepower of combat vehicles to concentrate combat power rapidly against the enemy. Combat power is generated by the massed employment of tanks and by enhancing the mobility of the forces through the use of assault amphibious vehicles and other ground mobility means. (MCRP 5-12C)

noncombatant evacuation operations—Operations directed by the Department of State, the Department of Defense, or other appropriate authority whereby noncombatants are evacuated from foreign countries when their lives are endangered by war, civil unrest, or natural disaster to safe havens or to the United States. Also called **NEO**. (JP 1-02)

on-call wave—See **wave**. (JP 1-02)

over-the-horizon amphibious operations—An operational initiative launched from beyond visual and radar range of the shoreline. (JP 1-02)

penetration—In land operations, a form of offensive which seeks to break through the enemy's defense and disrupt the defensive system. (JP 1-02)

petroleum, oils, and lubricants—A broad term which includes all petroleum and associated products used by the Armed Forces. Also called **POL**. (JP 1-02)

primary control officer—In amphibious operations, the officer embarked in a primary control ship assigned to control the movement of landing craft, amphibious vehicles, and landing ships to and from a colored beach. Also called **PCO**. (JP 1-02)

primary control ship—In amphibious operations, a ship of the task force designated to provide support for the primary control officer and a combat information center control team for a colored beach. Also called **PCS**. (JP 1-02)

pursuit—An offensive operation designed to catch or cut off a hostile force attempting to escape, with the aim of destroying it. (JP 1-02)

raid—An operation, usually small scale, involving a swift penetration of hostile territory to secure information, confuse the enemy, or to destroy installations. It ends with a planned withdrawal upon completion of the assigned mission. (JP 1-02)

rear area—For any particular command, the area extending forward from its rear boundary to the rear of the area assigned to the next lower level of command. This area is provided primarily for the performance of support functions. (JP 1-02)

rear area operations center—A command and control facility that serves as an area and/or subarea commander's planning, coordinating, monitoring, advising, and directing agency for area security operations. (JP 1-02)

rear area security—The measures taken before, during, and/or after an enemy airborne attack, sabotage action, infiltration, guerrilla action, and/or initiation of psychological or propaganda warfare to minimize the effects thereof. (MCRP 5-12C)

reconnaissance in force—An offensive operation designed to discover and/or test the enemy's strength or to obtain other information. (JP 1-02)

riverine operations—Operations conducted by forces organized to cope with and exploit the unique characteristics of a riverine area, to locate and destroy hostile forces, and/or to achieve or maintain control of the riverine area. Joint riverine operations combine land, naval, and air operations, as appropriate, and are suited to the nature of the specific riverine area in which operations are to be conducted. (JP 1-02)

scheduled wave—See **wave**. (JP 1-02)

screen—**1**. An arrangement of ships, aircraft and/or submarines to protect a main body or convoy. **2**. In cartography, a sheet of transparent film, glass, or plastic carrying a "ruling" or other regularly repeated pattern which may be used in conjunction with a mask, either photographically or photomechanically, to produce areas of the pattern. **3**. In surveillance, camouflage and concealment, any natural or artificial material, opaque to surveillance sensor(s), interposed between the sensor(s) and the object to be camouflaged or concealed. **4**. A security element whose primary task is to observe, identify, and report information, and which only fights in self-protection. See also flank guard; guard. **5**. (DOD only) A task to maintain surveillance; provide early warning to the main body; or impede, destroy, and harass enemy reconnaissance within its capability without becoming decisively engaged. (JP 1-02)

sea state—A scale that categorizes the force of progressively higher seas by wave height. This scale is mathematically co-related to the Pierson-Moskowitz scale and the relationship of wind to waves. (JP 1-02)

sector of fire—A defined area which is required to be covered by the fire of individual or crew served weapons or the weapons of a unit. (JP 1-02)

serial—**1**. An element or a group of elements within a series which is given a numerical or alphabetical designation for convenience in planning, scheduling, and control. **2**. A serial can be a group of people, vehicles, equipment, or supplies and is used in airborne, air assault, amphibious operations, and convoys. (JP 1-02)

serial assignment table—A table that is used in amphibious operations and shows the serial number, the title of the unit, the approximate number of personnel; the material, vehicles, or equipment in the serial; the number and type of landing craft and/or amphibious vehicles required to boat the serial; and the ship on which the serial is embarked. (JP 1-02)

spoiling attack—A tactical maneuver employed to seriously impair a hostile attack while the enemy is in the process of forming or assembling for an attack. Usually employed by armored units in defense by an attack on enemy assembly positions in front of a main line of resistance or battle position. (JP 1-02)

strong point—A key point in a defensive position, usually strongly fortified and heavily armed with automatic weapons, around which other positions are grouped for its protection. (JP 1-02)

suppressive fire—Fires on or about a weapons system to degrade its performance below the level needed to fulfill its mission objectives, during the conduct of the fire mission. (JP 1-02)

surf zone—The area of water from the surf line to the beach. (JP 1-02)

swell—Ocean waves that have traveled out of their fetch. Swell characteristically exhibits a more regular and longer period and has flatter crests than waves within their fetch. (JP 1-02)

turning movement—A variation of the envelopment in which the attacking force passes around or over the enemy's principal defensive positions to secure objectives deep in the enemy's rear to force the enemy to abandon his position or divert major forces to meet the threat. (JP 1-02)

wave—**1**. A formation of forces, landing ships, craft, amphibious vehicles or aircraft, required to beach or land about the same time. Can be classified as to type, function or order as shown: a. assault wave; b. boat wave; c. helicopter wave; d. numbered wave; e. on-call wave; f. scheduled wave. **2**. (DOD only) An undulation of water caused by the progressive movement of energy from point to point along the surface of the water. (JP 1-02)

Appendix O. References and Related Publications

Joint Publications (JPs)

JP 0-2	Unified Action Armed Forces (UNAAF)
JP 1-02	DOD Dictionary of Military and Associated Terms
JP 3-02	Joint Doctrine for Amphibious Operations
JP 3-02.1	Joint Doctrine for Landing Force Operations
JP 3-07	Joint Doctrine for Military Operations Other than War

Marine Corps Doctrinal Publications (MCDPs)

MCDP 1	Warfighting
MCDP 4	Logistics
MCDP 6	Command and Control

Marine Corps Warfighting Publications (MCWPs)

MCWP 3-15.1	Machine Guns and Machine Gun Gunnery
MCWP 3-17.1	River Crossing Operations
MCWP 3-17.3	MAGTF Breaching Operations
MCWP 3-31.5/NWP 3-02.1	Ship-To-Shore Movement
MCWP 3-35.4	Doctrine For Navy/Marine Corps Joint Riverine Operations
MCWP 3-35.6	Desert Operations
MCWP 3-37	MAGTF NBC Defense Operations
MCWP 3-37.2	NBC Protection
MCWP 3-37.3	NBC Decontamination
MCWP 3-40.3	Communications and Information Systems
MCWP 4-1	Logistics Operations
MCWP 5-1	Marine Corps Planning Process

Marine Corps Reference Publications (MCRPs)

MCRP 3-11.1A	Commander's Tactical Handbook
MCRP 3-35.1A	Small Unit Leader's Guide to Cold Weather Operations
MCRP 3-37A	NBC Field Handbook
MCRP 3-37.2B	Nuclear Contamination Avoidance
MCRP 4-11.3D	Naval Beach Group
MCRP 4-11.4A	Battlefield Damage Assessment and Repair
MCRP 5-12A	Operational Terms and Graphics

Marine Corps Technical Manuals (TMs)

TM 09674A-10/3A   Assault Amphibious Vehicle
TM 2350-10/1   Special Mission Kit For The AAV
TM 3-4230-204-12 & P   Operator's & Unit Maintenance Manual for Decontaminating
         Apparatus, Portable, ABC-M11
TM 3-4230-214-12 & P   Decontamination Apparatus, Portable, 14 Liter
TM 3-4230-228-10   Decontaminating Apparatus: Power Driven, Lightweight, M17

Marine Corps Technical Instruction (TI)

TI 10340-15/1D   Fuel Requirements Authorized Fuels for Engines

Naval Warfare Publication (NWP)

NWP 3-59.3   Surf Zone Operations

Army Field Manuals (FMs)

FM 3-4   NBC Protection
FM 3-7   NBC Field Handbook
FM 3-100   Chemical Operations Principles and Fundamentals
FM 5-100   Engineer Operations
FM 5-102   Countermobility
FM 7-7   The Mechanized Infantry Platoon and Squad (APC)
FM 20-32   Mine/Countermine Operations
FM 23-27   MK-19 40 mm Grenade Machine Gun Mod 3
FM 23-65   Browning Machine Gun Caliber .50 HB, M2
FM 34-130   Intelligence Preparation of the Battlefield
FM 44-80   Visual Aircraft Recognition
FM 71-1   Tank & Mechanized Infantry Company Team

www.ingramcontent.com/pod-product-compliance
Lightning Source LLC
Chambersburg PA
CBHW081058290526
45795CB00006B/1910